Thomas Carlyle

History of Friedrich II. of Prussia - Frederick the Great

Thomas Carlyle

History of Friedrich II. of Prussia - Frederick the Great

ISBN/EAN: 9783742839022

Manufactured in Europe, USA, Canada, Australia, Japa

Cover: Foto ©ninafisch / pixelio.de

Manufactured and distributed by brebook publishing software (www.brebook.com)

Thomas Carlyle

History of Friedrich II. of Prussia - Frederick the Great

HISTORY

OF

FRIEDRICH II. OF PRUSSIA,

CALLED

FREDERICK THE GREAT.

BY

THOMAS CARLYLE.

COPYRIGHT EDITION.

VOL. VI.

LEIPZIG

BERNHARD TAUCHNITZ

1862.

The Right of Translation is reserved.

CONTENTS

OF VOLUME VI.

BOOK XI.

FRIEDRICH TAKES THE REINS IN HAND. 1740.

CHAPTER	PAGE
I. PHENOMENA OF FRIEDRICH'S ACCESSION	3

Friedrich will make Men happy: Corn-Magazines, p. 9.
Abolition of Legal Torture, 12.
Will have Philosophers about him, and a real Academy of Sciences, 14.
And Every One shall get to Heaven in his own Way, 17.
Free Press, and Newspapers the best Instructors, 18.
Intends to be Practical withal, and every inch a King, 29.
Behaviour to his Mother; to his Wife, 31.
No Change in his Father's Methods or Ministries, 34.

II. THE HOMAGINGS.	43

Friedrich accepts the Homages, personally, in Three Places, p. 47.

III. FRIEDRICH MAKES AN EXCURSION, NOT OF DIRECT SORT, INTO THE CLEVE COUNTRIES	58

Friedrich strikes off to the left, and has a View of Strasburg for Two Days, p. 66.
Friedrich finds M. de Maupertuis; not yet M. de Voltaire, 80.

IV. VOLTAIRE'S FIRST INTERVIEW WITH FRIEDRICH	86

Particulars of First Interview, on severe Scrutiny, p. 92.
What Voltaire thought of the Interview Twenty Years afterwards, 94.
What Voltaire thought of the Interview at the Time, 98.

CONTENTS OF VOLUME VI.

CHAPTER	PAGE
V. AFFAIR OF HERSTAL	103

How the Herstallers had behaved to Friedrich Wilhelm, p. 105.
Friedrich takes the Rod out of Pickle, 109.
What Voltaire thought of Herstal, 115.

VI. RETURNS BY HANOVER; DOES NOT CALL ON HIS ROYAL UNCLE THERE 121

VII. WITHDRAWS TO REINSBERG, HOPING A PEACEABLE WINTER 130

Wilhelmina's Return-Visit, p. 131.
Unexpected News at Reinsberg, 136.

VIII. THE KAISER'S DEATH 139

IX. RESOLUTION FORMED AT REINSBERG IN CONSEQUENCE 148

Mystery in Berlin, for Seven Weeks, while the Preparations go on; Voltaire visits Friedrich to decipher it, but cannot, p. 152.
View of Friedrich behind the Veil, 158.
Excellency Botta has Audience; then Excellency Dickens, and others: December 6th, the Mystery is out, 163.
Masked Ball, at Berlin, 12-13th December, 168.

BOOK XII.

FIRST SILESIAN WAR, AWAKENING A GENERAL EUROPEAN ONE, BEGINS. 1740-1741.

I. OF SCHLESIEN, OR SILESIA 173

Historical Epochs of Schlesien; — after the Quads and Marchmen, p. 175.

II. FRIEDRICH MARCHES ON GLOGAU. . . . 181

Friedrich at Crossen, and still in his own Territory, 14th-16th Dec.; — steps into Schlesien, p. 183.
What Glogau, and the Government at Breslau, did upon it, 187.

CHAPTER		PAGE
	March to Weichau (Saturday 17th, and stay Sunday there); to Milkau (Monday 19th); get to Herrendorf, within sight of Glogau, Dec. 22d, 194.	
III.	PROBLEM OF GLOGAU.	204
	What Berlin is saying; what Friedrich is thinking, p. 208. Schwerin at Liegnitz; Friedrich hushes up the Glogau Problem, and starts with his best speed for Breslau, 214.	
IV.	BRESLAU UNDER SOFT PRESSURE.	219
	King enters Breslau; stays there, gracious and vigilant, Four Days (Jan. 2d—6th, 1741), p. 223.	
V.	FRIEDRICH PUSHES FORWARD TOWARDS BRIEG AND NEISSE.	227
	Friedrich comes across to Ottmachau; sits there, in survey of Neisse, till his Cannon come, p. 231.	
VI.	NEISSE IS BOMBARDED.	237
	Browne vanishes in a slight Flash of Fire, p. 244.	
VII.	AT VERSAILLES, THE MOST CHRISTIAN MAJESTY CHANGES HIS SHIRT, AND BELLEISLE IS SEEN WITH PAPERS.	246
	Of Belleisle and his Plans, p. 252.	
VIII.	PHENOMENA IN PETERSBURG.	261
IX.	FRIEDRICH RETURNS TO SILESIA.	273
	Skirmish of Baumgarten, 27th February 1741, p. 278. Aspects of Breslau, 282. Austria is standing to Arms, 286. The Young Dessauer captures Glogau (March 9th); the Old Dessauer, by his Camp of Göttin (April 2d), checkmates certain Designing Persons, 292. Friedrich takes the Field, with some Pomp; goes into the Mountains, — but comes fast back, 300.	
X.	BATTLE OF MOLLWITZ.	312
	Of Friedrich's Disappearance into Fairyland, in the interim; and of Maupertuis's Adventure, p. 336.	

CHAPTER	PAGE
XI. THE BURSTING FORTH OF BEDLAMS: BELLEISLE AND THE BREAKERS OF PRAGMATIC SANCTION	344

Who was to blame for the Austrian-Succession War? p. 349.
How Belleisle made Visit to Teutschland; and there was no fit Henry the Fowler to welcome him, 351.
Downbreak of Pragmatic Sanction; Manner of the chief Artists in handling their Covenants, 357.
Concerning the Imperial Election (*Kaiserwahl*) that is to be; Candidates for Kaisership, 367.
Teutschland to be carved into something of Symmetry, should the Belleisle Enterprises succeed, 372.
Belleisle on Visit to Friedrich; sees Friedrich besiege Brieg, with Effect, 376.

XII. SORROWS OF HIS BRITANNIC MAJESTY	385

1. Snatch of Parliamentary Eloquence by Mr. Viner (19th April 1741), p. 386.
2. Constitutional Historian on the Phenomenon of Walpole in England, 390.
3. Of the Spanish War, or the Jenkins's-Ear Question, 395.
Succinct History of the Spanish War, which began in 1739; and ended — When did it end? 399.

XIII. SMALL WAR: FIRST EMERGENCE OF ZIETHEN THE HUSSAR GENERAL INTO NOTICE	412

BOOK XI.

FRIEDRICH TAKES THE REINS IN HAND.

June — December 1740.

CHAPTER I.

PHENOMENA OF FRIEDRICH'S ACCESSION.

In Berlin, from Tuesday 31st May 1740, day of the late King's death, till the Thursday following, the post was stopped and the gates closed; no estafette can be despatched, though Dickens and all the Ambassadors are busy writing. On the Thursday, Regiments, Officers, principal Officials having sworn, and the new King being fairly in the saddle, estafettes and post-boys shoot forth at the top of their speed; and Rumour, towards every point of the compass, apprises mankind what immense news there is.*

A King's Accession is always a hopeful phenomenon to the public; more especially a young King's, who has been talked of for his talents and aspirings, — for his sufferings, were it nothing more, and whose *Anti-Macchiavel* is understood to be in the press. Vaguely everywhere there has a notion gone abroad that this young King will prove considerable. Here at last has a Lover of Philosophy got upon the throne, and great philanthropies and magnanimities are to be expected, think rash editors and idle mankind. Rash editors in England and elsewhere, we observe, are ready to believe that Friedrich has not only disbanded the Potsdam Giants; but means to "reduce the Prussian Army one half" or so, for ease (temporary ease, which we hope will be lasting) of parties concerned; and to

* Dickens (in State-Paper Office), 4th June 1740.

go much upon emancipation, political rose-water, and friendship to humanity, as we now call it.

At his first meeting of Council, they say, he put this question, "Could not the Prussian Army be reduced to 45,000?" The excellent young man. To which the Council had answered, "Hardly, your Majesty! The Jülich-and-Berg affair is so ominous hitherto!" These may be secrets, and dubious to people out of doors, thinks a wise editor; but one thing patent to the day was this, surely symbolical enough: On one of his Majesty's first drives to Potsdam or from it, a thousand children, — in round numbers a thousand of them, all with the *red string* round their necks, and liable to be taken for soldiers, if needed in the regiment of their Canton, — "a thousand children" met this young King at a turn of his road; and with shrill unison of wail, sang out: "Oh, deliver us from slavery," — from the red threads, your Majesty! Why should poor we be liable to suffer hardship for our Country or otherwise, your Majesty! Can no one else be got to do it? sang out the thousand children. And his Majesty assented on the spot, thinks the rash editor.* "Goose, Madam?" exclaimed a philanthropist projector once, whose scheme of sweeping chimneys by pulling a live goose down through them was objected to: "Goose, Madam? You can take two ducks, then, if you are so sorry for the goose!" — Rash editors think there is to be a reign of Astræa Redux in Prussia, by means of this young King; and forget to ask themselves, as the young King must by no means do, How far Astræa may be possible, for Prussia and him?

At home, too, there is prophesying enough, vague

* *Gentleman's Magazine* (London, 1740), x. 318; Newspapers, &c.

hope enough, which for most part goes wide of the mark. This young King, we know, did prove considerable; but not in the way shaped out for him by the public; — it was in far other ways! For no public in the least knows, in such cases: nor does the man himself know, except gradually and if he strive to learn. As to the public — "Doubtless," says a friend of mine, "doubtless it was the Atlantic Ocean "that carried Columbus to America; lucky for the "Atlantic, and for Columbus and us: but the Atlantic "did not quite vote that way from the first; nay *its* "votes, I believe, were very various at different stages "of the matter!" This is a truth which kings and men, not intending to be drift-logs or waste brine obedient to the Moon, are much called to have in mind withal, from perhaps an early stage of their voyage.

Friedrich's actual demeanour in these his first weeks, which is still decipherable if one study well, has in truth a good deal of the brilliant, of the popular, magnanimous; but manifests strong solid quality withal, and a head steadier than might have been expected. For the Berlin world is all in a rather Auroral condition; and Friedrich too is, — the chains suddenly cut loose, and such hopes opened for the young man. He has great things ahead; feels in himself great things, and doubtless exults in the thought of realising them. Magnanimous enough, popular, hopeful enough, with Voltaire and the highest of the world looking on: — but yet he is wise, too; creditably aware that there are limits, that this is a bargain, and the terms of it inexorable. We discern with pleasure the old veracity of character shining through this giddy new element;

that all these fine procedures are at least unaffected, to
a singular degree true, and the product of nature, on
his part; and that, in short, the complete respect for
Fact, which used to be a quality of his, and which is
among the highest and also rarest in man, has on no
side deserted him at present.

A trace of airy exuberance, of natural exultancy,
not quite repressible, on the sudden change to freedom
and supreme power from what had gone before: perhaps that also might be legible, if in those opaque
bead-rolls which are called Histories of Friedrich anything human could with certainty be read! He flies
much about from place to place; now at Potsdam, now
at Berlin, at Charlottenburg, Reinsberg; nothing loth
to run whither business calls him, and appear in
public: the gazetteer world, as we noticed, which has
been hitherto a most mute world, breaks out here and
there into a kind of husky jubilation over the great
things he is daily doing, and rejoices in the prospect
of having a Philosopher King; which function the
young man, only twenty-eight gone, cannot but wish
to fulfil for the gazetteers and the world. He is a
busy man; and walks boldly into his grand enterprise
of "making men happy," to the admiration of Voltaire
and an enlightened public far and near.

Bielfeld speaks of immense concourses of people
crowding about Charlottenburg, to congratulate, to
solicit, to &c.; tells us how he himself had to lodge
almost in outhouses, in that royal village of hope. His
emotions at Reinsberg, and everybody's while Friedrich
Wilhelm lay dying, and all stood like greyhounds on
the slip; and with what arrow-swiftness they shot away
when the great news came: all this he has already

described at wearisome length, in his fantastic semi-fabulous way.* Friedrich himself seemed moderately glad to see Bielfeld; received his highflown congratulations with a benevolent yet somewhat composed air; and gave him afterwards, in the course of weeks, an unexpectedly small appointment: To go to Hanover, under Truchsess von Waldburg, and announce our Accession. Which is but a simple, mostly formal service; yet perhaps what Bielfeld is best equal to.

The Britannic Majesty, or at least his Hanover people have been beforehand with this civility; Baron Münchhausen, no doubt by orders given for such contingency, had appeared at Berlin with the due compliment and condolence almost on the first day of the New Reign; first messenger of all on that errand; Britannic Majesty evidently in a conciliatory humour, — having his dangerous Spanish War on hand. Britannic Majesty in person, shortly after, gets across to Hanover; and Friedrich despatches Truchsess, with Bielfeld adjoined, to return the courtesy.

Friedrich does not neglect these points of good manners; along with which something of substantial may be privately conjoined. For example, if he had in secret his eye on Jülich and Berg, could anything be fitter than to ascertain what the French will think of such an enterprise? What the French; and next to them what the English, that is to say, Hanoverians, who meddle much in affairs of the Reich. For these reasons and others he likewise, probably with more study than in the Bielfeld case, despatches Colonel Camas to make his compliment at the French Court, and in an expert way take soundings there. Camas, a

* Bielfeld, i. 63-77; ib. 81.

fat sedate military gentleman, of advanced years, full of observation, experience and sound sense, — "with "one arm, which he makes do the work of two, and "nobody can notice that the other arm resting in his "coat-breast is of cork, so expert is he," — will do in this matter what is feasible; probably not much for the present. He is to call on Voltaire, as he passes, who is in Holland again, at the Hague for some months back; and deliver him "a little cask of Hungary Wine," which probably his Majesty had thought exquisite. Of which, and the other insignificant passages between them, we hear more than enough in the writings and correspondences of Voltaire about this time.

In such way Friedrich disposes of his Bielfelds; who are rather numerous about him now and henceforth. Adventurers from all quarters, especially of the literary type, in hopes of being employed, much hovered round Friedrich through his whole reign. But they met a rather strict judge on arriving; it cannot be said they found it such a Goshen as they expected.

Favour, friendly intimacy, it is visible from the first, avails nothing with this young King; beyond and before all things he will have his work done, and looks out exclusively for the man ablest to do it. Hence Bielfeld goes to Hanover, to grin out euphuisms, and make graceful court-bows to our sublime little Uncle there. On the other hand, Friedrich institutes a new Knighthood, *Order of Merit* so-called; which indeed is but a small feat, testifying mere hope and exuberance as yet; and may even be made worse than nothing, according to the Knights he shall manage to have. Happily it proved a successful new Order in this last all-essential particular; and, to the end of Friedrich's life, continued to be a great and coveted distinction among the Prussians.

Beyond doubt this is a radiant enough young Majesty; entitled to hope, and to be the cause of hope. Handsome, to begin with; decidedly well-looking, all say, and of graceful presence, though hardly five feet seven, and perhaps stouter of limb than the strict Belvedere standard.* Has a fine free expressive face; nothing of austerity in it; not a proud face, or not too proud, yet rapidly flashing on you all manner of high meanings.** Such a man, in the bloom of his years; with such a possibility ahead, and Voltaire and mankind waiting applausive! — Let us try to select, and extricate into coherence and visibility out of those Historical dustheaps, a few of the symptomatic phenomena, or physiognomic procedures of Friedrich in his first weeks of Kingship, by way of contribution to some Portraiture of his then inner-man.

Friedrich will make Men happy: Corn-Magazines.

On the day after his Accession, Officers and chief Ministers taking the Oath, Friedrich, to his Officers, "on whom he counts for the same zeal now which he

* Height, it appears, was five feet five inches (Rhenish), which in English measure is five feet seven or a hairsbreadth less. Preuss, twice over, by a mistake unusual with him, gives "five feet two inches three lines" as the correct cipher (which it is of *Napoleon's* measure in *French* feet); then settles on the above dimensions from unexceptionable authority (Preuss, *Buch für Jedermann*, i. 18; Preuss, *Friedrich der Grosse*, i. 39 and 419).
** "Wille's Engraving after Pesne" (excellent, both Picture and Engraving) is reckoned the best Likeness in that form.

2d June 1740.

"had witnessed as their comrade," recommends mildness of demeanour from the higher to the lower, and that the common soldier be not treated with harshness when not deserved: and to his Ministers he is still more emphatic, in the like or a higher strain. Officially announcing to them, by Letter, that a new Reign has commenced, he uses these words, legible soon after to a glad Berlin Public: "Our grand care will be, To "further the Country's wellbeing, and to make every "one of our subjects (*einen jeden unserer Unterthanen*) "contented and happy. Our will is, not that you strive "to enrich Us by vexation of Our subjects; but "rather that you aim steadily as well towards the ad-"vantage of the Country as Our particular interest, for-"asmuch as we make no difference between these two "objects," but consider them one and the same. This is written, and gets into print within the month; and his Majesty, that same day (Wednesday 2d June), when it came to personal reception, and actual taking of the Oath, was pleased to add in words, which also were printed shortly, this comfortable corollary: "My "will henceforth is, If it ever chance that my particular "interest and the general good of my Countries should "seem to go against each other, — in that case, my "will is, That the latter always be preferred."*

This is a fine dialect for incipient Royalty; and it is brand-new at that time. It excites an admiration in the then populations, which to us, so long used to it and to what commonly comes of it, is not conceivable at once. There can be no doubt the young King

---

* Dickens, Despatch, 4th June 1740; Preuss, *Friedrichs Jugend und Thronbesteigung* (Berlin, 1840), p. 325; — quoting from the Berlin Newspapers, of 28th June and 2d July 1740.

does faithfully intend to develop himself in the way of making men happy; but here, as elsewhere, are limits which he will recognise ahead, some of them perhaps nearer than was expected.

Meanwhile his first acts, in this direction, correspond to these fine words. The year 1740, still grim with cold into the heart of summer, bids fair to have a late poor harvest, and famine threatens to add itself to other hardships there have been. Recognising the actualities of the case, what his poor Father could not, he opens the Public Granaries, — a wise resource they have in Prussian countries against the year of scarcity; — orders grain to be sold out, at reasonable rates, to the suffering poor; and takes the due pains, considerable in some cases, that this be rendered feasible everywhere in his dominions. "Berlin, 2d June," is the first date of this important order; fine program to his Ministers, which, we read, is no sooner uttered, than some performance follows. An evident piece of wisdom and humanity; for which doubtless blessings of a very sincere kind rise to him from several millions of his fellow-mortals.

Nay furthermore, as can be dimly gathered, this scarcity continuing, some continuous mode of management was set on foot for the Poor; and there is nominated, with salary, with outline of plan and other requisites, as "Inspector of the Poor," to his own and our surprise, M. Jordan, late Reader to the Crown-Prince, and still much the intimate of his royal Friend. Inspector who seems to do his work very well. And in the November coming this is what we see: "One thousand poor old women, the destitute of Berlin, set to spin," at his Majesty's charges; vacant houses, hired for them in certain streets and suburbs, have been new-planked, partitioned, warmed; and spinning is there for any diligent female soul. There a thousand of them sit, under proper officers, proper wages, treatment; — and the hum of their poor spindles, and of their poor inarticulate old hearts, is a comfort, if one chance to think of it. — Of "distressed needlewomen" who cannot sew, nor be taught to do it; who, in private truth, are mutinous maid-servants come at last to the net upshot of their anarchies; of these, or of the like incurable phenomena, I hear nothing in Berlin; and can believe that, under this King, Indigence itself may still have something of a human aspect, not a brutal or diabolic as is commoner in some places! — This is one of Friedrich's first acts, this opening of the Corn-magazines, and arrangements for the Destitute;* and of this there can be no criticism. The sound of hungry pots set boiling, on judicious principles; the hum of those old women's spindles in the warm rooms: gods and men are well pleased to hear such sounds; and accept the same as part, real though infinitesimally small, of the sphere-harmonics of this Universe!

Abolition of Legal Torture.

Friedrich makes haste, next, to strike into Law-improvements. It is but the morrow after this of the Corn-magazines, by *Kabinets-Ordre* (Act of Parliament,

---

* *Helden-Geschichte*, i. 367. Rödenbeck, *Tagebuch aus Friedrichs des Grossen Regentenleben* (Berlin, 1840), i. 2, 26 (2d June, October, 1740): a meritorious, laborious, though essentially chaotic Book, unexpectedly futile of result to the reader; settles for each Day of Friedrich's Reign, so far as possible, where Friedrich was and what doing; fatally wants all index &c., as usual.

June—Sept. 1740.

such as they can have in that Country, where the Three Estates sit all under one Three-cornered Hat, and the debates are kept silent, and only the upshot of them, more or less faithfully, is made public), — by Cabinet Order, 3d June 1740, he abolishes the use of Torture in Criminal Trials.* Legal Torture, "Question" as they mildly call it, is at an end from this date. Not in any Prussian Court shall a "question" try for answer again by that savage method. The use of Torture had, I believe, fallen rather obsolete in Prussia; but now the very threat of it shall vanish, — the threat of it, as we may remember, had reached Friedrich himself, at one time. Three or four years ago, it is farther said, a dark murder happened in Berlin: Man killed one night in the open streets; murderer discoverable by no method, — unless he were a certain *Candidatus* of Divinity to whom some trace of evidence pointed, but who sorrowfully persisted in absolute and total denial. This poor Candidatus had been threatened with the rack; and would most likely have at length got it, had not the real murderer been discovered, — much to the discredit of the rack in Berlin. This Candidatus was only threatened; nor do I know when the last actual instance in Prussia was; but in enlightened France, and most other countries, there was as yet no scruple upon it. Barbier, the Diarist at Paris, some time after this, tells us of a gang of thieves there, who were regularly put to the torture; and "they blabbed too, *ils ont jasé*," says Barbier with official jocosity.**

* Preuss, *Friedrichs Jugend und Thronbesteigung* (Berlin, 1840, — a minor Book of Preuss's), p. 340. Rödenbeck, i. 14 ("3d June").

** Barbier, *Journal Historique du Règne de Louis XV* (Paris, 1849), ii. 338 (date "Dec. 1742").

Friedrich's Cabinet Order, we need not say, was greeted everywhere, at home and abroad, by three rounds of applause; — in which surely all of us still join; though the *per-contra* also is becoming visible to some of us, and our enthusiasm grows less complete than formerly. This was Friedrich's first step in Law-Reform, done on his fourth day of Kingship. A long career in that kind lies ahead of him; in reform of Law, civil as well as criminal, his efforts ended with life only. For his love of Justice was really great; and the mendacities and wiggeries, attached to such a necessary of life as Law, found no favour from him at any time.

Will have Philosophers about him, and a real Academy of Sciences.

To neglect the Philosophies, Fine Arts, interests of Human Culture, he is least of all likely. The idea of building up the Academy of Sciences to its pristine height, or far higher, is evidently one of those that have long lain in the Crown Prince's mind, eager to realise themselves. Immortal Wolf, exiled but safe at Marburg, and refusing to return in Friedrich Wilhelm's time, had lately dedicated a Book to the Crown Prince; indicating that perhaps, under a new Reign, he might be more persuadable. Friedrich makes haste to persuade; instructs the proper person, Reverend Herr Reinbeck, Head of the Consistorium at Berlin, to write and negotiate. "All reasonable conditions shall be granted" the immortal Wolf, — and Friedrich adds with his own hand as Postscript: "I request you (*Ihn*) to use all "diligence about Wolf. A man that seeks truth, and

June—Sept. 1740.

"loves it, must be reckoned precious in any human "society; and I think you will make a conquest in the "realm of truth if you persuade Wolf hither again."* This is of date June 6th; not yet a week since Friedrich came to be King. The Reinbeck-Wolf negotiation which ensued can be read in Büsching by the curious.** It represents to us a croaky, thrifty, long-headed old Herr Professor, in no haste to quit Marburg except for something better: "obliged to wear woollen shoes and leggings;" "bad at mounting stairs;" and otherwise needing soft treatment. Willing, though with caution, to work at an Academy of Sciences; — but dubious if the French are so admirable as they seem to themselves in such operations. Veteran Wolf, one dimly begins to learn, could himself build a German Academy of Sciences, to some purpose, if encouraged! This latter was probably the stone of stumbling in that direction. Veteran Wolf did not get to be President in the new Academy of Sciences; but was brought back, "streets all in triumph," to his old place at Halle; and there, with little other work that was heard of, but we hope in warm shoes and without much mounting of stairs, lived peaceably victorious the rest of his days.

Friedrich's thoughts are not of a German home-built Academy, but of a French one: and for this he already knows a builder; has silently had him in his eye, these two years past, — Voltaire giving hint, in the *Letter* we once heard of at Loo. Builder shall be that sublime Maupertuis; scientific lion of Paris, ever since his feat in the Polar regions, and the charming Narrative he

---

* In *Œuvres de Frédéric* (xxvii. n. 185), the Letter given.
** Büsching's *Beytrdge* (§ Freyherr von Wolf), i. 63-137.

gave of it. "What a feat, what a book!" exclaimed the Parisian cultivated circles, male and female, on that occasion; and Maupertuis, with plenty of bluster in him carefully suppressed, assents in a grandly modest way. His Portraits are in the Printshops ever since; one very singular Portrait, just coming out (at which there is some laughing): a coarse-featured, blusterous, rather triumphant-looking man, blusterous, though finely complacent for the nonce; in copious dressing-gown and fur cap; comfortably *squeezing* the Earth and her meridians flat (as if *he* had done it), with his left hand; and with the other, and its outstretched finger, asking mankind, "Are not you aware, then?" — "Are not we!" answers Voltaire by and by, with endless waggeries upon him, though at present so reverent. Friedrich, in these same days, writes this Autograph: which who of men or lions could resist?

To Monsieur de Maupertuis at Paris.

(No date; — dateable, June 1740.)

"My heart and my inclination excited in me, from the mo-
"ment I mounted the throne, the desire of having you here,
"that you might put our Berlin Academy into the shape you
"alone are capable of giving it. Come, then, come and insert
"into this wild crabtree the graft of the Sciences, that it may
"bear fruit. You have shown the Figure of the Earth to man-
"kind; show also to a King how sweet it is to possess such a
"man as you.

"Monsieur de Maupertuis, — *Votre très-affectionné*
"FÉDÉRIC (*sic*).*

This Letter, — how could Maupertuis prevent some accident in such a case? — got into the Newspapers;

* *Œuvres*, xvii. 1. 335. The fantastic "Fédéric," instead of "Fré-déric," is, by this time, the common signature to French Letters.

glorious for Friedrich, glorious for Maupertuis; and raised matters to a still higher pitch. Maupertuis is on the road, and we shall see him before long.

And every One shall get to Heaven in his own Way.

Here is another little fact which had immense renown at home and abroad, in those summer months and long afterwards.

June 22d, 1740, the *Geistliche Departement* (Board of Religion, we may term it) reports that the Roman-Catholic Schools, which have been in use these eight years past, for children of soldiers belonging to that persuasion, "are, especially in Ber- "lin, perverted, directly in the teeth of Royal Ordinance, 1732, "to seducing Protestants into Catholicism:" annexed, or ready for annexing, "is the specific Report of Fiscal-General to this "effect:" — upon which, what would it please his Majesty to direct us to do?

His Majesty writes on the margin these words, rough and ready, which we give with all their grammatical blotches on them; indicating a mind made up on one subject, which was much more dubious then, to most other minds, than it now is:

"*Die Religionen Müsen* (müssen) *alle Tollerirt* (tolerirt) "*werden, und Mus* (muss) *der Fiscal nuhr* (nur) *das Auge darauf* "*haben, das* (dass) *keine der andern abrug Tuhe* (Abbruch thue), "*den* (denn) *hier mus* (muss) *ein jeder nach seiner Fasson Selich* "(Façon selig) *werden.*" *

Which in English might run as follows:

"All Religions must be tolerated (*Tollerated*), and the "Fiscal must have an eye that none of them make unjust en- "croachment on the other; for in this Country every man must "get to Heaven in his own way."

* Preuss, *Thronbesteigung*, p. 333; Rödenbeck, *in die.*

Wonderful words; precious to the then leading spirits, and which (the spelling and grammar being mended) flew abroad over all the world; the enlightened Public everywhere answering his Majesty, once more, with its loudest "Bravissimo!" on this occasion. With what enthusiasm of admiring wonder, it is now difficult to fancy, after the lapse of sixscore years! And indeed, in regard to all these worthy acts of Human Improvement which we are now concerned with, account should be held (were it possible) on Friedrich's behalf, how extremely original, and bright with the splendour of new gold, they then were, and how extremely they are fallen dim, by general circulation, since that. Account should be held; and yet it is not possible, no human imagination is adequate to it, in the times we are now got into.

Free Press, and Newspapers the best Instructors.

Toleration, in Friedrich's spiritual circumstances, was perhaps no great feat to Friedrich: but what the reader hardly expected of him was Freedom of the Press, or an attempt that way! From England, from Holland, Friedrich had heard of Free Press, of Newspapers the best Instructors: it is a fact that he hastens to plant a seed of that kind at Berlin; sets about it "on the second day of his reign," so eager is he. Berlin had already some meagre *Intelligenz-Blatt* (Weekly or Thrice-Weekly Advertiser), perhaps two; but it is a real Newspaper, frondent with genial leafy speculation, and food for the mind, that Friedrich is intent upon: a "Literary-Political Newspaper," or were it even two Newspapers, one French, one German; and he rapidly makes the arrangements for it; despatches Jordan, on the second day, to seek some fit Frenchman. Arrangements are soon made: a Bookselling Printer, Haude, Bookseller once to the Prince-Royal, — whom we saw once in a domestic flash-of-lightning long ago,* — is encouraged to proceed with the improved German article, *Mercury* or whatever they called it; vapid Formey, a facile pen, but not a forcible, is the Editor sought out by Jordan for the French one. And, in short, No. 1 of Formey shows itself in print within a month;** and Haude and he, Haude picking up some grand Editor in Hamburg, do their best for the instruction of mankind.

In not many months, Formey, a facile and learned but rather vapid gentleman, demitted or was dismissed; and the Journals coalesced into one, or split into two again; and went I know not what road, or roads, in time coming, — none that led to results worth naming. Freedom of the Press, in the case of these Journals, was never violated, nor was any need for violating it. General Freedom of the Press Friedrich did not grant, in any quite Official or steady way; but in practice, under him, it always had a kind of real existence, though a fluctuating, ambiguous one. And we have to note, through Friedrich's whole reign, a marked disinclination to concern himself with Censorship, or the shackling of men's poor tongues and pens: nothing but some officious report that there was offence to Foreign Courts, or the chance of offence, in a poor man's pamphlet, could induce Friedrich to interfere with him

---

* *Antea*, Book vi. c. 7.
** "2d July 1740:" Preuss, *Thronbesteigung*, p. 330; and Formey, *Souvenirs*, i. 107, rectified by the exact Herr Preuss.

or it, — and indeed his interference was generally
against his Ministers for having wrong informed him,
and in favour of the poor Pamphleteer appealing at
the fountain-head.* To the end of his life, disgusting
Satires against him, *Vie Privée* by Voltaire, *Matinées
du Roi de Prusse*, and still worse Lies and Nonsenses,
were freely sold at Berlin, and even bore to be printed
there, Friedrich saying nothing, caring nothing. He
has been known to burn Pamphlets publicly, — one
Pamphlet we shall ourselves see on fire yet; — but it
was without the least hatred to them, and for official
reasons merely. To the last, he would answer his
reporting Ministers, "*La presse est libre* (Free press,
you must consider)!" — grandly reluctant to meddle
with the press, or go down upon the dogs barking at
his door. Those ill effects of Free Press (first stage of
the ill effects) he endured in this manner; but the good
effects seem to have fallen below his expectation.
Friedrich's enthusiasm for freedom of the press, prompt
enough, as we see, never rose to the extreme pitch,
and it rather sank than increased as he continued his
experiences of men and things. This of Formey and
the two Newspapers was the only express attempt he
made in that direction; and it proved a rather disappointing one. The two Newspapers went their way
thenceforth, Friedrich sometimes making use of them
for small purposes, once or twice writing an article
himself, of wildly quizzical nature, perhaps to be noticed
by us when the time comes; but are otherwise, except

---

* Anonymous (Laveaux), *Vie de Frédéric II, Roi de Prusse* (Strasbourg, 1787), iv. 82. A worthless, now nearly forgotten Book; but competent on this point, if on any; Laveaux (a handy fellow, fugitive Ex-Monk with fugitive Ex-Nun attached) having lived much at Berlin, always in the pamphleteering line.

for chronological purposes, of the last degree of insignificance to gods or men.

"Freedom of the Press," says my melancholic Friend, "is a noble thing; and in certain Nations, at "certain epochs, produces glorious effects, — chiefly in "the revolutionary line, where that has grown in"dispensable. Freedom of the Press is possible, where "everybody disapproves the least abuse of it; where "the 'Censorship' is, as it were, exercised by all the "world. When the world (as, even in the freest "countries, it almost irresistibly tends to become) is no "longer in a case to exercise that salutary function, "and cannot keep down loud unwise speaking, loud "unwise persuasion, and rebuke it into silence when"ever printed, Freedom of the Press will not answer "very long, among sane human creatures: and indeed, "in Nations not in an exceptional case, it becomes im"possible amazingly soon!" —

All these are phenomena of Friedrich's first week. Let these suffice as sample, in that first kind. Splendid indications surely; and shot forth in swift enough succession, flash following flash, upon an attentive world. Betokening, shall we say, what internal sea of splendour, struggling to disclose itself, probably lies in this young King; and how high his hopes go for mankind and himself? Yes, surely; — and introducing, we remark withal, the 'New Era,' of Philanthropy, Enlightenment and so much else; with French Revolution, and a "world well suicided" hanging in the rear! Clearly enough, to this young ardent Friedrich, foremost man of his Time, and capable of *doing* its inarticulate or dumb aspirings, belongs that questionable honour; and a very singular one it would have seemed to Friedrich, had he lived to see what it meant!

Friedrich's rapidity and activity, in the first months of his reign, were wonderful to mankind; as indeed through life he continued to be a most rapid and active King. He flies about; mustering Troops, Ministerial Boards, passing Edicts, inspecting, accepting Homages of Provinces; — decides and does, every day that passes, an amazing number of things. Writes many Letters, too; finds moments even for some verses; and occasionally draws a snatch of melody from his flute.

His Letters are copiously preserved; but, as usual, they are in swift official tone, and tell us almost nothing. To his Sisters he writes assurances; to his friends, his Suhms, Duhans, Voltaires, eager invitations, general or particular, to come to him. "My state has changed," is his phrase to Voltaire and other dear intimates; a tone of pensiveness, at first even of sorrow and pathos traceable in it; "Come to me," — and the tone, in an old dialect, different from Friedrich's, might have meant, "Pray for me." An immense new scene is opened, full of possibilities of good and bad. His hopes being great, his anxieties, the shadow of them, are proportionate. Duhan (his good old Tutor) does arrive, Algarotti arrives, warmly welcomed, both: with Voltaire there are difficulties; but surely he too will, before long, manage to arrive. The good Suhm, who had been Saxon Minister at Petersburg to his sorrow this long while back, got in motion soon enough; but, alas, his lungs were ruined by the Russian climate, and he did not arrive. Something pathetic still in those final *Letters* of Suhm. Passionately speeding on, like a spent steed struggling homeward; he has to pause at Warsaw, and in a few days dies there, — in a way mournful to Friedrich and us! To Duhan, and Duhan's children afterwards, he was punctually, not too lavishly, attentive; in like manner to Suhm's Nephews, whom the dying man had recommended to him. — We will now glance shortly at a second and contemporaneous phasis of Friedrich's affairs.

Intends to be Practical withal, and every inch a King.

Friedrich is far indeed from thinking to reduce his Army, as the Foreign Editor imagines. On the contrary, he is, with all industry, increasing it. He changed the Potsdam Giants into four regiments of the usual stature; he is busy bargaining with his Brother-in-law of Brunswick, and with other neighbours, for still new regiments; — makes up, within the next few months, Eight Regiments, an increase of, say, 16,000 men. It would appear he means to keep an eye on the practicalities withal; means to have a Fighting-Apparatus of the utmost potentiality, for one thing! Here are other indications.

We saw the Old Dessauer, in a sad hour lately, speaking beside the mark; and with what Olympian glance, suddenly tearless, the new King flashed out upon him, knowing nothing of "authority" that could reside in any Dessauer. Nor was that a solitary experience; the like befel wherever needed. Heinrich of Schwedt, the Ill Margraf, advancing with jocose countenance in the way of old comradeship, in those first days, met unexpected rebuff, and was reduced to gravity on the sudden: "*Jetzt bin ich König*, — My Cousin, I am now King!" a fact which the Ill Margraf could never get forgotten again. Lieutenant-General Schulenburg, too, the didactic Schulenburg, presuming on old familiarity, and willing to wipe out the misfortune of having once condemned us to death, which nobody is now upbraiding him with, rushes up from Landsberg, unbidden, to pay his congratulations and condolences, driven by irresistible exuberance of loyalty: to his astonishment, he is reminded (thing certain, manner of the thing not known), That an Officer cannot quit his post without order; that he, at this moment, ought to be in Landsberg!* Schulenburg has a hard old military face; but here is a young face too, which has grown unexpectedly rigorous. Fancy the blank look of little Schulenburg; the light of him snuffed out in this manner on a sudden. It is said he had thoughts of resigning, so indignant was he: no doubt he went home to Landsberg gloomily reflective, with the pipe-clay of his mind in such a ruinous condition. But there was no serious anger, on Friedrich's part; and he consoled his little Schulenburg, soon after, by expediting some promotion he had intended him. "Terribly proud young Majesty this," exclaim the sweet voices. And indeed, if they are to have a Saturnian Kingdom, by appearance it will be on conditions only!

Anticipations there had been, that old unkindnesses against the Crown Prince, some of which were cruel enough, might be remembered now: and certain people had their just fears, considering what account stood against them; others, *vice versâ*, their hopes. But

---

* Stenzel, iv. 41; Preuss, *Thronbesteigung:* &c.

neither the fears nor the hopes realised themselves; especially the fears proved altogether groundless. Derschau, who had voted Death in that Cöpenick Court-Martial, upon the Crown-Prince, is continued in his functions, in the light of his King's countenance, as if nothing such had been. Derschau, and all others so concerned; not the least question was made of them, nor of what they had thought or had done or said, on an occasion once so tragically vital to a certain man.

Nor is reward much regulated by past services to the Crown-Prince, or even by sufferings endured for him. "Shocking ingratitude!" exclaim the sweet voices here too, — being of weak judgment, many of them! Poor Katte's Father, a faithful old Soldier, not capable of being more, he does, rather conspicuously, make Feldmarschall, make Reichsgraf; happy, could these honours be a consolation to the old man. The Münchows of Cüstrin, — readers remember their kindness in that sad time; how the young boy went into petticoats again, and came to the Crown-Prince's cell with all manner of furnishings, — the Münchows, father and sons, this young gentleman of the petticoats among them, he took immediate pains to reward by promotion: eldest son was advanced into the General Directorium; two younger sons, to Majorship, to Captaincy, in their respective Regiments; him of the petticoats "he had already taken altogether to himself,"* — and of him we shall see a glimpse at Wilhelmina's shortly, as a "milkbeard (*jeune morveux*)" in personal attendance on his Majesty. This was a notable exception. And in effect there came good public service, eminent some of it, from these Münchows

* Preuss, i. 66.

in their various departments. And it was at length perceived to have been, in the main, because they were of visible faculty for doing work that they had got work to .do; and the exceptional case of the Münchows became confirmatory of the rule.

Lieutenant Keith, again, whom we once saw galloping from Wesel to save his life in that bad affair of the Crown-Prince's and his, was nothing like so fortunate. Lieutenant Keith, by speed on that Wesel occasion, and help of Chesterfield's Secretary, got across to England; got into the Portuguese service; and has there been soldiering, very silently, these ten years past, — skin and body safe, though his effigy was cut in four quarters and nailed to the gallows at Wesel; — waiting a time that would come. Time being come, Lieutenant Keith hastened home; appealed to his effigy on the gallows; — and was made a Lieutenant-Colonel merely, with some slight appendages, as that of *Stallmeister* (Curator of the Stables) and something else; — income still straitened, though enough to live upon.* Small promotion, in comparison with hope, thought the poor Lieutenant; but had to rest satisfied with it; and struggle to understand that perhaps he was fit for nothing bigger, and that he must exert himself to do this small thing well. Hardness of heart in high places! Friedrich, one is glad to see, had not forgotten the poor fellow, could he have done better with him. Some ten years hence, quite incidentally, there came to Keith, one morning, a fine purse of money from his Majesty, one pretty gift in Keith's experience; — much the topic in Berlin, while a certain solemn English Gentleman happened to be passing that

---

* Preuss, *Friedrich mit seinen Verwandten und Freunden,* p. 281.

way (whom we mean to detain a little by and by), who reports it for us with all the circumstances.*

Lieutenant Spaen too had got into trouble for the Crown-Prince's sake, though we have forgotten him again; had "admitted Katte to interviews," or we forget what; — had sat his "year in Spandau" in consequence; been dismissed the Prussian service, and had taken service with the Dutch. Lieutenant Spaen either did not return at all, or disliked the aspects when he did, and immediately withdrew to Holland again. Which probably was wise of him. At a late period, King Friedrich, then a great King, on one of his Cleve Journeys, fell in with Spaen; who had become a Dutch General of rank, and was of good manners and style of conversation: King Friedrich was charmed to see him; became his guest for the night; conversed delightfully with him, about old Prussian matters and about new; and in the colloquy never once alluded to that interesting passage in his young life and Spaen's.** Hard as polished steel! thinks Spaen perhaps; but, if candid, must ask himself withal, Are facts any softer, or the Laws of Kingship to a man that holds it? — Keith silently did his Lieutenant-Colonelcy with the appendages, while life lasted: of the Page Keith, his Brother, who indeed had blabbed upon the Prince, as we remember, and was not entitled to be clamorous, I never heard that there was any notice taken; and figure him to myself as walking with shouldered firelock, a private Fusileer, all his life afterwards, with many reflections on things bygone.***

* Sir Jonas Hanway: *Travels*, &c. (London, 1753), ii. 202. Date of the Gift is 1750.
** Nicolai: *Anekdoten*, vi. 178.
*** These and the other Prussian Keiths are all of Scotch extraction;

Old friendship, it would seem, is without weight in public appointments here: old friends are somewhat astonished to find this friend of theirs a King every inch! To old comrades, if they were useless, much more if they were worse than useless, how disappointing! "One wretched Herr" (name suppressed, but known at the time, and talked of, and whispered of), "who had, like several others, hoping to rise that way, "been industrious in encouraging the Crown-Prince's "vices as to women, was so shocked at the return he "now met, that in despair he hanged himself in Löbe-"jün" (Löbegun, Magdeburg Country): here is a case for the humane! —*

Friend Keyserling himself, "Cæsarion" that used to be, can get nothing, though we love him much; being an idle topsyturvy fellow with revenues of his own. Jordan, with his fine-drawn wit, French logics, *Literary Travels*, thin exactitude; what can be done for Jordan? Him also his new Majesty loves much; and knows that, without some official living, poor Jordan has no resource. Jordan, after some waiting and survey, is made "Inspector of the Poor;" — busy this Autumn looking out for vacant houses, and arrangements for the thousand spinning women; — continues to be employed in mixed literary services (hunting up of Formey, for Editor, was one instance), and to be in much real intimacy. That also was perhaps about the real amount of amiable Jordan. To get Jordan a living by planting him in some office which he could not do; to warm Jordan by burning our royal bed for

the Prussians, in natural German fashion, pronounce their name, *Kah-it* (English "*Kite*" with nothing of the y in it), as may be worth remembering in a more important instance.

* Küster: *Charakterzüge des* &c. *von Saldern* (Berlin, 1793), p. 63.

him: that had not entered into the mind of Jordan's royal friend. The Münchows he did promote; the Finks, sons of his Tutor Finkenstein: to these and other old comrades, in whom he had discovered fitness, it is no doubt abundantly grateful to him to recognise and employ it. As he notably does, in these and in other instances. But before all things he has decided to remember that he is King; that he must accept the severe laws of that trust, and do *it*, or not have done anything.

An inverse sign, pointing in the same way, is the passionate search he is making in Foreign Countries for such men as will suit him. In these same months, for example, he bethinks him of two Counts Schmettau, in the Austrian Service, with whom he had made acquaintance in the Rhine Campaign; of a Count Von Rothenburg, whom he saw in the French Camp there; and is negotiating to have them if possible. The Schmettaus are Prussian by birth, though in Austrian Service; them he obtains under form of an Order home, with good conditions under it; they came, and proved useful men to him. Rothenburg, a shining kind of figure in Diplomacy as well as Soldiership, was Alsatian German, foreign to Prussia; but him too Friedrich obtained, and made much of, as will be notable by and by. And in fact the soul of all these noble tendencies in Friedrich, which surely are considerable, is even this, That he loves men of merit, and does not love men of none; that he has an endless appetite for men of merit, and feels, consciously and otherwise, that they are the one thing beautiful, the one thing needful to him.

This, which is the product of all fine tendencies, is

likewise their centre or focus out of which they start again, with some chance of fulfilment; — and we may judge in how many directions Friedrich was willing to expand himself, by the multifarious kinds he was inviting, and negotiating for. Academicians, — and not Maupertuis only, but all manner of mathematical geniuses (Euler whom he got, 's Gravesande, Muschenbroek, whom he failed of); and Literary geniuses innumerable, first and last. Academicians, Musicians, Players, Dancers even; much more Soldiers and Civil-Service men: no man that carries any honest "*Can do*" about with him but may expect some welcome here! Which continued through Friedrich's reign; and involved him in much petty trouble, not always successful in the lower kinds of it. For his Court was the cynosure of ambitious creatures on the wing, or inclined for taking wing: like a lantern kindled in the darkness of the world; — and many owls impinged upon him; whom he had to dismiss with brevity.

Perhaps it had been better to stand by mere Prussian or German merit, native to the ground? Or rather, undoubtedly it had! In some departments, as in the military, the administrative, diplomatic, Friedrich was himself among the best of judges; but in various others he had mainly (mainly, by no means blindly or solely) to accept noise of reputation as evidence of merit; and in these, if we compute with rigour, his success was intrinsically not considerable. The more honour to him that he never wearied of trying. "A man that does not care for merit," says the adage, "cannot himself have any." But a King that does not care for merit, what shall we say of such a King! —

Behaviour to his Mother; to his Wife.

One other fine feature, significant of many, let us notice: his affection for his Mother. When his Mother addressed him as "Your Majesty," he answered, as the Books are careful to tell us: "Call me Son; that is the Title of all others most agreeable to me!" Words which, there can be no doubt, came from the heart. Fain would he shoot forth to greatness in filial piety, as otherwise; fain solace himself in doing something kind to his Mother. Generously, lovingly; though again with clear view of the limits. He decrees for her a Title higher than had been customary, as well as more accordant with his feelings; not "Queen Dowager," but "Her Majesty the Queen Mother." He decides to build her a new Palace; "under the Lindens" it is to be, and of due magnificence: in a month or two, he had even got bits of the foundation dug, and the Houses to be pulled down bought or bargained for:* — which enterprise, however, was renounced, no doubt with consent, as the public aspects darkened. Nothing in the way of honour, in the way of real affection heartily felt and demonstrated, was wanting to Queen Sophie in her widowhood. But, on the other hand, of public influence no vestige was allowed, if any was ever claimed; and the good kind Mother lived in her Monbijou, the centre and summit of Berlin society; and restricted herself wisely to private matters. She has her domesticities, family affections, readings, speculations; gives evening parties at Monbijou. One glimpse of her in 1742 we get, that of a perfectly

* Rödenbeck, p. 15 (30th June — 23d August 1740); and correct Stenzel (iv. 44).

private royal Lady; which though it has little meaning, yet as it is authentic, coming from Büsching's hand, may serve as one little twinkle in that total darkness, and shall be left to the reader and his fancy:

A Count Henkel, a Thüringian gentleman, of high speculation, high pietistic ways, extremely devout, and given even to writing of religion, came to Berlin about some Silesian properties, — a man I should think of lofty melancholic aspect; and, in severe type, somewhat of a lion, on account of his Book called "*Deathbed Scenes* in four Volumes." Came to Berlin; and on the 15th August 1742, towards evening (as the ever-punctual Büsching looking into Henkel's Papers gives it), "was presented to the Queen Mother; who retained him to "supper; supper not beginning till about ten o'clock. The "Queen Mother was extremely gracious to Henkel; but in- "vestigated him a good deal, and put a great many questions," not quite easy to answer in that circle, "as, Why he did not "play? What he thought of comedies and operas? What "Preachers he was acquainted with in Berlin? Whether he too "was a Writer of Books?" (covertly alluding to the *Deathbed Scenes*, notes Büsching). "And abundance of other question- "ing. She also recounted many fantastic anecdotes (*viel* "*Abenteuerliches*) about Count von Zinzendorf" (Founder of *Herrnhuth*, far-shining spiritual Paladin of that day, whom her Majesty thinks rather a spiritual Quixote); "and declared that "they were strictly true."* Upon which, *exit* Henkel, borne by Büsching, and our light is snuffed out.

This is one momentary glance I have met with of Queen Sophie in her Dowager state. The rest, though there were seventeen years of it in all, is silent to mankind and me; and only her death, and her Son's great grief about it, so great as to be surprising, is mentioned in the Books.

Actual painful sorrow about his Father, much more any new outburst of weeping and lamenting, is not on

* Büsching's *Beyträge*, iv. 27.

record, after that first morning. Time does its work; and in such a whirl of occupations, sooner than elsewhere: and the loved Dead lie silent in their mausoleum in our hearts, — serenely sad as Eternity, not in loud sorrow as of Time. Friedrich was pious as a Son, however he might be on other heads. To the last years of his life, as from the first days of his reign, it was evident in what honour he held Friedrich Wilhelm's memory; and the words "my Father," when they turned up in discourse, had in that fine voice of his a tone which the observers noted. "To his Mother "he failed no day, when in Berlin, however busy, to "make his visit; and he never spoke to her, except hat "in hand."

With his own Queen, Friedrich still consorts a good deal, in these first times; is with her at Charlottenburg, Berlin, Potsdam, Reinsberg, for a day or two, as occasion gives; sometimes at Reinsberg for weeks running, in the intervals of war and business: glad to be at rest amid his old pursuits, by the side of a kind innocent being familiar to him. So it lasts for a length of time. But these happy intervals, we can remark, grow rarer; whether the Lady's humour, as they became rarer, might not sink withal, and produce an acceleration in the rate of decline? She was thought to be capable of "pouting (*faire la fâchée*)," at one period! We are left to our guesses; there is not anywhere the smallest whisper to guide us. Deep silence reigns in all Prussian Books. — To feel or to suspect yourself neglected, and to become *more* amiable thereupon (in which course alone lies hope), is difficult for any Queen! Enough, we can observe these meetings, within two or three years, have become much rarer;

and perhaps about the end of the third or fourth year, they altogether cease; and pass merely into the formal character. In which state they continued fixed, liable to no uncertainty; and were transacted, to the end of Friedrich's life, with inflexible regularity as the annual reviews were. This is a curious section of his life; which there will be other opportunities of noticing. But there is yet no thought of it anywhere, nor for years to come; though fables to the contrary were once current in Books.*

No Change in his Father's Methods or Ministries.

In the old mode of Administration, in the Ministries, Government Boards, he made no change. These administrative methods of his wise Father's are admirable to Friedrich, who knows them well; and they continue to be so. These men of his Father's, them also Friedrich knows, and that they were well chosen. In methods or in men, he is inclined to make the minimum of alteration at present. One Finance Hofrath of a projecting turn, named Eckart, who had abused the last weak years of Friedrich Wilhelm, and much afflicted mankind by the favour he was in: this Eckart Friedrich appointed a commission to inquire into; found the public right in regard to Eckart, and dismissed him with ignominy, not with much other punishment. Minister Boden, on the contrary, high in the Finance Department, who had also been much grumbled at, Friedrich found to be a good man: and Friedrich not only retained Boden, but advanced him; and continued to make more and more use of him in

* Laveaux; &c.

time coming. His love of perfection in work done, his care of thrift, seemed almost greater than his late Father's had been, — to the disappointment of many. In the other Departments, Podewils, Thulmeyer and the rest, went on as heretofore; — only in general with less to do, the young King doing more himself than had been usual. Valori, "*mon gros Valori*, (my fat Valori)," French Minister here, whom we shall know better, writes home of the new King of Prussia: "He begins "his government, as by all appearance he will carry "it on, in a highly satisfactory way: everywhere traits "of benevolence, sympathy for his subjects, respect "shown to the memory of the Deceased,"* — no change made, where it evidently is not for the better.

Friedrich's "Three principal Secretaries of State," as we should designate them, are very remarkable. Three Clerks he found, or had known of, somewhere in the Public Offices; and now took, under some advanced title, to be specially his own Private Clerks: three vigorous long-headed young fellows, "Eichel, Schuhmacher, Lautensack" the obscure names of them;** out of whom, now and all along henceforth, he got immensities of work in that kind. They lasted all his life; and, of course, grew ever more expert at their function. Close, silent; exact as machinery; ever ready, from the smallest clear hint, marginal pencil-mark, almost from a glance of the eye, to clothe the Royal Will in official form, with the due rugged clearness and thrift of words. "Came punctually at four in the morning in summer, five in winter;" did daily the

* *Mémoires des Négociations du Marquis de Valori* (à Paris, 1820), i. 20 ("June 13th, 1740"). A valuable Book, which we shall often have to quote: edited in a lamentably ignorant manner.
** Rödenbeck, 15th June 1740.

day's work; and kept their mouths well shut. A very notable Trio of men; serving his Majesty and the Prussian Nation as Principal Secretaries of State, on those cheap terms; — nay almost as Houses of Parliament with Standing-Committees and appendages, so many *Acts* of Parliament, admittedly rather wise, being passed daily by his Majesty's help and theirs! — Friedrich paid them rather well; they saw no society; lived wholly to their work, and to their own families. Eichel alone of the Three was mentioned at all by mankind, and that obscurely; an "abstruse, reserved, longheaded "kind of man;" and "made a great deal of money in "the end," insinuates Büsching,* no friend of Friedrich's or his.

In superficial respects, again, Friedrich finds that the Prussian King ought to have a King's Establishment, and maintain a decent splendour among his neighbours, — as is not quite the case at present. In this respect he does make changes. A certain quantity of new Pages, new Goldsticks; some considerable, not too considerable, new-furbishing of the Royal Household, — as it were, a fair coat of new paint, with gilding not profuse, — brought it to the right pitch for this King. About "a hundred and fifty" new figures of the Page and Goldstick kind, is the reckoning given.** So many of these; and there is an increase of 16,000 to one's Army going on: that is the proportion noticeable. In the facts as his Father left them Friedrich persisted all his life; in the semblances or outer vestures he changed, to this extent for the present. — These are the Phenomena of Friedrich's Accession, noted by us.

* *Beyträge*, v. 238, &c.   ** *Helden-Geschichte*, I. 353.

Readers see there is radiance enough, perhaps slightly in excess, but of intrinsically good quality, in the Aurora of this new Reign. A brilliant valiant young King; much splendour of what we could call a *golden* or soft nature (visible in those "New-Era" doings of his, in those strong affections to his Friends); and also, what we like almost better in him, something of a *steel-bright* or stellar splendour (meaning, clearness of eyesight, intrepidity, severe loyalty to fact), — which is a fine addition to the softer element, and will keep *it* and its philanthropies and magnanimities well under rule. Such a man is rare in this world; how extremely rare such a man born King! He is swift and he is persistent; sharply discerning, fearless to resolve and perform; carries his great endowments lightly, as if they were not heavy to him. He has known hard misery, been taught by stripes; a light stoicism sits gracefully on him.

"What he will grow to?" Probably to something considerable. Very certainly to something far short of his aspirations; far different from his own hopes, and the world's concerning him. It is not we, it is Father Time that does the controlling and fulfilling of our hopes; and strange work he makes of them and us. For example, has not Friedrich's grand "New Era," inaugurated by him in a week, with the leading spirits all adoring, issued since in French Revolution and a "world well suicided," — the leading spirits much thrown-out in consequence! New Era has gone to great lengths since Friedrich's time; and the leading spirits do not now adore it, but yawn over it, or worse! Which changes to us the then aspect of Friedrich, and his epoch and his aspirations, a good deal. — On the whole, Friedrich will go his way, Time and the leading spirits going theirs; and, like the rest of us, will grow to what he can. His actual size is not great among the Kingdoms: his outward resources are rather to be called small. The Prussian Dominion at that date is, in extent, about Four-fifths of an England Proper, and perhaps not one-fifth so fertile: subject Population is well under Two Millions and a Half; Revenue not much above One Million Sterling, * — very small, were not thrift such a *vectigal*.

This young King is magnanimous; not much to be called ambitious, or not in the vulgar sense almost at all, — strange as it may sound to readers. His hopes at this time are many; — and among them, I perceive, there is not wanting secretly, in spite of his experiences, some hope that he himself may be a good deal "happier" than formerly. Nor is there any ascetic humour, on his part, to forbid trial. He is much determined to try. Probably enough, as we guess and gather, his agreeablest anticipations, at this time, were of Reinsberg: How, in the intervals of work well done, he would live there wholly to the Muses; have his chosen spirits round him, his colloquies, his suppers of the gods. Why not? There might be a King of Intellects conceivable withal; protecting, cherishing, practically guiding the chosen Illuminative Souls of this world. A new Charlemagne, the smallest new Charlemagne of Spiritual type, with *his* Paladins round him; how glorious, how salutary in the dim generations now going! — These too were

* The exact statistic cipher is, at Friedrich's Accession: *Prussian Territories*, 2,275 square miles German (56,875 English); *Population*, 2,240,000; *Annual Revenue*, 7,371,707 thalers 7 groschen (1,105,756*l*. without the pence). See Preuss, *Buch für Jedermann*, i. 49; Stenzel, iii. 692; &c.

hopes which proved signally futile. Rigorous Time could not grant these at all; — granted, in his own hard way, other things instead. But, all along, the Life-element, the Epoch, though Friedrich took it kindly and never complained, was ungenial to such a man.

"Somewhat of a rotten Epoch, this into which Friedrich "has been born, to shape himself and his activities royal and "other!" exclaims Smelfungus once: "In an older earnest "Time, when the eternally awful meanings of this Universe "had not yet sunk into dubieties to any one, much less into "levities or into mendacities, into huge hypocrisies carefully "regulated, — so luminous, vivid and ingenuous a young "creature had not wanted divine manna in his Pilgrimage "through Life. Nor, in that case, had he come out of it in "so lean a condition. But the highest man of us is born brother "to his Contemporaries; struggle as he may, there is no "escaping the family likeness. By spasmodic indignant con-"tradiction of them, by stupid compliance with them, — you "will inversely resemble, if you do not directly; like the "starling, you can't get out! — Most surely, if there do fall "manna from Heaven, in the given Generation, and nourish "in us reverence and genial nobleness day by day, it is blessed "and well. Failing that, in regard to our poor spiritual inter-"ests, there is sure to be one of two results: mockery, con-"tempt, disbelief, what we may call *short-diet* to the length of "very famine (which was Friedrich's case); or else slow-"poison, carefully elaborated and provided by way of daily "nourishment.

"Unhappy souls, these same! The slow-poison has gone "deep into them. Instead of manna, this long while back, "they have been living on mouldy corrupt meats sweetened by "sugar-of-lead; — or perhaps, like Voltaire, a few individuals "prefer hunger as the cleaner alternative; and in con-"temptuous, barren, mocking humour, not yet got the length "of geniality or indignation, snuff the east-wind by way of "spiritual diet. Pilgriming along on such nourishment, the "best human soul fails to become very ruddy! — Tidings "about Heaven are fallen so uncertain, but the Earth and her

"joys are still interesting: 'Take to the Earth and her joys;—
"let your soul go out, since it must; let your five senses and
"their appetites be well alive.' That is a dreadful 'Sham-
"Christian Dispensation' to be born under! You wonder at
"the want of heroism in the Eighteenth Century. Wonder
"rather at the degree of heroism it had; wonder how many
"souls there still are to be met with in it of some effective
"capability, though dieting in that way, — nothing else to be
"had in the shops about. Carterets, Belleisles, Friedrichs,
"Voltaires; Chathams, Franklins, Choiseuls: there is an
"effective stroke of work, a fine fire of heroic pride, in this
"man and the other; not yet extinguished by spiritual famine
"or slow-poison; so robust is Nature the mighty Mother! —
"But in general, that sad Gospel, 'Souls extinct, Stomachs
"well alive!' is the credible one, not articulately preached,
"but practically believed by the abject generations, and acted
"on as it never was before. What immense sensualities there
"were, is known; and also (as some small offset, though that
"has not yet begun in 1740) what immense quantities of Phy-
"sical Labour and contrivance were got out of mankind, in
"that Epoch and down to this day. As if, having lost its
"Heaven, it had struck desperately down into the Earth; as if
"it were a *beaver*-kind, and not a mankind any more. We had
"once a Barbarossa; and a world all grandly true. But from
"that to Karl VI., and *his* Holy Romish Reich in such a state
"of 'Holiness' —!" — I here cut short my abstruse Friend.

Readers are impatient to have done with these miscellaneous preludings, and to be once definitely under way, such a Journey lying ahead. Yes, readers; a Journey indeed! And, at this point, permit me to warn you that, where the ground, where Dryasdust and the Destinies, yield anything humanly illustrative of Friedrich and his Work, one will have to linger, and carefully gather it, even as here. Large tracts occur, bestrewn with mere pedantisms, diplomatic cobwebberies, learned marine-stores, and inhuman matter, over which we shall have to skip empty-handed: this also was among the sad conditions of our Enterprise, that it has to go now too slow and again too fast; not in proportion to natural importance of objects, but to several inferior considerations withal. So busy has perverse Destiny been on it; perverse Destiny, edacious Chance; — and the Dryasdusts, too, and Nightmares, in Prussia as elsewhere, we know how strong they are!

Friedrich's character in old age has doubtless its curious affinities, its disguised identities, with these prognostic features and indications of his youth: and to our readers, — if we do ever get them to the goal, of seeing Friedrich a little with their own eyes and judgments, — there may be pleasant contrasts and comparisons of that kind in store, one day. But the far commoner experience (which also has been my own), — here is Smelfungus's stern account of that:

"My friend, you will be luckier than I, if, after ten years, "not to say, in a sense, twenty years, thirty years, of reading "and rummaging in those sad Prussian Books, ancient and "new (which often are laudably authentic, too, and exact as to "details), you can gather any character whatever of Friedrich, "in any period of his life, or conceive him as a Human Entity "at all! It is strange, after such thousandfold writing, but it is "true, his History is considerably unintelligible to mankind at "this hour; left chaotic, enigmatic, in a good many points, — "the military part of it alone being brought to clearness, and "rendered fairly conceivable and credible to those who will "study. And as to the Man himself, or what his real Phy- "siognomy can have been —! — Well, it must be owned few "men were of such *rapidity* of face and aspect; so difficult to "seize the features of. In his action, too, there was such "rapidity, such secrecy, suddenness: a man that could not be "read, even by the candid, except as in flashes of lightning. "And then the anger of bystanders, *un*candid, who got hurt "by him; the hasty malevolences, the stupidities, the opa-

"cities: enough, in modern times, what is saying much, per-
"haps no man's motives, intentions, and procedure have been
"more belied, misunderstood, misrepresented, during his life.
"Nor, I think, since that, have many men fared worse, by the
"Limner or Biographic class, the favourable to him and the
"unfavourable; or been so smeared of and blotched of, and
"reduced to a mere blur and dazzlement of crosslights, in-
"coherences, incredibilities, in which nothing, not so much as
"a human nose, is clearly discernible by way of feature!" —
Courage, reader, nevertheless; on the above terms, let us
march according to promise.

CHAPTER II.

THE HOMAGINGS.

Young Friedrich, as his Father had done, considers it unnecessary to be crowned. Old Friedrich, first of the name, and of the King series, we did see crowned, with a pinch of snuff tempering the solemnities. That Coronation once well done suffices all his descendants hitherto. Such an expense of money, — of diluted mendacity too! Such haranguing, gesturing, symbolic fugling, all grown half-false: — avoid lying, even with your eyes, or knees, or the coat upon your back, so far as you easily can!"

Nothing of Coronation: but it is thought needful to have the *Huldigungen* (Homagings) done, the Fealties sworn; and the young Majesty in due course goes about, or gives directions, now here now there, in his various Provinces, getting that accomplished. But even in that, Friedrich is by no means strait-laced or punctilious; does it commonly by Deputy: only in three places, Königsberg, Berlin, Cleve, does he appear in person. Mainly by deputy; and always with the minimum of fuss, and no haranguing that could be avoided. Nowhere are the old *Stände* (Provincial Parliaments) assembled, now or afterwards: sufficient for this and for every occasion are the "Permanent Committees of the *Stände*;" nor is much speaking, unessential for despatch of business, used to these.

"*Stände*, — of Ritterschaft mainly, of Gentry small and "great, — existed once in all those Countries, as elsewhere,"

says one Historian; "and some of them, in Preussen for
"example, used to be rather loud, and inclined to turbulence,
"till the curb, from a judicious bridle-hand, would admonish
"them. But, for a long while past, — especially since the
"Great Elector's time, who got an 'Excise Law' passed, or the
"foundations of a good Excise Law laid;* and, what with
"Excise, what with Domain-Farms, had a fixed Annual
"Budget, which he reckoned fair to both parties, — they have
"been dying out for want of work; and, under Friedrich Wil-
"helm, may be said to have gone quite dead. What work
"was left for them? Prussian Budget is fixed, many things are
"fixed: why talk of them farther? The Prussian King,
"nothing of a fool like certain others," — which indeed is the
cardinal point, though my Author does not say so, — "is
"respectfully aware of the facts round him; and can listen to
"the rumours too, so far as he finds good. The King sees
"himself terribly interested to get into the right course in all
"things, and avoid the wrong one! Probably he does, in his
"way, seek 'wise Advice concerning the arduous matters of
"the Kingdom;' nay I believe he is diligent to have it of the
"wisest: — who knows if *Stände* would always give it wiser;
"especially *Stände* in the haranguing condition?" — Enough,
they are not applied to. There is no Freedom in that Country.
"No Freedom to speak of," continues he: "but I do a little
"envy them their Fixed Budget, and some other things. What
"pleasure there can be in having your household arrange-
"ments tumbled into disorder every new Year, by a new-
"contrived scale of expenses for you, I never could as-
"certain!" —

Friedrich is not the man to awaken Parliamentary
sleeping-dogs well settled by his Ancestors. Once or
twice, out of Preussen, in Friedrich Wilhelm's time,
there was heard some whimper, which sounded like
the beginning of a bark. But Friedrich Wilhelm was
on the alert for it: Are you coming in with your *Nie
Pozwalam* (your *Liberum Veto*), then? None of your
Polish vagaries here! "*Tout le pays sera ruiné* (the

* Preuss, iv. 432; and *Thronbesteigung*, pp. 379-383.

whole Country will be ruined)," say you? (Such had been the poor Marshal or Provincial *Speaker's* Remonstrance on one occasion): "I don't believe a word "of that. But I do believe the Government by *Junkers*" (Country Squires) "and *Nie Pozwalam* will be ruined," — as it is fully meant to be! "I am establishing the "King's Sovereignty like a rock of bronze *(Ich stabi-* "*lire die Souverainetät wie einen Rocher von Bronze),*" some extremely strong kind of rock!* This was one of Friedrich Wilhelm's marginalia in response to such a thing; and the mutinous whimper died out again. Parliamentary Assemblages are sometimes Collective Wisdoms, but by no means always so. In Magdeburg we remember what trouble Friedrich Wilhelm had with his unreasonable Ritters. Ritters there, in their assembled capacity, had the Reich behind them, and could not be dealt with like Preussen: but Friedrich Wilhelm, by wise slow methods, managed Magdeburg too, and reduced it to silence, or to words necessary for despatch of business.

In each Province, a Permanent Committee, — chosen I suppose, by King and Knights assenting; chosen I know not how, but admitted to be wisely chosen, — represents the once Parliament or *Stände;* and has its potency for doing good service in regard to all Provincial matters, from roads and bridges upwards, and is impotent to do the least harm. Roads and bridges, Church matters, repartition of the Landdues, Army matters, — in fact they are an effective non-haranguing Parliament, to the King's Deputy in every such Province; well calculated to illuminate and

---

* Förster, b. iii. (Urkundenbuch, i. 50); Preuss, iv. 420n. "*Nie Pozwalam*" (the formula of *Liberum Veto*) signifies, "I Don't Permit!"

forward his subaltern *Amtmen* and him. Nay, we observe it is oftenest in the way of gifts and solacements that the King articulately communicates with these Committees or their Ritterschafts. Projects for Draining of Bogs, for improved Highways, for better Husbandry; loans granted them, Loan-Banks established for the Province's behoof: — no need of parliamentary eloquence on such occasions, but of something far different.

It is from this quiescent, or busy but noiseless kind of *Stände* and Populations that Friedrich has his *Huldigung* to take; — and the operation, whether done personally or by deputy, must be an abundantly simple one. He, for his part, is fortunate enough to find everywhere the Sovereignty *established;* "rock of bronze" not the least shaken in his time. He will graciously undertake, by Written Act, which is read before the *Stände*, King or King's Deputy witnessing there, "To maintain the privileges" of his *Stände* and Populations; the *Stände* answer, on oath, with lifted hand, and express invocation of Heaven, That they will obey him as true subjects: And so, — doubtless with something of dining superadded, but no whisper of it put on record, — the *Huldigung* will everywhere very quietly transact itself.

The *Huldigung* itself is nothing to us, even with Friedrich there, — as at Königsberg, Berlin, Cleve, the three exceptional places. To which, nevertheless, let us briefly attend him, for the sake of here and there some direct glimpse we may get of the then Friedrich's actual physiognomy and ways. Other direct view, or the chance of such, is not conceded us out of those sad Prussian Books; which are very full on this of the *Huldigung*, if silent on so many other points.*

* Preuss, *Thronbesteigung*, p. 382.

CHAP. II.] THE HOMAGINGS. 47
7th July 1740.

Friedrich accepts the Homages, personally, in Three Places.

To Königsberg is his first excursion on this errand. Preussen has perhaps, or may be suspected of having, some remnants of sour humours left in it, and remembrances of *Stände* with haranguings, and even mutinies; there if anywhere the King in person may do good on such an occasion. He left Berlin, July 7th, bound thitherward; here is Note of that first Royal Tour, — specimen of several hundreds such, which he had to do in the course of the next Forty-five years.

"Friend Algarotti, charming talker, attended him; who "else, official and non-official, ask not. The Journey is to be "circuitous; to combine various businesses, and also to have "its amusements. They went by Cüstrin; glancing at old "known Country, which is at its greenest in this season. By "Cüstrin, across the Neumark, into Pommern; after that by "an intricate winding route; reviewing regiments, inspecting "garrisons, now here now there; doing all manner of in- "spections; talking I know not what; oftenest lodging with "favoured Generals, if it suited. Distance to Königsberg, by "the direct road, is about 500 miles; by this winding one, it "must have been 800: Journey thither took nine days in all. "Obliquely through Pommern, almost to the coast of the "Baltic; their ultimatum there a place called Köslin, where "they reviewed with strictness, — omitting Colberg, a small "Sea-Fortress not far rearward, time being short. Thence "into West-Preussen, into Polish Territory, and swiftly "across that; keeping Danzig and its noises wide enough to "the left: one night in Poland; and the next they are in Ost- "Preussen, place called Liebstadt, — again on home-ground, "and diligently reviewing there.

"The review at Liebstadt is remarkable in this, That the "regiments, one regiment especially, not being what was fit, a "certain Grenadier-Captain got cashiered on the spot; and "the old Commandant himself was soon after pensioned, and

"more gently sent his ways. So strict is his Majesty. Con-
"trariwise, he found Lieutenant-General von Katte's Garrison,
"at Angerburg, next day, in a very high perfection; and
"Colonel Posadowsky's regiment specially so; with which
"latter gentleman he lodged that night, and made him farther
"happy by the *Order of Merit:* Colonel Posadowsky, Garrison
"of Angerburg, far off in East Preussen, Chevalier of the
"Order of Merit henceforth, if we ever meet him again. To
"the good old Lieutenant-General von Katte, who no doubt
"dined with them, his Majesty handed, on the same occasion,
"a Patent of Feldmarschall; — intends soon to make him
"Graf; and did it, as readers know. Both Colonel and General
"attended him thenceforth, still by a circuitous route, to
"Königsberg, to assist in the solemnities there. By Gum-
"binnen, by Trakehnen, — the Stud of Trakehnen: that also
"his Majesty saw, and made review of; not without emotion,
"we can fancy, as the sleek colts were trotted out on those
"new terms! At Trakehnen, Katte and the Colonel would be
"his Majesty's guests, for the night they stayed. This is
"their extreme point eastward; Königsberg now lies a good
"way west of them. But at Trakehnen they turn; and, Satur-
"day 16th July 1740, after another hundred miles or so, along
"the pleasant valley of the Pregel, get to Königsberg: ready
"to begin business on Monday morning, — on Sunday if ne-
"cessary." *

On Sunday there did a kind of memorability occur: The *Huldigungs-Predigt* (Homage Sermon) by a reverend Herr Quandt, chief Preacher there. Which would not be worth mentioning, except for this circumstance, That his Majesty exceedingly admired Quandt, and thought him a most Demosthenic genius, and the best of all the Germans. Quandt's text was in these words: "*Thine are we, David, and on thy side, thou Son of* "*Jesse: Peace, peace be unto thee, and peace be to thine* "*helpers; for thy God helpeth thee.*" ** Quandt began, in a sonorous voice, raising his face with respectful

* From Preuss, *Thronbesteigung*, pp. 382, 385; Rödenbeck, p. 16; &c.
** *First Chronicles,* xii. 18.

enthusiasm to the King, "Thine are we, O Friedrich, "and on thy side, thou Son of Friedrich Wilhelm;" and so went on: sermon brief, sonorous, compact, and sticking close to its text. Friedrich stood immovable, gazing on the eloquent Demosthenic Quandt, with admiration heightened by surprise; — wrote of Quandt to Voltaire; and, with sustained enthusiasm, to the Public long afterwards; and to the end of his days was wont to make Quandt an exception, if perhaps almost the only one, from German barbarism, and disharmony of mind and tongue. So that poor Quandt cannot ever since get entirely forgotten, but needs always to be raked up again, for this reason when others have ceased: an almost melancholy adventure for poor Quandt and Another! —

The *Huldigung* was rather grand; Harangue and Counter-harangue permitted to the due length, and proper festivities following: but the *Stände* could not manage to get into vocal covenanting or deliberating at all; Friedrich before leaving Berlin had answered their hint or request that way, in these words: "We "are likewise graciously inclined to give to the said "*Stände*, before their Homaging, the same assurance "which they got from our Herr Father's Majesty, who "is now with God," — general assurance that their, and everybody's, "Rights shall be maintained" (as we see they are), — "with which, it is hoped (*hoffentlich*), "they will be content, and get to peace upon this "matter (*sich dabei beruhigen werden*)."* It will be best for them!

Friedrich gave away much corn here; that is, opened his Corn-Granaries, on charitable terms, and

* Preuss, *Thronbesteigung*, p. 380.

took all manner of measures, here as in other places, for relief of the scarcity there was. Of the illuminations, never so grand, the reader shall hear nothing. A "Torch Procession of the Students" turned out a pretty thing: — Students marching with torches, with fine wind-music, regulated enthusiasm, fine succinct Address to his Majesty; and all the world escorting, with its "Live Forever!" Friedrich gave the Students "a *Trink-Gelag* (Banquet of Liquors)," how arranged I do not know: and to the Speaker of the Address, a likely young gentleman with *Von* to his name, he offered an Ensigncy of Foot ("in Camas's Fusileer Regiment," — Camas now gone to Paris, embassying), which was joyfully accepted. Joyfully accepted; — and it turned out well for all parties; the young gentleman having risen, where merit was the rule of rising, and become Graf and Lieutenant-General, in the course of the next fifty years.*

Huldigung and Torch-Procession over, the Royal Party dashed rapidly off, next morning (21st July), homewards by the shortest route; and, in three days more, by Frankfurt on the Oder (where a glimpse of General Schwerin, a favourite General, was to be had), were safe in Berlin; received with acclamation, nay with "blessings and even tears" some say, after this pleasant Fortnight's Tour. General Schwerin, it is rumoured, will be made Feldmarschall straightway, the Münchows are getting so promoted as we said; edicts are coming out, much business speeding forward, and the tongues of men keep wagging.

Berlin *Huldigung*, — and indeed, by Deputy, that

* Preuss, *Thronlesteigung*, p. 367.

of nearly all the other Towns, — was on Tuesday, August 2d. At Berlin his Majesty was present in the matter: but, except the gazing multitudes, and hussar regiments, ranked in the Schloss-Platz and streets adjoining, there was little of notable in it; the upholstery arrangements thrifty in the extreme. His Majesty is prone to thrift in this of the Huldigung, as would appear; perhaps regarding the affair as scenic merely. Here, besides this of Berlin, is another instance just occurring. It appears, the Quedlinburg people, shut out from the light of the actual Royal Countenance, cannot do their Homaging by Deputy, without at least a Portrait of the King and of the Queen: How manage? asks the official Person. "Have a Couple of Daubs done in Berlin, three guineas apiece; send them these," answers the King!*

Here in the Berlin Schloss, scene the Large Hall within doors, there is a "platform raised three steps; "and on this, by way of a kind of throne, an armchair "covered with old black velvet;" the whole surmounted by a canopy also of old black velvet: not a sublime piece of upholstery; but reckoned adequate. Friedrich mounted the three steps; stood before the old chair, his Princes standing promiscuously behind it; his Ritters in quantity, in front and to right and left, on the floor. Some Minister of the Interior explains suitably, not at too great length, what they are met for; some junior Official, junior but of quality, responded briefly, for himself and his order, to the effect, "Yea, truly:" the *Huldigungs-Urkunde* (Deed of Homage) was then read by the proper Clerk, and the Ritters all

---

* "*On doit faire barbouiller de mauvaises copies à Berlin, la pièce d 20 écus.* — Fr." Preuss, ii. (Urkundenbuch, s. 222).

swore; audibly, with lifted hands. This is the Ritter Huldigung.

His Majesty then steps out to the Balcony, for Oath and Homage of the general Population. General population gave its oath, and "three great shouts over and above." "*Es lebe der König!*" thrice, with all their throats. Upon which a shower of Medals, "Homage-Medals," gold and silver (quantity not mentioned), rained down upon them, in due succession; and were scrambled for, in the usual way. "His Majesty," they write, and this is perhaps the one point worth notice, "his Majesty, contrary to custom and to etiquette, "remained on the Balcony, some time after the cere- "mony, perhaps a full half-hour;" — silent there, "with his look fixed attentively on the immeasurable "multitude before the Schloss; and seemed sunk in "deep reflection (*Betrachtung*):" — an almost awfully eloquent though inarticulate phenomenon to his Majesty, that of those multitudes scrambling and huzzahing there!*

These, with the Cleve one, are all the Homagings Friedrich was personally present at; the others he did by Deputy, all in one day (2d August); and without fuss. Scenic matters these; in which, except where he can, as in the Königsberg case, combine inspections and grave businesses with them, he takes no interest. However, he is now, for the sake chiefly of inspections and other real objects, bent on a Journey to Cleve;— the fellow of that to Königsberg: Königsberg, Preussen, the easternmost outlying wing of his long straggling Dominions; and then Cleve-Jülich, its counterpart on

* Preuss, *Thronbesteigung,* p. 389.

the south-western side, — there also, with such contingencies hanging over Cleve-Jülich, it were proper to make some mustering of the Frontier garrisons and affairs.* His Majesty so purposes: and we purpose again to accompany, — not for inspection and mustering, but for an unexpected reason. The grave Journey to Cleve has an appendage, or comic side-piece, hanging to it; more than one appendage; which the reader must not miss! — Before setting out, read these two Fractions, snatched from the Diplomatist Wastebag; looking well, we gain there some momentary view of Friedrich on the business side. Of Friedrich, and also of Another:

Sunday, 14th August 1740, Dickens, who has been reporting hitherto in a favourable, though in a languid exoteric manner, not being in any height of favour, England or he, — had express Audience of his Majesty; being summoned out to Potsdam for that end: "Sunday evening, about 7 P.M.," — Majesty intending to be off on the Cleve Journey to-morrow. Let us accompany Dickens. Readers may remember, George II. has been at Hanover for some weeks past; Bielfeld diligently grinning euphemisms and courtly graciosities to him; Truchsess hinting, on opportunity, that there are perhaps weighty businesses in the rear; which, however, on the Britannic side, seem loth to start. Britannic Majesty is much at a loss about his Spanish War, so dangerous for kindling France and the whole world upon him. In regard to which Prussia might be so important, for or against. — This, in compressed form, is what Dickens witnesses at Potsdam, that Sunday evening from 7 P.M.:

"Audience lasted above an hour: King turned directly "upon business; wishes to have 'Categorical Answers' as to "Three Points already submitted to his Britannic Majesty's "consideration. Clear footing indispensable between us.

* In regard to the Day of *Huldigung* at Cleve, which happily is not of the least moment to us, Preuss (*Thronbesteigung*, p. 390) and *Helden-Geschichte* (i. 423) seem to be in flat contradiction.

"What you want of me? say it, and be plain. What I want of you is, These three things:

"1º. Guarantee for Jülich and Berg. All the world knows *whose* these Duchies are. Will his Britannic Majesty guarantee me there? And if so, How, and to what lengths, will he proceed about it?

"2º. Settlement about Ost-Friesland. Expectancy of Ost-Friesland, soon to fall heirless, which was granted *me* long since, though Hanover makes hagglings, counter-claimings: I must have some Settlement about that.

"3º. The like about those perplexities in Mecklenburg. No difficulty there if we try heartily, nor is there such pressing haste about it.

"These are my three claims on England; and I will try to serve England as far in return, if it will tell me how. 'Ah, beware of throwing yourself into the arms of France!' modestly suggests Dickens. — 'Well, if France will guarantee me those Duchies, and you will not do anything?' answers his Majesty with a fine laugh: 'England I consider my most natural friend and ally; but I must know what there is to depend on there. Princes are ruled by their interest; cannot follow their feelings. Let me have an explicit answer; say, at Wesel, where I am to be on the 24th,'" — ten days hence. Britannic Majesty is at Hanover, and can answer within that time. "This he twice told 'me, Wesel, 24th,' in the course of our interview. Permit me to recommend the matter to your Lordship," — my Lord Harrington, now attending the Britannic Majesty.

"During the whole audience," adds Dickens, "the King was in extreme good humour; and not only heard with attention all the considerations I offered, but was not the least offended at any objections I made to what he said. It is undoubtedly the best way to behave with frankness to him." These last are Dickens's own words; let them modestly be a memorandum to your Lordship. This King goes himself direct to the point; and straightforwardness, as a primary condition, will profit your Lordship with him. *

Most true advice, this; — and would perhaps be followed, were it quite easy! But things are very complicated. And the Britannic Majesty, much plagued with Spanish War and Par-

* Dickens (in State-Paper Office), 17th August 1740.

liamentary noises in that unquiet Island, is doubtless glad to get away to Hanover for a little; and would fain be on holiday in these fine rural months. Which is not well possible either. Jenkins's Ear, rising at last like a fiery portent, has kindled the London Fog over yonder, in a strange way, and the murky stagnancy is all getting on fire; the English intent, as seldom any Nation was, to give the Spaniards an effectual beating. Which they hope they can, — though unexpected difficulties will occur. And, in the mean while, what a riddle of potentialities for his poor Majesty to read, and pick his way from!—

Bielfeld, in spite of all this, would fain be full of admiration for the Britannic Majesty. Confesses he is below the middle size, in fact a tiny little creature, but then his shape is perfect; leg much to be commended, — which his Majesty knows, standing always with one leg slightly advanced, and the Order of the Garter on it, that mankind may take notice. Here is Bielfeld's description faithfully abridged:

"Big blue eyes, perhaps rather of parboiled character, "though proud enough; eyes flush with his face or more, "rather *in relief* than on a level with it," — *à fleur de tête*, after the manner of a fish, if one might say so, and betokening such an intellect behind them! "Attitude constrained, leg advanced "in that way; his courtiers call it majestic. Biggish mouth, "strictly shut in the crescent or horse-shoe form (*fermée en* "*croissant*); curly wig (*à nœuds*, reminding you of lamb's- "wool, colour not known); eyebrows, however, you can see "are ashy-blond; general tint is fundamentally livid; but "when in good case, the royal skin will take tolerably bright "colours (*prend d'assez belles couleurs*). As to the royal mind "and understanding, what shall Bielfeld say? That his Ma- "jesty sometimes makes ingenious and just remarks, and is "laudably serious at all times, and can majestically hold his "tongue, and stand with advanced leg, and eyes rather more "than flush. Sense of his dignity is high, as it ought to be; "on great occasions you see pride and a kind of joy mantling "in the royal countenance. Has been known to make ex- "plosions, and to be very furious to Prince Fred and others, "when pricked into:— but, my friend, what mortal is exempt "from failings? Majesty reads the English Newspapers every "morning in bed, which are often biting. Majesty has his

"Walmoden, a Hanoverian Improper-Female, Countess of "Yarmouth so-called; quiet, autumnal, fair-complexioned, "stupid; who is much a comfort to him. She keeps out of "mischief, political or other; and gives Bielfeld a gracious nod "now and then." * Harrington is here too; — and Britannic Majesty and he are busy governing the English Nation on these terms. — We return now to the Prussian Majesty.

About six weeks after that of Dickens, — Cleve Journey and much else now ended, — Prätorius the Danish Envoy, whom we slightly knew at Reinsberg once, gives this testimony; writing home to an Excellency at Copenhagen, whose name we need not inquire into:

"To give your Excellency a just idea of the new Government here, I must observe that hitherto the King of Prussia "does as it were everything himself; and that, excepting the "Finance Minister von Boden, who preaches frugality, and "finds for that doctrine uncommon acceptance, almost greater "even than in the former reign, his Majesty allows no counselling from any Minister; so that Herr von Podewils, who "is now the working hand in the department of Foreign "Affairs, has nothing given him to do but to expedite the "orders he receives from the Cabinet, his advice not being "asked upon any matter; and so it is with the other Ministers. "People thought the loss of Herr von Thulmeyer," veteran Foreign Minister whom we have transiently heard of in the Double-Marriage time, and perhaps have even seen at London or elsewhere, ** " would be irreparable; so expert was he, and "a living archive in that business: however, his post seems to "have vanished with himself. His salary is divided between "Herr von Podewils," whom the reader will sometimes hear of again, "Kriegsrath (Councillor of War) von Ilgen," son of the old gentleman we used to know, " and Hofrath Sellentin who is "*Rendant of the Legations-Kasse*" (Ambassadors' Paymaster,

---

* Bielfeld, I. 158.
** Died, 4th August (Rödenbeck, p. 20).

we could guess, Ambassador Body having specialty of cash assigned it, comparable with the specialty of value received from it, in this strict frugal Country), — neither of which two latter names shall the reader be troubled with farther. "A "good many resolutions, and responses by the King, I have "seen: they combine laconic expression with an admirable "business eye (*Geschäftsblick*). Unhappily," — at least for us in the Diplomatic line, for your Excellency and me unhappily, — "there is nobody about the King who possesses his complete "confidence, or whom we can make use of in regard to the ne- "cessary introductions and preliminary movements. Hereby "it comes that, — as certain things can only be handled with "cautious foresight and circumlocution, and in the way of be- "ginning wide, — an Ambassador here is more thrown out of "his course than in any other Court; and knows not, though "his object were steadily in sight, what road to strike into for "getting towards it." *

* Preuss, *Thronbesteigung*, p. 877 (2d October 1740).

CHAPTER III.

FRIEDRICH MAKES AN EXCURSION, NOT OF DIRECT SORT, INTO THE CLEVE COUNTRIES.

KING Friedrich did not quite keep his day at Wesel; indeed this 24th was not the first day, but the last of several, he had appointed to himself for finis to that Journey in the Cleve Countries; Journey rather complex to arrange. He has several businesses ahead in those parts; and as usual, will group them with good judgment, and thrift of time. Not inspections merely, but amusements, meetings with ifriends, especially French friends: the question is, how to group them with skill, so that the necessary elements may converge at the right moment, and one shot kill three or four birds. This is Friedrich's fine way, perceptible in all these Journeys. The French friends, flying each on his own track, with his own load of impediments, Voltaire with his Madame for instance, are a difficult element in such problem; and there has been, and is, much scheming and corresponding about it, within the last month especially.

Voltaire is now at Brussels with his Du Châtelet, prosecuting that endless "lawsuit with the House of Honsbruck," — which he, and we, are both desirous to have done with. He is at the Hague, too, now and then; printing, about to print, the *Anti-Macchiavel;* corresponding, to right and left, quarrelling with Van Duren the Printer; lives, while there, in the *Vieille Cour*, in.the vast dusky rooms with faded gilding, and grand old Bookshelves "with the biggest spider-webs in Europe." Brussels is his place for Law-Consultations, general family residence; the Hague and that old spider-web Palace for correcting Proofsheets; doing one's own private studies, which we never quite neglect. Fain would Friedrich see him, fain he Friedrich; but there is a divine Emilie, there is a Maupertuis, there are — In short never were such difficulties, in the cooking of an egg with water boiling; and much vain correspondence has already been on that subject, as on others equally extinct. Correspondence which is not pleasant reading at this time; the rather as no reader can, without endless searching, even understand it. Correspondence left to us, not in the cosmic, elucidated or legible state; left mainly as the Editorial rubbish-waggons chose to shoot it; like a tumbled quarry, like the ruins of a sacked city; — avoidable by readers who are not forced into it!* Take the following select bricks as sample, which are of some use; the general Heading is,

King Friedrich to M. de Voltaire (at the Hague, or at Brussels).
"*Charlottenburg,* 12*th June* 1740. — * * My dear Voltaire, "resist no longer the eagerness I have to see you. Do in my "favour whatever your humanity allows. In the end of Au-"gust I go to Wesel, and perhaps farther. Promise that you "will come and join me; for I could not live happy, nor die "tranquil, without having embraced you! Thousand com-"pliments to the Marquise," divine Emilie. "I am busy with "both hands" (Corn-Magazines, Free Press, Abolition of Torture, and much else); "working at the Army with the "one hand, at the People and the Fine Arts with the other."
"*Berlin,* 5*th August* 1740. — * * I will write to Madame du "Châtelet, in compliance with your wish:" mark it, reader.

* Herr Preuss's edition (*Œuvres de Frédéric*, voll. xxi. xxii. xxiii.) has come out since the above was written: it is agreeably exceptional; being,

"To speak to you frankly concerning her journey, it is Vol-"taire, it is you, it is my Friend that I desire to see; and the "divine Emilie with all her divinity is only the Accessory of the "Apollo Newtonised.

"I cannot yet say whether I shall travel" (incognito into foreign parts a little) "or not travel;" there have been rumours, perhaps private wishes; but—** "Adieu, dear friend; "sublime spirit, first-born of thinking beings. Love me al-"ways sincerely, and be persuaded that none can love and "esteem you more than I. *Vale.* "FÉDÉRIC."

"*Berlin 6th August*" (which is next day). — "You will have "received a Letter from me dated yesterday; this is the second "I write to you from Berlin; I refer you to what was in the "other. If it must be (*faut*) that Emilie accompany Apollo, I "consent; but if I could see you alone, that is what I would "prefer. I should be too much dazzled; I could not stand so "much splendour all at once; it would overpower me. I "should need the veil of Moses to temper the united radiance "of your two divinities." * * In short, don't bring her, if you please.

"*Remusberg*" (poetic for *Reinsberg*), "*8th August* 1740. — "* * * My dear Voltaire, I do believe Van Duren costs you "more trouble and pains than you had with *Henri Quatre*. In "versifying the Life of a Hero, you wrote the history of your "own thoughts; but in coercing a scoundrel you fence with an "enemy who is not worthy of you." To punish him, and cut short his profits, "*print*, then, as you wish" (your own edition of the *Anti-Macchiavel*, to go along with his, and trip the feet from it). "*Faites rouler la presse;* erase, change, "correct; do as you see best; your judgment about it shall be "mine." — "In eight days I leave for" — (where thinks the reader? "*Dantzig*" deliberately print all the Editors, careful Preuss among them; overturning the terrestrial azimuths for us, and making day night!) — "for Leipzig, and reckon on "being at Frankfort on the 22d. In case you could be there, "I expect, on my passage, to give you lodging! At Cleve or "in Holland, I depend for certain on embracing you." *

for the first time, correctly printed, and the editor himself having mostly understood it,—though the reader still cannot, on the terms there allowed.
* Preuss, (*Œuvres de Frédéric*, xx. pp. 5, 19-21; Voltaire, *Œuvres*, lxxii. 226, &c. (not worth citing, in comparison).

Intrinsically the Friedrich correspondence at this time, with Voltaire especially, among many friends now on the wing towards Berlin and sending letters, has, — if you are forced into struggling for some understanding of it, and do get to read parts of it with the eyes of Friedrich and Voltaire, — has a certain amiability; and is nothing like so waste and dreary as it looks in the chaotic or sacked-city condition. Friedrich writes with brevity, oftenest on practicalities (the *Anti-Macchiavel*, the coming Interview, and the like), evidently no time to spare; writes always with considerable sincerity; with friendliness, much admiration, and an ingenuous vivacity, to M. de Voltaire. Voltaire, at his leisure in Brussels or the Old-Palace and its spiderwebs, writes much more expansively; not with insincerity, he either; — with endless airy graciosities, and ingenious twirls, and touches of flattering unction, which latter, he is aware, must not be laid on too thick. As thus:

In regard to the *Anti-Macchiavel*, — Sire, deign to give me your permissions as to the scoundrel of a Van Duren; well worth while, Sire, — "*it* is a monument for the latest poste-"rity; the only Book worthy of a King for these Fifteen "hundred years."

This is a strongish trowelful, thrown on direct, with adroitness; and even this has a kind of sincerity. Safer, however, to do it in the oblique or reflex way, — by Ambassador *Camas*, for example:

"I will tell you boldly, Sir" (you M. de Camas), "I put "more value on this Book (*Anti-Macchiavel*) than on the Em- "peror Julian's *Cæsar*, or on the *Maxims* of Marcus Aurelius," — I do indeed, having a kind of property in it withal! *

* Voltaire, *Œuvres,* lxxii. 280 (To Camas, 18th October 1740).

15th Aug. 1740.

In fact, Voltaire too is beautiful, in this part of the Correspondence; but much in a twitter, — the Queen of Sheba, not the sedate Solomon, in prospect of what is coming. He plumes himself a little, we perceive, to his d'Argentals and French Correspondents, on this sublime intercourse he has got into with a Crowned Head, the cynosure of mankind: — Perhaps even you, my best friend, did not quite know me, and what merits I had! Plumes himself a little; but studies to be modest withal; has not much of the peacock, and of the turkey has nothing, to his old friends. All which is very naïve and transparent; natural and even pretty, on the part of M. de Voltaire as the weaker vessel. — For the rest, it is certain Maupertuis is getting under way at Paris towards the Cleve rendezvous. Brussels, too, is so near these Cleve Countries; within two days good driving: — if only the times and routes would rightly intersect?

Friedrich's intention is by no means for a straight journey towards Cleve: he intends for Baireuth first, then back from Baireuth to Cleve, — making a huge southward *elbow* on the map, with Baireuth for apex or turning-point: — in this manner he will make the times suit, and have a convergence at Cleve. To Baireuth; — who knows if not farther? All summer there has gone fitfully a rumour, that he wished to see France; perhaps Paris itself incognito? The rumour, which was heard even at Petersburg,* is now sunk dead again; but privately, there is no doubt, a glimpse of the sublime French Nation would be welcome to Fried-

---

* Raumer's *Beitrdge* (English Translation, London, 1837), p. 15 Finch's Despatch, 24th June 1740).

17th Aug. 1740.

rich. He could never get to Travelling in his young time; missed his Grand Tour altogether, much as he wished it; and he is capable of pranks! — Enough, on Monday morning, 15th August 1740,* Friedrich and Suite leave Potsdam, early enough; go, by Leipzig, by the route already known to readers, through Coburg and the Voigtland regions; Wilhelmina has got warning, sits eagerly expecting her Brother in the Hermitage at Baireuth, gladdest of shrill sisters; and full of anxieties how her Brother would now be. The travelling party consisted, besides the King, of seven persons: Prince August Wilhelm, King's next Brother, Heir-apparent if there come no children, now a brisk youth of eighteen; Leopold Prince of Anhalt-Dessau, Old Dessauer's eldest, what we may call the "Young Dessauer;" Colonel von Borck, whom we shall hear of again; Colonel von Stille, already heard of (grave men of fifty, these two); milk-beard Münchow, an Adjutant, youngest of the promoted Münchows; Algarotti, indispensable for talk; and Fredersdorf, the House-steward and domestic Factotum, once Private in Schwerin's Regiment, whom Bielfeld so admired at Reinsberg, foreseeing what he would come to. One of Friedrich's late acts was to give Factotum Fredersdorf an Estate of Land (small enough, I fancy, but with country-house on it) for solace to the leisure of so useful a man, — studious of chemistry too, as I have heard. Seven in all, besides the King.** Direct towards Baireuth, incognito, and at the top of their speed. Wednesday, 17th, they actually arrive. Poor

---

* Rödenbeck, p. 15, slightly in error: see Dickens's Interview, *suprà*, p. 50.

** Rödenbeck, p. 19 (and for Chamberlain Fredersdorf's estate, p. 15).

Wilhelmina, she finds her Brother changed; — become a King in fact, and sternly solitary; alone in soul, even as a King must be!* —

"Algarotti, one of the first *beaux-esprits* of this age," as Wilhelmina defines him, — Friend Algarotti, the young Venetian gentleman of elegance, in dusky skin, in very white linen and frills, with his fervid black eyes, "does the expenses of the conversation." He is full of elegant logic, has speculations on the great world and the little, on Nature, Art, Papistry, Anti-Papistry, and takes up the Opera in an earnest manner, as capable of being a school of virtue and the moral sublime. His respectable Books on the Opera and other topics are now all forgotten, and crave not to be mentioned. To me he is not supremely beautiful, though much the gentleman in manners as in ruffles, and ingeniously logical: — rather yellow to me, in mind as in skin, and with a taint of obsolete Venetian Macassar. But to Friedrich he is thrice dear; who loves the sharp facetted cut of the man, and does not object to his yellow or Extinct-Macassar qualities of mind. Thanks to that wandering Baltimore for picking up such a jewel and carrying him Northward! Algarotti himself likes the North: here in our hardy climates, — especially at Berlin, and were his loved Friedrich *not* a King, — Algarotti could be very happy in the liberty allowed. At London, where there is no King, or none to speak of, and plenty of free Intelligences, Carterets, Lytteltons, young Pitts and the like, he is also well, were it not for the horrid smoke upon one's linen, and the little or no French of those proud Islanders.

Wilhelmina seems to like him here; is glad, at any

* Wilhelmina, ii. 322, 323.

rate, that he does the costs of conversation, better or worse. In the rest is no hope. Stille, Borck are accomplished military gentlemen; but of tacit nature, reflective, practical, rather than discursive, and do not waste themselves by incontinence of tongue. Stille, by his military Commentaries, which are still known to soldiers that read, maintains some lasting remembrance of himself: Borck we shall see engaged in a small bit of business before long. As to Münchow, the *jeune morveux* of an Aidecamp, he, though his manners are well enough, and he wears military plumes in his hat, is still an unfledged young creature, "bill still yellow," so to speak; — and marks himself chiefly by a visible hankering after that troublesome creature Marwitz, who is always coquetting. Friedrich's conversation, especially to my Wilhelmina, seems "*guindé*, set on stilts," likewise there are frequent cuts of banter in him; and it is painfully evident he distinguishes my Sister of Anspach and her foolish Husband, whom he has invited over hither in a most eager manner, beyond what a poor Wilhelmina with her old love can pretend to. Patience, my shrill Princess, Beauty of Baireuth and the world; let us hope all will come right again! My shrill Princess, — who has a melodious strength like that of war-fifes, too, — knows how to be patient; and veils many things, though of a highly unhypocritical nature.

These were Three great Days at Baireuth; Wilhelmina is to come soon, and return the visit at Berlin. To wait upon the King, known though incognito, "the Bishop of Bamberg" came driving over:* Schönborn, Austrian Kanzler, or who? His old City we once saw

* *Helden-Geschichte*, i. 419.

(and plenty of hanged malefactors swinging round it, during that *Journey to the Reich*);—but the Bishop himself never to our knowledge, Bishop being absent then. I hope it is the same Bishop of Bamberg whom a Friend of Büsching's, touring there about that same time, saw dining in a very extraordinary manner, with mediæval trumpeters, "with waiters in spurs and buff-belts:* if it is not, I have not the slightest shadow of acquaintance with him,—there have been so many Bishops of Bamberg with whom one wishes to have none! On the third day Friedrich and his company went away towards Würzburg; and Wilhelmina was left alone with her reflections. "I had had so much to "say to him; I had got nothing said at all:" alas, it is ever so. "The King was so changed, grown so much "bigger (*grandi*), you could not have known him again;" stands finely erect and at full breadth, every inch a King; his very stature, you would say, increased.—Adieu, my Princess, pearl of Princesses; all readers will expect your return-visit at Berlin, which is to be soon.

Friedrich strikes off to the left, and has a View of Strasburg for Two Days.

Through Würzburg, Frankfurt on the Mayn, speeds Friedrich;—Wilhelmina and mankind understand that it is homewards and to Cleve: but at Frankfurt, in deepest privacy, there occurs a sudden whirl southward,—up the Rhine-Valley; direct towards Strasburg, for a sight of France in that quarter! So has Friedrich decided,—not quite suddenly, on new Let-

* Büsching's *Beytrdge*;—Schlosser (*History of the Eighteenth Century*) also quotes the scene.

ters here, or new computations about Cleve; but by forethought taken at Baireuth, as rather appears. From Frankfurt to Strasburg, say 150 miles; from Strasburg home, is not much farther than from Frankfurt home: it can be done, then; husht! —

The incognito is to be rigorous: Friedrich becomes *Comte Dufour*, a Prussian-French gentleman; Prince August Wilhelm is Graf von Schaffgotsch, Algarotti is Graf von Pfuhl, Germans these two; what Leopold, the Young Dessauer called himself, — still less what the others, or whether the others were there at all, and not shoved on, direct towards Wesel, out of the way as is likelier, — can remain uncertain to readers and me. From Frankfurt, then, on Monday morning, 22d August 1740, as I compute, through old known Philipsburg-Campaign country, and the lines of Ettlingen and Stollhofen; there the royal Party speeds eagerly (weather very bad, as appears): and it is certain they are at Kehl on Tuesday evening; looking across the long Rhine Bridge, Strasburg and its steeples now close at hand.

This looks to be a romantic fine passage in the History of the young King; — though in truth it is not, and proves but a feeble story either to him or us. Concerning which, however, the reader, especially if he should hear that there exists precise Account of it, Two Accounts indeed, one from the King's own hand, will not fail of a certain craving to become acquainted with details. This craving, foolish rather than wise, we consider it thriftiest to satisfy at once; and shall give the King's *Narrative* entire, though it is a jingling lean scraggy Piece, partly rhyme, "in the manner of Bachaumont and La Chapelle;" written at the gallop, a few days hence, and despatched to Voltaire: — "You," dear Voltaire, "wish to know what I have "been about, since leaving Berlin; annexed you will "find a description of it," writes Friedrich.* Out of Voltaire's and other people's wastebaskets, it has at length been fished up, patch by patch, and pasted together by victorious modern Editors; and here it is again entire. The other Narrative, which got into the Newspapers soon after, is likewise of authentic nature, — Fassmann, our poor old friend, confirming it, if that were needful, — and is happily in prose.** Holding these two Pieces well together, and giving the King's, faithfully translated, in a complete state, it will be possible to satisfy foolish cravings, and make this Strasburg Adventure luminous enough.

King Friedrich to Voltaire (from Wesel, 2d September 1740), *chiefly in Doggerel, concerning the Run to Strasburg.****

"I have just finished a Journey, intermingled with singular "adventures, sometimes pleasant, sometimes the reverse. "You know I had set out for Baireuth," — *Bruxelles* the beautiful French Editor wrote, which makes Egyptian darkness of the Piece! — "to see a Sister whom I love no less than "esteem. On the road" (thither or thence; or likeliest, *there*), "Algarotti and I consulted the map, to settle our route for "returning by Wesel. Frankfurt on the Mayn comes always "as a principal stage; — Strasburg was no great roundabout: "we chose that route in preference. The *incognito* was de-"cided, names pitched upon" (Comte Dufour, and the others);

---
* *Œuvres*, xxii. 25 (Wesel, 2d September 1740).
** Given in *Helden-Geschichte*, i. 420-423; — see likewise Fassmann's *Merkwürdigster Regierungs-Antritt* (poor old Book on *Friedrich's Accession*); Preuss (*Thronbesteigung*, pp. 395-400; &c. &c.)
*** Part of it, incorrect, in Voltaire, *Œuvres* (scandalous Piece now called *Mémoires*, once *Vie Privée du Roi de Prusse*), ii. 24-26; finally, in Preuss, *Œuvres de Frédéric*, xiv. 156-161, the real and complete affair, — as fished up by victorious Preuss and others.

CHAP. III.] EXCURSION TO THE CLEVE COUNTRIES. 69
22d-25th Aug. 1740.

"story we were to tell: in fine all was arranged and concerted
"to a nicety as well as possible. We fancied we should get to
"Strasburg in three days," from Baireuth.

"But Heaven, which disposes of all "things,	*Mais le ciel, qui de tout dispose,*
"Differently regulated this thing.	*Régla différemment la chose.*
"With lank-sided coursers,	*Avec de coursiers efflanqués,*
"Lineal descendants from Rosi-"nante,	*En ligne droites issus de Rosinante,*
"With ploughmen in the dress of "postillions,	*Et des paysans en postillons masqués,*
"Blockheads of impertinent nature;	*Butors de race impertinente,*
"Our carriages sticking fast a hun-"dred times in the road,	*Notre carrosse en cent lieux accroché,*
"We went along with gravity at a "leisurely pace,	*Nous allions gravement, d'une allure indolente,*
"Knocking against the crags.	*Gravitant contre les rochers.*
"The atmosphere in uproar with "loud thunder,	*Les airs émus par le bruyant tonnerre,*
"The rain-torrents streaming over "the Earth	*Les torrents d'eau répandus sur la terre,*
"Threatened mankind with theDay "of Judgment [*very bad weather*],	*Du dernier jour menaçaient les humains;*
"And in spite of our impatience	*Et malgré notre impatience,*
"Four good days are, in penance,	*Quatre bons jours en pénitence*
"Lost forever in these jumblings.	*Sont pour jamais perdus dans les charrains.*

"Had all our fatalities been limited to stoppages of speed
"on the journey, we should have taken patience; but, after
"frightful roads, we found lodgings still frightfuller.

"For greedy landlords	*Car des hôtes intéressés,*
"Seing us pressed by hunger	*De la faim nous voyant pressés,*
"Did, in a more than frugal manner,	*D'une façon plus que frugale,*
"In their infernal hovels,	*Dans une chaumière infernale,*
"Poisoning instead of feeding,	*En nous empoisonnant, nous volaient*
"Steal from us our crowns.	*nos écus.*
"O age different" (in good cheer) "from that of Lucullus!	*O siècle différent des temps de Lucullus!*

"Frightful roads; short of victual, short of drink: nor was
"that all. We had to undergo a variety of accidents; and
"certainly our equipage must have had a singular air, for in
"every new place we came to, they took us for something
"different.

"Some took us for Kings,	Les uns nous prenaient pour des rois,
"Some for pickpockets well dis-"guised;	D'autres pour des filous courtois,
"Others for old acquaintances.	D'autres pour gens de connaissance;
"At times the people crowded out,	Parfois le peuple s'attroupait,
"Looked us in the eyes,	Entre les yeux nous regardait
"Like clowns impertinently curious.	En badauds curieux, remplis d'impertinence.
"Our lively Italian" (Algarotti) "swore;	Notre vif Italien jurait,
"For myself I took patience;	Pour moi je prenais patience,
"The young Count" (my gay younger Brother, eighteen at present) "quizzed and frolicked;	Le jeune Comte folâtrait,
"The big Count" (Heir-apparent of Dessau) "silently swung his "head,	Le grand Comte se dandinait,
"Wishing this fine Journey to "France,	Et ce beau voyage de France
"In the bottom of his heart, most "christianly at the Devil.	Dans le fond de son cœur chrétiennement damnait.

"We failed not, however, to struggle gradually along; at "last we arrived in that Stronghold, where" (as preface to the War of 1734, known to some of us) —

"Where the garrison, too supple,	Où la garnison, troupe flasque,
"Surrendered so piteously	Se rendit si piteusement
"After the first blurt of explosion	Après la première bourasque
"From the cannon of the French.	Du canon français foudroyant.

"You recognise Kehl in this description. It was in that fine "Fortress, — where, by the way, the breaches are still lying "unrepaired" (Reich being a slow corpus in regard to such things) — "that the Postmaster, a man of more foresight than "we, asked if we had got passports?

"No, said I to him; of passports	Non, lui dis-je, des passe-ports
"We never had the whim.	Nous n'eûmes jamais la folie.
"Strong ones I believe it would "need	Il en faudrait, je crois, des forts
"To recal, to our side of the limit,	Pour ressusciter à la vie
"Subjects of Pluto King of the Dead:	De chez Pluton le roi des morts;
"But, from the Germanic Empire	Mais de l'empire germanique
"Into the gallant and cynical abode	Au séjour galant et cynique
"Of Messieurs your pretty French-"men, —	De Messieurs vos jolis Français,

"A jolly and beaming air,	Un air rebondissant et frais,
"Rubicund faces, not ignorant of "wine,	Une face rouge et bachique,
"These are the passports which, le-"gible if you look on us,	Sont les passe-ports qu'en nos traits
"Our troop produces to you for that "end.	Vous produit ici notre clique.

"No, Messieurs, said the provident Master of Passports; "no salvation without passport. Seeing then that Necessity "had got us in the dilemma of either manufacturing passports "ourselves or not entering Strasburg, we took the former "branch of the alternative and manufactured one; — in which "feat the Prussian arms, which I had on my seal, were "marvellously furthersome."

This is a fact, as the old Newspapers and confirmatory Fassmann more directly apprise us. "The "Landlord" (or Postmaster) "at Kehl, having signified "that there was no crossing without Passport," Friedrich, at first somewhat taken aback, bethought him of his watch-seal with the Royal Arms on it; and soon manufactured the necessary Passport, signeted in due form; — which, however, gave a suspicion to the Innkeeper as to the quality of his Guest. After which, Tuesday evening, 23d August, "they at once got "across to Strasburg," says my Newspaper Friend, "and put up at the *Sign of the Raven* there." Or in Friedrich's own jingle:

"We arrived at Strasburg; and the Custom-house corsair, "with his inspectors, seemed content with our evidences.

"These scoundrels spied us,	Ces scélérats nous épiaient,
"With one eye reading our passport,	D'un œil le passe-port lisaient,
"With the other ogling our purse.	De l'autre lorgnaient notre bourse.
"Gold, which was always a resource,	L'or, qui toujours fut de ressource,
"Which brought Jove to the enjoy-"ment	Par lequel Jupin jouissait
"Of Danaë whom he caressed;	De Danaé, qu'il caressait;

"Gold, by which Cæsar governed	L'or, par qui César gouvernoit
"The world happy under his sway;	Le monde heureux sous son empire;
"Gold, more a divinity than Mars "or Love;	L'or, plus dieu que Mars et l'Amour,
"Wonder-working Gold introduced "us,	Le même or sut nous introduire,
"That evening, within the walls of "Strasburg."*	Le soir, dans les murs de Strasbourg.

Sad doggerel; permissible perhaps as a sample of the Friedrich manufacture, surely not otherwise! There remains yet more than half of it; readers see what their foolish craving has brought upon them! Doggerel out of which no clear story, such story as there is, can be had; though, except the exaggeration and contortion, there is nothing of fiction in it. We fly to the Newspaper, happily at least a prose composition, which begins at this point; and shall use the Doggerel henceforth as illustration only, or as repetition in the Friedrich-mirror, of a thing *otherwise* made clear to us:

Having got into Strasburg and the *Raven Hotel;* Friedrich now on French ground at last, or at least on Half-French, German-French, is intent to make the most of circumstances. The Landlord, with one of Friedrich's servants, is straightway despatched into the proper coffeehouses: to raise a supper-party of Officers; politely asks any likely Officer, "If he will not do a foreign Gentleman" (seemingly of some distinction, signifies Boniface) "the honour to sup with him at the Raven?" "No, by Jupiter!" answer the most, in their various dialects: "who is he that we should sup with him?" Three, struck by the singularity of the thing, undertake; and with these we must be content. Friedrich, — or call him M. le Comte Dufour, with Pfuhl, Schaffgotsch and such escort as we see, — politely apologises on the entrance of these Officers: "Many pardons, gentlemen, and many thanks. Knowing nobody; desirous of acquaintance: — since you are so good, how happy, by a little

* Given thus far, with several slight errors, in Voltaire, ii. 24-26; — the remainder, long unknown, had to be fished up, patch by patch (Preuss, (*Œuvres de Frédéric*, xiv. 159-161).

informality, to have brought brave Officers to keep me company, whom I value beyond other kinds of men!"

The Officers found their host a most engaging gentleman: his supper was superb, plenty of wine, "and one red kind they had never tasted before, and liked extremely;" — of which he sent some bottles to their lodging next day. The conversation turned on military matters, and was enlivened with the due sallies. This foreign Count speaks French wonderfully; a brilliant man, whom the others rather fear: perhaps something more than a Count? The Officers, loth to go, remembered that their two battalions had to parade next morning, that it was time to be in bed: "I will go to your review," said the Stranger Count: the delighted Officers undertake to come and fetch him, they settle with him time and method; how happy!

On the morrow, accordingly, they call and fetch him; he looks at the review; review done, they ask him to supper for this evening: "With pleasure!" and "walks with them about the Esplanade, to see the guard march by." Before parting, he takes their names, writes them in his tablets: says with a smile, "He is too much obliged ever to forget them." This is Wednesday, the 24th of August 1740; Field-Marshal Broglio is Commandant in Strasburg, and these obliging Officers are "of the regiment Piedmont," — their names on the King's tablets I never heard mentioned by anybody (or never till the King's Doggerel was fished up again). Field-Marshal Broglio my readers have transiently seen, afar off; — "galloping with only one boot," some say "almost in his shirt," at the Ford of Secchia, in those Italian campaigns, five years ago, the Austrians having stolen across upon him: — he had a furious gallop, with no end of ridicule, on that occasion; is now Commandant here; and we shall have a great deal more to do with him within the next year or two.

"This same day, 24th, while I" (the Newspaper volunteer Reporter or Own Correspondent, seemingly a person of some standing, whose words carry credibility in the tone of them) "was with Field-Marshal Broglio our Governor here, there "came two gentlemen to be presented to him; 'German Ca-"valiers' they were called; who, I now find, must have been "the Prince of Prussia and Algarotti. The Field-Marshal," — a rather high-stalking white-headed old military gentleman, bordering on seventy, of Piemontese air and breed, apt to be sudden and make flounderings, but the soul of honour, "was very polite to the two Cavaliers, and kept them to "dinner. After dinner there came a so-styled 'Silesian Noble- "man,' who likewise was presented to the Field-Marshal, and "affected not to know the other two: him I now find to have "been the Prince of Anhalt."

Of his Majesty's supper with the Officers that Wednesday, we are left to think how brilliant it was: his Majesty, we hear farther, went to the Opera that night, — the Polichinello or whatever the "Italian *Comödie*" was; — "and a little girl came "to his box with two lottery-tickets fifteen pence each, "begging the foreign Gentleman for the love of Heaven to "buy them of her; which he did, tearing them up at once, and "giving the poor creature four ducats," equivalent to two guineas, or say in effect even five pounds of the present British currency. The fame of this foreign Count and his party at The Raven is becoming very loud over Strasburg, especially in military circles. Our volunteer Own Correspondent proceeds (whom we mean to contrast with the Royal Doggerel by and by):

"Next morning," Thursday, 25th August, "as the Marshal "with above two hundred Officers was out walking on the "Esplanade, there came a soldier of the Regiment Luxem- "burg, who, after some stiff fugling motions, of the nature of "salutation partly, and partly demand for privacy, intimated "to the Marshal surprising news: That this Stranger in The "Raven was the King of Prussia in person; he, the soldier, at "present of the Regiment Luxemburg, had in other days be- "fore he deserted, been of the Prussian Crown Prince's regi- "ment; had consequently seen him in Berlin, Potsdam and "elsewhere a thousand times and more, and even stood sentry "where he was: the fact is beyond dispute, your Excellency! "said this soldier." — Whew!

Whereupon a certain Colonel, Marquis de Loigle, with or without a hint from Broglio, makes off for The Raven; introduces himself, as was easy; contrives to get invited to stay dinner, which also was easy. During dinner the foreign Gentleman expressed some wish to see their fortress. Colonel Loigle sends word to Broglio; Broglio despatches straightway an Officer and fine carriage: "Will the foreign Gentleman do me the honour?" The foreign Gentleman, still struggling for incognito, declines the uppermost seat of honour in the carriage; the two Officers, Loigle and this new one, insist on taking the inferior place. Alas, the incognito is pretty much out. Calling at some coffeehouse or the like on the road, a certain female, "Madame de Fienne," named the foreign Gentleman "Sire," — which so startled him that though he utterly declined such title, the two Officers saw well how it was.

"After survey of the works, the two attendant Officers had "returned to the Field-Marshal; and about 4 P.M. the high "Stranger made appearance there. But the thing had now "got wind, 'King of Prussia here incognito!' The place was "full of Officers, who came crowding about him: he escaped "deftly into the Maréchal's own Cabinet; sat there, an hour, "talking to the Maréchal" (little admiring the Maréchal's talk, as we shall find), "still insisting on the incognito," — to which Broglio, put out in his high paces by this sudden thing, and apt to flounder, as I have heard, was not polite enough to conform altogether. "What shall I do, in this sudden case?" poor Broglio is thinking to himself: "must write to Court; perhaps try to detain —" Friedrich's chief thought naturally is, One cannot be away out of this too soon. "Shan't we go to the Play, then, Monsieur le Maréchal? Play hour is come!" — Own Correspondent of the Newspaper proceeds:

"The Maréchal then went to the Play, and all his Officers "with him; thinking their royal prize was close at their heels. "Maréchal and Officers fairly ahead, coast once clear, their "royal prize hastened back to The Raven, paid his bill; "hastily summoning Schaffgotsch and the others within hear"ing; shot off like lightning; and was seen in Strasburg no "more. Algarotti, who was in the box with Broglio, heard "the news in the House; regretful rumour among the Officers, "'He is gone!' In about a quarter of an hour Algarotti too "slipt out; and vanished by extra post" — straight towards Wesel; but could not overtake the King (whose road, in the latter part of it, went zigzag, on business as is likely), nor see him again till they met in that Town.*

This is the Prose Truth of those Fifty or Eight-and-forty hours in Strasburg, which were so mythic

* From *Helden-Geschichte* (1. 420-424), &c.

and romantic at that time. Shall we now apply to the Royal Doggerel again, where we left off, and see the other side of the picture? Once settled in The Raven, within Strasburg's walls, the Doggerel continues:

"You fancy well that there was now something to exercise "my curiosity; and what desire I had to know the French Na- "tion in France itself.

"There I saw at length those French,	*Là je vis enfin ces Français,*
"Of whom you have sung the glories;	*Dont vous avez chanté la gloire;*
"A people despised by the English,	*Peuple méprisé des Anglais,*
"Whom their sad rationality fills "with black bile;	*Que leur triste raison remplit de bile noire;*
"Those French, whom our Germans "Reckon all to be destitute of sense;	*Ces Français, que nos Allemands Pensent tous privés de bon sens;*
"Those French, whose History con- "sists of Love-stories,	*Ces Français, dont l'amour pourrait dicter l'histoire,*
"I mean the wandering kind of "Love, not the constant;	*Je dis l'amour volage, et non l'amour constant;*
"Foolish this People, headlong, "high-going,	*Ce peuple fou, brusque et galant,*
"Which sings beyond endurance;	*Chansonnier insupportable,*
"Lofty in its good fortune, crawling "in its bad;	*Superbe en sa fortune, en son malheur rampant,*
"Of an unpitying extent of babble,	*D'un bavardage impitoyable,*
"To hide the vacancy of its igno- "rant mind.	*Pour cacher le creux d'un esprit ignorant.*
"Of the Trifling it is a tender lover;	*Tendre amant de la bagatelle,*
"The Trifling alone takes posses- "sion of its brain.	*Elle entre seule en sa cervelle;*
"People flighty, indiscreet, impru- "dent,	*Léger, indiscret, imprudent,*
"Turning like the weathercock to "every wind.	*Comme une girouette il revire à tout vent.*
"Of the ages of the Cæsars those of "the Louises are the shadow;	*Des siècles des Césars ceux des Louis sont l'ombre;*
"Paris is the ghost of Rome, take it "how you will.	*Rome efface Paris en tout sens, en tout point.*
"No, of those vile French you are "not one:	*Non, des vils Français vous n'êtes pas du nombre;*
"You think; they do not think at all.	*Vous pensez, ils ne pensent point.*

"Pardon, dear Voltaire, this definition of the French; at "worst, it is only of those in Strasburg I speak. To scrape

CHAP. III.] EXCURSION TO THE CLEVE COUNTRIES. 77
22d-25th Aug. 1740.

"acquaintance, I had to invite some Officers on our arrival,
"whom of course I did not know.

"Three of them came at once,	*Trois d'eux s'en vinrent a la fois.*
"Gayer, more content than Kings;	*Plus gais, plus contents que des rois,*
"Singing with rusty voice,	*Chantant d'une voix enrouée,*
"In verse, their amorous exploits,	*En vers, leurs amoureux exploits,*
"Set to a hornpipe.	*Ajustés sur une bourrée.*

"M. de la Crochardière and M. Malosa" (two names from
the tablets, third wanting) "had just come from a dinner
"where the wine had not been spared.

"Of their hot friendship I saw the "flame grow,	*De leur chaude amitié je vis croître la flamme,*
"The Universe would have taken us "for perfect friends:	*L'univers nous eût pris pour des amis parfaits;*
"But the instant of goodnight blew "out the business;	*Mais l'instant des adieux en détruisit la trame,*
"Friendship disappeared without "regrets,	*L'amitié disparut, sans causer des regrets,*
"With the games, the wine, the "table and the viands.	*Avec le jeu, le vin, et la table, et les mets.*

"Next day, Monsieur the Gouverneur of the Town and
"Province, Maréchal of France, Chevalier of the Orders of
"the King &c. &c., — Maréchal Duc de Broglio, in fact," who
was surprised at Secchia in the late War, —

"This General always surprised,	*Ce général toujours surpris,*
"Whom with regret young Louis" (your King)	*Qu'à regret le jeune Louis*
"Saw without breeches in Italy *	*Vit sans culottes en Italie,*
"Galloping to hide away his life	*Courir pour dérober sa vie*
"From the Germans, unpolite fight-"ers; —	*Aux Germains, guerriers impolis;*

"this General wished to investigate your Comte Dufour, —
"foreign Count, who the instant he arrives sets about inviting
"people to supper that are perfect strangers. He took the
"poor Count for a sharper; and prudently advised M. de la
"Crochardière not to be duped by him. It was unluckily the
"good Maréchal that proved to be duped.

* "With only one boot," was the milder rumour; which we adopted
(*supra*, vol. v. p. 41), but this sadder one, too, was current; and "Broglio's
breeches," or the vain aspiration after them, like a vanished ghost of
breeches, often enough turn up in the old Pamphlets.

"He was born for surprise. | Il était né pour la surprise.
"His white hair, his gray beard, | Ses cheveux blancs, sa barbe grise,
"Formed a reverend exterior. | Formaient un sage extérieur.
"Outsides are often deceptive: | Le dehors est souvent trompeur;
"He that, by the binding, judges | Qui juge par la reliure
"Of a Book and its Author | D'un ouvrage et de son auteur
"May, after a page of reading, | Dans une page de lecture
"Chance to recognise his mistake. | Peut reconnaître son erreur.

"That was my own experience; for of wisdom I could find "nothing except in his gray hair and decrepit appearance. "His first opening betrayed him; no great well of wit this "Maréchal,

"Who, drunk with his own gran-
  "deur, | Qui, de sa grandeur enivré,
"Informs you of his name and his
  "titles, | Décline son nom et ses titres,
"And authority as good as unlimited. | Et son pouvoir à rien borné.
"He cited to me all the records | Il me cita tous les registres
"Where his name is registered, | Où son nom est enregistré;
"Babbled about his immense power, | Bavard de son pouvoir immense,
"About his valour, his talents | De sa valeur, de ces talents
"So salutary to France; — | Si salutaires à la France:
"He forgot that, three years ago* | Il oubliait, passé trois ans,
"Men did not praise his prudence. | Qu'on ne louait pas sa prudence.

"Not satisfied with seeing the Maréchal, I saw guard "mounted

"By these Frenchmen, burning with
  "glory, | A ces Français brûlants de gloire,
"Who, on four sous a day, | Dotés de quatre sous par jour,
"Will make of Kings and of Heroes
  "the memory flourish: | Qui des rois, des héros font fleurir la mémoire,
"Slaves crowned by the hands of
  "Victory, | Esclaves couronnés des mains de la victoire,
"Unlucky herds whom the Court | Troupeaux malheureux que la cour
"Tinkles hither and thither by the
  "sound of fife and drum. | Dirige au seul bruit du tambour.

"That was my fated term. A deserter from our troops got "eye on me, recognised me and denounced me.

"This wretched, gallows-bird got
  "eye on me; | Ce malheureux pendard me vit,
"Such is the lot of all earthly things; | C'est le sort de toutes les choses;
"And so of our fine mystery | Ainsi de notre pot aux roses
"The whole secret came to light." | Tout le secret se découvrit.

* Six to a nearness, — "15th September 1734," if your Majesty will be exact.

Well; we must take this glimpse, such as it is, into the interior of the young man, — fine buoyant, pungent German spirit, road-ways for it very bad, and universal rain-torrents falling, yet with coruscations from a higher quarter; — and you can forget, if need be, the "Literature" of this young Majesty, as you would a staccato on the flute by him! In after months, on new occasion rising, "there was no end to his jibings and "bitter pleasantries on the ridiculous reception Broglio "had given him at Strasburg," says Valori,* — of which this Doggerel itself offers specimen.

"Probably the weakest Piece I ever translated?" exclaims one, who has translated several such. Nevertheless there is a straggle of pungent sense in it, — like the outskirts of lightning, seen in that dismally wet weather, which the Royal Party had. Its wit is very copious, but slashy, bantery, and proceeds mainly by exaggeration and turning topsyturvy; a rather barren species of wit. Of humour, in the fine poetic sense, no vestige. But there is surprising veracity, — truthfulness unimpeachable, if you will read well. What promptitude, too; — what funds for conversation, when needed! This scraggy Piece, which is better than the things people often talk to one another, was evidently written as fast as the pen could go. — "It is done, if such a Hand could have *done* it, in the "manner of Bachaumont and La Chapelle," says Voltaire scornfully, in that scandalous *Vie Privée;* — of which phrase this is the commentary, if readers need one:

"Some seventy or eighty years before that date, a M. "Bachaumont and a M. la Chapelle, his intimate, published,

* *Mémoires,* 1. 88.

"in Prose skipping off into dancings of Verse every now and "then, 'a charming *Relation* of a certain *Voyage* or Home "Tour' (whence or whither, or correctly when, this Editor "forgets),* which they had made in partnership. '*Relation*' "capable still of being read, if one were tolerably idle; — it "was found then to be charming, by all the world; and gave "rise to a new fashion in writing; which Voltaire often adopts, "and is supremely good at; and in which Friedrich, who is "also fond of it, by no means succeeds so well."

Enough, Friedrich got to Wesel, back to his business in a day or two; and had done, as we forever have, with the Strasburg Escapade and its Doggerel.

Friedrich finds M. de Maupertuis; not yet M. de Voltaire.

Friedrich got to Wesel on the 29th; found Maupertuis waiting there, according to appointment: an elaborately polite, somewhat sublime scientific gentleman; ready to "engraft on the Berlin crabtree," and produce real apples and Academics there, so soon as the King, the proprietor, may have leisure for such a thing. Algarotti has already the honour of some acquaintance with Maupertuis. Maupertuis has been at Brussels, on the road hither; saw Voltaire and even Madame, — which latter was rather a ticklish operation, owing to grudges and tiffs of quarrel that had risen, but it proved successful under the delicate guidance of Voltaire. Voltaire is up to oiling the wheels: "There you "are, Monsieur, like the" — (don't name What, though profane Voltaire does, writing to Maupertuis a month

---

* "First printed in 1665," say the Bibliographies; "but known to La Fontaine some time before." Good! — Bachaumont, practically an important and distinguished person, not literary by trade, or indeed otherwise than by ennui, was he that had given (some fifteen years before) the Nickname *Fronde* (Bickering of Schoolboys) to the wretched Historical Object which is still so designated in French annals.

ago) — "Three Kings running after you!" A new Pension to you from France; Russia outbidding France to have you; and then that *Letter* of Friedrich's, which is in all the Newspapers: "Three Kings,"— you plainly great man, Trismegistus of the Sciences called Pure! Madame honours you, has always done: one word of apology to the high female mind, it will work wonders; — côme now! —*

No reader guesses in our time what a shining celestial body the Maupertuis, who is now fallen so dim again, then was to mankind. In cultivated French society there is no such lion as M. Maupertuis since he returned from flattening the Earth in the Arctic regions. "The Exact Sciences, what else is there to depend on?" thinks French cultivated society: "and has not Monsieur done a feat in that line?" Monsieur, with fine ex-military manners, has a certain austere gravity, reticent loftiness and polite dogmatism, which confirms that opinion. A studious ex-military man, — was Captain of Dragoons once, but too fond of study, who is conscious to himself, or who would fain be conscious, that he is, in all points, mathematical, moral and other, the man. A difficult man to live with in society. Comes really near the limit of what we call genius, of originality, poetic greatness in thinking; — but never once can get fairly over said limit, though always struggling dreadfully to do so. Think of it! A fatal kind of man; especially if you have made a lion of him at any time. Of his envies, deep-hidden splenetic discontents and rages, with Voltaire's return for them, there will be enough to say in the ulterior stages.

* Voltaire, *Œuvres*, lxxii. 217, 216, 230 (Hague, 21st July 1740, and Brussels, 9th Aug. &c.).

He wears, — at least ten years hence he openly wears, though I hope it is not yet so flagrant, — "a red wig "with yellow bottom (*crinière jaune*);" and as Flattener of the Earth, is, with his own flattish red countenance and impregnable stony eyes, a man formidable to look upon, though intent to be amiable if you do the proper homage. As to the quarrel with Madame take this Note; which may prove illustrative of some thing's by and by:

Maupertuis is well known at Cirey; such a lion could not fail there. All manner of Bernouillis, Clairauts, high mathematical people, are frequent guests at Cirey: reverenced by Madame, — who indeed has had her own private Professor of Mathematics; one König from Switzerland (recommended by those Bernouillis), diligently teaching her the Pure Sciences this good while back, not without effect; and has only just parted with him, when she left on this Brussels expedition. A *bon garçon*, Voltaire says; though otherwise, I think, a little noisy on occasion. There has been no end of Madame's kindness to him, nay to his Brother and him, — sons of a Theological Professorial Syriac-Hebrew kind of man at Berne who has too many sons; and I grieve to report that this heedless König has produced an explosion in Madame's feelings, such as little beseemed him. On the road to Paris, namely, as we drove hitherward to the Honsbruck Lawsuit by way of Paris, in Autumn last, there had fallen out some dispute, about the monads, the *vis viva*, the infinitely little, between Madame and König; dispute which rose *crescendo* in disharmonious duet, and "ended," testifies M. de Voltaire, "in a scene *très désagréable*." Madame, with an effort, forgave the thoughtless fellow, who is still rather young, and is without malice. But thoughtless König, strong in his opinion about the infinitely little, appealed to Maupertuis: "Am not I right, Monsieur?" "*He* is right beyond question!" wrote Maupertuis to Madame; "somewhat drily," thinks Voltaire: and the result is, there is considerable rage in one celestial mind ever since against another male one in red wig and yellow bottom; and they are not on speaking terms, for a good many months past. Voltaire has his heart sore ("*j'en ai le cœur percé*") about it, needs to double-dose Maupertuis with flattery; and in fact has used the utmost diplomacy to effect some varnish of a reconcilement as Maupertuis passed on this occasion. As for König, who had studied in some Dutch university, he went by and by to be Librarian to the Prince of Orange; and we shall not fail to hear of him again, — once more upon the infinitely little.*

Voltaire too, in his way, is fond of these mathematical people; eager enough to fish for knowledge, here as in all elements, when he has the chance offered: this is much an interest of his at present. And he does attain sound ideas, outlines of ideas, in this province, — though privately defective in the due transcendency of admiration for it; — was wont to discuss cheerily with König, about *vis viva*, monads, gravitation and the infinitely little; above all, bows to the ground before the red-wigged Bashaw, Flattener of the Earth, whom for Madame's sake and his own he is anxious to be well with. "Fall on your face nine times, ye esoteric of only Impure Science!"— intimates Maupertuis to mankind. "By all means!" answers M. de Voltaire, doing it with alacrity; with a kind of loyalty, one can perceive, and also with a hypocrisy grounded on love of peace. If that is the nature of the Bashaw, and one's sole mode of fishing knowledge from him, why not? thinks M. de Voltaire. His patience with M. de Maupertuis, first and last, was very great. But we shall find it explode at length, a dozen years hence, in a conspicuous manner! —

"Maupertuis had come to us to Circy, with Jean "Bernouilli," says Voltaire; "and thenceforth Mau-"pertuis, who was born the most jealous of men, took "me for the object of this passion, which has always "been very dear to him."** Husht, Monsieur! — Here is a poor rheumatic kind of Letter, which illustrates the interim condition, after that varnish of reconcilement at Brussels:

* From *Œuvres de Voltaire*, ii. 126, lxxii. (20, 216, 230), lxiii. (229-239), &c. &c.
 ** *Vie Privée*.

Voltaire to M. de Maupertuis (at Wesel, waiting for the King, or with him rather).

"Brussels, 29th August (1740), 3d year since
"*the world flattened.*

"How the Devil, great Philosopher, would you have had "me write to you at Wesel? I fancied you gone from Wesel, "to seek the King of Sages on his Journey somewhere. I had "understood, too, they were so delighted to have you in that "fortified lodge (*bouge fortifié*) that you must be taking "pleasure there, for he that gives pleasure gets it.

"You have already seen the jolly Ambassador of the "amiablest Monarch in the world,"— Camas, a fattish man, on his road to Versailles (who called at Brussels here, with fine compliments, and a keg of Hungary Wine, as *you* may have heard whispered). "No doubt M. de Camas is with you. "For my own share, I think it is after you that he is running "at present. But in truth, at the hour while I say this, you "are with the King;" — a lucky guess; King did return to Wesel this very day. "The Philosopher and the Prince "perceive already that they are made for each other. You "and M. Algarotti will say, *Faciamus hic tria tabernacula*: as "to me, I can only make *duo tabernacula*," — profane Voltaire!

"Without doubt I would be with you if I were not at "Brussels; but my heart is with you all the same; and is the "subject, all the same, of a King who is formed to reign over "every thinking and feeling being. I do not despair that Ma-"dame du Châtelet will find herself somewhere on your route: "it will be a scene in a fairy tale; — she will arrive with a "*sufficient reason*" (as your Leibnitz says) "and with *monads*. "She does not love you the less though she now believes the "universe a *plenum*, and has renounced the notion of *void*. "Over her you have an ascendant which you will never lose. "In fine, my dear Monsieur, I wish as ardently as she to "embrace you the soonest possible. I recommend myself to "your friendship in the Court, worthy of you, where you now "are." — *Tout à vous,* somewhat rheumatic!*

* Voltaire, lxxii. p. 243.

Always an anxious almost tremulous desire to conciliate this big glaring geometrical bully in red wig. Through the sensitive transparent being of M. de Voltaire, you may see that feeling almost painfully busy in every Letter he writes to the Flattener of the Earth.

CHAPTER IV.

VOLTAIRE'S FIRST INTERVIEW WITH FRIEDRICH.

AT Wesel, in the rear of all this travelling excitement, Friedrich falls unwell; breaks down there into an aguish feverish distemper, which, for several months after, impeded his movements, would he have yielded to it. He has much business on hand, too, — some of it of prickly nature just now; — but is intent as ever on seeing Voltaire, among the first things. Diligently reading in the Voltaire-Friedrich Correspondence (which is a sad jumble of misdates and opacities, in the common editions),* this of the aguish condition frequently turns up; "Quartan ague," it seems; occasionally very bad: but Friedrich struggles with it; will not be cheated of any of his purposes by it.

He had a busy fortnight here; busier than we yet imagine. Much employment there naturally is of the usual Inspection sort; which fails in no quarter of his Dominions, but which may be particularly important here, in these disputed Berg-Jülich Countries, when the time of decision falls. How he does his Inspections we know; — and there are still weightier matters afoot here, in a silent way, of which we shall have to speak before long, and all the world will speak. Business enough, parts of it grave and silent, going on, and the

---

* Preuss (the recent latest Editor, and the only well-informed one, as we said) prints with accuracy; but cannot be *read* at all (in the sense of *understood*) without other light.

much that is public, miscellaneous, small: done, all of it, in a rapid punctual precise manner; — and always, after the crowded day, some passages of Supper with the Sages, to wind up with on melodious terms. A most alert and miscellaneously busy young King, in spite of the ague.

It was in these Cleve Countries, and now as probably as afterwards, that the light scene recorded in Laveaux's poor *History*, and in all the Anecdote-Books, transacted itself one day. Substance of the story is true; though the details of it go all at random, — somewhat to this effect:

"Inspecting his Finance Affairs, and questioning the "parties interested, Friedrich notices a certain Convent in "Cleve, which appears to have, payable from the Forest-dues, "considerable revenues bequeathed by the old Dukes, 'for "masses to be said on their behalf.' He goes to look at the "place; questions the Monks on this point, who are all drawn "out, in two rows, and have broken into *Te-Deum* at sight of "him: Husht! 'You still say those Masses, then?' 'Certainly "your Majesty!' — 'And what good does anybody get of "them?' 'Your Majesty, those old Sovereigns are to obtain "Heavenly mercy by them, to be delivered out of Purgatory "by them.' — 'Purgatory? It is a sore thing for the Forests, "all this while! And they are not yet out, those poor souls, "after so many hundred years of praying?' Monks have a "fatal apprehension, No. 'When will they be out, and the "thing complete?' Monks cannot say. 'Send me a courier "whenever it *is* complete!' sneers the King, and leaves them "to their *Te-Deum*."*

* C. Hildebrandt's Modern Edition of the (mostly dubious) *Anekdoten und Charakterzüge aus dem Leben Friedrichs des Grossen* (and a very ignorant and careless Edition it is; 6 voll. 12mo, Halberstadt, 1829), ii. 160; Laveaux (whom we already cited), *Vie de Frédéric*; &c. &c. Nicolai's *Anekdoten* alone, which are not included in this Hildebrandt Collection, are of sure authenticity; the rest, occasionally true, and often with a kind of *mythic* truth in them worth attending to, are otherwise of all degrees of dubiety, down to the palpably false and absurd.

Mournful state of the Catholic Religion so-called! How long must these wretched Monks go on doing their lazy thrice-deleterious torpid blasphemy; and a King, not histrionic but real, merely signify that he laughs at them and it? Meseems a heavier whip than that of satire might be in place here, your Majesty? The lighter whip is easier; — Ah yes, undoubtedly! cry many men. But horrible accounts are running up, enough to sink the world at last, while the heavier whip is lazily withheld, and lazy blasphemy, fallen torpid, chronic, and quite unconscious of being blasphemous, insinuates itself into the very heart's-blood of mankind! Patience, however; the heavy whip too is coming, — unless universal death be coming. King Friedrich is not the man to wield such whip. Quite other work is in store for King Friedrich; and Nature will not, by any suggestion of that terrible task, put him out in the one he has. He is nothing of a Luther, of a Cromwell; can look upon fakeers praying by their rotatory calabash, as a ludicrous platitude; and grin delicately as above, with the approval of his wiser contemporaries. Speed to him on his own course!

What answer Friedrich found to his English proposals, — answer due here on the 24th from Captain Dickens, — I do not pointedly learn; but can judge of it by Harrington's reply to that Despatch of Dickens's, which entreated candour and open dealing towards his Prussian Majesty. Harrington is at Herrenhausen, still with the Britannic Majesty there; both of them much at a loss about their Spanish War, and the French and other aspects upon it; "Suppose his Prussian Majesty were to give himself to France against us!" We will hope, not. Harrington's reply is to the effect,

2d-11th Sept. 1740.

"Hum, drum: — Berg and Jülich, say you? Impos-
"sible to answer; minds not made up here: — What
"will his Prussian Majesty do for *us?*" Not much, I
should guess, till something more categorical come
from you! His Prussian Majesty is careful not to
spoil anything by over-haste; but will wait and try
farther to the utmost, Whether England or France is
the likelier bargain for him.

Better still, the Prussian Majesty is intent to do
something for himself in that Berg-Jülich matter: we
find him silently examining these Wesel localities for
a proper "Entrenched Camp," Camp say of 40,000,
against a certain contingency that may be looked for.
Camp which will much occupy the Gazetteers when
they get eye on it. This is one of the concerns he
silently attends to, on occasion, while riding about in
the Cleve Countries. Then there is another small
item of business, important to do well, which is now in
silence diligently getting under way at Wesel; which
also is of remarkable nature, and will astonish the
Gazetteer and Diplomatic circles. This is the affair
with the Bishop of Liege, called also the Affair of
Herstal, which his Majesty has had privately laid up
in the corner of his mind, as a thing to be done during
this Excursion. Of which the reader shall hear anon,
to great lengths, — were a certain small preliminary
matter, Voltaire's Arrival in these parts, once off our
hands.

Friedrich's First Meeting with Voltaire! These
other high things were once loud in the Gazetteer and
Diplomatic circles, and had no doubt *they* were the
World's History; and now they are sunk wholly to the

Nightmares, and all mortals have forgotten them, — and it is such a task as seldom was to resuscitate the least memory of them, on just cause of a Friedrich or the like, so impatient are men of what is putrid and extinct: — and a quite unnoticed thing, Voltaire's First Interview, all readers are on the alert for it, and ready to demand of me impossibilities about it! Patience, readers. You shall see it, without and within, in such light as there was, and form some actual notion of it, if you will coöperate. From the circumambient inanity of Old Newspapers, Historical shot-rubbish, and unintelligible Correspondences, we sift out the following particulars, of this First Meeting, or actual Osculation of the Stars.

The Newspapers, though their eyes were not yet of the Argus quality now familiar to us, have been intent on Friedrich, during this Baireuth-Cleve Journey, especially since that sudden eclipse of him at Strasburg lately; forming now one scheme of route for him, now another; Newspapers, and even private friends, being a good deal uncertain about his movements. Rumour now ran, since his reappearance in the Cleve Countries, that Friedrich meant to have a look at Holland before going home. And that had, in fact, been a notion or intention of Friedrich's. "Holland? We could pass through Brussels on the way, and see Voltaire!" thought he.

In Brussels this was, of course, the rumour of rumours. As Voltaire's Letters, visibly in a twitter, still testify to us. King of Prussia coming! Madame du Châtelet, the "Princess Tour" (that is, Tour-and-Taxis), all manner of high Dames, are on the tiptoe. Princess Tour hopes she shall lodge this unparalleled Prince in her Palace: "You, Madame?" answers the Du Châtelet, privately, with a toss of her head: "His Majesty, I hope, belongs more to M. de Voltaire and me: he shall lodge here, please Heaven!" Voltaire, I can observe, has sublime hostelry arrangements chalked out for his Majesty, in case he go to Paris; which he doesn't, as we know. Voltaire is all on the alert, awake to the great contingencies far and near; the Châtelet-Voltaire breakfast-table, — fancy it on those interesting mornings, while the post comes round!*

Alas, in the first days of September, — Friedrich's Letter is dated "Wesel, 2d" (and has the *Strasburg Doggerel* enclosed in it), — the Brussels Postman delivers far other intelligence at one's door; very mortifying to Madame: "That his Majesty is fallen ill at "Wesel; has an aguish fever hanging on him, and "only hopes to come:" *Voilà*, Madame! — Next Letter, Wesel, Monday, 5th Sept., is to the effect: "Do still "much hope to come; tomorrow is my trembling day; if that prove to be off!" — Out upon it, that proves not to be off; that is on: next Letter, Tuesday, Sept. 6th, which comes by express (Courier dashing up with it, say on the Thursday following) is, — alas, Madame! — here it is:

King Friedrich to M. de Voltaire at Brussels.

"Wesel, 6th Sept. 1740.

"My dear Voltaire, — In spite of myself, I have to yield to "the Quartan Fever, which is more tenacious than a Jansenist; " and whatever desire I had of going to Antwerp and Brussels, "I find myself not in a condition to undertake such a journey "without risk. I would ask of you, then, if the road from "Brussels to Cleve would not to *you* seem too long for a meet-"ing; it is the one means of seeing you which remains to me.

* Voltaire, lxxii. 238-256 (Letters 22d August — 22d September 1740).

"Confess that I am unlucky: for now when I could dispose of "my person, and nothing hinders me from seeing you, the "fever gets its hand into the business, and seems to intend "disputing me that satisfaction.

"Let us deceive the fever, my dear Voltaire; and let me "at least have the pleasure of embracing you. Make my best "excuses" (polite, rather than sincere) "to Madame the *Mar-* "*quise*, that I cannot have the satisfaction of seeing her at "Brussels. All that are about me know the intention I was "in; which certainly nothing but the fever could have made "me change.

"Sunday next I shall be at a little Place near Cleve," — Schloss of Moyland, which, and the route to which, this Courier can tell you of; — "where I shall be able to possess you at "my ease. If the sight of you don't cure me, I will send for a "Confessor at once. Adieu; you know my sentiments and my "heart."* — Fédéric.

After which the Correspondence suddenly extinguishes itself: ceases for about a fortnight, — in the bad *mis*dated Editions even does worse; — and we are left to thick darkness, to our own poor shifts; Dryasdust being grandly silent on this small interest of ours. What is to be done?

Particulars of First Interview, on severe Scrutiny.

Here, from a painful Predecessor whose Papers I inherit, are some old Documents and Studies on the subject, — sorrowful collection, in fact, of what poor sparks of certainty were to be found hovering in that dark element; — which do at last (so luminous are *certainties* always, or "sparks" that will shine *steady*) coalesce into some feeble general twilight, feeble but indubitable; and even show the sympathetic reader *how* they were searched out and brought together. We number and label these poor Patches of Evidence on so small a matter; and leave them to the curious:

* Preuss,(Œuvres de Frédéric, xxii. 27.

11th Sept. 1740.

No. 1. *Date of the First Interview.* It is certain Voltaire did arrive at the little Schloss of Moyland, Sept. 11th, Sunday night, — which is the "Sunday" just specified in Friedrich's Letter. Voltaire had at once decided on complying, — what else? — and lost no time in packing himself: King's Courier on Thursday late; Voltaire on the road on Saturday early, or the night before. With Madame's shrill blessing (not the most musical in this vexing case), and plenty of fuss. "Was wont to travel in considerable style," I am told; "the innkeepers calling him "Your Lordship (*M. le Comte*).'" Arrives, sure enough, Sunday night; old Schloss of Moyland, six miles from Cleve; "moonlight," I find, — the Harvest Moon. Visit lasted three days.*

No. 2. *Voltaire's Drive thither.* Schloss Moyland: How far from Brussels, and by what route? By Louvain, Tirlemont, Tongres to Maestricht; then from Maestricht up the Maas (left bank) to Venlo, where cross; through Geldern and Goch to Cleve: between the Maas and Rhine this last portion. Flat damp country; tolerably under tillage; original constituents bog and sand. Distances I guess to be: To Tongres 60 miles and odd; to Maestricht 12 or 15, from Maestricht 75; in all 150 miles English. Two days' driving? There is equinoctial moon, and still above twelve hours of sunlight for "M. le Comte."

No. 3. *Of the Place Where.* Voltaire, who should have known, calls it "*petit Château de Meuse;*" which is a Castle existing nowhere but in Dreams. Other French Biographers are still more imaginary. The little Schloss of Moyland, — by no means "Meuse," nor even *Mörs*, which Voltaire probably means in saying *Château de Meuse*, — was, as the least inquiry settles beyond question, the place where Voltaire and Friedrich first met. Friedrich Wilhelm used often to lodge there in his Cleve journeys: he made thither for shelter, in the sickness that overtook him in friend Ginkel's house, coming home from the Rhine Campaign in 1734; lay there for several weeks after quitting Ginkel's. Any other light I can get upon it, is darkness visible. Büsching pointedly informs me,** "It is a Parish" (or patch of country under one priest), "and "Till *and* it are a Jurisdiction" (pair of patches under one

* Rödenbeck, p. 21; Preuss, &c. &c.
** *Erdbeschreibung*, v. 659, 677.

court of justice): — which does not much illuminate the inquiring mind. Small patch, this of Moyland, size not given; "was bought," says he, "in 1695, by Friedrich afterwards "First King, from the Family of Spaen," — we once knew a Lieutenant Spaen, of those Dutch regions, — "and was named a Royal Mansion ever thereafter." Who lived in it; what kind of thing was it, is it? *Altum silentium*, from Büsching and mankind. Belonged to the Spaens, fifty years ago; — some shadow of our poor banished friend the Lieutenant resting on it? Dim enough old Mansion, with "court" to it, with modicum of equipment; lying there in the moonlight; — did not look sublime to Voltaire on stepping out. So that all our knowledge reduces itself to this one point: of finding Moyland in the Map, with *date*, with *reminiscence* to us, hanging by it henceforth! Good.*

Mörs, — which is near the Town of Ruhrort, about midway between Wesel and Düsseldorf, — must be some forty miles from Moyland, forty-five from Cleve; southward of both. So that the place, "*à deux lieues de Clèves*," is, even by Voltaire's showing, this Moyland; were there otherwise any doubt upon it. "Château de *Meuse*," — hanging out a prospect of *Mörs* to us, — is bad usage to readers. Of an intelligent man, not to say a Trismegistus of men, one expects he will know in what town he is, after three days' experience, as here. But he does not always; he hangs out a mere "shadow of Mörs by "moonlight," till we learn better. Duvernet, his Biographer, even calls it "*Sleus-Meuse;*" some wonderful idea of Sluices and a River attached to it, in Duvernet's head!**

What Voltaire thought of the Interview Twenty Years afterwards.

Of the Interview itself, with general bird's-eye view of the Visit combined (in a very incorrect state), there is direct testimony by Voltaire himself. Voltaire

---

* Stieler's *Deutschland* (excellent Map in 25 Pieces), Piece 12. — Till is a mile or two north-east from Moyland; Moyland about 5 or 6 southeast from Cleve.

** Duvernet (2d *form* of him, — that is, Vie de Voltaire par T. J. D. V.), p. 117.

himself, twenty years after, in far other humour, all jarred into angry sarcasm, for causes we shall see by and by, — Voltaire, at the request of friends, writes down, as his Friedrich Reminiscences, that scandalous *Vie Privée* above spoken of, a most sad Document; and this is the passage referring to "the little Place in the neighbourhood of Cleve," where Friedrich now waited for him: errors corrected by our laborious Friend. After quoting something of that Strasburg Doggerel, the whole of which is now too well known to us, Voltaire proceeds:

"From Strasburg he," King Friedrich, "went to see his "Lower German Provinces; he said he would come and see "me incognito at Brussels. We prepared a fine house for him," — were ready to prepare such hired house as we had for him, with many apologies for its slight degree of perfection (*error first*), — "but having fallen ill in the little Mansion-"Royal of Meuse (*Château de Meuse*), a couple of leagues from "Cleve," — fell ill at Wesel; and there is no Château de *Meuse* in the world (*errors 2d and 3d*), — "he wrote to me that "he expected I would make the advances. I went, accord-"ingly, to present my profound homages. Maupertuis, who "already had his views, and was possessed with the rage of "being President to an Academy, had of his own accord," — no, being invited, and at my suggestion (*error 4th*), — "pre-"sented himself there; and was lodged with Algarotti and "Keyserling" (which latter, I suppose, had come from Berlin, not being of the Strasburg party, he) "in a garret of this "Palace.

"At the door of the court, I found, by way of guard, one "soldier. Privy-Councillor Rambonet, Minister of State" — (very subaltern man; never heard of him except in the Herstal Business, and here) "— was walking in the court; blowing in "his fingers to keep them warm." Sunday night, 11th September 1740; world all bathed in moonshine; and mortals mostly shrunk into their huts, out of the raw air. "He" Rambonet "wore big linen ruffles at his wrists, "very dirty" (visibly so in the moonlight? *Error 5th* extends *ad libitum* over all the following details); "a holed hat; an old official "periwig," — ruined into a totally unsymmetric state, as would seem, — "one side of which hung down into one of his "pockets, and the other scarcely crossed his shoulder. I was "told, this man was now entrusted with an affair of import- "ance here; and that proved true," — the Herstal Affair.

"I was led into his Majesty's apartment. Nothing but four "bare walls there. By the light of a candle, I perceived, in a "closet, a little trucklebed two feet and a half broad, on which "lay a little man muffled up in a dressing-gown of coarse blue "duffel: this was the King, sweating and shivering under a "wretched blanket there, in a violent fit of fever. I made my "reverence; and began the acquaintance by feeling his pulse, "as if I had been his chief physician. The fit over, he dressed "himself, and took his place at table. Algarotti, Keyserling, "Maupertuis, and the King's Envoy to the States-General" — one Räsfeld (skilled in *Herstal* matters, I could guess), — "we were of this supper, and discussed, naturally in a pro- "found manner, the Immortality of the Soul, Liberty, Fate, "the Androgynes of Plato" (the *Androgynoi*, or Men-Women, in Plato's *Convivium;* by no means the finest symbolic fancy of the divine Plato), — "and other small topics of that "nature."*

This is Voltaire's account of the Visit, — which included *three* "Suppers," all huddled into one by him here; — and he says nothing more of it; launching off now into new errors, about *Herstal*, the *Anti-Macchiavel*, and so forth: new and uglier errors, with much more of mendacity and serious malice in them, than in this harmless half-dozen now put on the score against him.

Of this Supper-Party, I know by face four of the guests: Maupertuis, Voltaire, Algarotti, Keyserling; — Räsfeld, Rambonet can sit as simulacra or mute accompaniment. Voltaire arrived on Sunday evening; stayed till Wednesday. Wednesday morning, 14th of the month, the Party broke up: Voltaire rolling off to left

* Voltaire, *Œuvres* (Piece once called *Vie Priv.'e*), ii. 26, 27.

hand, towards Brussels, or the Hague; King to right, on inspection business, and circuitously homewards. Three Suppers there had been, two busy Days intervening; discussions about Fate and the Androgynoi of Plato by no means the one thing done by Voltaire and the rest, on this occasion. We shall find elsewhere, "he declaimed his *Mahomet*" (sublime new Tragedy, not yet come out), in the course of these evenings, to the "speechless admiration" of his Royal Host, for one; and, in the daytime, that he even drew his pen about the Herstal Business, which is now getting to its crisis, and wrote one of the Manifestoes, still discoverable. And we need not doubt, in spite of his now sneering tone, that things ran high and grand here, in this paltry little Schloss of Moyland; and that those Three were actually Suppers of the Gods, for the time being.

"Councillor Rambonet," with the holed hat and unsymmetric wig, continues Voltaire in the satirical vein, "had mean-"while mounted a hired hack (*cheval de louage;*" mischievous Voltaire, I have no doubt he went on wheels, probably of his own): "he rode all night; and next morning, arrived at the "gates of Liége; where he took Act in the name of the King "his Master, whilst 2,000 men of the Wesel Troops laid Liége "under contribution. The pretext of this fine Marching of "Troops,"— not a pretext at all, but the assertion, correct in all points, of just claims long trodden down, and now made good with more spirit than had been expected,— "was cer-"tain rights which the King pretended to, over a suburb of "Liége. He even charged me to work at a Manifesto; and I "made one, good or bad; not doubting but a King with whom "I supped, and who called me his friend, must be in the right. "The affair soon settled itself, by means of a million of "ducats,"— nothing like the sum, as we shall see,— "which "he exacted by weight, to clear the costs of the Tour to "Strasburg, which, according to his complaint in that Poetic "Letter" (Doggerel above given), "were so heavy."

That is Voltaire's view; grown very corrosive after Twenty Years. He admits, with all the satire: "I na-"turally felt myself attached to him; for he had wit, "graces; and moreover he was a King, which always "forms a potent seduction, so weak is human nature. "Usually it is we of the writing sort that flatter Kings: "but this King praised me from head to foot, while the "Abbé Desfontaines and other scoundrels (*grédins*) "were busy defaming me in Paris at least once a "week."

What Voltaire thought of the Interview at the Time.

But let us take the contemporary account, which also we have at first hand; which is almost pathetic to read; such a contrast between ruddy morning and the storms of the afternoon! Here are Two Letters from Voltaire; fine transparent, human Letters, as his generally are: the first of them written directly on getting back to the Hague, and to the feeling of his eclipsed condition.

Voltaire to M. de Maupertuis (with the King).

"The Hague, 18th September 1740.

"I serve you, Monsieur, sooner than I promised; and that "is the way you ought to be served. I send you the answer of "M. Smith," — probably some German or Dutch *Schmidt*, spelt here in English, connected with the Sciences, say with water-carriage, the typographies, or one need not know what; — "you will see where the question stands.

"When we both left Cleve," — 14th of the month, Wednesday last; 18th is Sunday, in this old cobwebby Palace, where I am correcting *Anti-Macchiavel*, — "and you took to the right," — King, homewards, got to *Ham* that evening, — "I could have thought I was at the Last Judgment, where the "Bon Dieu separates the elect from the damned. *Divus Fre-*"*dericus* said to you, 'Sit down at my right hand in the Para-

"disc of Berlin;' and to me, 'Depart, thou accursed, into Holland.'

"Here I am accordingly in this phlegmatic place of punishment, far from the divine fire which animates the Friedrichs, the Maupertuis, the Algarottis. For God's love, do me the charity of some sparks in these stagnant waters where I am," — stiffening, cooling, — "stupefying to death. Instruct me of your pleasures, of your designs. You will doubtless see M. de Valori," — readers know de Valori; his Book has been published; edited, as too usual, by a Human Nightmare, ignorant of his subject and indeed of almost all other things, and liable to mistakes in every page; yet partly readable, if you carry lanterns, and love "*mon gros Valori:*" — "offer him, I pray you, my respects. If I do not write to him, the reason is, I have no news to send: I should be as exact as I am devoted, if my correspondence could be useful or agreeable to him.

"Won't you have me send you some Books? If I be still in Holland when your orders come, I will obey in a moment. I pray you do not forget me to M. de Keyserling," — Cæsarion whom we once had at Cirey; a headlong dusky little man of wit (library turned topsy-turvy, as Wilhelmina called him), whom we have seen.

"Tell me, I beg, if the enormous monad of Volfius," — (Wolf, would the reader like to hear about him? If so, he has only to speak!) — "is arguing at Marburg, at Berlin, or at Hall" (*Halle*, which is a very different place).

"Adieu, Monsieur: you can address your orders to me 'At the Hague:' they will be forwarded wherever I am; and I shall be, anywhere on earth, — Yours forever (*à vous pour jamais*)."*

Letter Second, of which a fragment may be given, is to one Cideville, a month later; all the more genuine as there was no chance of the King's hearing about this one. Cideville, some kind of literary Advocate at Rouen (who is wearisomely known to the reader of Voltaire's Letters), had done, what is rather an ende-

* Voltaire, lxxii. 252.

mical disorder at this time, some Verses for the King of Prussia, which he wished to be presented to his Majesty. The presentation, owing to accidents, did not take place; hear how Voltaire, from his cobweb Palace at the Hague, busy with *Anti-Macchiavel*, Van Duren and many other things, — 18th October 1740, on which day we find him writing many Letters, — explains the sad accident:

Voltaire to M. de Cideville (at Rouen).

"At the Hague, King of Prussia's Palace, 18th October 1740.

* * * "This is my case, dear Cideville. When you "sent me, enclosed in your Letter, those Verses (among which "there are some of charming and inimitable turn) for our "Marcus Aurelius of the North, I did well design to pay my "court to him with them. He was at that time to have "come to Brussels incognito: we expected him there; but the "Quartan Fever, which unhappily he still has, deranged all "his projects. He sent me a courier to Brussels," — mark that point, my Cideville; —"and so I set out to find him in "the neighbourhood of Cleve.

"It was there I saw one of the amiablest men in the world, "who forms the charm of society, who would be everywhere "sought after if he were not King; a philosopher without "austerity; full of sweetness, complaisance and obliging ways "(*agrémens*); not remembering that he is King when he meets "his friends; indeed so completely forgetting it that he made "me too almost forget it, and I needed an effort of memory to "recollect that I here saw sitting at the foot of my bed a "Sovereign who had an Army of 100,000 men. That was the "moment to have read your amiable Verses to him:" — yes; but then? — "Madame du Châtelet, who was to have sent "them to me, did not, *ne l'a pas fait*." Alas, no, they are still at Brussels, those charming Verses; and I, for a month past, am here in my cobweb Palace! But I swear to you, the instant I return to Brussels, I &c. &c.*

* lxxii. 282.

Finally, here is what Friedrich thought of it, ten days after parting with Voltaire. We will read this also (though otherwise ahead of us as yet); to be certified on all sides, and sated for the rest of our lives, concerning the Friedrich-Voltaire First Interview.

King Friedrich to M. Jordan (at Berlin).

"Potsdam, 24th September 1740.

"Most respectable Inspector of the poor, the invalids, "orphans, crazy people and Bedlams, — I have read with ma- "ture meditation the very profound Jordanic Letter which "was waiting here;" — and do accept your learned proposal.

"I have seen that Voltaire whom I was so curious to know; "but I saw him with the Quartan hanging on me, and my "mind as unstrung as my body. With men of his kind one "ought not to be sick; one ought even to be specially well, "and in better health than common, if one could.

"He has the eloquence of Cicero, the mildness of Pliny, "the wisdom of Agrippa; he combines, in short, what is to be "collected of virtues and talents from the three greatest men "of Antiquity. "His intellect is at work incessantly; every "drop of ink is a trait of wit from his pen. He declaimed his "*Mahomet* to us, an admirable Tragedy which he has done," — which the Official people smelling heresies in it ("tolera- "tion," "horrors of fanaticism," and the like) will not let him act, as readers too well know: — "he transported us out of "ourselves; I could only admire and hold my tongue. The "Du Châtelet is lucky to have him: for of the good things he "flings out at random, a person who had no faculty but me- "mory might make a brilliant Book. That Minerva has just "published her Work on *Physics:* not wholly bad. It was "König," — whom we know, and whose late tempest in a cer- tain teapot, — "that dictated the theme to her: she has ad- "justed, ornamented here and there with some touch picked "from Voltaire at her Suppers. The Chapter on Space is "pitiable; the" — in short she is still raw in the Pure Sciences, and should have waited. * * *

"Adieu, most learned, most scientific, most profound Jor- "dan, — or rather most gallant, most amiable, most jovial

"Jordan; — I salute thee, with assurance of all those old "feelings which thou hast the art of inspiring in every one "that knows thee. *Vale.*

"I write the moment of my arrival: be obliged to me, "friend; for I have been working, I am going to work still, "like a Turk, or like a Jordan."*

This is hastily thrown off for Friend Jordan, the instant after his Majesty's circuitous return home. Readers cannot yet attend his Majesty there, till they have brought the Affair of Herstal, and other remainders of the Cleve Journey, along with them.

* *Œuvres de Frédéric,* xvii. 71.

CHAPTER V.

AFFAIR OF HERSTAL.

This Rambonet, whom Voltaire found walking in the court of the old Castle of Moyland, is an official gentleman, otherwise unknown to History, who has lately been engaged in a Public Affair; and is now off again about it, "on a hired hack" or otherwise, — with very good instructions in his head. Affair which, though in itself but small, is now beginning to make great noise in the world, as Friedrich wends homewards out of his Cleve Journey. He has set it fairly alight, Voltaire and he, before quitting Moyland; and now it will go of itself. The Affair of Herstal, or of the Bishop of Liége; Friedrich's first appearance on the stage of politics. Concerning which some very brief notice, if intelligible, will suffice readers of the present day.

Heristal, now called Herstal, was once a Castle known to all mankind; King Pipin's Castle, who styled himself "Pipin of Heristal," before he became King of the Franks and begot Charlemagne. It lies on the Maas, in that fruitful Spa Country; left bank of the Maas, a little to the north of Liége; and probably began existence as a grander place than Liége (*Lüttich*), which was, at first, some Monastery dependent on secular Herstal and its grandeurs: — think only how the race has gone between these two entities; spiritual Liége now a big City, black with the smoke of forges and steam-mills; Herstal an insignificant Village, accidentally talked of for a few weeks in 1740, and no chance ever to be mentioned again by men.

Herstal, in the confused vicissitudes of a thousand years, had passed through various fortunes, and undergone change of owners often enough. Fifty years ago it was in the hands of the Nassau-Orange House; Dutch William, our English Protestant King, who probably scarce knew of his possessing it, was Lord of Herstal till his death. Dutch William had no children to inherit Herstal: he was of kinship to the Prussian House, as readers are aware; and from that circumstance, not without a great deal of discussion, and difficult "Division of the Orange Heritage," this Herstal had, at the long last, fallen to Friedrich Wilhelm's share; it and Neuchâtel, and the Cobweb Palace, and some other places and pertinents.

For Dutch William was of kin, we say; Friedrich I. of Prussia, by his Mother the noble Wife of the Great Elector, was full cousin to Dutch William: and the Marriage Contracts were express, — though the High Mightinesses made difficulties, and the collateral Orange branches were abundantly reluctant, when it came to the fulfilling point. For indeed the matter was intricate. Orange itself, for example, what was to be done with the Principality of Orange? Clearly Prussia's; but it lies imbedded deep in the belly of France: that will be a Cæsarean Operation for you! Had not Neuchâtel happened just then to fall home to France (or in some measure to France) and be heirless, Prussia's Heritage of Orange would have done little for Prussia! Principality of Orange was, by this chance, long since, mainly in the First King's time got settled:* but there needed many years more of good waiting, and of good pushing, on Friedrich Wilhelm's part; and it was not till 1732 that Friedrich Wilhelm got the Dutch Heritages finally brought to the square: Neuchâtel and Valengin, as aforesaid, in lieu of Orange; and now furthermore, that Old Palace at Loo (that *Vieille Cour* and biggest cobwebs), with pertinents, with Garden of Honslardik; and a string of items, bigger and less, not worth enumerating. Of the items, this Herstal was one;—and truly, so far as this went, Friedrich Wilhelm often thought he had better never have seen it, so much trouble did it bring him.

How the Herstallers had behaved to Friedrich Wilhelm.

The Herstal people, knowing the Prussian recruiting-system and other rigours, were extremely unwilling to come under Friedrich Wilhelm's sway, could they have helped it. They refused fealty, swore they never would swear; nor did they, till the appearance, or indubitable foreshine, of Friedrich Wilhelm's bayonets advancing on them from the East, brought compliance. And always after, spite of such quasi-fealty, they showed a pig-like obstinacy of humour; a certain insignificant, and as it were impertinent, deep-rooted desire to thwart, irritate and contradict the said Friedrich Wilhelm. Especially in any recruiting matter that might arise, knowing that to be the weak side of his Prussian Majesty. All this would have amounted to nothing, had it not been that their neighbour, the

---

* Neuchâtel, 3d November 1707, to Friedrich I., natives preferring him to "Fifteen other Claimants;" Louis XIV. loudly protesting: not till Treaty of Utrecht (14th March 1713, first month of Friedrich Wilhelm's reign) would Louis XIV., on cession of Orange, consent and sanction.

Prince Bishop of Liége, who imagined himself to have some obscure claims of sovereignty over Herstal, and thought the present a good opportunity for asserting these, was diligent to aid and abet the Herstal people in such their mutinous acts. Obscure claims; of which this is the summary, should the reader not prefer to skip it:

"The Bishop of Liége's claims on Herstal (which lie wrapt "from mankind in the extensive jungle of his law-pleadings, "like a Bedlam happily fallen extinct) seem to me to have "grown mainly from two facts more or less radical.

"*Fact first.* In Kaiser Barbarossa's time, year 1171, "Herstal had been given in pawn to the Church of Liége, for "a loan, by the then proprietor, Duke of Lorraine and Bra- "bant. Loan was repaid, I do not learn when, and the Pawn "given back; to the satisfaction of said Duke, or Duke's "Heirs; never quite to the satisfaction of the Church, which "had been in possession, and was loth to quit, after hoping "to continue. 'Give us back Herstal; it ought to be ours!' "unappeasable sigh or grumble to this effect is heard thence- "forth, at intervals, in the Chapter of Liége, and has not "ceased in Friedrich's time. But as the world, in its loud "thoroughfares, seldom or never heard, or could hear, such "sighing in the Chapter, nothing had come of it, — till —

"*Fact second.* In Kaiser Karl V.'s time, the Prince Bishop "of Liége happened to be a Natural Son of old Kaiser Max's; "— and had friends at headquarters, of a very choice nature. "Had, namely, in this sort, Kaiser Karl for Nephew or "Half-Nephew; and what perhaps was still better, as nearer "hand, had Karl's Aunt, Maria Queen of Hungary, then "Governess of the Netherlands, for Half-Sister. Liége, in "these choice circumstances, and by other good chances that "turned up, again got temporary clutch or half-clutch of "Herstal, for a couple of years (date 1546-'8, the Prince of "Orange, real proprietor, whose Ancestor had bought it for "money down, being then a minor); once, and perhaps a "second time in like circumstance; but had always to re- "nounce it again, when the Prince of Orange came to ma- "turity. And ever since, the Chapter of Liége sighs as be-

"fore, 'Herstal is perhaps in a sense ours. We had once
"'some kind of right to it!'—sigh inaudible in the loud
"public thoroughfares. That is the Bishop's claim. The
"name of him, if anybody care for it, is 'Georg Ludwig,
"'titular *Count of Berg*,' now a very old man: Bishop of Liége,
"he, and has been snatching at Herstal again, very eagerly
"by any skirt or tagrag that might happen to fly loose, these
"eight years past, in a rash and provoking manner;*—age
"eighty-two at present; poor old fool, he had better have sat
"quiet. There lies a rod in pickle for him, during these late
"months; and will be surprisingly laid on, were the time
"come!"

"I have Law Authority over Herstal, and power of judging there in the last appeal," said this Bishop:— "You!" thought Friedrich Wilhelm, who was far off, and had little time to waste.—"Any Prussian recruiter that behaves ill, bring him to me!" said the Bishop, who was on the spot. And accordingly it had been done; one notable instance two years ago: A Prussian Lieutenant locked in the Liége jail, on complaint of riotous Herstal; thereupon a Prussian Officer of rank (Colonel Kreutzen, worthy old Malplaquet gentleman) coming as Royal Messenger, not admitted to audience, nay laid hold of by the Liége bailiff instead; and other unheard-of procedures.** So that Friedrich Wilhelm had nothing but trouble with this petty Herstal, and must have thought his neighbour Bishop a very contentious highflying gentleman, who took great liberties with the Lion's whiskers, when he had the big animal at advantage.

The episcopal procedures, eight years ago, about the First Homaging of Herstal, had been of similar complexion; nor had other such failed in the interim,

* *Délices du Pais de Liége* (Liége, 1738); *Helden-Geschichte,* ii. 57-62.
** *Helden-Geschichte,* ii. 63-73.

though this last outrage exceeded them all. This last
began in the end of 1738; and span itself out through
1739, when Friedrich Wilhelm lay in his final sickness, less able to deal with it than formerly. Being a
peaceable man, unwilling to awaken conflagrations for
a small matter, Friedrich Wilhelm had offered, through
Kreutzen on this occasion, to part with Herstal
altogether; to sell it, "for 100,000 thalers," say
16,000*l.*, to the highflying Bishop, and honestly wash
his hands of it. But the highflying Bishop did not
consent, gave no definite answer; and so the matter
lay, — like an unsettled extremely irritating paltry
little matter, — at the time Friedrich Wilhelm died.

The Gazetteers and public knew little about these
particulars, or had forgotten them again; but at the
Prussian Court they were in lively remembrance.
What the young Friedrich's opinion about them had
been we gather from this succinct notice of the thing,
written seven or eight years afterwards, exact in all
points, and still carrying a breath of the old humour
in it. "A miserable Bishop of Liége thought it a
"proud thing to insult the late King. Some subjects
"of Herstal, which belongs to Prussia, had revolted;
"the Bishop gave them his protection. Colonel
"Kreutzen was sent to Liége, to compose the thing by
"treaty; credentials with him, full power, and all in
"order. Imagine it, the Bishop would not receive him!
"Three days, day after day, he saw this Envoy apply
"at his Palace, and always denied him entrance.
"These things had grown past endurance."* And
Friedrich had taken note of Herstal along with him,
on this Cleve Journey; privately intending to put

* Preuss, *Œuvres (Mém. de Brandenburg)*, ii. 53.

Herstal and the highflying Bishop on a suitabler footing, before his return from those countries.

For indeed, on Friedrich's Accession, matters had grown worse, not better. Of course there was Fealty to be sworn; but the Herstal people, abetted by the highflying Bishop, have declined swearing it. Apology for the past, prospect of amendment for the future, there is less than ever. What is the young King to do with this paltry little Hamlet of Herstal? He could, in theory, go into some Reichs-Hofrath, some Reichs-Kammergericht (kind of treble and tenfold English Court-of-Chancery, which has lawsuits 280 years old), — if he were a theoretic German King. He can plead in the Diets, and the Wetzlar Reichs-Kammergericht without end: "all German Sovereigns have power to send "their Ambassador thither, who is like a mastiff chained "in the backyard" (observes Friedrich elsewhere) "with "privilege of barking at the Moon," — unrestricted privilege of barking at the Moon, if that will avail a practical man, or King's Ambassador. Or perhaps the Bishop of Liége will bethink him, at last, what considerable liberty he is taking with some people's whiskers? Four months are gone; Bishop of Liége has not in the least bethought him: we are in the neighbourhood in person, with note of the thing in our memory.

Friedrich takes the Rod out of Pickle.

Accordingly the Rath Rambonet, whom Voltaire found at Moyland that Sunday night, had been over at Liége; went exactly a week before; with this message of very peremptory tenor from his Majesty:

4th-28th Sept. 1740.

To the Prince Bishop of Liége.

"Wesel, 4th September 1740.

"My Cousin, — Knowing all the assaults (*atteintes*) made "by you upon my indisputable rights over my free Barony of "Herstal; and how the seditious ringleaders there, for several "years past, have been countenanced (*bestärket*) by you in "their detestable acts of disobedience against me, — I have "commanded my Privy Councillor Rambonet to repair to "your presence, and in my name to require from you, within "two days, a distinct and categorical answer to this question: "Whether you are still minded to assert your pretended sover-"eignty over Herstal; and whether you will protect the rebels "at Herstal, in their disorders and abominable disobedience?

"In case you refuse, or delay beyond the term, the Answer "which I hereby of right demand, you will render yourself "alone responsible, before the world, for the consequences "which infallibly will follow. I am, with much consideration "— My Cousin, —

"Your very affectionate Cousin,
"FRIEDRICH." *

Rambonet had started straightway for Liége, with this missive; and had duly presented it there, I guess on the 7th, — with notice that he would wait forty-eight hours, and then return with what answer or no-answer there might be. Getting no written answer, or distinct verbal one; getting only some vague mumble-ment as good as none, Rambonet had disappeared from Liége on the 9th; and was home at Moyland when Voltaire arrived that Sunday evening, — just walking about to come to heat again, after reporting progress to the above effect.

Rambonet, I judge, enjoyed only one of those divine Suppers at Moyland; and dashed off again, "on hired hack" or otherwise, the very next morning; that contingency of No-answer having been the anticipated

* *Helden-Geschichte,* ii. 75, 111.

one, and all things put in perfect readiness for it. Rambonet's new errand was to "take act," as Voltaire calls it, "at the Gates of Liége," — to deliver at Liége a succinct Manifesto, Pair of Manifestoes, both in Print (ready beforehand), and bearing date that same Sunday, "Wesel, 11th September;" — much calculated to amaze his Reverence at Liége. Succinct good Manifestoes, said to be of Friedrich's own writing; the essential of the two is this:

Exposition of the Reasons which have induced his Majesty the King of Prussia to make just Reprisals on the Prince Bishop of Liége.

"His Majesty the King of Prussia, being driven beyond "bounds by the rude proceedings of the Prince Bishop of Liége, "has with regret seen himself forced to recur to the Method of "Arms, in order to repress the violence and affront which the "Bishop has attempted to put upon him. This resolution has "cost his Majesty much pain; the rather as he is, by principle "and disposition, far remote from whatever could have the "least relation to rigour and severity.

"But seeing himself compelled by the Bishop of Liége to "take new methods, he had no other course but to maintain "the justice of his rights (*la justice de ses droits*), and demand "reparation for the indignity done upon his Minister Von "Kreutzen, as well as for the contempt with which the Bishop "of Liége has neglected even to answer the Letter of the "King.

"As too much rigour borders upon cruelty, so too much "patience resembles weakness. Thus, although the King "would willingly have sacrificed his interests to the public "peace and tranquillity, it was not possible to do so in reference "to his honour; and that is the chief motive which has de-"termined him to this resolution, so contrary to his inten-"tions.

"In vain has it been attempted, by methods of mildness, "to come to a friendly agreement: it has been found, on the "contrary, that the King's moderation only increased the "Prince's arrogance; that mildness of conduct on one side "only furnished resources to pride on the other; and that, in "fine, instead of gaining by soft procedure, one was insen"sibly becoming an object of vexation and disdain.

"There being no means to have justice but in doing it for "oneself, and the King being Sovereign enough for such a "duty, — he intends to make the Prince of Liége feel how far "he was in the wrong to abuse such moderation so unworthily. "But in spite of so much unhandsome behaviour on the part "of this Prince, the King will not be inflexible; satisfied with "having shown the said Prince that he can punish him, and "too just to overwhelm him.

"Frédéric." *

"Wesel, September 11th, 1740."

Whether Rambonet insinuated his Paper-Packet into the Palace of Seraing, left it at the Gate of Liége (fixed by nail, if he saw good), or in what manner he "took act," I never knew; and, indeed, Rambonet vanishes from human History at this point: it is certain only that he did his Formality, say two days hence; — and that the Fact foreshadowed by it is likewise in the same hours, hour after hour, getting steadily done.

For the Manifestoes printed beforehand, dated Wesel, 11th September, were not the only thing ready at Wesel; waiting, as on the slip, for the contingency of No-answer. Major-General Borck, with the due battalions, squadrons and equipments, was also ready. Major-General Borck, the same who was with us at Baireuth lately, had just returned from that journey, when he got orders to collect 2,000 men, horse and foot, with the due proportion of artillery, from the Prussian Garrisons in these parts; and to be ready for marching with them, the instant the contingency of

* *Helden Geschichte*, ii. 77. Said to be by Friedrich himself (Stenzel, iv. 59).

No-answer arrives, — Sunday, 11th, as can be foreseen. Borck knows his route: To Maaseyk, a respectable Town of the Bishop's, the handiest for Wesel; to occupy Maaseyk and the adjoining "Counties of Lotz and Horn;" and lie there at the Bishop's charge till his Reverence's mind alter.

Borck is ready, to the last pontoon, the last munition-loaf; and no sooner is signal given of the No-answer come, than Borck, that same "Sunday, 11th," gets under way; marches, steady as clock-work, towards Maaseyk (fifty miles southwest of him, distance now lessening every hour); crosses the Maas, by help of his pontoons; is now in the Bishop's Territory, and enters Maaseyk, evening of "Wednesday, 14th," — that very day Voltaire and his Majesty had parted, going different ways from Moyland; and probably about the same hour while Rambonet was "taking act at the 'Gate of Liége," by nail-hammer or otherwise. All, goes punctual, swift, cog hitting pinion far and near, in this small Herstal Business; and there is no mistake made, and a minimum of time spent.

Borck's management was throughout good: punctual, quietly exact, polite, mildly inflexible. Fain would the Maaseyk Town-Raths have shut their gates on him; desperately conjuring him, "Respite for a few hours, till we send to Liége for instructions!" But it was to no purpose. "Unbolt, *ihr Herren;* swift, or the petard will have to do it!" Borck publishes his Proclamation, a mild-spoken rigorous Piece; signifies to the Maaseyk Authorities, That he has to exact a Contribution of 20,000 thalers (3,000*l.*) here, Contribution payable in three days; that he furthermore, while he continues in these parts, will need such and such rations, accommodations, allowances, — "fifty *louis* (say guineas) daily for his own private expenses," one item; — and, in mild rhadamanthine language, waves aside all remonstrance, refusal or delay, as superfluous considerations: Unless said Contribution and required supplies come in, it will be his painful duty to bring them in.*

The highflying Bishop, much astonished, does now eagerly answer his Prussian Majesty, "Was from home, was ill, thought he had answered; is the most ill-used of Bishops;" and other things of a hysteric character.** And there came forth, as natural to the situation, multitudinous complainings, manifestoings, applications to the Kaiser, to the French, to the Dutch, of a very shrieky character on the Bishop of Liége's part; sparingly, if at all noticed on Friedrich's: the whole of which we shall consider ourselves free to leave undisturbed in the rubbish-abysses, as henceforth conceivable to the reader. "*Sed spem stupende fefellit eventus*," shrieks the poor old Bishop, making moan to the Kaiser: "*ecce enim, præmissa duntaxat* one Letter," and little more, "the said King of Borussia has, with about "2,000 horse and foot, and warlike engines, in this "month of September, entered the Territory of Liége;"*** which is an undeniable truth, but an unavailing. Borck is there, and "2,000 good arguments with him," as Voltaire defines the phenomenon. Friedrich, except to explain pertinently what my readers already know, does not write or speak farther on the subject; and readers and he may consider the Herstal Affair, thus

---

* *Helden-Geschichte*, i. 427; ii. 113.
** Ibid. ii. 85, 86 (date, 16th September).
*** *Helden-Geschichte*, ii. p. 88.

set agoing under Borck's auspices, as in effect finished; and that his Majesty has left it on a satisfactory footing, and may safely turn his back on it, to wait the sure issue at Berlin before long.

What Voltaire thought of Herstal.

Voltaire told us he himself "did one Manifesto, good or bad," on this Herstal Business: — where is that Piece, then, what has become of it? Dig well in the realms of Chaos, rectifying stupidities more or less enormous, the Piece itself is still discoverable; and, were pieces by Voltaire less a rarity than they are, might be resuscitated by a good Editor, and printed in his *Works*. Lies buried in the lonesome rubbish-mountains of that *Helden-Geschichte*, — let a *Siste Viator*, scratched on the surface, mark where.* Apparently that is the Piece by Voltaire? Yes, on reading that, it has every internal evidence; distinguishes itself from the surrounding pieces, like a slab of compact polished stone, in a floor rammed together out of ruinous old bricks, broken bottles and mortar-dust; — agrees, too, if you examine by the miscroscope, with the external indications, which are sure and at last clear, though infinitesimally small; and is beyond doubt Voltaire's, if it were now good for much.

It is not properly a Manifesto, but an anonymous Memoir published in the Newspapers, explaining to impartial mankind, in a legible brief manner, what the old and recent History of Herstal, and the Troubles of Herstal, have been, and how chimerical and "null to the extreme of nullity (*nulles de toute nullité*)" this poor

* *Helden-Geschichte*, II. pp. 93-98.

Bishop's pretensions upon it are. Voltaire expressly piques himself on this Piece;* brags also how he settled "M. de Fénélon" (French Ambassador at the Hague), "who came to me the day before yesterday," much out of square upon the Herstal Business, till I pulled him straight. And it is evident (beautifully so, your Majesty) how Voltaire busied himself in the Gazettes and Diplomatic circles, setting Friedrich's case right; Voltaire very loyal to Friedrich and his Liége Cause at that time; — and the contrast between what his contemporary Letters say on the subject, and what his ulterior Pasquil called *Vie Privée* says, is again great.

The dull stagnant world, shaken awake by this Liége adventure, gives voice variously; and in the Gazetteer and Diplomatic circles it is much criticised, by no means everywhere in the favourable tone at this first blush of the business. "He had written an *Anti-Machiavel*," says the Abbé St. Pierre, and even says Voltaire (in the *Pasquil*, not the contemporary *Letters*), "and he acts thus!" Truly he does, Monsieur de Voltaire; and all men, with light upon the subject, or even with the reverse upon it, must make their criticisms. For the rest, Borck's "2,000 arguments" are there; which Borck handles well, with polite calm rigour: by degrees the dust will fall, and facts everywhere be seen for what they are.

As to the highflying Bishop, finding that hysterics are but wasted on Friedrich and Borck, and produce

---

* Letter to Friedrich! dateless, dateable "soon after 17th September;" which the rash dark Editors have by guess misdated "August;" or, what was safer for them, omitted altogether. *Œuvres de Voltaire* (Paris, 1818, 40 voll.) gives the Letter, xxxix. 442 (see also Ibid. 453, 463); later Editors, and even Preuss, take the safer course.

no effect with their 2,000 validities, he flies next to the Kaiser, to the Imperial Diet, in shrill-sounding Latin obtestations, of which we already gave a flying snatch: "Your *humilissimus* and *fidelissimus Vassallus*, and most obsequent Servant, Georgius Ludovicus; meek, modest, and unspeakably in the right: was ever Member of the Holy Roman Empire so snubbed, and grasped by the windpipe, before? O, help him, great Kaiser, bid the iron gripe loosen itself!"* The Kaiser does so, in heavy Latin rescripts, in German *Dehortatoriums* more than one, of a sulky, imperative, and indeed very lofty tenor; "Let Georgius Ludovicus go, foolish rash young Dilection (*Liebden*, not *Majesty*, we ourselves being the only Majesty), and I will judge between you; otherwise —!" said the Kaiser, ponderously shaking his Olympian wig, and lifting his gilt cane, or sceptre of mankind, in an Olympian manner. Here are some touches of his second sublimest *Dehortatorium* addressed to Friedrich, in a very compressed state: **

We Karl the Sixth, Kaiser of (*Titles enough*), * * * "Con-
"sidering these, in the Holy Roman Reich, almost unheard-
"of violent Doings (*Thätlichkeiten*), which We, in Our
"Supreme-Judge Office, cannot altogether justify, nor will
"endure..... We have the trust that you yourself will mag-
"nanimously see How evil counsellors have misled your Dilec-
"tion to commence your Reign, not by showing example of
"Obedience to the Laws appointed for all members of the
"Reich, for the weak and for the strong alike, but by such
"Doings (*Thathandlungen*) as in all quarters must cause a
"great surprise.

"We give your Dilection to know, therefore, That you
"must straightway withdraw those troops which have broken

* *Helden-Geschichte*, ii. 86-116.
** Ibid. ii. 127; a *first* and milder (ibid. 73).

"into the Liége Territory; make speedy restitution of all that
"has been extorted; — especially General von Borck to give
"back at once those 50 louis-d'or daily drawn by him, to re-
"nounce his demand of the 20,000 thalers, to make good all
"damage done, and retire with his whole military force
"(*Militz*) over the Liége boundaries; — and in brief that you
"will, by law or arbitration, manage to agree with the Prince
"Bishop of Liége, who wishes it very much. These things
"We expect from your Dilection, as Kurfürst of Branden-
"burg, within the space of Two Months from the Issuing of
"this; and remain," — Yours as you shall demean yourself,
"— KARL.

"Given at Wien, 4th of Oct. 1740." — The last Dehortatorium ever signed by Karl VI. In two weeks after, he ate
too many mushrooms, — and immense results followed!

Dehortatoriums had their interest, at Berlin and
elsewhere, for the Diplomatic circles; but did not produce the least effect on Borck or Friedrich; though
Friedrich noted the Kaiser's manner in these things,
and thought privately to himself, as was evident to the
discerning, "What an amount of wig on that old
gentleman!" A notable Kaiser's Ambassador, Herr
Botta, who had come with some Accession compliments,
in these weeks, was treated slightingly by Friedrich;
hardly admitted to Audience; and Friedrich's public
reply to the last Dehortatorium had almost something
of sarcasm in it: Evil counsellors, yourself, Most Dread
Kaiser! It is you that are "misled by counsellors,
"who might chance to set Germany on fire, were
"others as unwise as they!" Which latter phrase was
remarkable to mankind. — There is a long account
already run up between that old gentleman, with his
Seckendorfs, Grumkows, with his dull insolencies,
wiggeries, and this young gentleman, who has nearly
had his heart broken and his Father's house driven

mad by them! Borck remains at his post; rations duly delivered, and fifty louis a day for his own private expenses; and there is no answer to the Kaiser, or in sharp brief terms (about "chances of setting Germany on fire"), rather worse than none.

Readers see, as well as Friedrich did, what the upshot of this Affair must be; — we will now finish it off, and wash our hands of it, before following his Majesty to Berlin. The poor Bishop had applied, shrieking, to the French for help; — and there came some colloquial passages between Voltaire and Fénélon, if that were a result. He had shrieked in like manner to the Dutch, but without result of any kind traceable in that quarter: nowhere, except from the Kaiser, is so much as a *Dehortatorium* to be got. Whereupon the once highflying, now vainly shrieking Bishop discerns clearly that there is but one course left, — the course which has lain wide open for some years past, had not his flight gone too high for seeing it. Before three weeks are over, seeing how Dehortatoriums go, he sends his Ambassadors to Berlin, his apologies, proposals:* "Would not your Majesty perhaps consent to sell this Herstal, as your Father of glorious memory was pleased to be willing once?" —

Friedrich answers straightway to the effect: "Certainly! Pay me the price it was once already offered for: 100,000 thalers, *plus* the expenses since incurred. That will be 180,000 thalers, besides what you have spent already on General Borck's days' wages. To which we will add that wretched little fraction of Old

---

* Ambassadors arrived, 28th September; last Dehortatorium not yet out. Business was completed, 20th October (Rödenbeck *in diebus*).

28th Sept. 1740.

Debt, clear as noon, but never paid nor any part of it; 60,000 thalers, due by the See of Liége ever since the Treaty of Utrecht; 60,000, for which we will charge no interest: that will make 240,000 thalers, — 36,000*l.*, instead of the old sum you might have had it at. Produce that cash; and take Herstal, and all the dust that has risen out of it, well home with you."* The Bishop thankfully complies in all points; negotiation speedily done ("20th Oct." the final date): Bishop has not, I think, quite so much cash on hand; but will pay all he has, and 4 per centum interest till the whole be liquidated. His Ambassadors "get gold snuff-boxes;" and return mildly glad.

And thus, in some six weeks after Borck's arrival in those parts, Borck's function is well done. The noise of Gazettes and Diplomatic circles lays itself again; and Herstal, famous once for King Pipin, and famous again for King Friedrich, lapses at length into obscurity, which we hope will never end. Hope; — though who can say? *Roucoux*, quite close upon it, becomes a Battle-ground in some few years; and memorabilities go much at random in this world!

* Stenzel, iv. 60, who counts in gulden, and is not distinct.

CHAPTER VI.

RETURNS BY HANOVER; DOES NOT CALL ON HIS ROYAL UNCLE THERE.

FRIEDRICH spent ten days on his circuitous journey home; considerable inspection to be done, in Minden, Magdeburg, not to speak of other businesses he had. The old Newspapers are still more intent upon him, now that the Herstal Affair has broken into flame: especially the English Newspapers; who guess that there are passages of courtship going on between great George their King and him. Here is one fact, correct in every point, for the old London Public: "Letters "from Hanover say, that the King of Prussia passed "within a small distance of that City the 16th inst. "N. S., on his return to Berlin, but did not stop at "Herrenhausen;" — about which there has been such hoping and speculating among us lately.* A fact which the extinct Editor seems to meditate for a day or two; after which he says (partly in *italics*), opening his lips the second time, like a Friar Bacon's Head significant to the Public: "Letters from Hanover tell "us that the Interview, which it was said his Majesty "was to have with the King of Prussia, did not take "place, for certain *private reasons*, which our Cor- "respondent leaves us to guess at!"

It is well known Friedrich did not love his little

* *Daily Post*, 22d Sept. 1740; other London Newspapers from July 31st downwards.

Uncle, then or thenceforth; still less his little Uncle him: "What is this Prussia, rising alongside of us, higher and higher, as if it would reach our own sublime level!" thinks the little Uncle to himself. At present there is no quarrel between them; on the contrary, as we have seen, there is a mutual capability of helping one another, which both recognise; but will an interview tend to forward that useful result? Friedrich, in the intervals of an ague, with Herstal just broken out, may have wisely decided, No. "Our sublime little Uncle, of the waxy complexion, with the proudly staring fish-eyes, — no wit in him, not much sense, and a great deal of pride, — stands dreadfully erect, 'plumb and more,' with the Garter-leg advanced, when one goes to see him; and his remarks are not of an entertaining nature. Leave him standing there: to him let Truchsess and Bielfeld suffice, in these hurries, in this ague that is still upon us." Upon which the dull old Newspapers, Owls of Minerva that then were, endeavour to draw inferences. The noticeable fact is, Friedrich did, on this occasion, pass within a mile or two of his royal Uncle, without seeing him; and had not, through life, another opportunity; never saw the sublime little man at all, nor was again so near him.

I believe Friedrich little knows the thick-coming difficulties of his Britannic Majesty at this juncture; and is too impatient of these laggard procedures on the part of a man with eyes *à fleur-de-tête*. Modern readers too have forgotten Jenkins's Ear; it is not till after long study and survey that one begins to perceive the anomalous profundities of that phenomenon to the poor English Nation and its poor George II.

The English sent off, last year, a scanty Expedition,

"six ships of the line," only six, under Vernon, a fiery
Admiral, a little given to be fiery in Parliamentary
talk withal; and these did proceed to Porto-Bello on
the Spanish Main of South America; did hurl out on
Porto-Bello such a fiery destructive deluge, of gunnery
and bayonet-work, as quickly reduced the poor place
to the verge of ruin, and forced it to surrender with
whatever navy, garrison, goods and resources were in
it, to the discretion of fiery Vernon, — who does not
prove implacable, he or his, to a petitioning enemy.
Yes, humble the insolent, but then be merciful to them,
say the admiring Gazetteers. "The actual monster,"
how cheering to think, "who tore off Mr. Jenkins's
"Ear, was got hold of" (actual monster, or even three
or four different monsters who each did it, the "hold
got" being *mythical*, as readers see), "and naturally
"thought he would be slit to ribbons; but our people
"magnanimously pardoned him, magnanimously flung
"him aside out of sight;"* impossible to shoot a dog
in cold blood.

Whereupon Vernon returned home triumphant; and
there burst forth such a jubilation, over the day of
small things, as is now astonishing to think of. Had
the Termagant's own Thalamus and Treasury been
bombarded suddenly one night by redhot balls, Madrid
City laid in ashes, or Baby Carlos's Apanage extinguished from Creation, there could hardly have been
greater English joy (witness the "Porto-Bellos" they
still have, new Towns so named); so flamy is the murky
element growing on that head. And indeed had the
cipher of tar-barrels burnt, and of ale-barrels drunk,

---

* *Gentleman's Magazine*, x. 124, 145 (date of the Event is 3d Dec. x. s. 1739).

and the general account of wick and tallow spent in illuminations and in aldermanic exertions on the matter, been accurately taken, one doubts if Porto-Bello sold, without shot fired, to the highest bidder, at its flowriest, would have covered such a sum. For they are a singular Nation, if stirred up from their stagnancy; and are much in earnest about this Spanish War.

It is said there is now another far grander Expedition on the stocks; military this time as well as naval, intended for the Spanish Main; — but of that, for the present, we will defer speaking. Enough, the Spanish War is a most serious and most furious business to those old English; and, to us, after forced study of it, shines out like far-off conflagration, with a certain lurid significance in the then night of things. Night otherwise fallen dark and somniferous to modern mankind. As Britannic Majesty and his Walpoles have, from the first, been dead against this Spanish War, the problem is all the more ominous, and the dreadful corollaries that may hang by it the more distressing to the royal mind.

For example, there is known, or as good as known, to be virtually some Family Compact, or covenanted Brotherhood of Bourbonism, French and Spanish: political people quake to ask themselves, "How will the French keep out of this War, if it continue any length of time? And in that case, how will Austria, Europe at large? Jenkins's Ear will have kindled the Universe, not the Spanish Main only, and we shall be at a fine pass!" The Britannic Majesty reflects that if France take to fighting him, the first stab given will probably be in the accessiblest quarter and the intensely most sensitive, — our own Electoral Dominions where no Parliament plagues us, our dear native country, Hanover. Extremely interesting to know what Friedrich of Prussia will do in such contingency?

Well, truly it might have been King George's best bargain to close with Friedrich; to guarantee Jülich and Berg, and get Friedrich to stand between the French and Hanover; while George, with an England behind him, in such humour, went wholly into that Spanish Business, the one thing needful to them at present. Truly; but then again, there are considerations: "What *is* this Friedrich, just come out upon the world? What real fighting power has he, after all that ridiculous drilling and recruiting Friedrich Wilhelm made? Will he be faithful in bargain; is not, perhaps, from of old, his bias always toward France rather? And the Kaiser, what will the Kaiser say to it?" These are questions for a Britannic Majesty! Seldom was seen such an insoluble imbroglio of potentialities; dangerous to touch, dangerous to leave lying; — and his Britannic Majesty's procedures upon it are of a very slow intricate sort; and will grow still more so, year after year, in the new intricacies that are coming and be a weariness to my readers and me. For observe the simultaneous fact. All this while, Robinson at Vienna is dunning the Imperial Majesty to remember old Marlborough days and the Laws of Nature; and declare for us against France, in case of the worst. What an attempt! Imperial Majesty has no money; Imperial Majesty remembers recent days rather, and his own last quarrel with France (on the Polish-Election score), in which you Sea Powers cruelly stood neuter! One comfort, and pretty much one only, is left to a nearly bankrupt Imperial heart; that France does at any rate ratify Pragmatic Sanction, and instead of enemy to that inestimable Document has become friend, — if only she be well let alone. "Let well alone," says the sad Kaiser, bankrupt of heart as well as purse: "I have saved the Pragmatic, got Fleury to guarantee it; I will hunt wild swine and not shadows any more: ask me not!" And now this Herstal business; the Imperial Dehortatoriums, perhaps of a high nature, that are like to come? More hopeless proposition the Britannic Majesty never made than this to the Kaiser. But he persists in it, orders Robinson to persist; knocks at the Austrian door with one hand, at the Prussian or Anti-Austrian with the other; and gazes, with those proud fish-eyes, into perils and potentialities and a sea of troubles. Wearisome to think of, were not one bound to it! Here, from a singular *Constitutional History of England*, not yet got into print, are two Excerpts; which I will request the reader to try if he can take along with him, in view of much that is coming:

1. *A just War.* — "This War, which posterity scoffs at as "the *War for Jenkins's Ear*, was, if we examine it, a quite in- "dispensable one; the dim much-bewildered English, driven "into it by their deepest instincts, were, in a chaotic inarticu- "late way, right and not wrong in taking it as the Command- "ment of Heaven. For such, in a sense, it was; as shall by "and by appear. Not perhaps since the grand Reformation "Controversy, under Oliver Cromwell and Elizabeth, had "there, to this poor English People (who are essentially "dumb, *in*articulate, from the weight of meaning they have, "notwithstanding the palaver one hears from them in certain "epochs), been a more authentic cause of War. And, what "was the fatal and yet foolish circumstance, their Constitu- "tional Captains, especially their King, would never and "could never regard it as such; but had to be forced into it by

"the public rage, there being no other method left in the
"case.
"I say, a most necessary War, though of a most stupid
"appearance; such the fatality of it: — begun, carried on,
"ended, as if by a People in a state of somnambulism! More
"confused operation never was. A solid placid People,
"heavily asleep — (and *snoring* much, shall we say, and in-
"articulately grunting and struggling under indigestions,
"Constitutional and other? Do but listen to the hum of those
"extinct Pamphlets and Parliamentary Oratories of theirs!),
" — yet an honestly intending People; and keenly alive to any
"commandment from Heaven, that could pierce through the
"thick skin of them into their big obstinate heart. Such a
"commandment, then and there, was that monition about
"Jenkins's Ear. Upon which, so pungent was it to them,
"they started violently out of bed, into painful sleep-walk-
"ing; and went, for twenty years and more, clambering and
"sprawling about, far and wide, on the giddy edge of pre-
"cipices, over housetops and frightful cornices and parapets;
"in a dim fulfilment of the said Heaven's command. I reckon
"that this War, though there were intervals, Treaties of
"Peace more than one, and the War had various names, —
"did not end till 1763. And then, by degrees, the poor
"English Nation found that (at, say, a thousand times the
"necessary expense, and with imminent peril to its poor
"head, and all the bones of its body) it had actually suc-
"ceeded, — by dreadful exertions in its sleep! This will be
"more apparent by and by; and may be a kind of comfort to
"the sad English reader, drearily surveying such somnam-
"bulisms on the part of his poor ancestors."

2. *Two Difficulties.* — "There are Two grand Difficulties
"in this Farce-Tragedy of a War; of which only one, and
"that not the worst of the Pair, is in the least surmised by the
"English hitherto. Difficulty First, which is even worse than
"the other, and will surprisingly attend the English in all
"their Wars now coming, is: That their fighting-apparatus,
"though made of excellent material, cannot fight, — being in
"disorganic condition; one branch of it, especially the
"'Military' one, as they are pleased to call it, being as good
"as totally chaotic, and this in a quiet habitual manner, this
"long while back. With the Naval branch it is otherwise;

"which also is habitual there. The English almost as if by
"nature can sail, and fight, in ships; cannot well help doing
"it.' Sailors innumerable are bred to them; they are planted
"in the Ocean, opulent stormy Neptune clipping them in all
"his moods forever: and then by nature, being a dumb, much-
"enduring, much-reflecting, stout, veracious and valiant
"kind of People, they shine in that way of life, which speci-
"ally requires such. Without more forethought, they have
"sailors innumerable, and of the best quality. The English
"have among them also, strange as it may seem to the cursory
"observer, a great gift of organising; witness their Ark-
"wrights and others: and this gift they may often, in matters
"Naval more than elsewhere, get the chance of exercising.
"For a Ship's Crew, or even a Fleet, unlike a land Army, is
"of itself a unity, its fortunes disjoined, dependent on its
"own management; and it falls, moreover, as no land Army
"can, to the undivided guidance of one man, — who (by
"hypothesis, being English), has now and then, from of old,
"chanced to be an organising man; and who is always much
"interested to know and practise what *has* been well organised.
"For you are in contact with verities, to an unexampled de-
"gree, when you get upon the Ocean, with intent to sail on
"it, much more to fight on it; — bottomless destruction raging
"beneath you and on all hands of you, if you neglect, for any
"reason, the methods of keeping *it* down, and making it float
"you to your aim!

"The English Navy is in tolerable order at that period.
"But as to the English Army, — we may say it is, in a wrong
"sense, the wonder of the world, and continues so throughout
"the whole of this History and farther! Never before, among
"the rational sons of Adam, were Armies sent out on such
"terms, — namely without a General, or with no General
"understanding the least of his business. The English have
"a notion that Generalship is not wanted; that War is not an
"Art, as playing Chess is, as finding the Longitude, and
"doing the Differential Calculus are (and a much deeper Art
"than any of these); that War is taught by Nature, as eating
"is; that courageous soldiers, led on by a courageous Wooden
"Pole with Cocked-hat on it, will do very well. In the world
"I have not found opacity of platitude go deeper among any
"People. This is Difficulty First, — not yet suspected by an

20th—24th Sept. 1740.

"English People, capable of great opacity on some sub-
"jects.
"Difficulty Second is, That their Ministry, whom they
"had to force into this War, perhaps do not go zealously
"upon it. And perhaps even, in the above circumstances,
"they totally want knowledge how to go upon it, were they
"never so zealous! Difficulty Second might be much helped,
"were it not for Difficulty First. But the administering of war
"is a thing also that does not come to a man like eating. —
"This Second Difficulty, suspicion that Walpole and perhaps
"still higher heads want zeal, gives his Britannic Majesty in-
"finite trouble; and" —

— And so, in short, he stands there, with the Garter-
leg advanced, looking loftily into a considerable sea of
troubles, — that day when Friedrich drove past him,
Friday 16th September 1740, and never came so near
him again.

The next business for Friedrich was a Visit at
Brunswick, to the Affinities and Kindred, in passing;
where also was an important little act to be done: Betrothal of the young Prince, August Wilhelm, Heir-
Presumptive whom we saw in Strasburg, to a Princess
of that House, Louisa Amelia, younger Sister of Friedrich's own Queen. A modest promising arrangement;
which turned out well enough, — though the young
Prince, Father to the Kings that since are, was not
supremely fortunate otherwise.* After which, the
review at Magdeburg; and home on the 24th, there to
"be busy as a Turk or as a M. Jordan," — according
to what we read long since.

* Betrothal was 20th September 1740; Marriage, 5th January 1742
(Buchholz, i. 207).

CHAPTER VII.

WITHDRAWS TO REINSBERG, HOPING A PEACEABLE WINTER.

By this Herstal token, which is now blazing abroad, now and for a month to come, it can be judged that the young King of Prussia intends to stand on his own footing, quite peremptorily if need be; and will by no means have himself led about in Imperial harness, as his late Father was. So that a dull Public (Herrenhausen very specially), and Gazetteer Owls of Minerva everywhere, may expect events. All the more indubitably, when that spade-work comes to light in the Wesel Country. It is privately certain (the Gazetteers not yet sure about it, till they see the actual spades going), this new King does fully intend to assert his rights on Berg-Jülich; and will appear there with his iron ramrods, the instant old Kur-Pfalz shall decease, let France and the Kaiser say No to it or say Yes. There are, in fact, at a fit place, "Büderich, in the neighbourhood of Wesel," certain rampart-works, beginnings as of an Entrenched Camp, going on; — "for Review purposes merely," say the Gazetteers, *in italics.* Here, it privately is Friedrich's resolution, shall a Prussian Army, of the due strength (could be well nigh 100,000 strong if needful), make its appearance, directly on old Kur-Pfalz's decease, if one live to see such event.* France and the Kaiser will probably take good survey of that Büderich phenomenon before meddling.

* Stenzel, iv. 61.

To do his work like a King, and shun no peril and no toil in the course of what his work may be, is Friedrich's rule and intention. Nevertheless it is clear he expects to approve himself magnanimous rather in the Peaceable operations than in the Warlike; and his outlooks are, of all places and pursuits, towards Reinsberg and the Fine Arts, for the time being. His Public activity meanwhile they describe as "prodigious," though the ague still clings to him; such building, instituting, managing: Opera-House, French Theatre, Palace for his Mother; — day by day; many things to be recorded by Editor Formey, though the rule about them here is silence except on cause.

No doubt the ague is itself privately a point of moment. Such a vexatious paltry little thing, in this bright whirl of Activities, Public and other, which he continues managing in spite of it; impatient to be rid of it. But it will not go: there *it* reappears always, punctual to its "fourth day," — like a snarling street-dog, in the high Ball-room and Work-room. "He is drinking Pyrmont water;" has himself proposed Quinquina, a remedy just come up, but the Doctors shook their heads; has tried snatches of Reinsberg, too short; he intends soon to be out there for a right spell of country, there to be "happy," and get quit of his ague. The ague went, — and by a remedy which surprised the whole world, as will be seen!

Wilhelmina's Return-Visit.

Monday, 17th Oct., came the Baireuth Visitors; Wilhelmina all in a flutter, and tremor of joy and sorrow, to see her Brother again, her old kindred and the altered scene of things. Poor Lady, she is perceptibly more tremulous than usual; and her Narrative, not in dates only, but in more memorable points, dances about at a sad rate; interior agitations and tremulous shrill feelings shivering her this way and that, and throwing things topsy-turvy in one's recollection. Like the magnetic needle, shaky but stedfast (*agitée mais constante*). Truer nothing can be, points forever to the Pole; but also what obliquities it makes; will shiver aside in mad escapades, if you hold the paltriest bit of old iron near it, — paltriest clack of gossip about this loved Brother of mine! Brother, we will hope, silently continues to be Pole, so that the needle always comes back again; otherwise all would go to wreck. Here, in abridged and partly rectified form, are the phenomena witnessed:

"We arrived at Berlin the end of October" (Monday 17th, as above said.) "My younger Brothers, followed by the "Princes of the Blood and by all the Court, received us at the "bottom of the stairs. I was led to my apartment, where I "found the Reigning Queen, my Sisters" (Ulrique, Amelia), "and the Princesses" (of the Blood, as above, Schwedt and the rest). "I learned with much chagrin that the King was "ill of tertian ague" (quartan; but that is no matter). "He "sent me word that, being in his fit, he could not see me; but "that he depended on having that pleasure to-morrow. The "Queen Mother, to whom I went without delay, was in a dark "condition; rooms all hung with their lugubrious drapery; "everything yet in the depth of mourning for my Father. "What a scene for me! Nature has her rights; I can say with "truth, I have almost never in my life been so moved as on "this occasion." Interview with Mamma, — we can fancy it, — "was of the most touching." Wilhelmina had been absent eight years. She scarcely knows the young ones again, all so grown; — finds change on change; and that Time, as he always is, has been busy. That night the Supper-Party was exclusively a Family one.

Her Brother's welcome to her on the morrow, though ardent enough, she found deficient in sincerity, deficient in several points; as indeed a Brother up to the neck in business, and just come out of an ague-fit, does not appear to the best advantage. Wilhelmina noticed how ill he looked, so lean and broken-down (*maigre et défait*) within the last two months; but seems to have taken no account of it farther, in striking her balances with Friedrich. And indeed in her Narrative of this Visit, not, we will hope, in the Visit itself, she must have been in a high state of magnetic deflection, — pretty nearly her maximum of such, discoverable in those famous *Memoirs*, — such a tumult is there in her statements, all gone to ground-and-lofty tumbling in this place; so discrepant are the still ascertainable facts from this topsy-turvy picture of them, sketched by her four years hence (in 1744). The truest of magnetic needles; but so sensitive, if you bring foreign iron near it!

Wilhelmina was loaded with honours by an impartial Berlin Public, that is, Court-Public; "but, all being in "mourning, the Court was not brilliant. The Queen Mother "saw little company, and was sunk in sorrow; — had not the "least influence in affairs, so jealous was the new King of his "Authority, — to the Queen Mother's surprise," says Wilhelmina. For the rest, here is a King "becoming "truly unpopular" (or, we fancy so, in our deflected state, and judging by the rumour of cliques); "a general dis- "content reigning in the Country, love of his subjects pretty "much gone; people speaking of him in no measured "terms" (in certain cliques). "Cares nothing about those "who helped him as Prince Royal, say some; others complain "of his avarice" (meaning steady vigilance in outlay) "as "surpassing the late King's; this one complained of his "violences of temper (*emportemens*); that one of his suspicions, "of his distrust, his haughtinesses, his dissimulation" (meaning polite impenetrability when he saw good). Several circumstances, known to Wilhelmina's own experience, compel Wilhelmina's assent on those points. "I would have spoken "to him about them, if my Brother of Prussia" (young August Wilhelm, betrothed the other day) "and the Queen "Regnant had not dissuaded me. Farther on I will give the "explanation of all this," — never did it anywhere. "I beg "those who may one day read these *Memoirs*, to suspend their "judgment on the character of this great Prince till I have "developed it."* Oh my Princess, you are true and bright, but you are shrill; and I admire the effect of atmospheric electricity, not to say, of any neighbouring marine-store shop, or miserable bit of broken pan, on one of the finest magnetic needles ever made and set trembling!

Wilhelmina is incapable of deliberate falsehood; and this her impression or reminiscence, with all its exaggeration, is entitled to be heard in evidence so far. From this, and from other sources, readers will assure themselves that discontents were not wanting; that King Friedrich was not amiable to everybody at this time, — which indeed he never grew to be at any other time. He had to be a King; that was the trade he followed, not the quite different one of being amiable all round. Amiability is good, my Princess; but the question rises, "To whom? — for example, to the young gentleman who shot himself in Löbegun?" There are young gentlemen and old, sometimes in considerable quantities, to whom, if you were in your duty, as a King of men (or even as a "King of one man and his affairs," if that is all your kingdom), you should have been hateful instead of amiable! That is a stern truth; too much forgotten by Wilhelmina and others. Again, what a deadening and killing circumstance is it in the career of amiability, that you are bound *not* to be communicative of your inner man, but perpetually and strictly the reverse! It may be doubted if a good King can be amiable; certainly he cannot in any but the noblest ages, and then only to a select few. I should guess Friedrich was at no time fairly loved, not by

* Wilhelmina, ii. 326.

those nearest to him. He was rapid, decisive; of wiry compact nature; had nothing of his Father's amplitudes, simplicities; nothing to sport with and fondle, far from it. Tremulous sensibilities, ardent affections; these we clearly discover in him, in extraordinary vivacity; but he wears them under his polished panoply, and is outwardly a radiant but metallic object to mankind. Let us carry this along with us in studying him; and thank Wilhelmina for giving us hint of it in her oblique way. — Wilhelmina's love for her Brother rose to quite heroic pitch in coming years, and was at its highest when she died. That continuation of her *Memoirs* in which she is to develop her Brother's character, was never written: it has been sought for, in modern times; and a few insignificant pages, with evidence that there is not, and was not, any more, are all that has turned up.*

Incapable of falsity prepense, we say; but the known facts, which stand abundantly on record if you care to search them out, are merely as follows: Friedrich, with such sincerity as there might be, did welcome Wilhelmina on the morrow of her arrival; spoke of Reinsberg, and of air and rest, and how pleasant it would be; rolled off next morning, having at last gathered up his businesses, and got them well in hand, to Reinsberg accordingly; whither Wilhelmina, with the Queen Regnant and others of agreeable quality, followed in two days; intending a long and pleasant spell of country out there. Which hope was tolerably fulfilled, even for Wilhelmina, though there did come unexpected interruptions, not of Friedrich's bringing.

* Pertz: *Über die Denkwürdigkeiten der Markgräfin von Bayreuth* (Paper read in the *Akademie der Wissenschaften*, Berlin, 25th April 1850).

Unexpected News at Reinsberg.

Friedrich's pursuits and intended conquests, for the present, are of peaceable and even gay nature. French Theatre, Italian Opera-House, these are among the immediate outlooks. Voltaire, skilled in French acting, if anybody ever were, is multifariously negotiating for a Company of that kind, — let him be swift, be successful.* An Italian Opera there shall be; the House is still to be built: Captain Knobelsdorf, who built Reinsberg, whom we have known, is to do it. Knobelsdorf has gone to Italy on that errand; "went by "Dresden, carefully examining the Opera-House there, "and all the famed Opera-Houses on his road." Graun, one of the best judges living, is likewise off to Italy, gathering singers. Our Opera too shall be a successful thing, and we hope, a speedy. Such are Friedrich's outlooks at this time.

A miscellaneous pleasant company is here; Truchsess and Bielfeld, home from Hanover, among them; Wilhelmina is here;—Voltaire himself perhaps coming again. Friedrich drinks his Pyrmont waters; works at his public businesses all day, which are now well in hand, and manageable by couriers; at evening he appears in company, and is the astonishment of everybody; brilliant, like a new-risen sun, as if he knew of no illness, knew of no business, but lived for amusement only. "He intends Private Theatricals withal, and is "getting ready Voltaire's *Mort de César*."** These were pretty days at Reinsberg. This kind of life lasted seven or eight weeks, — in spite of interruptions

---

* Letters of Voltaire (*passim*, in these months).
** Preuss, *Thronbesteigung*, p. 415.

of subterranean volcanic nature, some of which were surely considerable. Here, in the very first week, coming almost volcanically, is one, which indeed is the sum of them all.

Tuesday forenoon, 25th October 1740, Express arrives at Reinsberg; direct from Vienna five days ago; finds Friedrich under eclipse, hidden in the interior, labouring under his ague-fit: question rises, Shall the Express be introduced, or be held back? The news he brings is huge, unexpected, transcendent, and may agitate the sick King. Six or seven heads go wagging on this point, — who by accident are nameable, if readers care: "Prince August Wilhelm," lately betrothed; "Graf Truchsess," home from Hanover; "Colonel Graf von Finkenstein," Old Tutor's Son, a familiar from boyhood upwards; "Baron Pöllnitz," kind of chief Goldstick now, or Master of the Ceremonies, not too witty, but the cause of wit; "Jordan, Bielfeld," known to us; and lastly "Fredersdorf," Majordomo and Factotum, who is grown from Valet to be Purse-Keeper, confidential Manager, and almost friend, — a notable personage in Friedrich's History. They decide, "Better wait!"

They wait accordingly; and then, after about an hour, the trembling-fit being over, and Fredersdorf having cautiously preluded a little, and prepared the way, the Despatch is delivered, and the King left with his immense piece of news. News that his Imperial Majesty Karl VI. died, after short illness, on Thursday the 20th last. Kaiser dead: House of Hapsburg, and its Five Centuries of tough wrestling, and uneasy Dominancy in this world, ended, gone to the distaff:

— the counter-wrestling Ambitions and Cupidities not dead; and nothing but Pragmatic Sanction left between the fallen House and them! Friedrich kept silence; showed no sign how transfixed he was to hear such tidings; which, he foresaw, would have immeasurable consequences in the world.

One of the first was, that it cured Friedrich of his ague. It braced him (it, and perhaps "a little quinquina which he now insisted on") into such a tensity of spirit as drove out his ague like a mere hiccup; quite gone in the course of next week; and we hear no more of that importunate annoyance. He summoned Secretary Eichel, "Be ready in so many minutes hence;" rose from his bed, dressed himself;* — and then, by Eichel's help, sent off expresses for Schwerin his chief General, and Podewils his chief Minister. A resolution, which is rising or has risen in the Royal mind, will be ready for communicating to these Two by the time they arrive, on the second day hence. This done, Friedrich, I believe, joined his company in the evening; and was as light and brilliant as if nothing had happened.

* Preuss, *Thronbesteigung,* p. 416.

CHAPTER VIII.

THE KAISER'S DEATH.

THE Kaiser's death came on the Public unexpectedly; though not quite so upon observant persons, closer at hand. He was not yet fifty-six out; a firm-built man; had been of sound constitution, of active, not intemperate habits: but in the last six years, there had come such torrents of ill-luck rolling down on him, he had suffered immensely, far beyond what the world knew of; and to those near him, and anxious for him, his strength seemed much undermined. Five years ago, in summer 1735, Robinson reported, from a sure hand: "Nothing can equal the Emperor's agitation "under these disasters" (brought upon him by Fleury and the Spaniards, as afterclap to his Polish-Election feat). "His good Empress is terrified, many times, he "will die in the course of the night, when singly with "her he gives a loose to his affliction, confusion and "despair." Sea-Powers will not help; Fleury and mere ruin will engulf! "What augments this agitation is "his distrust in every one of his own Ministers, except "perhaps Bartenstein,"* — who is not much of a support either, though a gnarled weighty old stick in his way ("Professor at Strasburg once"): not interesting to us here. The rest his Imperial Majesty considers to be of sublimated blockhead type, it appears. Prince Eugene had died lately, and with Eugene all good fortune.

* Robinson to Lord Harrington, 5th July 1735 (in State-Paper Office).

And then, close following, the miseries of that Turk War, crashing down upon a man! They say, Duke Franz, Maria Theresa's Husband, nominal Commander in those Campaigns, with the Seckendorfs and Wallises under him going such a road, was privately eager to have done with the Business, on any terms, lest the Kaiser should die first, and leave it weltering. No wonder the poor Kaiser felt broken, disgusted with the long Shadow-Hunt of Life; and took to practical field-sports rather. An Army that cannot fight, War-Generals good only to be locked in Fortresses, an Exchequer that has no money; after such wagging of the wigs, and such Privy-Councilling and such War-Councilling: — let us hunt wild-swine, and not think of it! That, thank Heaven, we still have; that, and Pragmatic Sanction well engrossed, and generally sworn to by mankind, after much effort! —

The outer Public of that time, and Voltaire among them more deliberately afterwards, spoke of "mushrooms," an "indigestion of mushrooms;" and it is probable there was something of mushrooms concerned in the event. Another subsequent Frenchman, still more irreverent, adds to this of the "excess of mushrooms," that the Kaiser made light of it. "When the "Doctors told him he had few hours to live, he would "not believe it; and bantered his Physicians on the "sad news. 'Look me in the eyes,' said he; 'have I "the air of one dying? When you see my sight grow-"ing dim, then let the sacraments be administered, "whether I order or not.'" Doctors insisting, the Kaiser replied: "'Since you are foolish fellows, who know "neither the cause nor the state of my disorder, I "command that, once I am dead, you open my body, "to know what the matter was; you can then come "and let me know!'"* — in which also there is perhaps a glimmering of distorted truth, though, as Monsieur mistakes even the day ("18th October," says he, not 20th), one can only accept it as rumour from the outside.

Here, by an extremely sombre domestic Gentleman of great punctuality and great dulness, are the authentic particulars, such as it was good to mention in Vienna circles.** An extremely dull Gentleman, but to appearance an authentic; and so little defective in reverence that he delicately expresses some astonishment at Death's audacity this year, in killing so many Crowned Heads. "This year 1740," says he, "though the weather "throughout Europe had been extraordinarily fine," or fine for a cold year, "had already witnessed several "Deaths of Sovereigns: Pope Clement XII., Friedrich "Wilhelm of Prussia, the Queen Dowager of Spain" (Termagant's old stepmother, not Termagant's self by a great way). "But that was not enough: unfathom-"able Destiny ventured now on Imperial Heads (*wagte* "*sich auch an Kaiserkronen*): Karl VI., namely, and "Russia's great Monarchess:" — an audacity to be remarked. Of Russia's great Monarchess (Czarina Anne, with the big cheek) we will say nothing at present; but of Karl VI. only, — abridging much, and studying arrangement:

"Thursday, October 13th, returning from Halbthurn, a "Hunting Seat of his," over in Hungary some fifty miles, "to

* *Anecdotes Germaniques* (Paris, 1769), p. 692.
** (Anonymous) *Des &c. Römischen Kaiser's Carl VI. Leben und Thaten* (Frankfurt und Leipzig, 1741), pp. 220-227.

"the Palace Favorita at Vienna, his Imperial Majesty felt
"slightly indisposed," — indigestion of mushrooms or whatever it was: had begun *at* Halbthurn the night before, we
rather understand, and was the occasion of his leaving. "The
"Doctors called it cold on the stomach, and thought it of no
"consequence. In the night of Saturday, it became alarm-
"ing;" inflammation, thought the Doctors, inflammation of
the liver, and used their potent appliances, which only made
the danger come and go; "and on the Tuesday, all day, the
"Doctors did not doubt his Imperial Majesty was dying."
('Look me in the eyes; pack of fools; you will have to dissect
me, you will then know:' Any truth in all that? No matter.)

"At noon of that Tuesday he took the Sacrament, the
"Pope's Nuncio administering. His Majesty showed uncom-
"monly great composure of soul, and resignation to the
"Divine Will;" being indeed 'certain,' — so he expressed it
to "a principal Official Person sunk in grief" (Bartenstein,
shall we guess?), who stood by him — 'certain of his cause,'
not afraid in contemplating that dread Judgment now near:
'Look at me! A man that is certain of his cause can enter
'on such a Journey with good courage and a composed mind
'(*mit gutem und gelassenem Muth*).' To the Doctors, dubitating
what the disease was, he said, 'If Gazelli,' my late worthy
Doctor, 'were still here, you would soon know; but as it is,
'you will learn it when you dissect me;' — and once asked
to be shown the Cup where his heart would lie after that
operation.

"Sacrament being over," Tuesday afternoon, "he sent for
"his Family, to bless them each separately. He had a long
"conversation with Grand Duke Franz," titular of Lorraine,
actual of Tuscany, "who had assiduously attended him, and
"continued to do so, during the whole illness. The Grand
"Duke's Spouse," — Maria Theresa, the noble-hearted and
the overwhelmed; who is now in an interesting state again
withal; a little Kaiserkin (Joseph II.) coming in five months;
first child, a little girl, is now two years old; — "had been
"obliged to take to bed three days ago; laid up of grief and
"terror (*vor Schmerzen und Schrecken*), ever since Sunday the
"16th. Nor would his Imperial Majesty permit her to enter
"this death-room, on account of her condition, so important
"to the world: but his Majesty, turning towards that side

"where her apartment was, raised his right hand, and com-
"manded her Husband, and the Archduchess her younger
"Sister, to tell his Theresa, That he blessed her herewith,
"notwithstanding her absence." Poor Kaiser, poor Theresa!
"Most distressing of all was the scene with the Kaiserin. The
"night before, on getting knowledge of the sad certainty, she
"had fainted utterly away (*starke Ohnmacht*), and had to be
"carried into the Grand Duchess's (Maria Theresa's) "room.
"Being summoned now with her Children, for the last blessing,
"she cried as in despair, 'Do not leave me, Your Dilection,
"do not (*Ach Euer Liebden verlassen mich doch nicht*)!'" Poor
good souls! "Her Imperial Majesty would not quit the room
"again, but remained to the last."
"Wednesday 19th, all day, anxiety, mournful suspense;"
poor weeping Kaiserin and all the world waiting; the
inevitable visibly struggling on. "And in the night of that
"day" (night of 19th-20th Oct. 1740), "between one and two
"in the morning, Death snatched away this most invaluable
"Monarch (*den preiswürdigsten Monarchen*) in the 56th year of
'his life;" and Kaiser Karl VI., and the House of Hapsburg
and its Five tough Centuries of good and evil in this world had
ended. The poor Kaiserin "closed the eyes" that could now
no more behold her; "kissed his hands; and was carried out
"more dead than alive."*

A good affectionate Kaiserin, I do believe; honourable, truthful, though unwitty of speech, and converted
by Grandpapa in a peculiar manner. For her Kaiser
too, after all, I have a kind of love. Of brilliant

* Anonymous, *ut suprà*, pp. 220-227. — Adelung, *Pragmatische Staats-
geschichte* (Gotha, 1762-1767), ii. 120. *Johan Christoph* Adelung: the same
who did the *Dictionary* and many other deserving Books; here is the precise Title: "*Pragmatische Staatsgeschichte Europens*," that is, "Documentary "History of Europe, from Kaiser Karl's Death, 1740, till Peace of
"Paris, 1763." A solid, laborious and meritorious Work, of its kind; extremely extensive (9 voll. 4to, some of which are double and even treble),
mostly in the undigested, sometimes in the quite uncooked or raw condition; perhaps about a fifth part of it consists of "Documents" proper,
which are skippable. It cannot help being dull, waste, dreary, but is
everywhere intelligible (excellent Indexes too), — and offers an unhappy
reader by far the best resource attainable for survey of that sad Period.

articulate intellect there is nothing; nor of inarticulate (as in Friedrich Wilhelm's case) anything considerable: in fact his Shadow-Hunting, and Duelling with the Termagant, seemed the reverse of wise. But there was something of a high proud heart in it, too, if we examine; and even the Pragmatic Sanction, though in practice not worth one regiment of iron ramrods, indicates a profoundly fixed determination, partly of loyal nature, such as the gods more or less reward. "He had been a great builder," say the Histories; "was a "great musician, fit to lead orchestras, and had com- "posed an Opera," — poor Kaiser. There came out large traits of him, in Maria Theresa again, under an improved form, which were much admired by the world. He looks, in his Portraits, intensely serious; a handsome man, stoically grave; much the gentleman, much the Kaiser or Supreme Gentleman. As, in life and fact, he was; "something solemn in him, even when he laughs," the people used to say. A man honestly doing his very best with his poor Kaisership, and dying of chagrin by it. "On opening the body, the liver-region "proved to be entirely deranged; in the place where "the gall-bladder should have been, a stone of the size "of a pigeon's egg was found grown into the liver, "and no gall-bladder now there."

That same morning, with earliest daylight, "Thurs- "day 20th, six A.M.," Maria Theresa is proclaimed by her Heralds over Vienna: "According to Pragmatic "Sanction, Inheritress of all the" &c. &c.; — Sovereign Archduchess of Austria, Queen of Hungary and Bohemia, for chief items. "At seven her Majesty took the Oath "from the Generals and Presidents of Tribunals, —

"said, through her tears, 'All was to stand on the old "footing, each in his post,'" — and the other needful words. Couriers shoot forth towards all Countries; — one express courier to Regensburg, and the Enchanted Wiggeries there, to say That a New Kaiser will be needed; *Reichs*-Vicar or Vicars (Kur-Sachsen and whoever more, for they are sometimes disagreed about it) will have to administer in the interim.

A second courier we saw arrive at Reinsberg; he likewise may be important. The Bavarian Minister, Karl Albert Kur-Baiern's man, shot off his express, like the others: answer is, by return of courier, or even earlier (for a messenger was already on the road), Make protest! "We Kur-Baiern solemnly protest against Pragmatic Sanction, and the assumption of such Titles by the Daughter of the late Kaiser. King of Bohemia, and in good part even of Austria, it is not you, Madam, but of right *we*; as, by Heaven's help, it is our fixed resolution to make good!" Protest was presented, accordingly, with all the solemnities, without loss of a moment. To which Bartenstein and the Authorities answered "Pooh-pooh," as if it were nothing. It is the first ripple of an immeasurable tide or deluge in that kind, threatening to submerge the new Majesty of Hungary; — as had been foreseen at Reinsberg; though Bartenstein and the Authorities made light of it, answering "Pooh-pooh," or almost "Ha-ha," for the present.

Her Hungarian Majesty's chief Generals, Seckendorf, Wallis, Neipperg, sit in their respective prisonwards at this time (from which she soon liberates them): Kur-Baiern has lodged protest; at Reinsberg there will be an important resolution ready: — and in the Austrian Treasury (which employs 40,000 persons, big and little) there is of cash or available resource, 100,000 florins, that is to say, 10,000*l.* net.* And unless Pragmatic sheepskin hold tighter than some persons expect, the affairs of Austria and of this young Archduchess are in a threatening way.

His Britannic Majesty was on the road home, about Helvoetsluys or on the sea for Harwich, that night the Kaiser died; of whose illness he had heard nothing. At London, ten days after, the sudden news struck dismally upon his Majesty and the Political Circles there: "No help, then, from that quarter, in our Spanish War; perhaps far other than help!" — Nay, certain Gazetteers were afraid the grand new Anti-Spanish Expedition itself, which was now, at the long last, after such confusions and delays, lying ready, in great strength, Naval and Military, would be countermanded, — on Pragmatic-Sanction considerations, and the crisis probably imminent.** But it was not countermanded; it sailed all the same, "November 6th" (seventh day after the bad news); and made towards — Shall we tell the reader, what is Officially a dead secret, though by this time well guessed at by the Public, English and also Spanish? — towards Carthagena, to reinforce fiery Vernon, in the tropical latitudes; and overset Spanish America, beginning with that important Town!

* Mallath, *Geschichte des Oestreichischen Kaiserstaat*: (Hamburg, 1850), v. 8.
** London Newspapers (31st Oct. — 6th Nov. 1740).

Commodore Anson, he also, after long fatal delays, is off, several weeks ago;* round Cape Horn; hoping (or perhaps already not hoping) to coöperate from the Other Ocean, and be simultaneous with Vernon, — on these loose principles of keeping time! Commodore Anson does, in effect, make a Voyage which is beautiful, and to mankind memorable; but as to keeping tryste with Vernon, the very gods could not do it on those terms!

* 29th (18th) September 1740.

CHAPTER IX.

RESOLUTION FORMED AT REINSBERG IN CONSEQUENCE.

THURSDAY 27th October, two days after the Expresses went for them, Schwerin and Podewils punctually arrived at Reinsberg. They were carried into the interior privacies, "to long conferences with his Majesty "that day, and for the next four days; Majesty and "they even dining privately together;" grave business of state, none guesses how grave, evidently going on. The resolution Friedrich laid before them, fruit of these two days since the news from Vienna, was probably the most important ever formed in Prussia, or in Europe during that Century: Resolution to make good our Rights on Silesia, by this great opportunity, the best that will ever offer. Resolution which had sprung, I find, and got to sudden fixity in the head of the young King himself; and which met with little save opposition from all the other sons of Adam, at the first blush and for long afterwards. And, indeed, the making of it good (of it, and of the immense results that hung by it) was the main business of this young King's Life henceforth; and cost him Labours like those of Hercules, and was in the highest degree momentous to existing and not yet existing millions of mankind, — to the readers of this History especially!

It is almost touching to reflect how unexpectedly, like a bolt out of the blue, all this had come upon Friedrich; and how it overset his fine program for the winter at Reinsberg, and for his Life generally. Not the Peaceable magnanimities, but the Warlike, are the thing appointed Friedrich this winter, and mainly henceforth. Those "*golden* or soft radiances" which we saw in him, admirable to Voltaire and to Friedrich, and to an esurient philanthropic world, — it is not those, it is "the *steel-bright* or stellar kind," that are to become predominant in Friedrich's existence: grim hail-storms, thunders and tornado for an existence to him, instead of the opulent genialities and halcyon weather, anticipated by himself and others! Indisputably enough, to us if not yet to Friedrich, "Reinsberg and Life to the Muses" are done. On a sudden, from the opposite side of the horizon, see, miraculous Opportunity, rushing hitherward, — swift, terrible, clothed with lightning like a courser of the gods: dare you clutch *him* by the thunder-mane, and fling yourself upon him, and make for the Empyrean by that course rather? Be immediate about it, then; the time is now, or else never! — No fair judge can blame the young man that he laid hold of the flaming Opportunity in this manner, and obeyed the new omen. To seize such an Opportunity, and perilously mount upon it, was the part of a young magnanimous King, less sensible to the perils, and more to the other considerations, than one older would have been.

Schwerin and Podewils were, no doubt, astonished to learn what the Royal purpose was; and could not want for commonplace objections many and strong, had this been the scene for dwelling on them, or dressing them out at eloquent length. But they knew well this was not the scene for doing more than, with eloquent modesty, hint them; that the Resolution, being already taken, would not alter for commonplace; and

that the question now lying for honourable members
was, How to execute it? It is on this, as I collect,
that Schwerin and Podewils in the King's company
did, with extreme intensity, consult during those four
days; and were, most probably, of considerable use to
the King, though some of their modifications adopted
by him turned out, not as they had predicted, but as
he. On all the Military details and outlines, and
on all the Diplomacies of this business, here are two
Oracles extremely worth consulting by the young
King.

To seize Silesia is easy: a Country open on all but
the south side; open especially on our side, where a
battalion of foot might force it; the three or four fortresses, of which only two, Glogau and Neisse, can be
reckoned strong, are provided with nothing as they
ought to be; not above 3,000 fighting men in the
whole Province, and these little expecting fight. Silesia
can be seized: but the maintaining of it? — We must
try to maintain it, thinks Friedrich.

At Reinsberg it is not yet known that Kur-Baiern
has protested; but it is well guessed he means to do
so, and that France is at his back in some sort. Kur-Baiern, probably Kur-Sachsen and plenty more, France
being secretly at their back. What low condition
Austria stands in, all its ready resources run to the
lees, is known; and that France, getting lively at
present with its Belleisles and adventurous spirits not
restrainable by Fleury, is always on the watch to bring
Austria lower; — capable, in spite of Pragmatic
Sanction, to snatch the golden moment, and spring

hunter-like on a moribund Austria, were the hunting-dogs once out, and in cry. To Friedrich it seems unlikely the Pragmatic Sanction will be a Law of Nature to mankind, in these circumstances. His opinion is, "the old political system has expired with the Kaiser." Here is Europe, burning in one corner of it by Jenkins's Ear, and such a smoulder of combustible material awakening nearer hand: will not Europe, probably, blaze into general War; Pragmatic Sanction going to waste sheepskin, and universal scramble ensuing? In which he who has 100,000 good soldiers, and can handle them, may be an important figure in urging claims, and keeping what he has got hold of! —

Friedrich's mind, as to the fact, is fixed; seize Silesia we will: but as to the manner of doing it, Schwerin and Podewils modify him. Their counsel is: "Do not step out in hostile attitude at the very first, saying, 'These Duchies, Liegnitz, Brieg, Wohlau, "'Jägerndorf, are mine, and I will fight for them;' say "only, 'Having, as is well known, interests of various "kinds in this Silesia, I venture to take charge of it "in the perilous times now come, and will keep it safe "for the real owner.' Silesia seized in this fashion," continue they, "negotiate with the Queen of Hungary; offer her help, large help in men and money, against her other enemies; perhaps she will consent to do us right?" — "She never will consent," is Friedrich's opinion. "But it is worth trying?" urge the Ministers. — "Well," answers Friedrich, "be it in that form; that is the soft-spoken cautious form: any form will do, if the fact be there." That is understood to have been the figure of the deliberation in this conclave at Reinsberg, during the four days.* And now it remains only to fix the Military details, to be ready in a minimum of time; and to keep our preparations and intentions in impenetrable darkness from all men, in the interim. Adieu, Messieurs.

And so, on the 1st of November, fifth morning since they came, Schwerin and Podewils, a world of new business silently ahead of them, return to Berlin, intent to begin the same. All the Kings will have to take their resolution on this matter; wisely, or else unwisely. King Friedrich's, let it prove the wisest or not, is notably the rapidest, — complete, and fairly entering upon action, on November 1st. At London the news of the Kaiser's death had arrived the day before; Britannic Majesty and Ministry, thrown much into the dumps by it, much into the vague, are nothing like so prompt with their resolution on it. Somewhat sorrowfully in the vague. In fact, they will go jumbling hither and thither for about three years to come, before making up their minds to a resolution: so intricate is the affair to the English Nation and them. Intricate indeed; and even imaginary, — definable mainly as a bottomless abyss of nightmare dreams to the English Nation and them! Productive of strong somnambulisms, as my friend has it! —

Mystery in Berlin, for Seven Weeks, while the Preparations go on; Voltaire visits Friedrich to decipher it, but cannot.

Podewils and Schwerin gone, King Friedrich, though still very busy in working-hours, returns to his society

---

* Stenzel (from what sources he does not clearly say, no doubt from sources of some authenticity) gives this as summary of it, iv. 61-65.

and its gaieties and brilliancies; apparently with increased appetite after these four days of abstinence. Still busy in his working-hours, as a King must be; couriers coming and going, hundreds of businesses despatched each day; and in the evening what a relish for society, — Prätorius is quite astonished at it. Music, dancing, play-acting, suppers of the gods, "not "done till four in the morning sometimes," these are the accounts Prätorius hears at Berlin. "From all persons who return from Reinsberg," writes he, the "unanimous report is, That the King works, the whole "day through, with an assiduity that is unique; and "then, in the evening, gives himself to the pleasures "of society, with a vivacity of mirth and sprightly "humour which makes those Evening-Parties charm"ing."* So it had to last, with frequent short journeys on Friedrich's part, and at last with change to Berlin as headquarters, for about seven weeks to come, — till the beginning of December, and the day of action, namely. A notable little Interim in Friedrich's History and that of Europe.

Friedrich's secret, till almost the very end, remained impenetrable; though, by degrees, his movements excited much guessing in the Gazetteer and Diplomatic world everywhere. Military matters do seem to be getting brisk in Prussia; arsenals much astir; troops are seen mustering, marching, plainly to a singular degree. Marching towards the Austrian side, towards Silesia, some note. Yes; but also towards Cleve, certain detachments of troops are marching, — do not men see? And the Entrenchment at Büderich in those parts, that is getting forward withal, — though pri-

* Excerpt, in Preuss, *Thronbesteigung,* p. 418.

vately there is not the least prospect of using it, in these altered circumstances. Friedrich already guesses that if he could get Silesia, so invaluable on the one skirt of him, he will probably have to give up his Berg-Jülich claims on the other: I fancy he is getting ready to do so, should the time come for such alternative. But he labours at Büderich, all the same, and "improves the roads in that quarter," — which at least may help to keep an inquisitive public at bay. These are seven busy weeks on Friedrich's part, and on the world's: constant realities of preparation, on the one part, industriously veiled; on the other part, such shadows, guessings, spyings, spectral movements above ground and below; Diplomatic shadows fencing, Gazetteer shadows rumouring; — dreams of a world as if near awakening to something great! "All Officers on "furlough have been ordered to their posts," writes Bielfeld, on those vague terms of his: "On arriving at Ber- "lin, you notice a great agitation in all departments of "the State. The regiments are ordered to prepare their "equipages, and to hold themselves in readiness for "marching. There are magazines being formed at Frank- "furt-on-the-Oder and at Crossen," — handy for Silesia, you would say? "There are considerable trains "of Artillery getting ready; and the King has frequent "conferences with his Generals."* The authentic fact is: "By the middle of November, Troops, to the extent "of 30,000 and more, had got orders to be ready for "marching in three weeks hence;" their public motions very visible ever since, their actual purpose a mystery to all mortals except Three.

---

* Bielfeld, i. 165 (Berlin, 30th November, is the date he puts to it).

Towards the end of November, it becomes the prevailing guess that the business is immediate, not prospective; that Silesia may be in the wind, not Jülich and Berg. Which infinitely quickens the shadowy rumourings and Diplomatic fencings of mankind. The French have their special Ambassador here; a Marquis de Beauvau, observant military gentleman, who came with the Accession Compliment some time ago, and keeps his eyes well open, but cannot see through millstones. Fleury is intensely desirous to know Friedrich's secret; but would fain keep his own (if he yet have one), and is himself quite tacit and reserved. To Fleury's Marquis de Beauvau Friedrich is very gracious; but in regard to secrets, is for a reciprocal procedure. Could not Voltaire go and try? It is thought Fleury had let fall some hint to that effect, carried by a bird of the air. Sure enough Voltaire does go; is actually on visit to his royal Friend, "six days with him at "Reinsberg;" perhaps near a fortnight in all (20 November — 2 December or so), hanging about those Berlin regions, on the survey. Here is an unexpected pleasure to the parties; — but in regard to penetrating of secrets, an unproductive one!

Voltaire's ostensible errand was, To report progress about the *Anti-Macchiavel*, the Van Duren nonsense; and, at any rate, to settle the Money-accounts on these and other scores; and to discourse Philosophies, for a day or two, with the First of Men. The real errand, it is pretty clear, was as above. Voltaire has always a wistful eye towards political employment, and would fain make himself useful in high quarters. Fleury and he have their touches of direct Correspondence now and then; and obliquely, there are always intermediates and channels. Small hint, the slightest twinkle of Fleury's eyelashes, would be duly speeded to Voltaire, and set him going. We shall see him expressly missioned hither, on similar errand, by and by; though with as bad success as at present.

Of this his First Visit to Berlin, his Second to Friedrich, Voltaire in the *Vie Privée* says nothing. But in his *Siècle de Louis XV*, he drops, with proud modesty, a little foot-note upon it: "The Author was with the "King of Prussia at that time; and can affirm that "Cardinal de Fleury was totally astray in regard to the "Prince he had now to do with." To which a *date* slightly wrong is added; the rest being perfectly correct.* No other details are to be got anywhere, if they were of importance; the very dates of it in the best Prussian Books are all slightly awry. Here, by accident, are two poor flint-sparks caught from the dust whirlwind, which yield a certain sufficing twilight, when put in their place; and show us both sides of the matter, the smooth side and the seamy:

1. *Friedrich to Algarotti, at Berlin.* From "Reinsberg, 21st Nov.," showing the smooth side.

"My dear Swan of Padua, Voltaire has arrived; all "sparkling with new beauties, and far more sociable than at "Cleve. He is in very good humour; and makes less com-"plaining about his ailments than usual. Nothing can be "more frivolous than our occupations here:" mere verse-making, dancing, philosophising, then card-playing, dining, flirting; merry as birds on the bough (and Silesia *invisible*, except to oneself and two others).**

* (*Œuvres* (Siècle de Louis XV, c. 6), xxviii. 74.
** *Œuvres de Frédéric*, xviii. 25.

2. *Friedrich to Jordan, at Berlin.* "Ruppin, 28th November."

* * "Thy Miser" (Voltaire, now gone to Berlin, of whom Jordan is to send news, as of all things else), "thy Miser shall "drink to the lees of his insatiable desire (*sic*) to enrich him- "self: he shall have the 3,000 thalers (450*l.*). He was with "me six days: that will be at the rate of 150 thalers (75*l.*) "a-day. That is paying dear for one's merry-andrew) *c'est* "*bien payer un fou*); never had court-fool such wages be- "fore." *

Which latter, also at first hand, shows us the seamy side. And here, finally, with date happily appended, is a poetic snatch, in Voltaire's exquisite style, which with the response gives us the medium view:

Voltaire's Adieu ("*Billet de Congé,* 2 December 1740").

"*Non, malgré vos vertus, non, malgré vos appas,*
"*Mon âme n'est point satisfaite;*
"*Non, vous n'êtes qu'une coquette,*
"*Qui subjuguez les cœurs, et ne vous donnez pas.*"

FRIEDRICH'S RESPONSE.

"*Mon âme sent le prix de vos divins appas;*
"*Mais ne présumez point qu'elle soit satisfaite.*
"*Traître, vous me quittez pour suivre une coquette;*
"*Moi je ne vous quitterais pas.*" **

— Meaning, perhaps, in brief English: *V.* "Ah, you are but a beautiful coquette; you charm away our hearts, and do not give your own" (won't tell me your secret at all)! *F.* "Treacherous Lothario, it is you that quit me for a coquette" (your divine Emilie; and won't stay here, and be of my Academy); "but however —!" — Friedrich looked hopingly on the French,

* Ib. xvii. 72. Particulars of the money-payment (travelling expenses chiefly, rather exorbitant, and *this* journey added to the list; and no whisper of the considerable Van-Duren moneys, and copyright of *Anti-Macchiavel*, in abatement.) are in Rödenbeck, t. 27. Exact sum paid is 3,300 thalers; 2,000 a good while ago, 1,300 at this time, which settles the greedy bill.

** (*Œuvres de Frédéric* (xiv. 167); *Œuvres de Voltaire;* &c. &c.

but could not give his secret except by degrees and with reciprocity. Some days hence he said to Marquis de Beauvau, in the Audience of leave, a word which was remembered.

View of Friedrich behind the Veil.

As to Friedrich himself, since about the middle of November his plans seem to have been definitely shaped out in all points; Troops so many, when to be on march, and how; no important detail uncertain since then. November 17th, he jots down a little Note, which is to go to Vienna, were the due hour come, by a special Ambassador, one Count Gotter acquainted with the ground there; and explain to her Hungarian Majesty, what his exact demands are, and what the exact services he will render. Of which important little Paper readers shall hear again. Gotter's demands are at first to be high: Our Four Duchies, due by law so long; these and even more, considering the important services we propose; this is to be his first word; — but, it appears, he is privately prepared to put up with Two Duchies, if he can have them peaceably: Duchies of Sagan and Glogau, which are not of the Four at all, but which lie nearest us, and are far below the value of the Four, to Austria especially. This intricate point Friedrich has already settled in his mind. And indeed it is notably the habit of this young King to settle matters with himself in good time: and in regard to all manner of points, he will be found, on the day of bargaining about them, to have his own resolution formed and definitely fixed; — much to his advantage over conflicting parties who have theirs still flying loose.

Another thing of much concernment is, To secure himself from danger of Russian interference. To this end he despatches Major Winterfeld to Russia, a man well known to him; — day of Winterfeld's departure is not given; day of his arrival in Petersburg is "19th December" just coming. Russia, at present, is rather in a staggering condition; hopeful for Winterfeld's object. On the 28th of October last, only eight days after the Kaiser, Czarina Anne of Russia, she with the big cheek, once of Courland, had died; "audacious Death," as our poor friend had it, "venturing upon another Crowned Head" there. Bieren her dear Courlander, once little better than a Horse-groom, now Duke of Courland, Quasi-Husband to the late Big Cheek, and thereby sovereign of Russia, this long while past, is left Official Head in Russia. Poor little Anton Ulrich and his august Spouse, well enough known to us, have indeed produced a Czar Iwan, some months ago, to the joy of mankind: but Czar Iwan is in his cradle; Father and Mother's function is little other than to rock the cradle of Iwan; Bieren to be Regent and Autocrat over him and them in the interim. To their chagrin, to that of Feldmarschal Münnich and many others: the upshot of which will be visible before long. Czarina Anne's death had seemed to Friedrich the opportune removal of a dangerous neighbour, known to be in the pay of Austria: here now are new mutually hostile parties springing up; chance, surely, of a bargain with some of them? He despatches Winterfeld on this errand; — probably the fittest man in Prussia for it. How soon and perfectly Winterfeld succeeded, and what Winterfeld was, and something of what a Ru· ·ia he found it, we propose to mention by and by.

These, and all points of importance, Friedrich has settled with himself some time ago. What his own private thoughts on the Silesian Adventure are, readers will wish to know, since they can at first hand. Hear Friedrich himself, whose veracity is unquestionable to such as know anything of him:

"This Silesian Project fulfilled all his (the King's) political "views," — summed them all well up into one head. "It was "a means of acquiring reputation; of increasing the power of "the State; and of terminating what concerned that long-"litigated question of the Berg-Jülich Succession;" — can be sure of getting that, at lowest; intends to give that up, if necessary.

"Meanwhile, before entirely determining, the King weighed "the risks there were in undertaking such a War, and the ad-"vantages that were to be hoped from it. On one side, pre-"sented itself the potent House of Austria, not likely to want "resources with so many vast Provinces under it; an Em-"peror's Daughter attacked, who would naturally find allies "in the King of England, in the Dutch Republic, and so "many Princes of the Empire who had signed the Pragmatic "Sanction." Russia was, — or had been, and might again be, — in the pay of Vienna. Saxony might have some clippings from Bohemia thrown to it, and so be gained over. Scanty Harvest, 1740, threatened difficulties as to provisioning of troops. "The risks were great. One had to apprehend "the vicissitudes of war. A single battle lost might be de-"cisive. The King had no allies; and his troops, hitherto "without experience, would have to front old Austrian "soldiers, grown gray in harness, and trained to war by so "many campaigns.

"On the other side were hopeful considerations," — four in number: *First*, Weak condition of the Austrian Court, Treasury empty, War-Apparatus broken in pieces; inexperienced young Princess to defend a disputed succession, on those terms. *Second*, There *will* be allies; France and England always in rivalry, both meddling in these matters, King is sure to get either the one or the other. *Third*, Silesian War lies handy to us, and is the only kind of Offensive War that does; Country bordering on our frontier, and with the Oder running through it as a sure highroad for everything. *Fourth*, "What suddenly turned the balance," or at least what kept it steady in that posture, — "news of the Czarina's death ar-"rives:" Russia has ceased to count against us; and become a manageable quantity. On, therefore! —

"Add to these reasons," says the King, with a candour which has not been well treated in the History Books, "Add to "these reasons, an Army ready for acting; Funds, Supplies "all found" (lying barrelled in the Schloss at Berlin); — "and "perhaps the desire of making oneself a name," from which few of mortals able to achieve it are exempt in their young time: "all this was cause of the War which the King now en-"tered upon." *

"Desire to make himself a name; how shocking!" exclaim several Historians. "Candour of confession that "he may have had some such desire; how honest!" is what they do not exclaim. As to the justice of his Silesian Claims, or even to his own belief about their justice, Friedrich affords not the least light which can be new to readers here. He speaks, when business requires it, of "those known rights" of his, and with the air of a man who expects to be believed on his word; but it is cursorily, and in the business way only; and there is not here or elsewhere the least pleading: — a man, you would say, considerably indifferent to our belief on that head; his eye set on the practical merely. "Just Rights? What are rights, never so just, which you cannot make valid? The world is full of such. If you have rights and can assert them into facts, do it; that is worth doing!" —

We must add two Notes, two small absinthine drops, bitter but wholesome, administered by him to the Old Dessauer; whose gloomy wonder over all this

* *Œuvres de Frédéric* (Histoire de mon Temps), i. 128.

military whirl of Prussian things, and discontent that he, lately the head authority, has never once been spoken to on it, have been great. Guessing, at last, that it was meant for Austria, a Power rather dear to Leopold, he can suppress himself no longer; but breaks out into Cassandra prophesyings, which have piqued the young King, and provoke this return::

1. "*Reinsberg*, 24*th November* 1740. — I have received your "Letter, and seen with what inquietude you view the ap-"proaching march of my Troops. I hope you will set your "mind at ease on that score; and wait with patience what I in-"tend with them and you. I have made all my dispositions; "and Your Serenity will learn, time enough, what my orders "are, without disquieting yourself about them, as nothing has "been forgotten or delayed." — FRIEDRICH.

Old Dessauer, cut to the bone, perceives he will have to quit that method and never resume it; writes next how painful it is to an old General to see himself neglected, as if good for nothing, while his scholars are allowed to gather laurels. Friedrich's answer is of soothing character:

2. "*Berlin*, 2*d December* 1740. — You may be assured I "honour your merits and capacity as a young Officer ought to "honour an old one, who has given the world so many proofs "of his talent (*Dexterität*); nor will I neglect Your Serenity on "any occasion when you can help me by your good counsel "and coöperation." But it is a mere "bagatelle" this that I am now upon; though, next year, it may become serious. For the rest, Saxony being a neighbour whose intentions one does not know, I have privately purposed Your Serenity should keep an outlook that way, in my absence. Plenty of employment coming for Your Serenity. "But as to this pre-"sent Expedition, I reserve it for myself alone; that the world "may not think the King of Prussia marches with a Tutor to "the Field." — , FRIEDRICH.*

* Orlich: *Geschichte der Schlesischen Kriege* (Berlin, 1841), i. 38, 39.

And therewith Leopold, eagerly complying, has to rest satisfied; and beware of too much freedom with this young King again.

"Berlin, December 2d," is the date of that last Note to the Dessauer; date also of Voltaire's *Adieu* with the *Response;* — on which same day, "Friday, December 2d," as I find from the Old Books, his Majesty, quitting the Reinsberg sojourn, "had arrived in Berlin about 2 P.M.; accompanied by Prince August Wilhelm" (betrothed at Brunswick lately); "such a crowd on the streets as if they had never seen "him before." He continued at Berlin or in the neighbourhood thenceforth. Busy days these; and Berlin a much-whispering City, as Regiment after Regiment marches away. King soon to follow, as is thought, — "who himself sometimes deigns to take the Regiments "into highest own eye-shine, *Höchst-eigenen Augen-*"*schein*" (that is, to review them), say the reverential Editors. December 6th — But let us follow the strict sequence of Phenomena at Berlin.

Excellency Botta has Audience; then Excellency Dickens, and others: December 6th, the Mystery is out.

Of course her Hungarian Majesty, and her Bartensteins and Ministries, heard enough of those Prussian rumours, interior Military activities, and enigmatic movements; but they seem strangely supine on the matter; indeed they seem strangely supine on such matters; and lean at ease upon the Sea-Powers, upon Pragmatic Sanction and other Laws of Nature. But at length even they become painfully interested as to Friedrich's intentions; and despatch an Envoy to sift him a little: an expert Marchese di Botta, Genoese by birth, skilful in the Russian and other intricacies; who was here at Berlin lately, doing the Accession Compliment (rather ill received at that time), and is fit for the job. Perhaps Botta will penetrate him? That is becoming desirable, in spite of the gay Private Theatricals at Reinsberg, and the Berlin Carnival Balls he is so occupied with.

England is not less interested, and the diligent Sir Guy is doing his best; but can make out nothing satisfactory; — much the reverse indeed; and falls into angry black anticipations. "Nobody here, great or "small," says his Excellency, "dares make any repre-"sentation to this young Prince against the measures "he is pursuing; though all are sensible of the con-"fusion which must follow. A Prince who had the "least regard to honour, truth and justice, could not "act the part he is going to do." Alas, no, Excellency Dickens! "But it is plain his only view was, to "deceive us all, and conceal for a while his ambitious "and mischievous designs."* "Never was such dis-"simulation!" exclaims the Diplomatic world everywhere, being angered at it, as if it were a vice on the part of a King about to invade Silesia. Dissimulation, if that mean mendacity, is not the name of the thing; it is the art of wearing a polite cloak of darkness, and the King is little disturbed what name they call it.

Botta did not get to Berlin till December 1st, had no Audience till the 5th; — by which time it is becoming evident to Excellency Dickens, and to everybody, that Silesia is the thing meant. Botta hints as much in that first Audience, December 5th: "Terrible

* Despatch, 29th November — 3d December 1740: Raumer, p. 58.

roads, those Silesian ones, your Majesty!" says Botta, as if historically merely, but with a glance of the eye. "Hm," answers his Majesty in the same tone, "the worst that comes of them is a little mud!" — Next day, Dickens had express Audience, "Berlin, Tuesday 6th:" a smartish, somewhat flurried Colloquy with the King; which, well abridged, may stand as follows:

Dickens. * * "Indivisibility of the Austrian Monarchy, Sire!" — *King.* "Indivisibility? What do you mean?" — *Dickens.* "The maintenance of the Pragmatic Sanction."— *King.* "Do you intend to support it? I hope not; for such is not my intention." (There is for you!) * * *

Dickens. "England and Holland will much wonder at the measures your Majesty was taking, at the moment when your Majesty proposed to join with them, and were making friendly proposals!" (Has been a deceitful man, Sir Guy, at least an impenetrable; — but this latter is rather strong on your part!) 'What shall I write to England?' ("When I "mentioned this," says Dickens, "the King grew red in the "face," eyes considerably flashing, I should think.)

King. "You can have no instructions to ask that question! And if you had, I have an answer ready for you. England has no right to inquire into my designs. Your great Sea-Armaments, did I ask you any questions about them? No; I was and am silent on that head; only wishing you good luck, and that you may not get beaten by the Spaniards." (Dickens hastily draws in his rash horns again; after a pass or two, King's natural colour returns.) * *

King. "Austria as a Power is necessary against the Turks. But in Germany, what need of Austria being so superlative? Why should not, say, Three Electors united be able to oppose her? * * * Monsieur, I find it is your notion in England, as well as theirs in France, to bring other Sovereigns under your tutorage, and lead them about. Understand that I will not be led by either. * * Tush, *you* are like the Athenians, who, when Philip of Macedon was ready to invade them, spent their time in haranguing!"

Dickens. * * "Berg and Jülich, if we were to guarantee them?" *King.* "Hm. Don't so much mind that Rhine Country:

difficulties there, — Dutch always jealous of one. But, on the other Frontier, neither England nor Holland could take umbrage," — points clearly to Silesia then, your Excellency Dickens?*

Alas, yes! Troops and military equipments are, for days past, evidently wending towards Frankfurt, towards Crossen, and even the Newspapers now hint that something is on hand in that quarter. Nay, this same day, *Tuesday 6th December*, there has come out brief Official Announcement, to all the Foreign Ministers at Berlin, Excellency Dickens among them, "That his "Royal Majesty, our most all-gracious Herr, has taken "the resolution to advance a Body of Troops into "Schlesien,"— rather out of friendly views towards Austria (much business lying between us about Schlesien), not out of hostile views by any means, as all Excellencies shall assure their respective Courts.** Announcement which had thrown the Excellency Dickens into such a frame of mind, before he got his Audience to-day! —

Saturday following, which was December 10th, Marquis de Beauvau had his Audience of leave; intending for Paris shortly: Audience very gracious; covertly hinting, on both sides, more than it said; ending in these words, on the King's side, which have become famous: "Adieu, then, M. le Marquis. I believe "I am going to play your game; if the aces fall to me, "we will share (*Je vais, je crois, jouer votre jeu: si les* "*as me viennent, nous partagerons*)!" ***

To Botta, all this while, Friedrich strove to be specially civil; took him out to Charlottenburg, that

* Raumer (from State-Paper Office), pp. 63, 64.
** Copy of the Paper, in *Helden-Geschichte*, i. 447.
*** Voltaire, *Œuvres* (Siècle de Louis XV, c. 6), xxviii. 74.

same Saturday, with the Queen and other guests; but Botta, and all the world, being now certain about Silesia, and that no amount of mud, or other terror on the roads, would be regarded, Botta's thoughts in this evening party are not of cheerful nature. Next day, Sunday, December 11th, he too gets his Audience of leave; and cannot help bursting out, when the King plainly tells him what is now afoot, and that the Prussian Ambassador has got instructions what to offer upon it at Vienna. "Sire, you are going to ruin the "House of Austria," cried Botta, "and to plunge your- "self into destruction (*vous abîmer*) at the same time!" —"Depends on the Queen," said Friedrich, "to accept "the Offers I have made her." Botta sank silent, seemed to reflect, but gathering himself again, added with an ironical air and tone of voice, "They are fine "Troops, those of yours, Sire. Ours have not the "same splendour of appearance; but they have looked "the wolf in the face. Think, I conjure you, what you "are getting into!" Friedrich answered with vivacity, a little nettled at the ironical tone of Botta, and his mixed sympathy and menace: "You find my troops are "beautiful; perhaps I shall convince you they are "good too." Yes, Excellency Botta, goodish troops; and very capable "to look the wolf in the face," — or perhaps in the tail too, before all end! "Botta "urged and entreated that at least there should be "some delay in executing this project. But the King "gave him to understand that it was now too late, and "that the Rubicon was passed."*

The secret is now out, therefore; Invasion of Silesia certain and close at hand. "A day or two

* Friedrich's own Account (*Œuvres*, ii. 57).

before marching," may have been this very day when Botta got his audience, the King assembled his Chief Generals, all things ready out in the Frankfurt-Crossen region yonder; and spoke to them as follows; briefly and to the point:

"Gentlemen, I am undertaking a War, in which I have no "allies but your valour and your goodwill. My cause is just; "my resources are what we ourselves can do; and the issue lies "in Fortune. Remember continually the glory which your "Ancestors acquired in the plains of Warsaw, at Fehrbellin, "and in the Expedition to Preussen" (across the Frische Haf "on ice, that time). "Your lot is in your own hands: dis-"tinctions and rewards wait upon your fine actions which shall "merit them.

"But what need have I to excite you to glory? It is the one "thing you keep before your eyes; the sole object worthy of "your labours. We are going to front troops who, under Prince "Eugene, had the highest reputation. Though Prince Eugene "is gone, we shall have to measure our strength against brave "soldiers: the greater will be the honour if we can conquer. "Adieu, go forth. I will follow you straightway, to the rendez-"vous of glory which awaits us."*

Masked Ball, at Berlin, 12*th* - 13*th December.*

On the evening of Tuesday 12th, there was, as usual, Masked (or Half-Masked) Ball, at the Palace. As usual; but this time it has become mentionable in World-History. Bielfeld, personally interested, gives us a vivid glance into it; — which, though pretending to be real and contemporaneous, is unfortunately *mythical* only, and done at a great interval of years (dates, and even slight circumstances of fact, refusing to conform); — which, however, for the truth there is in it, we will give, as better than nothing. Bielfeld's pretended date is, "Berlin, 15th December;" should

* *Œuvres de Frédéric,* ii. 58.

have been 14th, — wrong by a day, after one's best effort!

"*Berlin, 15th December* 1740. As for me, dear Sister, I am "like a shuttlecock whom the Kings of Prussia and of England "hit with their rackets, and knock to and fro. The night be-"fore last, I was at the Palace Evening Party (*Assemblée*); "which is a sort of Ball, where you go in domino, but without "mask on the face. The Queen was there, and all the Court. "About eight o'clock the King also made his appearance. His "Majesty, noticing M. de G**" (that is *de Guidiken*, or Guy "Dickens), "English Minister, addressed him; led him into the "embrasure of a window, and talked alone with him for more "than an hour" (uncertain, probably apocryphal this). "I "threw, from time to time, a stolen glance at this dialogue, "which appeared to me to be very lively. A moment after, "being just dancing with Madame the Countess de — *Three-*"*Asterisks*, — I felt myself twitched by the domino; and turn-"ing, was much surprised to see that it was the King; who "took me aside, and said, 'Are your boots oiled (*Vos bottes* "*sont-elles graissées*, Are you ready for a journey)?' I replied, "'Sire, they will always be so for your Majesty's service.' — "'Well, then, Truchsess and you are for England; the day "'after tomorrow you go. Speak to M. de Podewils!' — "This was said like a flash of lightning. His Majesty passed "into another apartment; and I, I went to finish my minuet "with the Lady; who had been not less astonished to see me "disappear from her eyes, in the middle of the dance, than I "was at what the King said to me." * Next morning, I —

The fact is, next morning, Truchsess and I began preparation for the Court of London, — and we did there, for many months afterwards, strive our best to keep the Britannic Majesty in some kind of tune, amid the prevailing discord of events; — fact interesting to some. And the other fact, interesting to everybody, though Bielfeld has not mentioned it, is, That King Friedrich, the same next morning, punctually "at the

* Bielfeld, i. 167, 168.

stroke of 9," rolled away Frankfurt-ward, — into the First Silesian War! Tuesday, "13th December, this "morning the King, privately quitting the Ball, has "gone" (after some little snatch of sleep, we will hope) "for Frankfurt, to put himself at the head of his "Troops."* Bellona his companion for long years henceforth, instead of Minerva and the Muses, as he had been anticipating.

Hereby is like to be fulfilled (except that Friedrich himself is perhaps this "little stone") what Friedrich prophesied to his Voltaire, the day after hearing of the Kaiser's Death: "I believe there will, by June next, "be more talk of cannon, soldiers, trenches, than of "actresses, and dancers for the ballet. This small "Event changes the entire system of Europe. It is "the little stone which Nebuchadnezzar saw, in his "dream, loosening itself, and rolling down on the "Image made of Four Metals, which it shivers to "ruin." **

---

* Dickens (in State-Paper Office), 13th December 1740; see also *Helden-Geschichte*, i. 452; &c. &c.

** Friedrich to Voltaire, busy gathering actors at that time, 26th Oct. 1740 (*Œuvres de Frédéric*, xxii. 49).

BOOK XII.

FIRST SILESIAN WAR, AWAKENING A GENERAL EUROPEAN ONE, BEGINS.

December 1740—May 1741.

CHAPTER I.

OF SCHLESIEN, OR SILESIA.

SCHLESIEN, what we call Silesia, lies in elliptic shape, spread on the top of Europe, partly girt with mountains, like the crown or crest to that part of the Earth; — highest table-land of Germany or of the Cisalpine Countries; and sending rivers into all the seas. The summit or highest level of it is in the south-west; longest diameter is from north-west to south-east. From Crossen, whither Friedrich is now driving, to the Jablunka Pass, which issues upon Hungary, is above 250 miles; the *axis*, therefore, or longest diameter, of our Ellipse we may call 250 English miles; — its shortest or conjugate diameter, from Friedland in Bohemia (Wallenstein's old Friedland), by Breslau across the Oder to the Polish Frontier, is about 100. The total area of Schlesien is counted to be some 20,000 square miles, nearly the third of England Proper.

Schlesien, — will the reader learn to call it by that name, on occasion? for in these sad Manuscripts of ours the names alternate, — is a fine, fertile, useful and beautiful Country. It leans sloping, as we hinted, to the East and to the North; a long curved buttress of Mountains ("*Riesengebirge*, Giant Mountains," is their best-known name in foreign countries) holding it up on the South and West sides. This Giant-Mountain Range, — which is a kind of continuation of the Saxon-Bohemian "Metal Mountains (*Erzgebirge*)" and of the straggling Lausitz Mountains, to westward of these, — shapes itself like a bill-hook (or elliptically, as was said): handle and hook together may be some 200 miles in length. The precipitous side of this is, in general, turned outwards, towards Böhmen, Mähren, Ungarn (Bohemia, Moravia, Hungary, in our dialects); and Schlesien lies inside, irregularly sloping down, towards the Baltic and towards the utmost East. From the Bohemian side of these Mountains there rise Two Rivers: Elbe, tending for the West; Morawa for the South; — Morawa, crossing Moravia, gets into the Donau, and thence into the Black-Sea; while Elbe, after intricate adventures among the mountains, and then prosperously across the plains, is out, with its many ships, into the Atlantic. Two rivers, we say, from the Bohemian or steep side: and again, from the Silesian side, there rise other Two, the Oder and the Weichsel (*Vistula*); which start pretty near one another in the South-East, and, after wide windings, get both into the Baltic, at a good distance apart.

For the first thirty, or in parts, fifty miles from the Mountains, Silesia slopes somewhat rapidly; and is still to be called a Hill-country, rugged extensive elevations diversifying it: but after that, the slope is gentle, and at length insensible, or noticeable only by the way the waters run. From the central part of it, Schlesien pictures itself to you as a plain; growing ever flatter, ever sandier, as it abuts on the monotonous endless sand-flats of Poland, and the Brandenburg territories; nothing but Boundary Stones with their brass inscriptions marking where the transition is; and only some Fortified Town, not far off, keeping the door of the Country secure in that quarter.

On the other hand, the Mountain part of Schlesien is very picturesque; not of Alpine height anywhere (the Schnee-Koppe itself is under 5,000 feet), so that verdure and forest wood fail almost nowhere among the Mountains; and multiplex industry, besung by rushing torrents and the swift young rivers, nestles itself high up; and from wheat-husbandry, madder and maize husbandry, to damask-weaving, metallurgy, charcoal-burning, tar-distillery, Schlesien has many trades, and has long been expert and busy at them to a high degree. A very pretty Ellipsis, or irregular Oval, on the summit of the European Continent; — "like the palm of a left-hand well stretched-out, with the Riesengebirge for thumb!" said a certain Herr to me, stretching out his arm in that fashion towards the north-west. Palm, well stretched-out, measuring 250 miles; and the cross way 100. There are still beavers in Schlesien; the Katzbach River has gold grains in it, a kind of Pactolus not now worth working; and in the scraggy lonesome pine-woods, grimy individuals, with kindled mounds of pine-branches and smoke carefully kept down by sods, are sweating out a substance which they inform you is to be tar.

Historical Epochs of Schlesien; — after the Quads and Marchmen.

Who first lived in Schlesien, or lived long since in it, there is no use in asking, nor in telling if one knew. "The *Quadi* and the Lygii," says Dryasdust, in a groping manner: Quadi and consorts, in the fifth or sixth Century, continues he with more confidence, shifted Rome-ward, following the general track of contemporaneous mankind; weak remnant of Quadi was thereupon overpowered by Slavic populations, and their Country became Polish, which the eastern rim of it still essentially is. That was the end of the Quadi in those parts, says History. But they cannot speak nor appeal for themselves; History has them much at discretion. Rude burial urns, with a handful of ashes in them, have been dug up in different places; these are all the Archives and Histories the Quadi now have. It appears their name signifies *Wicked*. They are those poor Quadi (*Wicked People*) who always go along with the Marcomanni (*Marchmen*), in the beadroll Histories one reads; and I almost guess they must have been of the same stock: "Wickeds and Borderers;" considered, on both sides of the Border, to belong to the Dangerous Classes in those times. Two things are certain: First, *quad* and its derivatives have, to this day, in the speech of rustic Germans, something of that meaning, — "nefarious," at least "injurious," "hateful, and to be avoided:" for example, *quad*del, "a nettle-burn;" *quet*schen, "to smash" (say, your thumb while hammering); &c. &c. And then a second thing: The Polish equivalent word is *Zle* (Büsching says *Zlezi*); hence *Zle*zien, *Schle*sien, meaning merely *Bad*-land, Quadland, what we might call *Damag*itia, or Country where you get into Trouble. That is the etymology, or what passes for such. As to the History of Schlesien, hitherwards of these burial urns dug up in different places, I notice, as not yet entirely buriable, Three Epochs.

First Epoch; Christianity: A.D. 966. Introduction of Christianity; to the length of founding a Bishoprick that year, so hopeful were the aspects; "Bishoprick of Schmoger" (Schm*a*gram, dim little Village still discoverable on the Polish frontier, not far from the Town of Namslau); Bishoprick which, after one removal farther inward, got across the Oder, to "*Wratislav*," which we now call Breslau; and sticks there, as Bishoprick of Breslau, to this day. Year 966: it was in Adalbert, our Prussian Saint and Missionary's younger time. Preaching, by zealous Polacks, must have been going on, while Adalbert, Bright in Nobleness, was studying at Magdeburg, and ripening for high things in the general estimation. This was a new gift from the Polacks, this of Christianity; an infinitely more important one than that nickname of "*Zlezien*," or "*Damagitia*," stuck upon the poor Country, had been.

Second Epoch; Get gradually cut loose from Poland: A.D. 1139-1159. Twenty years of great trouble in Poland, which were of lasting benefit to Schlesien. In 1139 the Polack King, a very potent Majesty whom we could name but do not, died; and left his Dominions shared by punctual bequest among his five sons. Punctual bequest did avail: but the eldest Son (who was King, and had Schlesien with much else to his share) began to encroach, to grasp; upon which the others rose upon him, flung him out into exile; redivided; and hoped now they might have quiet. Hoped, but were disappointed; and could come to no sure bargain for the next twenty years,—not till "the eldest brother," first author of these strifes, "died an exile in Holstein," or was just about dying, and had agreed to take Schlesien for all claims, and be quiet thenceforth.

His, this eldest's, Three Sons did accordingly, in 1159, get Schlesien instead of him; their uncles proving honourable. Schlesien thereby was happy enough to get cut loose from Poland, and to continue loose; steering a course of its own;—parting farther and farther from Poland and its habits and fortunes. These Three Sons, of the late Polish Majesty who died in exile in Holstein, are the "Piast Dukes," much talked of in Silesian Histories: of whose merits I specify this only, That they so soon as possible strove to be German. They were Progenitors of all "the Piast Dukes," Proprietors of Schlesien thenceforth, till the last of them died out in 1675,—and a certain *Erbverbrüderung* they had entered into could not take effect at that time. Their merits as Sovereign Dukes seem to have been considerable; a certain piety, wisdom and nobleness of mind not rare among them; and no doubt it was partly their merit, if partly also their good luck, that they took to Germany, and leant thitherward; steering looser and looser from Poland, in their new circumstances. They themselves by degrees became altogether German; their Countries, by silent immigration, introduction of the arts, the composures and sobrieties, became essentially so. On the eastern rim there is still a Polack remnant, its territories very sandy, its condition very bad; remnant which surely ought to cease its Polack jargon, and learn some dialect of intelligible Teutsch, as the first condition of improvement. In all other parts, Teutsch reigns; and Schlesien is a green abundant Country; full of metallurgy, damask-weaving, grain-husbandry, instead of gasconade, gilt anarchy, rags, dirt, and *Nie Pozwalam.*

A.D. 1327; *Get completely cut loose.* The Piast Dukes, who soon ceased to be Polish, and hung rather upon Bohemia, and thereby upon Germany, made a great step in that direction, when King Johann, old *Ich-Dien* whom we ought to recollect, persuaded most of them, all of them but two, "*pretio ac prece,*" to become Feudatories (Quasi-Feudatories, but of a sovereign sort) to his Crown of Bohemia. The two who stood out, resisting prayer and price, were the Duke of Jauer and the Duke of Schweidnitz, — lofty-minded gentlemen, perhaps a thought too lofty. But these also Johann's son, little Kaiser Karl IV., "marrying their heiress," contrived to bring in; — one fruitful adventure of little Karl's, among the many wasteful he made, in the German Reich. Schlesien is henceforth a bit of the Kingdom of Bohemia; indissolubly hooked to Germany; and its progress in the arts and composures, under wise Piasts with immigrating Germans, we guess to have become doubly rapid.*

Third Epoch; Adopt the Reformation: A.D. 1414-1517. Schlesien, hanging to Bohemia in this manner, extensively adopted Huss's doctrines; still more extensively Luther's; and that was a difficult element in its lot, though, I believe, an unspeakably precious one. It cost above a Century of sad tumults, Zisca Wars; nay above Two Centuries, including the sad Thirty-years War; — which miseries, in Bohemia Proper, were sometimes very sad and even horrible. But Schlesien, the outlying Country, did, in all this, suffer less

---

* Büsching, *Erdbeschreibung,* viii. 725; Hübner, t. 94.

than Bohemia Proper; and did *not* lose its Evangelical Doctrine in result, as unfortunate Bohemia did, and sink into sluttish "fanatical torpor, and big Crucifixes of japanned Tin by the wayside," though in the course of subsequent years, named of Peace, it was near doing so. Here are the steps, or unavailing counter-steps, in that latter direction:

A.D. 1537. Occurred, as we know, the *Erbverbrüderung;* Duke of Liegnitz, and of other extensive heritages, making Deed of Brotherhood with Kur-Brandenburg; — Deed forbidden, and so far as might be, rubbed out and annihilated by the then King of Bohemia, subsequently Kaiser, Ferdinand I., Karl V.'s Brother. Duke of Liegnitz had to give up his parchments, and become zero in that matter: Kur-Brandenburg entirely refused to do so; kept his parchments, to see if they would not turn to something.

A.D. 1624. Schlesien, especially the then Duke of Liegnitz (great-grandson of the *Erbverbrüderung* one), and poor Johann George, Duke of Jägerndorf, cadet of the then Kur-Brandenburg, went warmly ahead into the Winter-King project, first fire of the Thirty-years War; sufferings from Papal encroachment, in high quarters, being really extreme. Warmly ahead; and had to smart sharply for it; — poor Johann George with forfeiture of Jägerndorf, with *Reiches-Acht* (Ban of the Empire), and total ruin; fighting against which he soon died. Act of Ban and Forfeiture was done tyrannously, said most men; and it was persisted in equally so, till men ceased speaking of it; — Jägerndorf Duchy, fruit of the Act, was held by Austria, ever after, in defiance of the Laws of the Reich. Religious Oppression lay heavy on Protestant Schlesien thenceforth; and many lukewarm individualities were brought back to Orthodoxy by that method, successful in the diligent skilled hands of Jesuit Reverend Fathers, with fiscals and soldiers in the rear of them.

A.D. 1648. Treaty of Westphalia mended much of this, and set fair limits to Papist encroachment; — had said Treaty been kept: but how could it? By Orthodox Authority, anxious to recover lost souls, or at least to have loyal subjects, it was publicly kept in name; and tacitly, in substance, it was violated more and more. — Of the "Blossoming of Silesian Literature," spoken of in Books; of the Poet Opitz, Poets Logau, Hoffmannswaldau, who burst into a kind of Song

12*

better or worse at this Period, we will remember nothing; but request the reader to remember it, if he is tunefully given, or thinks it a good symptom of Schlesien.

A.D. 1707. Treaty of Altranstädt: between Kaiser Joseph I. and Karl XII. Swedish Karl, marching through those parts, — out of Poland, in chase of August the Physically Strong, towards Saxony, there to beat him soft, — was waited upon by Silesian Deputations of a lamentable nature; was entreated, for the love of Christ and His Evangel, to "Protect us poor Protestants, and get the Treaty of Westphalia observed on our behalf, and fair play shown!" Which Karl did; Kaiser Joseph, with such weight of French War lying on him, being much struck with the tone of that dangerous Swede. The Pope rebuked Kaiser Joseph for such compliance in the Silesian matter: "Holy Father," answered this Kaiser (not of distinguished orthodoxy in the House), "I am too glad he did not ask me to become Lutheran; I know not how I should have helped myself!*"

These are the Three Epochs; — most things, in respect of this Third or Reformation Epoch, stepping steadily downward hitherto. As to the Fourth Epoch, dating "13th Dec. 1740," which continues, up to our day and farther, and is the final and crowning Epoch of Silesian History, — read in the following Chapters.

* Pauli, *Allgemeine Preussische Staats-Geschichte* (viii. 298-592); Büsching, *Erdbeschreibung* (viii. 700-39); &c. — Heinrich Wuttke, *Friedrichs des Grossen Besitzergreifung von Schlesien* (Seizure of Silesia by Friedrich, 2 voll. Leipzig, 1843), I mention only lest ingenuous readers should be tempted by the Title to buy it. Wuttke begins at the Creation of the World; and having, in two heavy volumes, at last struggled down close to the *Besitzergreifung* or Seizure in question, calls halt; and stands (at ease, we will hope) immovably there for the seventeen years since.

CHAPTER II.

FRIEDRICH MARCHES ON GLOGAU.

AT what hour Friedrich ceased dancing on that famous Ball-night of Bielfeld's, and how long he slept after, or whether at all, no Bielfeld even mythically says: but next morning, as is patent to all the world, Tuesday 13th December 1740, at the stroke of nine, he steps into his carriage; and with small escort rolls away towards Frankfurt-on-Oder;* out upon an Enterprise which will have results for himself and others.

Two youngish military men, Adjutants-General both, were with him, Wartensleben, Borck; both once fellow Captains in the Potsdam Giants, and much in his intimacy ever since. Wartensleben we once saw at Brunswick, on a Masonic occasion; Borck, whom we here see for the first time, is not the Colonel Borck (properly Major-General) who did the Herstal Operation lately; still less is he the venerable old Minister, Marlborough Veteran, and now Field-Marshal Borck, whom Hotham treated with, on a certain occasion. There are numerous Borcks always in the King's service; nor are these three, except by loose cousinry, related to one another. The Borcks all come from Stettin quarter; a brave kindred, and old enough, — "Old as the Devil, *Das ist so old als de Borcken und de Düwel*," says the Pomeranian Proverb; — the Adjutant-General, a junior member of the clan, chances to be the notablest of them at this moment. Wartens-

---
* *Helden-Geschichte*, 1. 452; Preuss, *Thronbesteigung*, p. 456.

leben, Borck, and a certain Colonel von der Golz, whom also the King much esteems, these are his company on this drive. For escort, or guard of honour out of Berlin to the next stages, there is a small body of Hussars, Life-guard and other Cavalry, "perhaps 500 horse in all."

They drive rapidly, through the gray Winter; reach Frankfurt on the Oder, sixty miles or more; where no doubt there is military business waiting. They are forward, on the morrow, for dinner, forty miles farther, at a small Town called Crossen, which looks over into Silesia; and is, for the present, headquarters to a Prussian Army, standing ready there and in the environs. Standing ready, or hourly marching in, and rendezvousing; now about 28,000 strong, horse and foot. A Rearguard of Ten or Twelve Thousand will march from Berlin in two days, pause hereabouts, and follow according to circumstances: Prussian Army will then be some 40,000 in all. Schwerin has been Commander, manager and mainspring of the business hitherto: henceforth it is to be the King; but Schwerin under him will still have a Division of his own.

Among the Regiments, we notice "Schulenburg Horse-Grenadiers," — come along from Landsberg hither, these Horse-Grenadiers, with little Schulenburg at the head of them; — "Dragoon Regiment Bayreuth," "Lifeguard Carbineers," "Derschau of Foot;" and other Regiments and figures slightly known to us, or that will be better known.[*] Rearguard, just getting under way at Berlin, has for leaders the Prince of Holstein-Beck ("Holstein-*Vaisselle*," say wags, since

[*] List in *Helden-Geschichte*, i. 453.

the Principality went all to *Silver-Plate*) and the Hereditary Prince of Anhalt-Dessau, whom we called the Young Dessauer, on the Strasburg Journey lately: Rearguard, we say, is of 12,000; main Army is 28,000; Horse and Foot are in the proportion of about 1 to 3. Artillery "consists of 20 three-pounders; 4 twelve- "pounders; 4 howitzers (*Haubitzen*); 4 big mortars, "calibre fifty-pounds; and of Artillerymen 166 in "all."

With this Force the young King has, on his own basis (pretty much in spite of all the world, as we find now and afterwards), determined to invade Silesia, and lay hold of the Property he has long had there; — not computing, for none can compute, the sleeping whirlwinds he may chance to awaken thereby. Thus lightly does a man enter upon Enterprises which prove unexpectedly momentous, and shape the whole remainder of his days for him; crossing the Rubicon as it were in his sleep. In Life, as on railways at certain points, — whether you know it or not, there is but an inch, this way or that, into what tram you are shunted; but try to get out of it again! "The man is mad, *cet homme-là est fol!*" said Louis XV. when he heard it.*

Friedrich at Crossen, and still in his own Territory,
14th-16th Dec.; — steps into Schlesien.

At all events, the man means to try; — and is here dining at Crossen, noon of Wednesday the 14th;

* Raumer, *Beiträge* (English Translation, called *Frederick II. and his Times*; from *British Museum and State-Paper Office;* — a very indistinct poor Book, in comparison with what it might have been), p. 73 (24th Dec. 1740).

certain important persons, — especially two Silesian Gentlemen, deputed from Grünberg, the nearest Silesian Town, who have come across the border on business, — having the honour to dine with him. To whom his manner is lively and affable; lively in mood, as if there lay no load upon his spirits. The business of these two Silesian Gentlemen, a Baron von Hocke one of them, a Baron von Kestlitz the other, was To present, on the part of the Town and Amt of Grünberg, a solemn Protest against this meditated entrance on the Territory of Schlesien; Government itself, from Breslau, ordering them to do so. Protest was duly presented; Friedrich, as his manner is, and continues to be on his march, glances politely into or at the Protest; hands it, in silence, to some page or secretary to reposit in the due pigeon-hole or waste-basket; and invites the two Silesian Gentlemen to dine with him; as, we see, they have the honour to do. "He (*Er*) lives near Grünberg, then, Mein Herr von Hocke?" "Close to it, *Ihro Majestät*. My poor mansion, Schloss of Deutsch-Kessel, is some fifteen miles hence; how infinitely at your Majesty's service, should the march prove inevitable, and go that way!" — "Well, perpaps!" I find Friedrich did dine, the second day hence, with one of these Gentlemen; and lodged with the other. Government at Breslau has ordered such Protest, on the part of the Frontier populations and Official persons; and this is all that comes of it.

During these hours, it chanced that the big Bell of Crossen dropped from its steeple, — fulness of time, or entire rottenness of axletree, being at last completed, at this fateful moment. Perhaps an ominous thing? Friedrich, as Cæsar and others have done, cheerfully interprets the omen to his own advantage: "Sign that the High is to be brought low!" says Friedrich. Were the march-routes, wagon-trains, and multifarious adjustments perfect to the last item here at Crossen, he will with much cheerfulness step into Silesia, independent of all Grünberg Protests and fallen Bells.

On the second day he does actually cross; "the "regiments marching in, at different points; some "reaching as far as 25 miles in." It is Friday 16th Dec. 1740; there has a game begun which will last long! They went through the Village of Lüsgen; that was the first point of Silesian ground ("Circle of Schwiebus," our old friend, is on the left near by); and "Schwerin's regiment was the foremost." Others cross more to the left or right; "marching through the Vil-"lage of Lessen," and other dim Villages and little Towns, round and beyond Grünberg; all regiments and divisions bearing upon Grünberg and the Great Road; but artistically portioned out,— several miles in breadth (for the sake of quarters), and, as is generally the rule, about a day's march in length. This evening nearly the whole Army was on Silesian ground.

Printed "Patent" or Proclamation, briefly assuring all Silesians, of whatever rank, condition or religion, "'That we have come as friends to them, and will protect all persons in their privileges, and molest no peaceable mortal," is posted on Church-doors, and extensively distributed by hand. Soldiers are forbidden, "under penalty of the rods," Officers under that of "cassation with infamy," to take anything, without first bargaining and paying ready money for it. On these terms the Silesian villages cheerfully enough accept their new guests, interesting to the rural mind; and though the billetting was rather heavy, "as many as 24 soldiers to a common Farmer (*Gärtner*)," no complaints were made. In one Schloss, where the owners had fled, and no human response was to be had by the wayworn soldiery, there did occur some breakages and impatient kickings about; which it grieved his Majesty to hear of, next morning; — in one, not in more.

Official persons, we perceive, study to be absolutely passive. This was the Bürgermeister's course at Grünberg to-night; Grünberg, first Town on the Frontier, sets an example of passivity which cannot be surpassed. Prussian troops being at the Gate of Grünberg, Bürgermeister and adjuncts sitting in a tacit expectant condition in their Townhall, there arrives a Prussian Lieutenant requiring of the Bürgermeister the Key of said Gate. "To deliver such Key? Would to God I durst, "Mein Herr Lieutenant; but how dare I! There is the "Key lying: but to *give* it — You are not the Queen "of Hungary's Officer, I doubt?" — The Prussian Lieutenant has to put out hand, and take the Key; which he readily does. And on the morrow, in returning it, when the march recommences, there are the same phenomena: Bürgermeister or assistants dare not for the life of them touch that Key: It lay on the table; and may again, in the course of Providence, come to lie! — The Prussian Lieutenant lays it down accordingly, and hurries out, with a grin on his face. There was much small laughter over this transaction; Majesty himself laughing well at it. Higher perfection of passivity no Bürgermeister could show.

The march, as readers understand, is towards Glogau; a strongish Garrison Town, now some 40 miles ahead; the key of Northern Schlesien. Grünberg (where my readers once slept for the night, in the late King's time, though they have forgotten it) is the first and only considerable Town on the hither side of Glogau. On to Glogau, I rather perceive, the Army is in good part provisioned before starting: after Glogau — we must see. Bread-wagons, Baggage-wagons, Ammunition-and-Artillery-wagons, all is in order; Army artistically portioned out. That is the form of march; with Glogau ahead. King, as we said above, dines with his Baron von Hocke, at the Schloss of Deutsch-Kessel, short way beyond Grünberg, this first day: but he by no means loiters there; — cuts across, a dozen miles westward, through a country where his vanguard on its various lines of march ought to be arriving; — and goes to lodge, at the Schloss of Schweinitz, with his other Baron, the Von Kestlitz, of Wednesday at Crossen.* This is Friday 16th December, his first night on Silesian ground.

What Glogau, and the Government at Breslau, did upon it.

Silesia, in the way of resistance, is not in the least prepared for him. A month ago, there were not above 3,000 Austrian Foot and 600 Horse in the whole Province: neither the military Governor Count Wallis, nor the Imperial Court, nor any Official Person near or far, had the least anticipation of such a Visit. Count Wallis, who commands in Glogau, did in person, nine or ten days ago, as the rumours rose ever higher, run over to Crossen; saw with his eyes the undeniable there; and has been zealously endeavouring ever since, what *he* could, to take measures. Wallis is

* *Helden-Geschichte,* i. 459.

now shut in Glogau; his second, the now Acting Governor, General Browne, a still more reflective man, is doing likewise his utmost; but on forlorn terms, and without the least guidance from Court. Browne has, by violent industry, raked together, from Mähren and the neighbouring countries, certain fractions which raise his Force to 7,000 Foot: these he throws, in small parties, into the defensible points; or, in larger, into the Chief Garrisons. New Cavalry he cannot get; the old 600 Horse he keeps for himself, all the marching Army he has.*

Fain would he get possession of Breslau, and throw in some garrison there; but cannot. Neither he nor Wallis could compass that. Breslau is a City divided against itself, on this matter; full of emotions, of expectations, apprehensions for and against. There is a Supreme Silesian Government (*Ober-Amt*, "Head-Office," kind of Austrian Vice-Royalty) in Breslau; and there is, on Breslau's own score, a Town-Rath; strictly Catholic both these, Vienna the breath of their nostrils. But then also there are forty-four Incorporated Trades; Oppressed-Protestant in majority; to whom Vienna is not breath, but rather the want of it. Lastly, the City calls itself Free; and has crabbed privileges still valid; a "*jus præsidii*" (or right to be one's own garrison) one of them, and the most inconvenient just now. Breslau is a *Reichs-Stadt*; in theory, sovereign member of the Reich, and supreme over its own affairs, even as Austria itself: — and the truth is, old Theory and new Fact, resolved not to quarrel, have lapsed into one another's arm in a quite inextricable way, in

* Particulars in *Helden-Geschichte*, i. 465; total of Austrian Force seems to be 7,800 horse and foot.

Breslau as elsewhere! With a Head Government which can get no orders from Vienna, the very Town-Rath has little alacrity, inclines rather to passivity like Grünberg; and a silent Population threatens to become vocal if you press upon it.

Breslau, that is to say the *Ober-Amt* there, has sent courier on courier to Vienna for weeks past: not even an answer;—what can Vienna answer, with Kur-Baiern and others threatening war on it, and only 10,000*l.* in its National Purse? Answer at last is, "Don't bother! Danger is not so near. Why spend money on couriers, and get into such a taking?" General Wallis came to Breslau, after what he had seen at Crossen; and urged strongly, in the name of self-preservation, first law of Nature, to get an Austrian real Garrison introduced; wished much (horrible to think of!) "the suburbs should be burnt, and better ramparts raised:" but could not succeed in any of these points, nor even mention some of them in a public manner. "You shall have a Protestant for commandant," suggested Wallis; "there is Count von Roth, Silesian-Lutheran, an excellent Soldier!" — "Thanks," answered they, "we can defend ourselves; we had rather not have any!" And the Breslau Burghers have, accordingly, set to drill themselves; are bringing out old cannon in quantity; repairing breaches; very strict in sentry-work: "Perfectly able to defend our City, — so far as we see good!" — Tuesday last, December 13th (the very day Friedrich left Berlin), as this matter of the Garrison, long urged by the Ober-Amt, had at last been got agreed to by the Town-Rath, "on proviso of consulting the Incorporated Trades," or at least consulting their Guild-Masters, who are usually a silent folk, — the Guild-Masters suddenly became in part vocal; and their Forty-four Guilds unusually so: — and there was tumult in Breslau, in the Salz-Ring (big central Square or marketplace, which they call *Ring*) such as had not been; idle population, and guild-brethren of suspicious humour, gathering in multitudes into and round the fine old Town-hall there; questioning, answering, in louder and louder key; at last bellowing quite in alt; and on the edge of flaming into one knew not what: * — till the matter of Austrian Garrison (much more, of burning the suburbs!) had to be dropt; settled in what way we see.

Head Government (*Ober-Amt*) has, through its Northern official people, sent Protest, strict order to the Silesian Population to look sour on the Prussians: — and we saw, in consequence, the Two Silesian Gentlemen did dine with Friedrich, and he has returned their visits; and the Mayor of Grünberg would not touch his keys. Head Government is now redacting a "Patent," or still more solemn Protest of its own; which likewise it will affix in the Salz-Ring here, and present to King Friedrich: and this, — except "despatching by boat down the river a great deal of meal to Glogau," which was an important quiet thing, of Wallis's enforcing, — is pretty much all it can do. No Austrian Garrison can be got in ("Perfectly able to defend ourselves!") — let Government and Wallis or Browne contrive as they may. And as to burning the suburbs, better not whisper of that again. Breslau feels, or would fain feel itself "perfectly able;" — has at any rate no wish to be bombarded; and contains

* *Helden-Geschichte*, i. 469.

privately a great deal of Protestant humour. Of all which, Friedrich, it is not doubted, has notice more or less distinct; and quickens his march the more.

General Browne is at present in the Southern parts; an able active man and soldier; but with such a force what can he attempt to do? There are three strong places in the Country, Glogau, then Brieg, both on the Oder river; lastly Neisse, on the Neisse river, a branch of the Oder (one of the *four* Neisse rivers there are in Germany, mostly in Silesia, — not handy to the accurate reader of German Books). Browne is in Neisse; and will start into a strange stare when the flying post reaches him: Prussians actually on march! Debate with them, if debate there is to be, Browne himself must contrive to do; from Breslau, from Vienna, no Government Supreme or Subordinate can yield his 8,000 and him the least help.

Glogau, as we saw, means to defend itself; at least General Wallis the Commandant does, in spite of the Glogau public; and is, with his whole might, digging, palisading, getting-in meal, salt meat and other provender; — likewise burning suburbs, uncontrollable he, in the small place; and clearing down the outside edifices and shelters, at a diligent rate. Yesterday, 15th December, he burnt down the "three Oder-Mills, which "lie outside, the big suburban Tavern, also the *Ziegel-* "*Scheune* (Tile-Manufactory)," and other valuable buildings, careless of public lamentation, — fire catching the Town itself, and needing to be quenched again.* Nay, he was clear for burning down, or blowing up, the Protestant Church, indispensable sacred edifice

* *Helden-Geschichte,* i. 473-5.

which stands outside the walls: "Prussians will make a blockhouse of it!" said Wallis. A chief Protestant, Baron von Something, begged passionately for only twelve hours of respite, — to lay the case before his Prussian Majesty. Respite conceded, he and another chief Protestant had posted off accordingly; and did the next morning (Friday 16th), short way from Crossen, meet his Majesty's carriage; who graciously pulled up for a few instants, and listened to their story. "*Meine* "*Herren*, you are the first that ask a favour of me on "Silesian ground; it shall be done you!" said the King; and straightway despatched, in polite style, his written request to Wallis, engaging to make no military use whatever of said Church, "but to attack by the other side, if attack were necessary." Thus his Majesty saved the Church of Glogau; which of course was a popular act. Getting to see this Church himself a few days hence, he said, "Why, it must come down at any rate, and be rebuilt; so ugly a thing!"

Wallis is making strenuous preparation; forces the inhabitants, even the upper kinds of them, to labour day and night by relays, in his rampartings, palisadings; is for burning all the adjacent Villages, — and would have done it, had not the peasants themselves turned out in a dangerous state of mind. He has got together about 1,000 men. His powder, they say, is fifty years old; but he has eatable provender from Breslau, and means to hold out to the utmost. Readers must admit that the Austrian military, Graf von Wallis to begin with, — still more, General Browne, who is a younger man and has now the head charge, — behave well in their present forsaken condition. Wallis (Graf *Franz Wenzel* this one, not to be confounded with an older Wallis heard of in the late Turk War) is of Scotch descent, — as all these Wallises are; "came to Austria long generations ago; *Reichsgrafs* since 1612:" — Browne is of Irish; age now thirty-five, ten years younger than Wallis. Read this Note on the distinguished Browne:

"A German-Irish Gentleman, this General (ultimately "Fieldmarshal) Graf von Browne; one of those sad exiled "Irish Jacobites, or sons of Jacobites, who are fighting in "foreign armies; able and notable men several of them, and "this Browne considerably the most so. We shall meet him "repeatedly within the next eighteen years. Maximilian-"Ulysses Graf von Browne: I said he was born German; "Basel his birthplace (23d October 1705), Father also a "soldier: he must not be confounded with a contemporary "Cousin of his, who is also 'Fieldmarshal Browne,' but serves "in Russia, Governor of Riga for a long time in the coming "years. This Austrian General, Fieldmarshal Browne, will "by and by concern us somewhat; and the reader may take "note of him.

"Who the Irish Brothers Browne, the Fathers of these "Marshals Browne, were? I have looked in what Irish Peer-"ages and printed Records there were, but without the least "result. One big dropsical Book, of languid quality, called "*King James's Irish Army-List*, has multitudes of Brownes and "others, in an indistinct form; but the one Browne wanted, "the one Lacy, almost the one Lally, like the part of *Hamlet*, "are omitted. There are so many Irish in the like case with "these Brownes. A Lacy we once slightly saw or heard of; "busy in the Polish-Election time, — besieging Dantzig (in-"vesting Dantzig, that Münnich might besiege it); — that "Lacy, 'Governor of Riga,' whom the *Russian* Browne will "succeed, is also Irish: a conspicuous Russian man; and will "have a Son Lacy, conspicuous among the Austrians. Ma-"guires, Ogilvies (of the Irish stock), Lieutenants 'Fitz-"geral;' very many Irish; and there is not the least distinct "account to be had of any of them."*

* For *Browne*, see "Anonymous of Hamburg" (so I have had to label a J. F. S. *Geschichte des* &c. — in fact, History of Seven-Years War, in

Let us attend his Majesty on the next few marches towards Glogau, to see the manner of the thing a little; after which it will behove us to be much more summary, and stick by the main incidents.

March to Weichau (Saturday 17th, and stay Sunday there); to Milkau (Monday 19th); get to Herrendorf, within sight of Glogau, Dec. 22d.

Friedrich's march proceeds with speed and regularity. Strict discipline is maintained; all things paid for, damage carefully avoided: "We come, not as invasive enemies of you or of the Queen of Hungary, but as protective friends of Silesia and of her Majesty's rights there; — her Majesty once allowing us (as it is presumable she will) our own rights in this Province, no man shall meddle with hers, while we continue here." To that effect runs the little "Patent," or initiatory Proclamation, extensively handed out, and posted in public places, as was said above; and the practice is conformable.

To all men, coming with Protests or otherwise, we

---

successive volumes, done chiefly by the scissors; Leipzig and Frankfurt, 1759 et seqq.), i. 123-131 n.: elaborate Note of eight pages there; intimating withal that he, J. F. S., wrote the "*Life of Browne;*" a Book I had in vain sought for; and can now guess to consist of those same elaborate eight pages, *plus* water and lathering to the due amount. Anonymous "of Hamburg," I call my J. F. S., — having fished him out of the dust abysses in that City: a very poor take; yet worth citing sometimes, being authentic, as even the darkest Germans generally are. — For a glimpse of *Lacy* (the Elder Lacy), see Büsching, *Beytrāge*, vi. 162. — For *Wallis* (tombstone Note on Wallis), see (among others who are copious in that kind of article, and keep large *sacks* of it, in admired disorder) Anonymous Seyfarth, *Geschichte Friedrichs des Andern* (Leipzig, 1784-1788), i. 112 n.; and Anonymous, *Leben der &c. Marie Theresie* (Leipzig, 1781), 27 n.: laboriously authentic Books both; essentially *Dictionaries,* — stuffed as into a row of blind *sacks.*

perceive, the young King is politeness itself; giving clear answer, and promise which will be kept, on the above principle. Nothing angers him except that gentlemen should disbelieve, and run away. That a mansion be found deserted by its owners, is the one evil omen for such mansion. Thus, at the Schloss of Weichau (across the "Black Ochel" and the "White," muddy streams which saunter eastward towards the Oder there, nothing yet running westward for the Bober, our other limitary river), next night after Schweinitz, second night in Silesia, there was no Owner to be met with; and the look of his Majesty grew *finster* (dark); remembering what had passed yesternight, in like case, at that other Schloss from which the owner with his best portable furniture had vanished. At which Schloss, as above noticed, some disorders were committed by angry parties of the march; — doors burst open (doors standing impudently dumb to the rational proposals made them!), inferior remainders of furniture smashed into firewood, and the like, — no doubt to his Majesty's vexation. Here at Weichau stricter measures were taken: and yet difficulties, risks were not wanting; and the *Amtmann* (Steward of the place) got pulled about, and once even a stroke or two. Happily the young Herr of Weichau appeared in person on the morrow, hearing his Majesty was still there: "Papa is old; lives at another Schloss; could not wait upon your Majesty; nor, till now, could I have that honour." — "Well; lucky that you have come: stay dinner!" Which the young Count did, and drove home in the evening to reassure Papa; his Majesty continuing there another night, and the risk over.*

* *Helden-Geschichte,* i. 459.

This day, Sunday 18th, the Army rests; their first Sunday in Silesia, while the young Count pays his devoir: and here in Weichau, as elsewhere, it is in the Church, Catholic nearly always, that the Heretic Army does its devotions, safe from weather at least: such the Royal Order, they say; which is taken note of, by the Heterodox and by the Orthodox. And ever henceforth, this is the example followed; and in all places where there is no Protestant Church and the Catholics have one, the Prussian Army-Chaplain assembles his buff-belted audience in the latter: "No offence, Reverend Fathers; but there are hours for us, and hours for you; and such is the King's Order." There is regular divine-service in this Prussian Army; and even a good deal of inarticulate religion, as one may see on examining.

Country Gentlemen, Town Mayors and other civic Authorities, soon learn that on these terms they are safe with his Majesty: march after march he has interviews with such, to regulate the supplies, the necessities and accidents of the quartering of his Troops. Clear, frank, open to reasonable representation, correct to his promise; in fact, industriously conciliatory and pacificatory: such is Friedrich to all Silesian men. Provincial Authorities, who can get no instructions from Headquarters; Vienna saying nothing, Breslau nothing, and Deputy-Governor Browne being far south in Neisse, — are naturally in difficulties: How shall they act? Best not to act at all, if one can help it; and follow the Mayor of Grünberg's unsurpassable pattern! —

"These Silesians," says an Excerpt I have made, "are "still in majority Protestant; especially in this Northern por-

"tion of the Province: they have had to suffer much on that
"and other scores; and are secretly or openly in favour of the
"Prussians. Official persons, all of the Catholic creed, have
"leant heavy, not always conscious of doing it, against Pro-
"testant rights. The Jesuits, consciously enough, have been
"and are busy with them; intent to recal a Heretic Popula-
"tion, by all methods fair and unfair. We heard of
"Charles XII.'s interference, three-and-thirty years ago; and
"how the Kaiser, hard bested at that time, had to profess
"repentance and engage for complete amendment. Amend-
"ment did, for the moment, accordingly take place. Treaty
"of Westphalia in all its stipulations, with precautionary im-
"provements, was reënacted as Treaty of Altranstädt; with
"faithful intention of keeping it too, on Kaiser Joseph's part,
"who was not a superstitious man: 'Holy Father, I was too
"glad he did not demand my own conversion to the Protestant
"Heresy, bested as I am, — with Louis Quatorze and Com-
"pany upon the neck of me!' Some improvement of per-
"formance, very marked at first, did ensue upon this Altran-
"städt Treaty. But the sternly accurate Karl of Sweden
"soon disappeared from the scene; Kaiser Joseph of Austria
"soon disappeared; and his Brother, Karl VI., was a much
"more orthodox person.

"The Austrian Government, and Kaiser Karl's in parti-
"cular, is not to be called an intentionally unjust one; the
"contrary, I rather find; but it is, beyond others, ponderous;
"based broad on such multiplex formalities, old habitudes;
"and *gravitation* has a great power over it. In brief, Official
"human nature, with the best of Kaisers atop, flagitated con-
"tinually by Jesuit Confessors, does throw its weight on a
"certain side: — the sad fact is, in a few years the brightness
"of that Altranstädt improvement began to wax dim; and
"now, under long Jesuit manipulation, Silesian things are
"nearly at their old pass; and the patience of men is heavily
"laden. To see your Chapel made a Soldiers' Barrack, your
"Protestant School become a Jesuit one — Men did not then
"think of revolting under injuries; but the poor Silesian
"weaver, trudging twenty miles for his Sunday sermon; and
"perceiving that, unless their Mother could teach the art of
"reading, his boys, except under soul's peril, would now

"never learn it: such a Silesian could not want for reflections.
"Voiceless, hopeless, but heavy; and dwelling secretly, as
"under nightmare, in a million hearts. Austrian Officiality,
"wilfully unjust, or not wilfully so, is admitted to be in a
"most heavy-footed condition; can administer nothing well.
"Good Government in any kind is not known here: Possibly
"the Prussian will be better; who can say?

"The secret joy of these populations, as Friedrich ad-
"vances among them, becomes more and more a manifest
"one. Catholic Officials do not venture on any definite hope,
"or definite balance of hope and fear; but adopt the Mayor
"of Grünberg's course, and study to be passive and silent.
"The Jesuit-Priest kind are clear in their minds for Austria;
"but think, Perhaps Prussia itself will not prove very tyran-
"nous? At all events, be silent; it is unsafe to stir. We
"notice generally, it is only in the Southern or Mountain re-
"gions of Silesia, where the Catholics are in majority, that
"the population is not ardently on the Prussian side. Passive,
"if they are on the other side; accurately passive at lowest,
"this it is prescribed all prudent men to be."

On the 18th, while divine service went on at Weichau, there was at Breslau another phenomenon observable. Provincial Government in Breslau had, at length, after intense study, and across such difficulties as we have no idea of, got its "Patent," or carefully worded Protestation against Prussia, brought to paper; and does, this day, with considerable solemnity, affix it to the Rathhaus door there, for the perusal of mankind; despatching a Copy for his Prussian Majesty withal, by two Messengers of dignity. It has needed courage screwed to the sticking-place to venture on such a step, without instruction from Headquarters; and the utmost powers of the Official mind have been taxed to couch this Document in language politely ambiguous, and yet strong enough; — too strong, some of us now think it. In any case, here it now is; Provincial Government's bolt, so to speak, is shot. The affixing took place under dark weather-symptoms; actual outburst of thunder and rain at the moment, not to speak of the other surer omens. So that, to the common mind at Breslau, it did not seem there would much fruit come of this difficult performance. Breslau is secretly a much agitated City; and Prussian Hussar Parties, shooting forth to great distances ahead, were, this day for the first time, observed within sight of it.

And on the same Sunday we remark further, what is still more important: Herr von Gotter, Friedrich's special Envoy to Vienna, has his first interview with the Queen of Hungary, or with Grand-Duke Franz the Queen's Husband and Co-Regent; and presents there, from Friedrich's own hand, written we remember when, brief distinct Note of his Prussian Majesty's actual Proposals and real meaning in regard to this Silesian Affair. Proposals anxiously conciliatory in tone, but the heavy purport of which is known to us: Gotter had been despatched, time enough, with these Proposals (written above a month ago); but was instructed not to arrive with them, till after the actual entrance into Silesia. And now the response to them is —? As good as nothing; perhaps worse. Let that suffice us at present. Readers, on march for Glogau, would grudge to pause over State-papers, though we shall have to read this of Friedrich's at some freer moment.

Monday 19th, before daybreak, the Army is astir again, simultaneously wending forward; spread over wide areas, like a vast cloud (potential thunder in it) steadily advancing on the winds. Length of the Army, artistically portioned out, may be ten or fifteen miles, breadth already more, and growing more; Schwerin always on the right or western wing, close by the Bober River as yet, through Naumburg and the Towns on that side, — Liegnitz and other important Towns lying ahead for Schwerin, still farther apart from the main Body, were Glogau once settled.

So that the march is in Two Columns; Schwerin, with the westernmost small column, intending towards Liegnitz, and thence ever farther southward, with his right leaning on the high lands which rise more and more into mountains as you advance. Friedrich himself commands the other column, has his left upon the Oder, in a country mounting continually towards the South, but with less irregularity of level, and generally flat as yet. From beginning to end, the entire field of march lies between the Oder and its tributary the Bober; climbing slowly towards the sources of both. Which two rivers, as the reader may observe, form here a rectangular or trapezoidal space, ever widening as we go southward. Both rivers, coming from the Giant Mountains, hasten directly north; but Oder, bulging out easterly in his sandy course, is obliged to turn fairly westward again; and at Glogau, and a good space farther, flows in that direction; — till once Bober strikes in, almost at right angles, carrying Oder with *him*, though he is but a branch, straight northward again. Northward, but ever slower, to the swollen Pommern regions, and sluggish exit into the Baltic there.

One of the worst features is the state of the weather. On Sunday, at Breslau, we noticed thunder bursting out on an important occasion; "ominous," some men thought; — omen, for one thing, that the weather was breaking. At Weichau, that same day, rain began, — the young Herr of Weichau, driving home to Papa from dinner with Majesty, would get his share of it;— and on Monday 19th, there was such a pour of rain as kept most wayfarers, though it could not the Prussian Army, within doors. Rain in plunges, fallen. and falling, through that blessed day; making roads into mere rivers of mud. The Prussian hosts marched on, all the same. Headquarters, with the Van of the wet Army, that night, were at Milkau; — from which place we have a Note of Friedrich's for Friend Jordan, perhaps producible by and by. His Majesty lodged in some opulent Jesuit Establishment there. And indeed he continued there, not idle, under shelter, for a couple of days. The Jesuits, by their two head men, had welcomed him with their choicest smiles; to whom the King was very gracious, asking the two to dinner as usual, and styling them "Your Reverence." Willing to ingratiate himself with persons of interest in this Country; and likes talk, even with Jesuits of discernment.

On the morrow (20th), came to him, here at Milkau, — probably from some near stage, for the rain was pouring worse than ever, — that Breslau "Patent," or strongish Protestation, by its two Messengers of dignity. The King looked over it, "without visible anger" or change of countenance; "handed it," we expressly see, "to a Page to reposit" in the proper waste-basket; — spoke politely to the two gentlemen; asked each or one of them, "Are you of the Ober-Amt at Breslau, then?" — using the style of *Er* (He). — "No, your Majesty;

we are only of the Land-Stände" (Provincial Parliament, such as it is). "Upon which" (do you mark!) "his Majesty became still more polite; asked them to "dinner, and used the style of *Sie*." For their *Patent*, now lying safe in its waste-basket, he gave them signed receipt; no other answer.

Rain still heavier, rain as of Noah, continued through this Tuesday, and for days afterwards: but the Prussian hosts, hastening towards Glogau, marched still on. This Tuesday's march, for the rearward of the Army, 10,000 foot, and 2,000 horse; march of ten hours long, from Weichau to the hamlet Milkau (where his Majesty sits busy and affable), — is thought to be the wettest on record. Waters all out, bridges down, the Country one wild lake of eddying mud. Up to the knee for many miles together; up to the middle for long spaces; sometimes even up to the chin or deeper, where your bridge was washed away. The Prussians marched through it, as if they had been slate or iron. Rank and file, nobody quitted his rank, nobody looked sour in the face; they took the pouring of the skies, and the red seas of terrestrial liquid, as matters that must be; cheered one another with jocosities, with choral snatches (tobacco, I consider, would not burn); and swashed unweariedly forward. Ten hours some of them were out, their march being twenty or twenty-five miles; ten to fifteen was the average distance come. Nor, singular to say, did any loss occur; except of *almost* one poor Army-Chaplain, and altogether of one poor Soldier's Wife; — sank dangerously both of them, beyond redemption she, taking the wrong side of some bridge-parapet. Poor Soldier's Wife, she is not named to me at all; and has no history save this, and that "she was of the regiment Bredow." But I perceive she washed herself away in a World-Transaction; and there was one rough Bredower, who probably sat sad that night on getting to quarters. His Majesty surveyed the damp battalions on the morrow (21st), not without sympathy, not without satisfaction; allowed them a rest-day here at Milkau, to get dry and bright again; and gave them "fifteen thalers a company," which is about nine-pence apiece, with some words of praise.*

Next day, Thursday 22d, his Majesty and they marched on to Herrendorf; which is only five miles from Glogau, and near enough for Headquarters, in the now humour of the place. Wallis has his messenger at Herrendorf, "Sorry to warn your Majesty, That if there be the least hostility committed, I shall have to resist it to the utmost." Headquarters continue six days at Herrendorf, Army (main body, or left Column, of the Army) cantoned all round, till we consider what to do.

As to the right Column, or Schwerin's Division, that, after a rest-day or two, gathers itself into more complete separation here, tucking-in its eastern skirts; and gets on march again, by its own route. Steadily southward; — and from Liegnitz, and the upland Countries, there will be news of Schwerin and it before long. Rain ending, there ensued a ringing frost; — not favourable for Siege-operations on Glogau: — and Silesia became all of flinty glass, with white peak to the South-west, whither Schwerin is gone.

* *Helden-Geschichte,* i. 482.

CHAPTER III.

PROBLEM OF GLOGAU.

FRIEDRICH was over from Herrendorf with the first daylight, "reconnoitring Glogau, and rode up to the very glacis;" scanning it on all sides.* Since Wallis is so resolute, here is an intricate little problem for Friedrich, with plenty of corollaries and conditions hanging to it. Shall we besiege Glogau, then? We have no siege-cannon here. Time presses, Breslau and all things in such crisis; and it will take time. By what methods *could* Glogau be besieged? — Readers can consider what a blind many-threaded coil of things, heaping itself here in wide welters round Glogau, and straggling to the world's end, Friedrich has on hand: probably those six days, of Headquarters at Herrendorf, were the busiest he had yet had.

One thing is evident, there ought to be siege-cannon got straightway; and, still more immediate, the right posts and battering-places should be ready against its coming. — "Let the Young Dessauer with that Rearguard, or Reserve of 10,000, which is now at Crossen, come up and assist here," orders Friedrich; "and let him be swift, for the hours are pregnant!" On farther reflexion, perhaps on new rumours from Breslau, Friedrich perceives that there can be no besieging of Glogau at this point of time; that the Reserve, Half of the Reserve, must be left to "mask" it;

* *Helden-Geschichte,* i. 484.

to hold it in strict blockade, with starvation daily advancing as an ally to us, and with capture by bombarding possible when we like. That is the ultimate decision; — arrived at through a welter of dubieties, counter-poisings and perilous considerations, which we now take no account of. A most busy week; Friedrich incessantly in motion, now here now there; and a great deal of heavy work got well and rapidly done. The details of which, in these exuberant Manuscripts, would but weary the reader. Choosing of the proper posts and battering-places (post "on the other side of the River," "on this side of it," "on the Island in the middle of it"), and obstinate entrenching and preparing of the same in spite of frost; "wooden bridge built" farther up; with "regulation of the river-boats, the Polish Ferry," and much else: all this we omit; and will glance only at one pregnant point, by way of sample:

* * "Most indispensable of all, the King has to provide
"Subsistences; — and enters now upon the new plan, which
"will have to be followed henceforth. The Provincial Chief-
"men (*Landes-Ältesten*, Land's-*Eldests*, their title) are sum-
"moned, from nine or ten Circles which are likely to be inter-
"ested: they appear punctually, and in numbers, — lest con-
"tumacy worsen the inevitable. King dines them, to start
"with; as many as 'ninety-five covers,' — day not given, but
"probably one of the first in Herrendorf; not Christmas itself,
"one hopes!

"Dinner done, the ninety-five Land's-Eldest are instructed
"by proper parties, What the Infantry's ration is, in meat, in
"bread, exact to the ounce; what the Cavalry's is, and that
"of the Cavalry's Horse. Tabular statement, succinct, cor-
"rect, clear to the simplest capacity, shows what quotities of
"men on foot, and of men on horseback, or men with draught-
"cattle, will march through their respective Circles; Land's-
"Eldests conclude what amount of meal and butcher's meat it

"will be indispensable to have in readiness;—what Land's-
"Eldest can deny the fact? These Papers still exist, at least
"the long-winded Summary of them does: and I own the
"reading of it far less insupportable than that of the moun-
"tains of Proclamatory, Manifesto and Diplomatic matter.
"Nay it leaves a certain wholesome impression on the mind,
"as of business thoroughly well done; and a matter, capable
"if left in the chaotic state, of running to all manner of depths
"and heights, compendiously forced to become cosmic in this
"manner.

"These Land's-Eldest undertake, in a mildly resigned or
"even hopeful humour. They will manage as required, in
"their own Circles; will communicate with the Circles farther
"on; and everywhere the due proviants, prestations, further-
"ances, shall be got together by fair apportionment on the
"Silesian Community, and be punctually ready as the Army
"advances. Book-keeping there is to be, legible record of
"everything; on all hands 'quittance' for everything furn-
"ished: and a time is coming, when such quittance, pre-
"sented by any Silesian man, will be counted money paid by
"him, and remitted at the next tax-day, or otherwise made
"good. Which promise also was accurately kept, the hoped-
"for time having come. It must be owned the Prussian Army
"understands business; and, with brevity, reduces to a minimum
"its own trouble, and that of other people, non-fighters, who
"have to do with it. Non-fighters, I say; to fighters we hope it
"will give a respectable maximum of trouble when applied to!"*

The Gotter Negotiation at Vienna, which we saw
begin there that wet Sunday, is now fast ending, as
good as ended; without result except of a negative
kind. Gotter's Proposals, — would the reader wish to
hear these Proposals, which were so intensely interesting at one time? They are fivefold; given with great
brevity by Friedrich, by us with still greater:

1º. "Will fling myself heartily into the Austrian scale, and
"endeavour for the interest of Austria in this Pragmatic matter,
"with my whole strength against every comer.

* *Helden-Geschichte*, i. 492-499.

2º. "Will make treaty with Vienna, with Russia and the "Sea-Powers, to that effect.

3º. "Will help by vote, and with whole amount of interest "will endeavour, to have Grand-Duke Franz, the Queen's Hus-"band, chosen Kaiser; and to maintain such choice against all "and sundry. Feel myself strong enough to accomplish this "result; and may, without exaggeration, venture to say it shall "be done.

4º. "To help the Court of Vienna in getting its affairs into "good order and fencible condition, — will present to it, on the "shortest notice, Two Million Gulden (200,000*l.*) ready "money." — Infinitely welcome this Fourth Proposition; and indeed all the other Three are welcome: but they are saddled with a final condition, which pulls down all again. This, which is studiously worded, politely evasive in phrase, and would fain keep old controversies asleep, though in substance it is so fatally distinct, — we give in the King's own words:

5º. "For such essential services as those to which I bind "myself by the above very onerous conditions, I naturally re-"quire a proportionate recompense; some suitable assurance, "as indemnity for all the dangers I risk, and for the part (*rôle*) "I am ready to play: in short, I require hereby the entire and "complete cession of all Silesia, as reward for my labours and "dangers which I take upon myself in this course now to be "entered upon for the preservation and renown of the House "of Austria;" — Silesia all and whole; and we say nothing of our "rights" to it; politely evasive to her Hungarian Majesty, though in substance we are so fatally distinct.*

These were Friedrich's Proposals; written down with his own hand at Reinsberg, five or six weeks ago (November 17th is the date of it); in what mood, and how wrought upon by Schwerin and Podewils, we saw above. Gotter has fulfilled his instructions 'in regard to this important little Document; and now the effect of it is —? — Gotter can report no good effect what-

* Preuss, *Thronbesteigung*, p. 451; "from Olenschlager, *Geschichte des Interregni*" (Frankfurt, 1746), "i. 134."

ever. "Be cautious," Friedrich instructs him farther; "modify that Fifth Proposal; I will take less than the whole, 'if attention is paid to my just claims on Schlesien.'" To that effect writes Friedrich once or twice. But it is to no purpose; nor can Gotter, with all his industry, report other than worse and worse. Nay, he reports before long, not refusal only, but refusal with mockery: "How strange that his Prussian Majesty, "whose official post in Germany, as Kur-Brandenburg "and Kaiser's Chamberlain, has been to present ewer "and towel to the House of Austria, should now set up "for prescribing rules to it!" A piece of wit, which could not but provoke Friedrich; and warn him that negotiation on this matter might as well terminate. Such had been his own thought, from the first; but in compliance with Schwerin and Podewils he was willing to try.

Better for Maria Theresa, and for all the world how much better, could she have accepted this Fifth Proposition! But how could she, — the high Imperial Lady, keystone of Europe, though by accident with only a few pounds of ready money at present? Twenty years of bitter fighting, and agony to herself and all the world, were necessary first; a new Fact of Nature having turned up, a new European Kingdom with real King to it; *not* recognisable as such, by the young Queen of Hungary or by any other person, till it do its proofs.

What Berlin is saying; what Friedrich is thinking.

What Friedrich's own humour is, what Friedrich's own inner man is saying to him, while all the world so babbles about his Silesian Adventure? Of this too there are, though in diluted state, some glimmerings to be had, — chiefly in the Correspondence with Jordan.

Ingenious Jordan, Inspector of the Poor at Berlin, — his thousand old women at their wheels humming pleasantly in the background of our imaginations, though he says nothing of that, — writes twice a week to his Majesty: pleasant gossipy Letters, with an easy respectfulness not going into sycophancy anywhere; which keep the campaigning King well abreast of the Berlin news and rumours: something like the essence of an Old Newspaper; not without worth in our present Enterprise. One specimen, if we had room!

Jordan to the King (successively from Berlin — somewhat abridged).

No. 1. "*Berlin*, 14*th December* 1740" (day after his Majesty left). "Everybody here is on tiptoe for the Event; of which "both origin and end are a riddle to the most. I am charmed "to see a part of your Majesty's Dominions in a state of Pyr- "rhonism; the disease is epidemical here at present. Those "who, in the style of theologians, consider themselves en- "titled to be certain, maintain That your Majesty is expected "with religious impatience by the Protestants, and that the "Catholics hope to see themselves delivered from a multitude "of imposts which cruelly tear up the beautiful bosom of their "Church. You cannot but succeed in your valiant and stoical "Enterprise, since both religion and worldly interest rank "themselves under your flag.

"Wallis," Austrian Commandant in Glogau, "they say, "has punished a Silesian Heretic of enthusiastic turn, as "blasphemer, for announcing that a new Messiah is just "coming. I have a taste for that kind of martyrdom. — "Critical persons consider the present step as directly op- "posed to certain maxims in the *Anti-Macchiavel*.

"The word *Manifesto*" — (your Majesty's little *Patent* on

entering Silesia, which no reader shall be troubled with at present) — "is the burden of every conversation. Rumour "goes, there is a short Piece of the kind to come out to-day, by "way of preface to a large complete exposition, which a "certain Jurisconsult is now busy with. People crowd to the "Bookshops for it, as if looking out for a celestial pheno-"menon that had been predicted. — This is the beginning of "my Gazette; can only come out twice a week, owing to the "arrangement of the Posts. Friday, the day your Majesty "crosses into Silesia, I shall spend in prayer and devotional "exercises: Astronomers pretend that Mars will that day "enter" — no matter what.

Note, The above Manifesto rumour is correct; Jurisconsult is ponderous Herr Ludwig, Kanzler (Chancellor) of Halle University, monster of law learning, — who has money also, and had to help once with a House in Berlin for one Nüssler, a son-in-law of his, transiently known to us; — ponderous Ludwig, matchless or difficult to match in learning of this kind, will write ample enough Deductions (which lie in print still, to the extent of tons weight), and explain the *Erbverbrüderung* and violence done upon it, so that he who runs may read. Postpone him to a calmer time.

No. 2. "*Berlin, Saturday,* 17*th December.*' Manifesto has "appeared," — can be seen, under thick strata of cobwebs, in many Books;* is not worth reading now: Incontestable rights which our House has for ages had on Schlesien, and which doubtless the Hungarian Majesty will recognise; not the slightest injury intended, far indeed from that; and so on! — "people are surprised at its brevity; and, studying it "as theologians do a passage of Scripture, can make almost "nothing of it. Clear as crystal, says one; dextrously obscure "by design, says another.

"Rumour that the Grand-Duke of Lorraine," Maria Theresa's Husband, "was at Reinsberg, incognito lately," — Grand-Duke a concerting party, think people looking into the thing with strong spectacles on their nose! "M. de "Beauvau" (French Ambassador Extraordinary, to whom the aces were promised if they came) "said one thing that sur-

* In *Helden-Geschichte,* 1. 448, 453 (what Jordan now alludes to); *ib.* 559-592 ("Deduction" itself, Ludwig in all his strength, some three weeks hence); in *Olenschlager* (doubtless); in &c. &c.

"prised me: 'What put the King on taking this step, I do not know; but perhaps it is not such a bad one.' Surprising news that the Elector of Saxony, King of Poland, is fallen into inconsolable remorse for changing his religion" (to Papistry, on Papa's hest, many long years ago); "and that it is not to the Pope, but to the King of Prussia, that he opens his heart to steady his staggering orthodoxy." Very astonishing to Jordan. "One thing is certain, all Paris rings with your Majesty's change of religion" (over to Catholicism, say those astonishing people, first conjurors of the universe)!

No. 3. "*Berlin, 20th December.* M. de Beauvau," French Ambassador, "is gone. Ended, yesterday, his survey of the "Cabinet of Medals; charmed with the same: charmed too, as the public is, with the rich present he has got from said Cabinet" (coronation medal or medals in gold, I could guess): "people say the King of France's Medal given to our M. de Camas is nothing to it.

"Rumour of alliance between your Majesty and France with Sweden," — premature rumour. Item "Queen of Hungary dead in child-birth;" — ditto with still more emphasis! "The day before yesterday, in all churches, was prayer to Heaven for success to your Majesty's arms; interest of the Protestant religion being the one cause of the War, or the only one assigned by the reverend gentlemen. At sound of these words, the zeal of the people kindles: 'Bless God for raising such a Defender! Who dared suspect our King's indifference to Protestantism?'"

A right clever thing this last (*O le beau coup d'état*)! exclaims Jordan, — though it is not clever or the contrary, not being dramatically prearranged, as Jordan exults to think. Jordan, though there are dregs of old devotion lying asleep in him, which will start into new activity when stirred again, is for the present a very unbelieving little gentleman, I can perceive. — This is the substance of public rumour at Berlin for one week. Friedrich answers:

"*To M. Jordan, at Berlin.*

"*Quarter at Milkau, towards Glogau, 19th December* 1740" (comfortable Jesuit-Establishment at Milkau, Friedrich just got in, out of the rain). — "Seigneur Jordan, thy Letter has

"given me a deal of pleasure, in regard to all these talkings
"thou reportest. Tomorrow" (not tomorrow, nor next day;
wet troops need a rest) "I arrive at our last station this side
"Glogau, which place I hope to get in a few days. All
"favours my designs; and I hope to return to Berlin, after
"executing them gloriously and in a way to be content with.
"Let the ignorant and the envious talk; it is not they that
"shall ever serve as loadstar to my designs; not they, but
"Glory" (*la Gloire;* Fame, depending not on them): "with
"the love of that I am penetrated more than ever; my troops
"have their hearts big with it, and I answer to thee for suc-
"cess. Adieu, dear Jordan. Write me all the ill that the
"public says of thy Friend, and be persuaded that I love and
"will esteem thee always." — F.

Jordan to the King.

No. 4. "*Berlin*, 24*th December.* Your Majesty's Letter
"fills me with joy and contentment. The Town declared
"your Majesty to be already in Breslau; founding on some
"Letter to a Merchant here. Ever since they think of your
"Majesty acting for Protestantism, they make you step along
"with strides of Achilles to the ends of Silesia. — Foreign
"Courts are all rating their Ambassadors here for not finding
"you out.

"Wolf," his negotiations concluded at last, "has entered
"Halle almost like the triumphant Entry to Jerusalem. A con-
"course of pedants escorted him to his house. Lange" (his
old enemy, who accused him of Atheism and other things)
"has called to see him, and loaded him with civilities, to the
"astonishment of the old Orthodox." There let him rest, well
buttoned in gaiters, and avoiding to mount stairs. * *
"Madame de Roucoulle has sent me the three objects ad-
"joined, for your Majesty's behoof," — woollen achievements,
done by the needle, good against the winter weather for one
she nursed. The good old soul. Enough now of Jordan.*

Voltaire, who left Berlin 2d or 3d December, seems
to have been stopt by overflow of rivers about Cleve,
then to have taken boat; and is, about this very time,

* *Œuvres de Frédéric,* xvii. 75-78.

writing to Friedrich "from a vessel on the Coasts of Zealand, where I am driven mad." (Intends, privately, for Paris before long, to get his *Mahomet* acted, if possible.) To Voltaire, here is a Note coming!

King to M. de Voltaire (at Brussels, if once got thither).

"*Quarter of Herrendorf in Silesia,* 23d *December* 1740. "My dear Voltaire, — I have received two of your Letters; "but could not answer sooner; I am like Charles Twelfth's "Chess-King, who was always kept on the move. For a fort-"night past, we have been continually afoot and under way, "in such weather as you never saw.

"I am too tired to reply to your charming Verses; and "shivering too much with cold to taste all the charm of them: "but that will come round again. Do not ask poetry from a "man who is actually doing the work of a wagoner, and some-"times even of a wagoner stuck in the mud. Would you like "to know my way of life? We march from seven in the morn-"ing till four in the afternoon. I dine then; afterwards I "work, I receive tiresome visits; with these comes a detail of "insipid matters of business. 'Tis wrongheaded men, puncti-"liously difficult, who are to be set right; heads too hot "which must be restrained, idle fellows that must be urged, "impatient men that must be rendered docile, plunderers to "restrain within the bounds of equity, babblers to hear bab-"bling, dumb people to keep in talk: in fine, one has to drink "with those that like it, to eat with those that are hungry; "one has to become a Jew with Jews, a Pagan with Pagans.

"Such are my occupations; — which I would willingly "make over to another, if the Phantom they call Fame "(*Gloire*) did not rise on me too often. In truth it is a great "folly, but a folly difficult to cast away when once you are "smitten by it." (Phantom of *Gloire* somewhat rampant in those first weeks; let us see whether it will not lay itself again, for evermore, before long!)

"Adieu, my dear Voltaire; may Heaven preserve from "misfortune the man I should so like to sup with at night, after "fighting in the morning! The Swan of Padua" (Algarotti, with his big hook-nose and dusky solemnly greedy counte-nance) "is going, I think, to Paris, to profit by my absence;

"the Philosopher Geometer" (big Maupertuis, in red wig and yellow frizzles, vainest of human kind) "is squaring curves; poor little Jordan" (with the kindly hazel eyes, and pen that pleasantly gossips to us) "is doing nothing, or probably some-"thing near it. Adieu once more, dear Voltaire; do not "forget the absent who love you. — Fédéric."*

Schwerin at Liegnitz; Friedrich hushes up the Glogau Problem, and starts with his best speed for Breslau.

Meanwhile, on the Western road, and along the foot of the snowy peaks over yonder, Schwerin with the small Right column is going prosperously forwards. Two columns always, as the reader recollects, — two parallel military currents, flowing steadily on, shooting out estafettes, or horse-parties, on the right and left; steadily submerging all Silesia as they flow forward. Left column or current is in slight pause at Glogau here; but will directly be abreast again. On Tuesday 27th, Schwerin is within wind of Liegnitz; on Wednesday morning, while the fires are hardly lighted, or the smoke of Liegnitz risen among the Hills, Schwerin has done his feat with the usual deftness: Prussian grenadiers came softly on the sentry, softly as a dream; but with sudden levelling of bayonets, sudden beckoning. "To your Guardhouse!" — and there, turn the key upon his poor company and him. Whereupon the whole Prussian column marches in; tramp tramp, without music, through the streets: in the Marketplace they fold themselves into a ranked mass, and explode into wind-harmony and rolling of drums. Liegnitz, mostly in nightcap, looks cautiously out of window: it is a deed done, *ihr Herren;* Liegnitz ours, better late than never; and after so many years, the King has his

* *Œuvres de Frédéric,* xxii. 57.

own again. Schwerin is sumptuously lodged in the Jesuits' Palace: Liegnitz, essentially a Protestant Town, has many thoughts upon this event, but as yet will be stingy of speaking them.

Thus is Liegnitz managed. A pleasant Town, amid pleasant hills on the rocky Katzbach; of which swift stream, and other towns and passes on it, we shall yet hear more. Population, silently industrious in weaving and otherwise, is now above 14,000; was then perhaps about half that number. Patiently inarticulate, by no means bright in speech or sentiment; a much-enduring, steady-going, frugal, pious and very desirable people.

The situation of Breslau, all this while, is very critical. Much bottled emotion in the place; no Austrian Garrison admissible; Authorities dare not again propose such a thing, though Browne is turning every stone for it, — lest the emotion burst bottle, and take fire. I have dim account that Browne has been there, has got 300 Austrian dragoons into the Dom Insel (*Cathedral Island;* "Not in the City, you perceive!" says General Browne: "no, separated by the Oder, on both sides, from the rest of the City; that stately mass of edifices, and good military post"); — and had hoped to get the suburbs burnt, after all. But the bottled emotion was too dangerous. For, underground, there are *Anti-*Brownes: one especially; a certain busy Deblin, Shoemaker by craft, whom Friedrich speaks of, but gives no name to; this zealous Cordwainer, Deblin, and he is not the only individual of like humour, operates on the guild-brothers and lower populations;*
things seem to be looking worse and worse for the

* Preuss, *Thronbesteigung,* p. 469; *Œuvres de Frédéric,* ii. 61.

Authorities, in spite of General Browne and his activities and dragoons.

What the issue will be? Judge if Friedrich wished the Young Dessauer come! Friedrich's Hussar parties (or Schwerin's, instructed by Friedrich) go to look if the Breslau suburbs are burnt. Far from it, if Friedrich knew; — the suburbs merely sit quaking at such a proposal, and wish the Prussians were here. "But there is time ahead of us," said everybody at Breslau; "Glogau will take some sieging!" Browne, in the course of a day or two, — guessing, I almost think, that Glogau was not to be besieged, — ranked his 300 Austrian dragoons, and rode away; sending the Austrian State-Papers, in half a score of wagons, ahead of him. "Archives of Breslau!" cried the general population, at sight of these wagons; and largely turned out, with emotion again like to unbottle itself. "Mere Tax-Ledgers, and records of the Government Offices; come and convince yourselves!" answered the Authorities. And the ten wagons went on; calling at Ohlau and Brieg, for farther lading of the like kind. Which wagons the Prussian light horse chased, but could not catch. On to Mähren went these Archive-wagons; to Brünn, far over the Giant Mountains; — did not come back for a long while, nor to their former Proprietor at all!

Tuesday 27th, Leopold the Young Dessauer does finally arrive, with his Reserve, at Glogau: never man more welcome; such a fermentation going on at Breslau, — known to Friedrich, and what it will issue in, if he delay, not known. With despatch, Leopold is put into his charge; posts all yielded to him; orders given,

— blockade to be strictness itself, but no fighting if avoidable; "starvation will soon do it, two months at most," hopes Friedrich, too sanguine as it proved: — and with earliest daylight on the 28th, Friedrich's Army, Friedrich himself in the van as usual, is on march again; at its best speed for Breslau. Read this Note for Jordan:

Friedrich to M. Jordan, at Berlin.

"*Herrendorf*, 27*th Dec.* 1740. Sieur Jordan, — I march "to-morrow for Breslau; and shall be there in four days," — (three, it happened; there rising, as would seem, new reason for haste). "You Berliners" (of the 24th last) "have a spirit "of prophecy, which goes beyond me. In fine, I go my road; "and thou wilt shortly see Silesia ranked in the list of our "Provinces. Adieu; this is all I have time to tell thee. Reli-"gion" (Silesian Protestantism, and Breslau's Cordwainer), "religion and our brave soldiers will do the rest.

"Tell Maupertuis I grant those Pensions he proposes for "his Academicians; and that I hope to find good subjects for "that dignity in the Country where I am, withal. Give him "my compliments. — FÉDÉRIC."

The march was of the swiftest, — swifter even than had been expected; — which, as Silesia is all ringing glass, becomes more achievable than lately. But certain regiments outdid themselves in marching; "in three marches, near upon seventy miles," with their baggage jingling in due proximity. Through Gläsersdorf, thence through Parchwitz, Neumarkt, Lissa, places that will be better known to us; — on Saturday, last night of the Year, his Majesty lodged at a Schloss called Pilsnitz, five miles to west of Breslau; and van-ward regiments, a good few, quartered in the Western and Southern suburbs of Breslau itself; suburbs decidedly glad to see them, and escape conflagration. The Town-gates are hermetically shut; — plenty of emotion bottled in the 100,000 hearts within. The sentries on the walls presented arms; nay, it is affirmed, some could not help exclaiming, "*Willkommen, Ihr Lieben Herrn* (Welcome, dear Sirs)!"*

Colonel Posadowsky (active Horse Colonel whom we have seen before, who perhaps has been in Breslau before) left orders "at the Scultet Garden-House," that all must be ready and the rooms heated, his Majesty intending to arrive here, early on the morrow. Which happened accordingly; Majesty alighting duly at said Garden-House, near by the Schweidnitz Gate, — I fancy almost before break of day.

* *Helden-Geschichte*, 1. 534.

CHAPTER IV.

BRESLAU UNDER SOFT PRESSURE.

THE issue of this Breslau transaction is known, or could be stated in few words; nor is the manner of it such as would, for Breslau's sake, deserve many. But we are looking into Friedrich, wish to know his manners and aspects; and here, ready to our hand, a Paper turns up, compiled by an exact person with better leisure than ours, minutely detailing every part of the affair. This Paper, after the question, Burn or insert? is to have the lot of appearing here, with what abridgments are possible:

"*Sunday*, 1*st January* 1741. The King having established "himself in Herrn Scultet's Garden-House, not far from the "Schweidnitz Gate, there began a delicate and great opera-"tion. The Prussians, in a soft cautious manner, in the gray "of the morning, push out their sentries towards the Three "Gates on this side of the Oder; seize any 'Excise House,' or "the like, that may be fit for a post; and softly put 'twenty "grenadiers' in it. All this before sunrise. Breslau is rigidly "shut; Breslau thought always it could stand upon its guard, "if attacked;—is now, in Official quarters, dismally uncertain "if it can; general population becoming certain that it cannot, "and waiting anxious on the development of this grand "drama.

"About 7 A.M. a Prussian subaltern advancing within cry "of the Schweidnitz Gate, requests of the Town-guard there, "To send him out a Town-Officer. Town-Officer appears; is "informed, 'That Colonels Posadowsky and Borck, Com-"missioners or plenipotentiary Messengers from his Prussian "Majesty, desire admittance to the Chief Magistrate of Bres-

"'lau, for the purpose of signifying what his Prussian Majesty's "'instructions are.' Town Officer bows, and goes upon his "'errand. Town-Officer is some considerable time before he "'can return; City Authorities being, as we know, various, "'partly Imperial, partly Civic; elderly; and some of them "'gone to church, — for matins, or to be out of the way. "'However, he does at last return; admits the two Colonels, "'and escorts them honourably, to the Chief *Raths-Syndic* "'(Lord-Mayor) old Herr von Gutzmar's; where the poor old "''President of the *Ober-Amt*' (Von Schaffgotsch the name of "'this latter) is likewise in attendance.

"'Prussian Majesty's proposals are of the mildest sort: "''Nothing demanded of Breslau but the plainly indispensable "'and indisputable, That Prussia be in it what Austria has "'been. In all else, *status quo*. Strict neutrality to Breslau, "'respect for its privileges as a Free City of the Reich; pro-"'tection to all its rights and privileges whatsoever. Shall be "'guarded by its own Garrison; no Prussian soldier to enter "'except with side-arms; only 30 guards for the King's person, "'who will visit the City for a few days; — intends to form a "'Magazine, with guard of 1,000 men, but only outside the "'City: no requisitions; ready money for everything. Chief "'Syndic Gutzmar and President Schaffgotsch shall consider "'these points.'* Syndic and President answer, Surely! "'Cannot, however, decide till they have assembled the Town-"'Rath; the two Herren Colonels will please to be guests of "'Breslau, and lodge in the City till then.

"And they lodged, accordingly, in the '*Grosse Ring*' "(called also *Salz-Ring*, big Central Square, where the Rath-"haus is); and they made and received visits, — visited "especially the Chief President's Office, the Ober-Amt, and "signified there, that his Prussian Majesty's expectation was, "They would give some account of that rather high Procla-"mation or 'Patent' they had published against him the other "day, amid thunder and lightning here, and what they now "thought would be expedient upon it? All in grave official "terms, but of such a purport as was not exhilarating to every-"body in those Ober-Amt localities.

"*Monday morning*, 2d *January*. The Rath is assembled; "and consults, — consults at great length. *Rath*-House and

* *Helden-Geschichte*, 1. 537.

2d Jan. 1741.

Syndic Gutzmar, 'in such crisis, would fain have advice
"from *Amt*-House or President Schaffgotsch; but can get
"none: considerable coming and going between them: at
"length, about 3 in the afternoon, the Treaty is got drawn
"up; is signed by the due Breslau hands, and by the two
"Prussian Colonels,— which latter ride out with it, about 4 of
"the clock; victorious after thirty hours. Straight towards
"the Scultet Garden ride they; Town-guard presenting Arms,
"at the Schweidnitz Gate; nay Town-band breaking out into
"music, which is never done but to Ambassadors and high
"people. By thirty hours of steady soft pressure, they have
"brought it thus far.

"Friedrich had waited patiently all Sunday, keeping
"steady guard at the Gates; but on Monday, naturally, the
"thirty hours began to hang heavy: at all events, he perceived
"that it would be well to facilitate conclusions a little from
"without. Breslau stands on the West, more strictly speaking,
"on the South side of the Oder, which makes an elbow here,
"and thus bounds it, or mostly bounds it, on two sides. The
"big drab-coloured River spreads out into Islands, of a con-
"fused sort, as it passes; which are partly built upon, and con-
"stitute suburbs of the Town, — stretching over, here and
"there, into straggles of farther suburb beyond the River,
"where a road with its bridge happens to cross for the Eastern
"parts. The principal of these Islands is the *Dom Insel*,"
— known to General Browne and us, — "on which is the Ca-
"thedral, and the *Close* with rich Canons and their edifices;
"Island filled with strong high architecture; and a superior
"military post.

"Friedrich has already as good as possessed himself of the
"Three landward Gates, which look to the south and to the
"west; the riverward Gates, or those on the north and the
"east, he perceives that it were good now also to have; these,
"and even perhaps something more? 'Gather all the river-
"boats, make a bridge of them across the Oder; push across
"the Oder; push across 400 men:' this is done on Monday
"morning, under the King's own eye. This done, 'March up
"to that riverward Gate, and also to that other, in a mild but
"dangerous-looking manner; hew the beams of said Gate in
"two; start the big locks; fling wide open said Gate and
"Gates:' this too is done; Town-guard looking mournfully

"on. This done, 'March forward swiftly, in two halves, "without beat of drum, — whitherward you know!'

"Those three hundred Austrian Dragoons, we saw them "leave the Dom Island, three days ago; there are at present "only Six Men, of the Bishop's Guard, walking under arms "there, — at the end of the chief bridge, on the Townward "side of their Dom Island. See, Prussian caps and muskets, "ye six men under arms! The six men clutch at their draw- "bridge, and hastily set about hoisting: — alas, another "Prussian corps, which has come privately by the eastern (or "Country-ward) Bridge, King himself with it, taps them on "the shoulder at this instant; mildly constrains the six into "their guardhouse: the drawbridge falls; 400 Prussian "grenadiers take quiet possession of the Dom Island: King "may return to the Scultet Garden, having quickened the "lazy hours in this manner. To such of the Canons as he came "upon, his Majesty was most polite; they most submiss. The "six soldiers of the drawbridge, having spoken a little loud, — "still more a too zealous beef-cater of old Schaffgotsch's "found here, who had been very loud, — were put under "arrest; but more for form's sake; and were let go, in a day or "two."

Nothing could be gentler on Friedrich's part, and on that of his Two Colonels, than this delicate operation throughout: — and at 4 P.M., after thirty hours of waiting, it is done, and nobody's skin scratched. Old Syndic Gutzmar, and the Town-Rath, urged by perils and a Town Population who are Protestant, have signed the Surrender with goodwill, at least with resignation, and a feeling of relief. The Ober-Amt Officials have likewise had to sign; full of all the silent spleen and despondency which is natural to the situation: spleen which, in the case of old Schaffgotsch, weak with age, becomes passionately audible here and there. He will have to give account of that injurious Proclamation, or Queen's "Patent," to this King that has now come.

King enters Breslau; stays there, gracious and vigilant, Four Days (Jan. 2d-6th, 1741).

In the Royal Entrance which took place next day, note these points. Syndic Gutzmar and the Authorities came out, in grand coaches, at 8 in the morning; had to wait a while; the King, having ridden away to look after his manifold affairs, did not get back till 10. Town Guard and Garrison are all drawn out; Gates all flung open, Prussian sentries withdrawn from them, and from the Excise-houses they had seized: King's Kitchen-and-Proviant Carriages (four mules to each, with bells, with uncommonly rich housings): King's Body-Coach very grand indeed, and grandly escorted, the Thirty Bodyguards riding ahead; but nothing in it, only a most superfine cloak "lined wholly with ermine" flung upon the seat. Other Coaches, more or less grandly escorted; Head Cupbearers, Seneschals, Princes, Margraves: — but where is the King? King had ridden away, a second time, with chief Generals, taking survey of the Town Walls, round as far as the *Ziegel-Thor* (Tile-Gate, extreme south-east, by the river-edge): he has thus made the whole circuit of Breslau; — unwearied in picking up useful knowledge, "though it was very cold," while that Procession of Coaches went on.

At noon, his Majesty, thrifty of time, did enter: on horseback, Schwerin riding with him; behind him miscellaneous chief Officers; Borck and Posadowsky among others; some miscellany of Page-people following. With this natural escort, he rode in; Town-Major (commandant of Town-guard), with drawn sword, going ahead; — King wore his usual Cocked Hat, and practical

Blue Cloak, both a little dimmed by service: but his gray horse was admirable; and Four scarlet Footmen, grand as galoon and silver fringe could make them, did the due magnificence in dress. He was very gracious; saluting to this side and to that, where he noticed people of condition in the windows. "Along Schweidnitz Street, across the Great Ring, down Albrecht Street." He alighted, to lodge, at the Count-Schlegenberg House; which used to be the Austrian Cardinal von Sinzendorf, Primate of Silesia's hired lodging, — Sinzendorf's furniture is put gently aside, on this new occasion. King came on the balcony; and stood there for some minutes, that everybody might see him. The "immense shoutings," Dryasdust assures me, have been exaggerated; and I am warned not to believe the *Kriegs-Fama* such and such a Number, except after comparing it with him. — That day there was dinner of more than thirty covers, Chief Syndic Gutzmar and other such guests; but as to the viands, says my friend, these, owing to the haste, were nothing to speak of.*

Dinner, better and better ordered, King more and more gracious, so it continued all the four days of his Majesty's stay: — on the second day he had to rise suddenly from table, and leave his guests with an apology; something having gone awry, at one of the Gates. Awry there, between the Town Authorities and a General Jeetz of his, — who is on march across the River at this moment (on what errand we shall hear), and a little mistakes the terms. His Majesty puts Jeetz right; and even waits, till he see his Brigade and him clear across. A junior Schaffgotsch,** not the

* *Helden-Geschichte,* l. 545-548.   ** Ib. ll. 159.

inconsolable Schaffgotsch senior, but his Nephew, was one of the guests this second day; an ecclesiastic, but of witty fashionable type, and I think a very worthless fellow, though of a family important in the Province. Dinner falls about noon; does not last above two hours or three, so that there is space for a ride ("to the Dom," the first afternoon, "four runners" always), and for much in-door work, before the supper-hour.

As the Austrian Authorities sat silent in their place, and gave no explanation of that "Patent," affixed amid thunder and lightning, — they got orders from his Majesty to go their ways next day; and went. In behalf of old President von Schaffgotsch, a chief of the Silesian Nobility, and man much loved, the Breslau people, and men from every guild and rank of society, made petition. That he should be allowed to continue in his Town House here. Which "first request of yours" his Majesty, with much grace, is sorry to be obliged to refuse. The suppressed, and insuppressible, weak indignation of old Schaffgotsch is visible on the occasion; nor, I think, does Friedrich take it ill; only sends him out of the way with it, for the time. The Austrian Ober-Amt vanished bodily from Breslau in this manner; and never returned. Proper "War-Commission (*Feld-Kriegs-Commissariat*)," with Münchow, one of those skilful Cüstrin Münchows, at the top of it, organised itself instead; which, almost of necessity, became Supreme Government in a City ungoverned otherwise: — and truly there was little regret of the Ober-Amt, in Breslau; and ever less, to a marked extent, as the years went on.

On the 5th of January (fourth and last night here), his Majesty gave a grand Ball. Had hired, or Colonel

Posadowsky instead of him had hired, the Assembly Rooms (*Redouten-Saal*) for the purpose: "Invite all the the Nobility high and low;" — expense by estimate is a ducat (half-guinea) each; do it well, and his Majesty will pay. About 6 in the evening, his Majesty in person did us the honour to drive over; opened the Ball with Madam the Countess von Schlegenberg (I should guess, a Dowager Lady), in whose house he lodges. I am not aware that his Majesty danced much farther; but he was very condescending, and spoke and smiled up and down; — till, about 10 P.M., an Officer came in with a Letter. Which Letter his Majesty having read, and seemingly asked a question or two in regard to, put silently in his pocket, as if it were a finished thing. Nevertheless, after a few minutes, his Majesty was found to have silently withdrawn; and did not return, not even to supper. Perceiving which, all the Prussian official people gradually withdrew; though the dancing and supping continued not the less, to a late hour.*

"Open the Austrian Mail-bag (*Felleisen*); see a little what they are saying over there!" Such order had evidently been given, this night. In consequence of which people wrote by Dresden, and not the direct way, in future; wishing to avoid that openable *Felleisen*. Next morning, January 6th, his Majesty had left for Ohlau, — early I suppose; though there proved to be nothing dangerous ahead there, after all

* *Helden-Geschichte,* i. 557.

CHAPTER V.

FRIEDRICH PUSHES FORWARD TOWARDS BRIEG AND NEISSE.

OHLAU is a pleasant little Town, two marches south-east of Breslau; with the Ohlau River on one side, and the Oder on the other; capable of some defence, were there a garrison. Brieg the important Fortress, still on the Oder, is some fifteen miles beyond Ohlau; after which, bending straight south and quitting Oder, Neisse the still more important may be thirty miles: — from Breslau to Neisse, by this route (which is *bow*, not *string*), sixty-five or seventy miles. One of my Topographers yields this Note, if readers care for it:

"Ohlau River, an insignificant drab-coloured stream, rises "well south of Breslau, about Strehlen; makes, at first, direct "westward towards the Oder; and then, when almost close "upon it, breaks off to north, and saunters along, irregularly "parallel to Oder, for twenty miles farther, before it can fall "fairly in. To this circumstance both Breslau and a Town of "Ohlau owe their existence; Towns, both of them, 'between "the waters,' and otherwise well seated; Ohlau sheltering "itself in the attempted outfall of its little river; Breslau "clustering itself about the actual outfall: both very defensible "places in the old rude time, and good for trade in all times. "Both Oder and Ohlau Rivers have spilt and spread themselves into islands and deltas, a good deal, at their place of "meeting; and even have changed their courses, and cut out "new channels for themselves, in the sandy country; making "a very intricate watery network of a site for Breslau: and "indeed the Ohlau River here, for centuries back, has been "compelled into wide meanderings, mere filling of rampart-

"ditches, so that it issues quite obscurely, and in an artificial "engineered condition, at Breslau."

Ohlau had been expected to make some defence; General Browne having thrown 300 men into it, and done what he could for the works. And Ohlau did at first threaten to make some; but thought better of it over night, and in effect made none; but was got (morning of January 9th) on the common terms, by merely marching up to it in minatory posture. "Prisoners of War, if you make resistance; Free Withdrawal" (Liberty to march away, arms shouldered, and not serve against us for a year), "if you have made none;" this is the common course, where there are Austrian Soldiers at all; the course where none are, and only a few Syndics sit, with their Town-Key laid on the table, a prey to the stronger hand, we have already seen.

From Ohlau, proper Detachment, under General Kleist is pushed forward to summon Brieg; Jeetz from the other side of the river (whom we saw crossing at Breslau the other day, interrupting his Majesty's dinner) is to coöperate with Kleist in that enterprise, — were the Country once cleared on his, Jeetz's, east side of Oder; especially were Namslau once had, a small Town and Castle over there, which commands the Polish and Hungarian road. Friedrich's hopes are buoyant; Schwerin is swiftly rolling forward to rightward, nothing resisting him; Detachment is gone from Schwerin, over the Hills, to Glatz (the *Grafschaft*, or County Glatz, an Appendage to Schlesien), under excellent guidance; under guidance, namely, of Colonel Camas, who has just come home from his Parisian Embassy, and got launched among the wintry Mountains, on a new operation, — which, however, proves of non-effect for the present.*

Indeed, it is observable that southward of Breslau the dispute, what dispute there can be, properly begins; and that General Browne is there, and shows himself a shining man in this difficult position. It must be owned, no General could have made his small means go farther. Effective garrisons, 1,600 each, put into Brieg and Neisse; works repaired, magazines collected, there and elsewhere; the rest of his poor 7,000 thriftily sprinkled about, in what good posts there are, and "capable of being got together in six hours;" a superior soldier, this Browne, though with a very bad task; and seems to have inspired everybody with something of his own temper. So that there is marching, detaching, miscellaneous difficulty for Friedrich in this quarter, more than had been expected. If the fate of Brieg and Neisse be inevitable, Browne does wonders to delay it.

Of the Prussian marches in these parts, recorded by intricate Dryasdust, there was no point so notable to me as this unrecorded one: the Stone Pillar which, I see, the Kleist Detachment was sure to find, just now, on the march from Ohlau to Brieg; last portion of that march, between the village of Briesen and Brieg. The Oder, flowing on your left hand, is hereabouts agreeably clothed with woods: the country, originally a swamp, has been drained, and given to the plough, in an agreeable manner; and there is an excellent road paved with solid whinstone, — quarried in Strehlen,

---

* *Helden-Geschichte,* i. 678; Orlich, *Geschichte der beiden Schlesischen Kriege,* i. 49.

twenty miles away, among the Hills to the right yonder, as you may guess, — road very visible to the Prussian soldier, though he does not ask where quarried. These beautiful improvements, beautiful humanities, — were done by whom? "Done in 1584," say the records, by "George the Pious;" Duke of Liegnitz, Brieg, and Wohlau; 156 years ago. "Pious" his contemporaries called this George; — he was son of the *Erbverbrüderung* Duke, who is so important to us; he was grandfather's grandfather of the last Duke of all; after whom it was we that should have got these fine Territories; they should all have fallen to the Great Elector, had not the Austrian strong hand provided otherwise. George did these plantations, recoveries to the plough; made this perennial whinstone road across the swamps; upon which, notable to the roughest Prussian (being "twelve feet high by eight feet square"), rises a Hewn Mass with this Inscription on it, — not of the name or date of George; but of a thought of his, which is not without a pious beauty to me:

> *Straverunt alii nobis, nos Posteritati;*
> *Omnibus at Christus stravit ad astra viam.*
>
> Others have made roads for us; we make them for still others:
> Christ made a road to the stars for us all.*

I know not how many Brandenburgers of General Kleist's Detachment, or whether any, read this Stone; but they do all rustle past it there, claiming the Heritage of this Pious George; and their mute dim interview with him, in this manner, is a thing slightly more memorable than orders of the day, at this date.

It was on the 11th, two days after Ohlau, that

* Zöllner, *Briefe über Schlesien,* i. 175; Hübner, i. t. 101.

General Kleist summoned Brieg; and Brieg answered resolutely, No. There is a garrison of 1,600 here, and a proper magazine: nothing for it but to "mask" Brieg too; Kleist on this side the River, Jeetz on that, — had Jeetz once done with Namslau, which he has not by any means. Namslau's answer was likewise stiffly in the negative; and Jeetz cannot do Namslau, at least not the Castle, all at once; having no siege-cannon. Seeing such stiffness everywhere, Friedrich writes to Glogau, to the Young Dessauer, "Siege-artillery hither! Swift, by the Oder; you don't need it where you are!" — and wishes it were arrived, for behoof of Neisse and these stiff humours.

Friedrich comes across to Ottmachau; sits there, in survey of Neisse, till his Cannon come.

The Prussians met with serious resistance, for the first time (9th January, same day when Ohlau yielded), at a place called Ottmachau; a considerable little Town and Castle on the Neisse River, not far west of Neisse Town, almost at the very south of Silesia. It lay on the route of Schwerin's Column; long distances ahead of Liegnitz, — say, by straight highway a hundred miles; — during which, to right and to left, there had been nothing but submission hitherto. No resistance was expected here either, for there was not hope in any; only that Browne had been here; industrious to create delay till Neisse were got fully ready. He is, by every means, girding up the loins of Neisse for a tight defence; has put 1,600 men into it, with proper stores for them, with a resolute skilful Captain at the top of them: assiduous Browne had been at Ottmachau, as the outpost of Neisse, a day or two before; and, they say, had admonished them "Not to yield on any terms, for he would certainly come to their relief." Which doubtless he would have done, had it been in his power; but how, except by miracle, could it be? On the 9th of January, when Schwerin comes up, Browne is again waiting hereabouts. Again in defensive posture, but without force to undertake anything; stands on the Southern Uplands, with Böhmen and Mähren and the Giant Mountains at his back; — stands, so to speak, defensive at his own House-door, in this manner; and will have, after *seeing* Ottmachau's fate and Neisse's, to duck in with a slam! At any rate, he had left these Towns in the above firm humour, screwed to the sticking-place; and had then galloped elsewhither to screw and prepare.

And so the Ottmachau Austrians, "260 picked grenadiers" (400 dragoons there also at first were, who, after flourishing about on the outskirts as if for fighting, rode away), fire "*desperat*," says my intricate friend;* entirely refusing terms from Schwerin; kill twelve of his people (Major de Rège, distinguished Engineer Major, one of them): so that Schwerin has to bring petards upon them, four cannon upon them; and burst-in their Town Gate, almost their Castle Gate, and pretty much their Castle itself; — wasting three days of his time upon this paltry matter. Upon which they do signify a willingness for "Free Withdrawal." "No, *ihr Herren*," answers Schwerin; "not now; after such mad explosion. His Majesty will have to settle it." Majesty, who is by this time not far off, comes over to Ottmachau (January 12th); gives words of rebuke, rebuke not very inexorable; and admits

* *Helden-Geschichte*, 1. 672-677; Orlich, 1. 50.

them Prisoners of War. "The officers were sent to Cüstrin, common men to Berlin;" the usual arrangement in such case. Ottmachau Town belongs to the Right Reverend von Sinzendorf, Bishop of Breslau, and Primate; whose especial Palace is in Neisse; though he "commonly sends his refractory Priests to "do their penance in the Schloss at Ottmachau here," — and, I should say, had better himself make terms, and come out hitherward, under present aspects.

Friedrich continues at Ottmachau; head-quarters there thenceforth, till he see Neisse settled. On the morrow, 13th, he learns that the Siege Artillery is at Grotkau; well forward towards Neisse; half way between Brieg and it. Same day, Colonel Camas returns to him out of Glatz; five of his men lost; and reports That Browne has had the roads torn up, that Glatz is mere ice and obstruction, and that nothing can be made of it at this season. Good news alternating with not so good.

The truth is, Friedrich has got no Strong Place in Schlesien; all strengths make unexpected defence; paltry little Namslau itself cannot be quite taken, Castle cannot, till Jeetz get his siege artillery, — which does not come along so fast as that to Neisse does. Here is an Excerpt from my Dryasdust, exact though abridged, concerning Jeetz:

"*January* 24*th*, 1741. Prussians, masters of the Town for "a couple of weeks back, have got into the Church at Nams-"lau, into the Cloister; are preparing plank floors for batteries, "cutting loop-holes; diligent as possible, — siege-guns now at "last just coming. The Castle fires fiercely on them, makes "furious sallies, steals six of our oxen, — makes insolent "gestures from the walls; at least one soldier does, this day.

"'Sir, may I give that fellow a shot?' asks the Prussian sentry "'Do, then,' answers his Major: 'too insolent that one!' And "the sentry explodes on him; brings him plunging down, head "foremost (*herunter pürzelte*); the too insolent mortal, silent "enough thenceforth."* — Jeetz did get his cannon, though not till now, this very day I think; and then, in a couple of days more, Jeetz finished-off Namslau ("officers to Cüstrin, common men to Berlin"); and thereupon blockades the Eastern side of Brieg, joining hands with Kleist on the Western: whereby Brieg, like Glogau, is completely masked, — till the season mend.

Friedrich, now that his artillery is come, expects no difficulty with Neisse. A "paltry hamlet (*bicoque*)," he playfully calls it; and, except this, Silesia is now his. Neisse got (which would be the desirable thing), or put under "mask" as Glogau is, and as Brieg is being, Austria possesses not an inch of land within these borders. Here are some Epistolary snatches; still in the light style, not to say the flimsy and uplifted; but worth giving, so transparent are they; off hand, like words we had heard his Majesty *speak*, in his high mood:

King to M. Jordan, at Berlin (Two successive Letters).

1º. "*Ottmachau, 14th January* 1741" (second day after our arrival there). "My dear Monsieur Jordan, my sweet Monsieur "Jordan, my quiet Monsieur Jordan, my good, my benign, my "pacific, my humanest Monsieur Jordan, — I announce to Thy "Serenity the conquest of Silesia; I warn thee of the bombard- "ment of Neisse" (just getting ready), "and I prepare thee "for still more important projects; and instruct thee of the "happiest successes that the womb of Fortune ever bore.

"This ought to suffice thee. Be my Cicero as to the justice "of my cause, and I will be thy Cæsar as to the execution. "Adieu: thou knowest whether I am not, with the most cordial "regard, thy faithful friend. F."

* *Helden-Geschichte*, 1. 703.

2°. "*Ottmachau*, 17*th January* 1741. I have the honour to "inform Your Humanity that we are christianly preparing to "bombard Neisse; and that if the place will not surrender of "good will, needs must that it be beaten to powder (*nécessité* "*sera de l'abimer*). For the rest, our affairs go the best in the "world; and soon thou wilt hear nothing more of us. For, in "ten days, it will all be over; and I shall have the pleasure of "seeing you and hearing you, in about a fortnight.

"I have seen neither my Brother" (August Wilhelm, not "long ago at Strasburg with us, and betrothed since then) "nor Keyserling: I left them at Breslau, not to expose them to "the dangers of war. They perhaps will be a little angry; "but what can I do? — The rather as, on this occasion, one "cannot share in the glory, unless one is a mortar!

"Adieu, M. le Conseiller" (*Poor's-Rath*, so styled). "Go "and amuse yourself with Horace, study Pausanias, and be "gay over Anacreon. As to me, who for amusement have "nothing but merlons, fascines and gabions,* I pray God to "grant me soon a pleasanter and peacefuller occupation, "and you health, satisfaction and whatever your heart "desires. — F."**

King Friedrich to M. le Comte Algarotti (gone on a journey).

"*Ottmachau*, 17*th January* 1741" (same day as the above to "Jordan). "I have begun to settle the Figure of Prussia: the "outline will not be altogether regular; for the whole of Sile-"sia is taken, except one miserable hamlet (*bicoque*), which "perhaps I shall have to keep blockaded till next spring.

"Up to this time, the whole conquest has cost only Twenty "Men, and Two Officers, one of whom is the poor De Rège, "whom you have seen at Berlin," — De Rège, Engineer Major, killed here at Ottmachau, in Schwerin's late tussle.

"You are greatly wanting to me here. So soon as you have "talked that business over, write to me about it." (What is the business? Whither is the dusky Swan of Padua gone?) "In all these three hundred miles I have found no human

---

* Merlons are mounds of earth placed behind the solid or blind parts of the parapet (that is, between the embrasures) of a Fortification; fascines are bundles of brushwood for filling up a ditch; gabions, baskets filled with earth, to be ranged in defence till you get trenches dug.

** *Œuvres de Frédéric,* xvii. 84.

"creature comparable to the Swan of Padua. I would
"willingly give ten cubic leagues of ground for a genius
"similar to yours. But I perceive I was about entreating you
"to return fast, and join me again, — while you are not yet
"arrived where your errand was. Make haste to arrive, then;
"to execute your commission, and fly back to me. I wish you
"had a Fortunatus Hat; it is the only thing defective in your
"outfit.

"Adieu, dear Swan of Padua: think, I pray you, sometimes
"of those who are getting themselves cut in slices" (*échiner*,
chined) "for the sake of glory here, and above all do not
"forget your friends who think a thousand times of you. —
"FÉDÉRIC."*

The object of the dear Swan's journey, or even the whereabouts of it, cannot be discovered without difficulty; and is not much worth discovering. "Gone to Turin," we at last make out, "with secret commissions:"** desirable to sound the Sardinian Majesty a little, who is Doorkeeper of the Alps, between France and Austria, and opens to the best bidder? No great things of a meaning in this mission, we can guess, or Algarotti had not gone upon it, — though he is handy, at least, for keeping it unnoticed by the Gazetteer species. Nor was the Swan successful, it would seem; the more the pity for our Swan! However he comes back safe; attends Friedrich in Silesia, and in the course of next month readers will see him, if any reader wished it.

* *Œuvres de Frédéric,* xviii. 28.
** Denina: *La Prusse Littéraire* (Berlin, 1790), i. 198. A poor vague Book; only worth consulting in case of extremity.

CHAPTER VI.

NEISSE IS BOMBARDED.

NEISSE, which Friedrich calls a paltry hamlet (*bicoque*), is a pleasant strongly-fortified Town, then of perhaps 6 or 8,000 inhabitants, now of double that number; stands on the left or north bank of the Neisse, — at this day, on both banks. Pleasant broad streets, high strong houses, mostly of stone. Pleasantly encircled by green Hills, northward buttresses of the Giant Mountains; itself standing low and level, on rich ground much inclined to be swampy. A lesser river, Biele, or Bielau, coming from the South, flows leisurely enough into the Neisse, — filling all the Fortress ditches, by the road. Orchard-growth and meadow-growth are lordly (*herrlich*); a land rich in fruit, and flowing with milk and honey. Much given to weaving, brewing, stocking-making; and, moreover, trades greatly in these articles, and above all in Wine. Yearly on St. Agnes Day, "21st January, if not a Sunday," there is a Wine-fair here; Hungarian, of every quality from Tokay downward, is gathered here for distribution into Germany and all the Western Countries. While you drink your Tokay, know that it comes through Neisse. St. Agnes Day falls but unhandily this year; and I think the Fair will, as they say, *ausbleiben*, or not be held.

Neisse is a Nest of Priests (*Pfaffen-Nest*), says Friedrich once; which came in this way. About 600 years ago, an ill-conditioned Heir-Apparent of the

Liegnitz Sovereign to whom it then belonged, quarrelled with his Father, quarrelled slightly with the Universe; and, after moping about for some time, went into the Church. Having Neisse for an apanage already his own, he gave it to the Bishop of Breslau; whose, in spite of the old Father's protestings, it continued, and continues. Bishops of Breslau are made very grand by it; Bishops of Breslau have had their own difficulties here. Thus once (in our Perkin-Warbeck time, A.D. 1497), a Duke of Oppeln, sitting in some Official Conclave or meeting of magnates here, — zealous for country privilege, and feeling himself insufferably put upon, — started up, openly defiant of Official men; glaring wrathfully into Duke Casimir of Teschen (Bohemian-Austrian Captain of Silesia), and into the Bishop of Breslau himself; nay at last, flashed out his sword upon those sublime dignitaries. For which, by and by, he had to lay his head on the block, in the great square here; and died penitent, we hope.

This place, my Dryasdust informs me, had many accidents by floodage and by fire; was seized and re-seized in the Thirty-Years War especially, at a great rate: Saxon Arnheim, Austrian Holk, Swedish Torstenson; no end to the battering and burning poor Neisse had, to the big ransoms "in new Reichsthalers and 300 casks of wine." But it always rebuilt itself, and began business again. How happy when it could get under some effectual Protector, of the Liegnitz line, of the Austrian-Bohemian line, and this or the other battering, just suffered, was to be the last for some time! — Here again is a battering coming on it; the first of a series that are now imminent.

The reader is requested to look at Neisse; for

besides the Tokay wine, there will things arrive there.
— Neisse River, let us again mention, is one of Four
bearing that name, and all belonging to the Oder: —
could not they be labelled, then, or *numbered*, in some
way? This Neisse, which we could call Neisse the
First (and which careful readers may as well make
acquaintance with on their Map, where too they will
find Neisse the *Second*, "the *Wüthende* or Roaring
Neisse," and two others which concern us less), rises
in the "Western Snow-Mountains (*Schneegebirg*),"
South-Western or Glatz district of the Giant Mountains; drains Glatz County and grows big there: washes
the Town of Glatz; then eastward by Ottmachau, by
Neisse Town; whence turning rather abruptly north
or north-east, it gets into the Oder not far south of
Brieg.

Neisse as a Place of Arms, the chief Fortress of
Silesia and the nearest to Austria, is extremely desirable
for Friedrich; but there is no hope of it without some
kind of Siege; and Friedrich determines to try in that
way. From Ottmachau, accordingly, and from the
other sides, the Siege-Artillery being now at hand, due
force gathers itself round Neisse, Schwerin taking
charge; and for above a week there is demonstrating
and posting, summoning and parleying; and then, for
three days, with pauses intervening, there is extremely
furious bombardment, red-hot at times: "Will you
yield, then?" — with steady negative from Neisse.
Friedrich's quarter is at Ottmachau, twelve miles off;
from which he can ride over, to see and superintend.
The fury of his bombardment, which naturally grieved
him, testifies the intensity of his wish. But it was to

no purpose. The Commandant, Colonel von Roth (the same who was proposed for Breslau lately, a wise head and a stout, famed in defences) had "poured water on his ramparts," after well repairing them, — made his ramparts all ice and glass; — and done much else. Would the reader care to look for a moment? Here, from our waste Paper-masses, is abundance, requiring only to be abridged:

"*January* 1741: *Monday 9th — Wednesday 11th.* Monday "9th, — day when that sputter at Ottmachau began, — "Prussian light-troops appeared transiently on the heights "about Neisse, for the first time. Directly on sight of whom, "Commandant Roth assembled the Burghers of the place; "took a new Oath of Fidelity from one and all; admonished " them to do their utmost, as they should see him do. The " able-bodied and likeliest of them (say about 400) he has had "arranged into Militia Companies, with what drill there could "be in the interim; and since his coming, has employed every "moment in making ready. Wednesday 11th, he locks all the " Gates, and stands strictly on his guard. The inhabitants "are mostly Catholic; with sumptuous Bishops of Breslau, "with *Kreuzherren* (imaginary Teutsch or other Ritters with "some reality of money), with Jesuit Dignitaries, Church and "Quasi-Church Officialities, resident among them: popula-"tion, high and low, is inclined by creed to the Queen of "Hungary. Commandant Roth has only 1,200 regular "soldiers; at the outside 1,600 men under arms: but he has "gunpowder, he has meal; experience also and courage; and "hopes these may suffice him for a time. One of the most "determined Commandants; expert in the defence of strong "places. A born Silesian (not Saxon, as some think), — and "is of the Augsburg Confession; but that circumstance is not "important here, though at Breslau Browne thought it was.

"*Thursday*, 12*th.* The Prussians, in regular force, appear "on the Kaninchen Berg (Cony Hill, so - called from its "rabbits), south of the River, evidently taking post there. "Roth fires a signal shot; the Southern Suburbs of Neisse, as "preappointed, go up in flame; crackle high and far; in a

15th Jan. 1741.

"lamentable manner (*erbärmlich*), through the grim winter "air." This is the day Friedrich came over to Ottmachau, and settled the sputter there.

"Next day, and next again, the same phenomena at "Neisse; the Prussians edging ever nearer, building their "batteries, preparing to open their cannonade. Whereupon "Roth burns the remaining Suburbs, with lamentable crackle; "on all sides now are mere ashes. Bishop's Mill, Franciscan "Cloister, Bishop's Pleasure-garden, with its summer-houses; "Bishop's Hospital, and several Churches: Roth can spare "none of these things, with the Prussians nestling there. "Surely the Bishop himself, respectable Cardinal Graf von "Sinzendorf, had better get out of these localities while time "yet is?" 'Saturday 14th,' that was the day Friedrich, at Ottmachau, wrote as above to Jordan (Letter No. 1), while the Neisse Suburbs crackled lamentably, twelve miles off, "Schwerin gets order to break up, in person, from Ottmachau "to-morrow, and begin actual business on the Kaninchen Hill "yonder.

"*Sunday* 15*th.* Schwerin does; marches across the River; "takes post on the south side of Neisse: notable to the Sunday "rustics. Nothing but burnt villages and black walls for "Schwerin, in that Cony-Hill quarter, and all round; and "Roth salutes him with one twenty-four pounder, which did "no hurt. And so the cannonade begins, Sunday 15th; and "intermittently, on both sides of the River, continues, always "bursting out again at intervals, till Wednesday; a mere "preliminary cannonade on Schwerin's part; making noise, "doing little hurt: intended more to terrify, but without effect "that way on Roth or the Townsfolk. The poor Bishop did, "on the second day of it, come out, and make application to "Schwerin; was kindly conducted to his Majesty, who "happened to be over there; was kept to dinner; and easily "had leave to retire to Freywalde, a Country-House he has, "in the safe distance.* There let him be quiet, well out of "these confused batterings and burnings of property.

"His Majesty's headquarter is at Ottmachau, but in two "hours he can be here any day; and looks into everything; "sorry that the cannonade does not yet answer. And remnants "of suburbs are still crackling into flame; high Country-

* *Helden-Geschichte,* i. 683.

"Houses of Kreuzherren, of Jesuits; a fanatic people "seemingly all set against us. 'If Neisse will not yield of "good-will, needs is it must be beaten to powder,' wrote his "Majesty to Jordan in these circumstances, as we read above. "Roth is sorry to observe, the Prussians have still one good "Bishop's-mansion, in a place called the Karlau (Karl-"Meadow), with the Bishop's winter fuel all ready stacked "there; but strives to take order about the same.

"*Wednesday* 18*th*. This day two provocations happened. "First in the morning by his Majesty's order, Colonel Borck "(the same we saw at Herstal) had gone with a Trumpeter "towards Roth; intending to inform Roth how mild the terms "would be, how terrible the penalty of not accepting them. "But Roth or Roth's people singularly disregard Borck and "his Parley Trumpet; answer its blasts by musketry; fire upon "it, nay again fire worse when it advances a step farther; on "these terms Borck and Trumpet had to return. Which much "angered his Majesty at Ottmachau that evening; as was na-"tural. Same evening, our fine quarters in the Karlau "crackled up in flame, the Bishop's winter firewood all along "with it: this was provocation second. Roth had taken order "with the Karlau; and got a resolute Butcher to do the feat, "under pretext of bringing us beef. It is piercing cold; only "blackened walls for us now in the Karlau or elsewhere. His "Majesty, naturally much angered, orders for the morrow a "dose of bombshells and red-hot balls. Plant a few mortars "on the North side too, orders his Majesty.

"*Thursday*, 19*th*. Accordingly, by 8 of the clock, cannon "batteries re-awaken with a mighty noise, and red-hot balls "are noticeable; and at 10 the actual bombarding bursts out, "terrible to hear and see; — first shell falling in Haubitz the "Clothier's shop, but being happily got under. Roth has his "City Militia companies, organised with waterhoses for "quenching of the red-hot balls; in which they became expert. "So that though the fire caught many houses they always put "it out. Late in the night, hearing no word from Roth, the "Prussians went to bed.

"*Friday* 20*th*. Still no word; on which, about 4 P.M., the "Prussian batteries awaken again: volcanic torrent of red-hot "shot and shells, for seven hours; still no word from Roth. "About 11 at night his Majesty again sends a Drum (Parley

"Trumpet or whatever it is) to the Gate; formally summons "Roth; asks him, 'If he has well considered what this can lead "to? Especially what he, Roth, meant by firing on our first "Trumpet on Wednesday last?' Roth answered, 'That as to "the Trumpet, he had not heard of it before. On the other "hand, that this mode of sieging by red-hot balls seems a little "unusual; for the rest, that he has himself no order or intention "but that of resisting to the last.' Some say the Drum here- "upon by order talked of 'pounding Neisse into powder, mere "child's play hitherto;' to which Roth answered only by "respectful dumb-show.

Saturday 21st — Monday 23d. Midnight of Friday — "Saturday, on this answer coming, the fire-volcanoes open "again;— nine hours long; shells, and red-hot material, in "terrible abundance. Which hit mostly the Churches, "Jesuits' Seminariums and Collegiums; but produced no "change in Roth. From 9 A.M. the batteries are silent. Silent "still, next morning: Divine Service may proceed, if it like. "But at 4 of the afternoon, the batteries awaken worse than "ever; from seven to nine bombs going at once. Universal "rage, of noise and horrid glare, making night hideous, till "10 of the clock; Roth continuing inflexible. This is the last "night of the Siege."

Friedrich perceived that Roth would not yield; that the utter smashing down of Neisse might more concern Friedrich than Roth;— that, in fine, it would be better to desist till the weather altered. Next day, "Monday 23d, between noon and 1 o'clock," the Prussians drew back;— converted the siege into a blockade. Neisse to be masked, like Brieg and Glogau (Brieg only half done yet, Jeetz without cannon till tomorrow, 24th, and little Namslau still gesticulating): "'The only thing "one could try upon it was bombardment. A Nest of "Priests (*Pfaffen-Nest*); not many troops in it: but it "cannot well be forced at present. If spring were here, "it will cost a fortnight's work."*

* *Friedrich to the Old Dessauer*: Fraction of Letter (Ottmachau, 16th-

A noisy business; "King's high person much ex-"posed: a bombardier and then a sergeant were killed "close by him, though in all he lost only five men."*

Browne vanishes in a slight Flash of Fire.

Browne all this while has hung on the Mountain-side, witnessing these things; sending stores towards Glatz south-westward, and "ruining the ways" behind them; waiting what would become of Neisse. Neisse done, Schwerin is upon him; Browne makes off South-eastward, across the Mountains, for Moravia and home; Schwerin following hard. At a little place called Grätz,** on the Moravian border, Browne faced round, tried to defend the Bridge of the Oppa, sharply though without effect; and there came (January 25th) a hot sputter between them for a few minutes:—after which Browne vanished into the interior, and we hear, in these parts, comparatively little more of him, during this War. Friend and foe must admit that he has neglected nothing; and fairly made the best of a bad business here. He is but an interim General, too; his Successor just coming; and the Vienna Board of War is frequently troublesome, — to whose windy specula-tions Browne replies with sagacious scepticism, and here and there a touch of veiled sarcasm, which was

21st January 1741) cited by Orlich, i. 51; — from the Dessau Archives, where Herr Orlich has industriously been. To all but strictly military people these pieces of Letters are the valuable feature of Orlich's Book; and a general reader laments that it does not all consist of such, properly elucidated and labelled into accessibility.

* *Helden-Geschichte*. i. 680-690.

** The name, in old Slavic speech, signifies *Town*; and there are many *Grätzes*: *Königingrätz* (*Queen's*, which for brevity is now generally called *Königsgrätz*, in Bohemia); Grätz in Styria; *Windischgrätz* (Wendish-town), &c.

not likely to conciliate in high places. Had her Hungarian Majesty been able to retain Browne in his post, instead of poor Neipperg who was sent instead, there might have been a considerably different account to give of the sequel. But Neipperg was Tutor (War-Tutor) to the Grand-Duke; Browne is still of young standing (age only thirty-five), with a touch of veiled sarcasm; and things must go their course.

In Schlesien, Schwerin is now to command in chief; the King going off to Berlin for a little, naturally with plenty of errand there. The Prussian Troops go into Winter-quarters; spread themselves wide; beset the good points, especially the Passes of the Hills, — from Jägerndorf, eastward to the Jablunka leading towards Hungary; — nay they can, and before long do, spread into the Moravian Territories, on the other side; and levy contributions, the Queen proving unreasonable.

It was Monday 23d, when the Siege of Neisse was abandoned: on Wednesday, Friedrich himself turns homeward; looks into Schweidnitz, looks into Liegnitz; and arrives at Berlin as the week ends, — much acclamation greeting him from the multitude. Except those Three masked Fortresses, capable of no defence to speak of, were Winter over, Silesia is now all Friedrich's, — has fallen wholly to him in the space of about Seven Weeks. The seizure has been easy; but the retaining of it, perhaps he himself begins to see more clearly, will have difficulties! From this point, the talk about *gloire* nearly ceases in his Correspondence. In those seven weeks he has, with *gloire* or otherwise, cut out for himself such a life of labour as no man of his Century had.

CHAPTER VII.

AT VERSAILLES, THE MOST CHRISTIAN MAJESTY CHANGES HIS SHIRT, AND BELLEISLE IS SEEN WITH PAPERS.

WHILE Friedrich was so busy in Silesia, the world was not asleep around him; the world never is, though it often seems to be, round a man and what action he does in it. That Sunday morning, First Day of the Year 1741, in those same hours while Friedrich, with energy, with caution, was edging himself into Breslau, there went on in the Court of Versailles an interior Phenomenon; of which, having by chance got access to it face to face, we propose to make the reader participant before going farther.

Readers are languidly aware that phenomena do go on round their Friedrich; that their busy Friedrich, with his few Voltaires and renowned persons, are not the only population of their Century, by any means. Everybody is aware of that fact; yet, in practice, almost everybody is as good as not aware; and the World all round one's Hero is a darkness, a dormant vacancy. How strange when, as here, some waste Paper-spill (so to speak) turns up, which you can *kindle;* and, by the brief flame of it, bid a reader look with his own eyes! — From Herr Doctor Büsching, who did the *Geography* and about a Hundred other Books, — a man of great worth, almost of genius, could he have elaborated his Hundred Books into Ten (or distilled, into flasks of aquavitæ, what otherwise

Jan. 1741.

lies tumbling as tanks of mash and wort, now run very sour and malodorous); — it is from Herr Büsching that we gain the following rough Piece, illuminative if one can kindle it:

The Titular-Herr Baron Anton von Geusau, a gentleman of good parts, scholastic by profession, and of Protestant creed, was accompanying as Travelling Tutor, in those years, a young Graf von Reuss. Graf von Reuss is one of those indistinct Counts Reuss, who always call themselves "Henry;" and, being now at the eightieth and farther, with uncountable collateral Henrys intertwisted, are become in effect anonymous, or of nomenclature inscrutable to mankind. Nor is the young one otherwise of the least interest to us; — except that Herr Anton, the Travelling Tutor, punctually kept a Journal of everything. Which Journal, long afterwards, came into the hands of Büsching, also a punctual man; and was by him abridged, and set forth in print in his *Beyträge*. Offering at present a singular daguerreotype glimpse of the then actual world, wherever Graf von Reuss and his Geusau happened to be. Ninetenths of it, even in Büsching's Abridgment, are now fallen useless and wearisome; but to one studying the days that then were, even the effete commonplace of it occasionally becomes alive again. And how interesting to catch, here and there, a Historical Figure on these conditions; Historical Figure's very self, in his work-day attitude; eating his victuals; writing, receiving letters, talking to his fellow-creatures; unaware that Posterity, miraculously, through some chink of the Travelling Tutor's producing, has got its eye upon him!

"*Sunday,* 1*st January* 1741, Geusau and his young Gentle-
"man leave Paris, at 5 in the morning, and drive out to Ver-
"sailles; intending to see the ceremonies of Newyear's day
"there. Very wet weather it had been, all Wednesday, and
"for days before;* but on this Sunday, Newyear's morning,
"all is ice and glass; and they slid about painfully by lamp-
"light, — with unroughened horses, and on the Hilly or Meu-

* See in *Barbier* (II. 283 et sqq.), what terrible Noah-like weather it had been; big houses, long in soak, tumbling down at last into the Seine; *châsse of St. Geneviève* brought out (two days ago), December 30th, to try it by miracle; &c. &c.

"don road, having chosen that as fittest, the waters being out;
"— not arriving at Court till 9. Nor finding very much to
"comfort them, except on the side of curiosity, when there.
"Ushers, *Introducteurs*, Cabinet Secretaries, were indeed
"assiduous to oblige; and the King's Levee will be: but if you
"follow it to the Chapel Royal to witness high mass, you must
"kneel at elevation of the host; and this, as reformed
"Christians, Reuss and his Tutor cannot undertake to do.
"They accept a dinner invitation (12 the hour) from some
"good Samaritan of Quality; and, for sights, will content
"themselves with the King's Levee itself, and generally with
"what the King's Ante-chamber, and the Œil-de-Bœuf, can
"exhibit to them. The Most Christian King's Levee" (*Lever*,
"literally here his Getting out of Bed) "is a daily miracle of
"these localities, only grander on Newyear's day; and it is to
"the following effect:

"'Till Majesty please to awaken, you saunter in the Salle
"des Ambassadeurs; whole crowds jostling one another there;
"gossiping together in a diligent, insipid manner;" gossip all
reported; snatches of which have acquired a certain flavour
by long keeping; — which the reader shall imagine. "Mean-
"while you keep your eye on the Grate of the Inner Court,
"which as yet is only ajar, Majesty inaccessible as yet. Behold,
"at last, Grate opens itself wide; sign that Majesty is out of
"bed; that the privileged of mankind may approach, and see
"the miracles." Geusau continues, abridged by Büsching
and us:

"The whole Assemblage passed now into the King's Ante-
"room; had to wait there about half an hour more, before the
"King's bedroom was opened. But then at last, lo you, —
"there is the King, visible to Geusau and everybody, 'wash-
"ing his hands.' Which effected itself in this way. 'The
"King was seated; a gentleman-in-waiting knelt before him,
"and held the Ewer, a square vessel silver-gilt, firm upon the
"King's breast; and another gentleman-in-waiting poured
"water on the King's hands.' Merely an official washing, we
"perceive; the real, it is to be hoped, had, in a much more
"effectual way, been going on during the half-hour just
"elapsed. After washing, the King rose for an instant; had
"his dressing-gown, a grand yellow silky article with silver
"flowerings, pulled off, and flung round his loins; upon which

"he sat down again, and," — observe it, ye privileged of mankind, — "the Change of Shirt took place! 'They put the "clean shirt down over his head,' says Anton, 'and plucked "up the dirty one from within, so that of the naked skin you "saw little or nothing.'" Here is a miracle worth getting out of bed to look at!

"His Majesty now quitted chair and dressing-gown; stood "up before the fire; and, after getting on the rest of his cloth- "ing, which, on account of Czarina Anne's death" (readers remember that) "was of violet or mourning colour, he had the "powder-mantle thrown round him, and sat down at the "Toilette to have his hair frizzled. The Toilette, a table "with white cover shoved into the middle of the room, had on "it a mirror, a powder-knife, and" — no mortal cares what. "The King," what all mortals note as they do the heavenly omens, "is somewhat talky; speaks sometimes with the Dutch "Ambassador, sometimes with the Pope's Nuncio, who seems "a jocose kind of gentleman; sometimes with different French "Lords, and at last with the Cardinal Fleury also, — to whom, "however, he does not look particularly gracious," — not particularly, this time. These are the omens; happy who can read them! — "Majesty then did his morning-prayer, assisted "only by the common Almoners-in-waiting (Cardinal took no "hand, much less any other); Majesty knelt before his bed, "and finished the business 'in less than six seconds.' After "which mankind can ebb out to the Ante-room again; pay "their devoir to the Queen's Majesty, which all do; or wait "for the Transit to Morning Chapel, and see Mesdames of "France and the others flitting past in their sedans.

"Queen's Majesty was already altogether dressed," says Geusau, almost as if with some disappointment; "all in black; "a most affable courteous Majesty; stands conversing with "the Russian Ambassador, with the Dutch ditto, with the "Ladies about her, and at last, 'in a friendly and merry "tone,' with old Cardinal Fleury. Her Ladies, when the "Queen spoke with them, showed no constraint at all; leant "loosely with their arms on the fire-screens, and took things "easy. Mesdames of France" — Geusau saw Mesdames. Poor little souls, they are the *Loque*, the *Cochon* (Rag, Pig, so Papa would call them, dear Papa), who become tragically visible again in the Revolution time: — all blooming young children as yet (Queen's Majesty some Thirty-seven gone), and little dreaming what lies fifty years ahead! King Louis's career of extraneous gallantries, which ended in the Parc-aux-Cerfs, is now just beginning: think of that too; and of her Majesty's fine behaviour under it; so affable, so patient, silent, now and always!— "In a little while, their Majesties go along "the Great Gallery to Chapel;" whither the Protestant mind cannot with comfort accompany.*

This is the daily miracle done at Versailles to the believing multitude; only that on Newyear's day, and certain supreme occasions, the shirt is handed by a Prince of the Blood, and the towel for drying the royal hands by a ditto, with other improvements; and the thing comes out in its highest power of effulgence, — especially if you could see high mass withal. In the Antechamber and Œil-de-Bœuf, Geusau, among hundreds of phenomena fallen dead to us, saw the Four following, which have still some life:

1⁰. Many Knights of the Holy Ghost (*Chevaliers du Saint Esprit*) are about; magnificently piebald people, indistinct to us, and fallen dead to us: but there, among the company, do not we indisputably see, "in full Cardinal's costume," Fleury the ancient Prime Minister talking to her Majesty. Blandly smiling; soft as milk, yet with a flavour of alcoholic wit in him here and there. That is a man worth looking at, had they painted him at all. Red hat, red stockings; a serenely definite old gentleman, with something of prudent wisdom, and a touch of imperceptible jocosity at times; mildly inexpugnable in manner: this King, whose Tutor he was twenty years ago, still looks to him as his father; Fleury is the real King of France at present. His age is eighty-seven gone; the King's is thirty (seven years younger than his Queen): and the Cardinal has red stockings and red hat; veritably there, successively in both Antechambers, seen by Geusau, January 1st, 1741: that is all I know.

2⁰. The Prince de Clermont, a Prince of the Blood,

* Büsching, *Beyträge*, ii. 59-78.

"handed the shirt," *teste* Geusau. Some other Prince, notable to Geusau, and to us nameless, had the honour of the "towel:" but this Prince de Clermont, a dissolute fellow of wasted parts, kind of Priest, kind of Soldier too, is seen visibly handing the shirt there; — whom the reader and I, if we cared about it, shall again see, getting beaten by Prince Ferdinand, at Crefeld, within twenty years hence. These are points first and second, slightly noticeable, slightly if at all.

Of the actual transit to High Mass, transit very visible in the Great Gallery or Œil-de-Bœuf, why should a human being now say anything? Queen, poor Stanislaus's Daughter, and her Ladies, in their sublime sedans, one flood of jewels, sail first; next sails King Louis, shirt warm on his back, with "Thirty-four Chevaliers of the Holy Ghost" escorting; next "the Dauphin" (Boy of eleven, Louis XVI.'s Father), and "Mesdames of France, with" — But even Geusau stops short. Protestants cannot enter that Chapel, without peril of idolatry; wherefore Geusau and Pupil kept strolling in the general Œil-de-Bœuf, — and "the Dutch Ambassador approved of it," he for one. And here now is another point, slightly noticeable:

3º. High Mass over, his Majesty sails back from Chapel, in the same magnificently piebald manner; and vanishes into the interior; — leaving his Knights of the Holy Ghost, and other Courtier-multitude, to simmer about, and ebb away as they found good. Geusau and his young Reuss had now the honour of being introduced to various people; among others "to the Prince de Soubise." Prince de Soubise: frivolous, insignificant being; of whom I have no portrait that is not nearly blank, and content to be so; — though Herr von Geusau would have one, with features and costume to it, when he heard of the Beating at Rossbach, long after! Prince de Soubise is pretty much a blank to everybody; — and no sooner are we loose of him, than (what every reader will do well to note)

4º. Our Herren Travellers are introduced to a real Notability: Monseigneur, soon to be Maréchal, the Comte de Belleisle; whom my readers and I are to be much concerned with, in time coming. "A tall lean man (*langer hagerer Mann*), without much air of quality," thinks Geusau; but with much swift intellect and energy, and a distinguished character, whatever Geusau might think. "Comte de Belleisle "was very civil; but apologised, in a courtly and kind way, "for the hurry he was in; regretting the impossibility of "doing the honours to the Comte de Reuss in this Country, — "his, Belleisle's, Journey into Germany, which was close at "hand, overwhelming him with occupations and engagements "at present. And indeed, even while he spoke to us," says Geusau, "all manner of Papers were put into his hand."*

"Journey to Germany, Papers put into his hand:" there is perhaps no Human Figure in the world, this Sunday (except the one Figure now in those same moments over at Breslau, gently pressing upon the locked Gates there), who is so momentous for our Silesian Operations: and indeed he will kindle all Europe into delirium; and produce mere thunder and lightning, for seven years to come, — with almost no result in it, except Silesia! A tall lean man; there stands he, age now fifty-six, just about setting out on such errand. Whom one is thankful to have seen for a moment, even in that slight manner.

Of Belleisle and his Plans.

Charles Louis Auguste Fouquet, Comte de Belleisle, is Grandson of that Intendant Fouquet, sumptuous Financier, whom Louis XIV. at last threw out, and locked into the Fortress of Pignerol, amid the Savoy Alps, there to meditate for life, which lasted thirty years longer. It was never understood that the sumptuous Fouquet had altogether stolen public moneys, nor indeed rightly what he had done to merit Pignerol; and always, though fallen somehow into such dire disfavour, he was pitied and respected by a good portion of the public. "Has angered Colbert,"

* Büsching, ii. 79: see Barbier, ii. 282, 287.

said the public; "dangerous rivalry to Colbert; that is what has brought Pignerol upon him."

Out of Pignerol that Fouquet never came; but his Family bloomed up into light again; had its adventures, sometimes its troubles, in the Regency time, but was always in a rising way: — and here, in this tall lean man getting papers put into his hand, it has risen very high indeed. Going as Ambassador Extraordinary to the Germanic Diet, "To assist good neighbours, as a neighbour and Most Christian Majesty should, in choosing their new Kaiser to the best advantage:" that is the official colour his mission is to have. Surely a proud mission; — and Belleisle intends to execute it in a way that will surprise the Germanic Diet and mankind. Privately, Belleisle intends that he, by his own industries, shall himself choose the right Kaiser, such Kaiser as will suit the Most Christian Majesty and him; he intends to make a new French thing of Germany in general; and carries in his head plans of an amazing nature! He and a Brother he has, called the Chevalier de Belleisle, who is also a distinguished man, and seconds M. le Comte with eloquent fire and zeal in all things, are grandsons of that old Fouquet, and the most shining men in France at present. France little dreams how much better it perhaps were, had they also been kept safe in Pignerol! —

The Count, lean and growing old, is not healthy; is ever and anon tormented, and laid up for weeks, with rheumatisms, gouts and ailments: but otherwise he is still a swift ardent elastic spirit; with grand schemes, with fiery notions and convictions, which captivate and hurry-off men's minds, more than eloquence could, so intensely true are they to the Count himself; — and then his Brother the Chevalier is always there to put them into the due language and logic, where needed.* A magnanimous highflown spirit; thought to be of supreme skill both in War and in Diplomacy; fit for many things; and is still full of ambition to distinguish himself, and tell the world at all moments, "*Me voilà;* World, I too am here!" — His plans, just now, which are dim even to himself, except on the hither skirt of them, stretch out immeasurable, and lie piled up high as the skies. The hither skirt of them, which will suffice the reader at present, is:

That your Grand-Duke Franz, Maria Theresia's Husband, shall in no wise, as the world and Duke Franz expect, be the Kaiser chosen. Not he, but another who will suit France better: "Kur-Sachsen perhaps, the so-called King of Poland? Or say it were Karl Albert Kur-Baiern, the hereditary friend and dependant of France? We are not tied to a man: only, at any and at all rates, not Grand-Duke Franz." This is the grand, essential and indispensable point; alpha and omega of points; very clear this one to Belleisle, — and towards this the first steps, if as yet only the first, are also clear to him. Namely that "the 27th of February next," — which is the time set by Kur-Mainz and the native Officials for the actual meeting of their Reichstag to begin Election Business, will be too early a time; and must be got postponed.**

---

* Voltaire, xxviii. 74; xxix. 392; &c.
** Adelung, ii. 185 ("27th February — 1st March 1741, at Frankfurt-on-Mayn," appointed by Kur-Mainz, "Arch-Chancellor of the *Reich*," under date November 3d, 1740): — ib. 236 ("Delay for a month or two," suggests Kur-Pfalz, on January 12th, seconded by others in the French interest); — upon which the appointment, after some arguing, collapsed into the vague,

Postponed; which will be possible, perhaps for long; one knows not for how long: that is a first step definitely clear to Belleisle. Towards which, a preliminary to it and to all the others in a dimmer state, there is a second thing clear, and has even been officially settled (all but the day): That, in the mean while, and surely the sooner the better, he, Belleisle, Most Christian Majesty's Ambassador Extraordinary to the Reichstag coming, — do, in his most dazzling and persuasive manner, make a Tour among German Courts. Let us visit, in our highest and yet in our softest splendour, the accessible German Courts, especially the likely or well-disposed: Mainz, Köln, Trier, these, the Three called Spiritual, lie on our very route; then Pfalz, Baiern, Sachsen: — we will tour diligently up and down; try whether, by optic machinery and art-magic of the mind, one cannot bring them round.

In all these preliminary steps and points, and even in that alpha and omega of excluding Grand-Duke Franz, and getting a Kaiser of his own, Belleisle succeeded. With painful results to himself and to millions of his fellow-creatures, — to readers of this History, among others. And became in consequence the most famous of mankind; and filled the whole world with rumour of Belleisle, in those years. — A man of such intrinsic distinction as Belleisle, whom Friedrich afterwards deliberately called a great Captain, and the only Frenchman with a genius for war; and who, for some time, played in Europe at large a part like that of Warwick the Kingmaker: how has he fallen into such oblivion? Many of my readers never heard of

and there ensued delay enough; actual Election not till **January 24th, 1742.**

him before; nor, in writing or otherwise, is there symptom that any living memory now harbours him, or has the least approach to an image of him! "For the times are babbly," says Goethe, "And then again the times are dumb:

> "*Denn geschwätzig sind die Zeiten,*
> "*Und sie sind auch wieder stumm.*"

Alas, if a man sow only chaff, in never so sublime a manner, with the whole Earth and the long-eared populations looking on, and chorally singing approval, rendering night hideous, — it will avail him nothing. And that, to a lamentable extent, was Belleisle's case. His scheme of action was in most felicitously just accordance with the national sense of France, but by no means so with the Laws of Nature and of Fact; his aim, grandiose, patriotic, what you will, was unluckily false and not true. How could "the times" continue talking of him? They found they had already talked too much. Not to say that the French Revolution has since come; and has blown all that into the air, miles aloft, — where even the solid part of it, which must be recovered one day, much more the gaseous, which we trust is forever irrecoverable, now wanders and whirls; and many things are abolished, for the present, of more value than Belleisle! —

For my own share, being, as it were, forced accidentally to look at him again, I find in Belleisle a really notable man; far superior to the vulgar of noted men, in his time or ours. Sad destiny for such a man! But when the general Life-element becomes so unspeakably phantasmal as under Louis XV., it is difficult for any man to be real; to be other than a play-actor, more or less eminent and artistically dressed. Sad enough, surely, when the truth of your relation to the Universe, and the tragically earnest meaning of your Life, is quite lied out of you, by a world sunk in lies; and you can, with effort, attain to nothing but to be a more or less splendid lie along with it! Your very existence all become a vesture, a hypocrisy and hearsay; nothing left of you but this sad faculty of sowing chaff in the fashionable manner! After Friedrich and Voltaire, in both of whom, under the given circumstances, one finds a perennial reality, more or less, — Belleisle is next; none *fails* to escape the mournful common lot by a nearer miss than Belleisle.

Beyond doubt, there are in this man the biggest projects any French head has carried, since Louis XIV. with his sublime periwig first took to striking the stars. How the indolent Louis XV. and the pacific Fleury have been got into this sublimely adventurous mood? By Belleisle chiefly, men say; — and by King Louis's first Mistresses, blown upon by Belleisle; poor Louis having now, at length, left his poor Queen to her reflections, and taken into that sad line, in which by degrees he carried it so far. There are three of them, it seems; — the first female souls that could ever manage to kindle, into flame or into smoke, in this or any other kind, that poor torpid male soul: those Mailly Sisters, three in number (I am shocked to hear), successive, nay in part simultaneous! They are proud women, especially the two younger; with ambition in them, with a bravura magnanimity, of the theatrical or operatic kind; of whom Louis is very fond. "To raise France to its place, your Majesty; the top of the Universe, namely!" "Well; if it could be done, — and quite without trouble?" thinks Louis. Bravura magnanimity, blown upon by Belleisle, prevails among these high Improper-Females, and generally in the Younger Circles of the Court; so that poor old Fleury has had no choice but to obey it or retire. And so Belleisle stalks across the Œil-de-Bœuf in that important manner, visibly to Geusau; and is the shining object in Paris, and much the topic there at present.

A few weeks hence, he is farther, — a little out of the common turn, but not beyond his military merits or capabilities, — made Maréchal de France;[*] by way of giving him a new splendour in the German Political World, and assisting in his operations there, which depend much upon the laws of vision. French epigrams circulate in consequence, and there are witty criticisms; to which Belleisle, such a dusky world of Possibility lying ahead, is grandly indifferent. Maréchal de France; — and Geusau hears (what is a fact) that there are to be "thirty young French Lords in his suite;" his very "Livery," or mere plush retinue, "to consist of 110 persons;" such an outfit for magnificence as was never seen before. And in this equipment, "early in March" (exact day not given), magnificence of outside corresponding to grandiosity of faculty and idea, Belleisle, we shall find, does practically set off towards Germany; — like a kind of French Belus, or God of the Sun; capable to dazzle weak German Courts, by optical machinery, and to set much rotten thatch on fire! —

"There are curious daguerreotype glimpses of old Paris "to be found in that Notebook of Geusau's,' says another Ex- "cerpt; "which come strangely home to us, like reality at "first-hand; — and a rather unexpected Paris it is, to most

[*] *Fastes de Louis XV,* i. 356 (12th February 1741).

"readers; many things then alive there, which are now deep
"underground. Much Jansenist Theology afloat: grand
"French Ladies piously eager to convert a young Protestant
"Nobleman like Reuss; sublime Dorcases, who do not rouge,
"or dress high, but eschew the evil world, and are thrifty for
"the Poor's sake, redeeming the time. There is a Cardinal
"de Polignac, venerable sage and ex-political person, of
"astonishing erudition, collector of Antiques (with whom we
"dined); there is the Chevalier Ramsay, theological Scotch
"Jacobite, late Tutor of the young Turenne. So many
"shining persons, now fallen indistinct again. And then,
"besides gossip, which is of mild quality, and in fair propor-
"tion, — what talk, casuistic and other, about the Moral
"Duties, the still feasible Pieties, the Constitution Unigenitus!
"All this alive, resonant at dinner-tables of Conservative
"stamp; the Miracles of Abbé Pâris much a topic there: —
"and not a whisper of Infidel Philosophies; the very name of
"Voltaire not once mentioned in the Reuss section of Parisian
"things.

"There is rumour now and then of a 'Comte de Rothen-
"bourg,' conspicuous in the Parisian circles; a shining mili-
"tary man, but seemingly in want of employment; who has
"lost in gambling, within the last four years, upwards of
"50,000*l.* (1,300,000 livres, the exact cipher given). This is
"the Graf von Rothenburg whom Friedrich made acquaint-
"ance with, in the Rhine Campaign six years ago, and has
"ever since had in his eye; — whom, in a few weeks hence,
"Friedrich beckons over to him into the Prussian States:
"'Hither, and you shall have work!' Which Rothenburg
"accepts; with manifold advantage to both parties: — one
"of Friedrich's most distinguished friends for the rest of
"his life.

"Of Cardinal Polignac there is much said, and several
"dinners with him are transacted, dialogue partly given: a
"pious wise old gentleman really, in his kind (age now
"eighty-four); looking mildly forth upon a world just about
"to overset itself and go topsy-turvy, as he sees it will. His
"*Anti-Lucretius* was once such a Poem! — but we mention him
"here because his fine Cabinet of Antiques came to Berlin on
"his death, Friedrich purchasing; and one often hears of it

"(if one cared to hear) from the Prussian Dryasdust in sub-
"sequent years.*

"Of Friedrich's unexpected Invasion of Silesia there are
"also talkings and surmisings, but in a mild indifferent tone,
"and much in the vague. And in the best-informed circles it
"is thought Belleisle will manage to *have* Grand-Duke Franz,
"the Queen of Hungary's Husband, chosen Kaiser, and, in
"some mild good way, put an end to all that;"— which is far
indeed from Belleisle's intention!

* Came to Charlottenburg, August 1742 (old Polignac had died, November last, ten months after those Geusau times): cost of the Polignac Cabinet was 40,000 thalers (6,000*l.*) say some, 90,000 livres (under 4,000*l.*) say others; cheap at either price; — and, by chance, came opportunely, "a fire having just burnt down the Academy Edifice," and destroyed much ware of that kind. Rödenbeck, i. 73; Seyfarth (Anonymous), *Geschichte Friedrichs des Andern*, i. 230.

CHAPTER VIII.

PHENOMENA IN PETERSBURG.

I KNOW not whether Major Winterfeld, who was sent to Petersburg in December last, had got back to Berlin in February, now while Friedrich is there: but for certain the good news of him had, That he had been completely successful, and was coming speedily, to resume his soldier duties in right time. As Winterfeld is an important man (nearly buried into darkness in the dull Prussian Books), let us pause for a moment on this Negotiation of his; — and on the mad Russian vicissitudes which preceded and followed, so far as they concern us. Russia, a big demi-savage neighbour next door, with such caprices, such humours and interests, is always an important, rather delicate object to Friedrich; and Fortune's mad wheel is plunging and canting in a strange headlong way there, of late. Czarina Anne, we know, is dead; the Autocrat of All the Russias following the Kaiser of the Romans within eight days. Iwan, her little Nephew, still in swaddling-clothes, is now Autocrat of All the Russias if he knew it, poor little red-coloured creature; and Anton Ulrich and his Mecklenburg Russian Princess — But let us take up the matter where our Notebooks left it, in Friedrich Wilhelm's time:

"Czarina Anne with the big cheek," continues that Notebook,* "was extremely delighted to see little Iwan; but en-

* Suprà, vol. v. p. 265.

"joyed him only two months; being herself in dying circum-
"stances. She appointed little Iwan her Successor, his Mother
"and Father to be Guardians over him; but one Bieren (who
"writes himself Biron, and 'Duke of Courland,' being Cza-
"rina's Quasi-Husband these many years) to be Guardian, as
"it were, over both them and him. Such had been the trucu-
"lent insatiable Bieren's demand on his Czarina. 'You are
"running on your destruction,' said she, with tears; but com-
"plied, as she had been wont.

"Czarina Anne died, 28th October 1740; leaving a Czar
"in his cradle; little Czar Iwan of two months, with Mother
"and Father to preside over him, and to be themselves pre-
"sided over by Bieren, in this manner.* This was the first
"great change for Anton Ulrich; but others greater are
"coming. Little Anton, readers know, is Friedrich's Brother-
"in-law, much patronised by Austria; Anton's spouse is the
"Half-Russian Princess Catherine of Mecklenburg (now
"wholly Russian, and called Princess Anne), whom Friedrich
"at one time thought of applying for, in his distress about a
"Wife. These two, will they side with Prussia, will they side
"with Austria? It was hardly worth inquiry, had not For-
"tune's wheel made suddenly a great cant, and pitched them
"to the top, for the time being.

"Bieren lasted only twenty days. He was very high and
"arbitrary upon everybody; Anne and Anton Ulrich suffering
"naturally most from him. They took counsel with Feld-
"marschall Münnich on the matter; who, after study, de-
"clared it a remediable case. Friday 18th November, Mün-
"nich had, by invitation, to dine with Duke Bieren; Münnich
"went accordingly that day, and dined; Duke looking a little
"flurried, they say: and the same evening, dinner being quite
"over, and midnight come, Münnich had his measures all
"taken, soldiers ready, warrant in hand; — and arrested
"Bieren in his bed; mere Siberia, before sunrise, looming
"upon Bieren. Never was such a change as this from 18th
"day to 19th with a supreme Bieren. Our friend Mannstein,
"excellent punctual Aide-de-Camp of Münnich, was the exe-
"cutor of the feat; and has left punctual record of it, as he

---

* Mannstein, pp. 264-267 (28th October, by Russian or Old Style, is
"17th;" we translate, in this and other cases, Russian or English, into
New Style, unless the contrary is indicated).

"does of every thing, — what Bieren said, and what Madam "Bieren, who was a little obstreperous on the occasion.* "What side Anton Ulrich and Spouse will take in a quarrel "between Prussia and Austria, is now well worth asking.

"Anton Ulrich and Wife Anne, that is to say, 'Regent "Anne' and 'Generalissimo Anton Ulrich,' now ruled, with "Münnich for right-hand man; and these were high times for "Anton Ulrich, Generalissimo and Czar's-Father; who indeed "was modest, and did not often interfere in words, though "grieved at the foolish ways his Wife had. An indolent flabby "kind of creature, she, unfit for an Autocrat; sat in her pri- "vate apartments, all in a huddle of undress; had foolish "notions, — especially had soubrettes who led her about by "the ear. And then there was a 'Princess Elizabeth,' Cousin- "german of Regent Anne, — daughter, that is to say, last "child there now was, of Peter the Great and his little brown "Catherine: — who should have been better seen to. Harm- "less foolish Princess, not without cunning; young, plump, "and following merely her flirtations and her orthodox devo- "tions; very orthodox and soft, but capable of becoming "dangerous, as a centre of the disaffected. As 'Czarina Eli- "zabeth,' before long, and ultimately as '*infâme Catin du* "*Nord,*' she —" But let us not anticipate!

It was in this posture of affairs, about a month after it had begun, that Winterfeld arrived in Petersburg; and addressed himself to Münnich, on the Prussian errand. Winterfeld was Münnich's Son-in-law (properly stepson-in-law, having married Münnich's stepdaughter, a Fräulein von Malzahn, of good Prussian kin); was acquainted with the latitudes and longitudes here, and well equipped for the operation in hand. To Madam Münnich, once Madam Malzahn, his Mother-in-law, he carried a diamond ring of 1,200*l.*, "small testimony of his Prussian Majesty's regard to so high a Prussian Lady;" to Münnich's Son and Madam's a present of 3,000*l.* on the like score: and the wheels

* Mannstein, p. 268.

being oiled in this way, and the steam so strong (son Winterfeld an ardent man, father Münnich the like, supreme in Russia, and the thing itself a salutary thing), the diplomatic speed obtained was great. Winterfeld had arrived in Petersburg December 19th: Treaty of Alliance to the effect, "Firm friends and good neighbours, we Two, Majesties of Prussia and of All the Russias; will help each the other, if attacked, with 12,000 men," — was signed on the 27th: whole Transaction, so important to Friedrich, complete in eight days. Austrian Botta, directly on the heel of those unsatisfactory Dialogues about Silesian roads, about troops that were pretty, but had never looked the wolf in the face, — had rushed off, full speed, for Petersburg, in hopes of running athwart such a Treaty as Winterfeld's, and getting one for Austria instead. But he arrived too late; and perhaps could have done nothing had he been in time. Botta tried his utmost for years afterwards, above ground and below, to obstruct and reverse this thing; but it was to no purpose, and even to less; and only, in result, brought Botta himself into flagrant diplomatic trouble and scandal; which made noise enough in the then Gazetteer world, and was the finale of Botta's Russian efforts,[*] though not worth mentioning now. The Russian Notebook continues:

"Münnich, supreme in Russia since Bieren's removal, had "wise counsels for the Regent Anne and her Husband; though "perhaps, being a high old military gentleman, he might be "somewhat abrupt in his ways. And there were domestic "Ostermanns, foreign Bottas, La Chétardies, and dangerous "Intriguers and Opposition figures, to improve any grudge

[*] Adelung, iii. ɪɪ. 289; Mannstein, p. 375 ("Lapuschin Plot," of Botta's raising; found out, "August 1743;" — Botta put in arrest, &c.).

"that might arise. Sure enough, in March 1741, Feldmarschall
"Münnich was forbid the Court (some Ostermann succeeding
"him there): 'Ever true to your Two Highnesses, though no
"longer needed;'— and withdrew, in a lofty friendly strain;
"his Son continuing at Court, though Papa had withdrawn.
"Supreme Münnich had lasted about four months; Supreme
"Bieren hardly three weeks; — and Siberia is still agape.

"Münnich being gone to his own Town-Mansion, and Re-
"gent Anne sitting in hers in a huddle of undress; little ac-
"cessible to her longheaded melancholic Ostermann, and too
"accessible to her Livonian maid; with poor little Anton
"Ulrich pouting and remonstrating, but unable to help, —
"this state of matters, with such intrigues undermining it,
"could not last forever. And had not Princess Elizabeth been
"of indolent luxurious nature, intent upon her prayers and
"flirtations, it would have ended sooner even than it did.
"Princess Elizabeth had a Surgeon called L'Estoc; a Marquis
"de la Chétardie, a highflown French Excellency (who used
"to be at Berlin, to our young Friedrich's delight), was her —
"What shall I say? La Chétardie himself had no scruple to
"say it! These two plotted for her; these were ready, —
"could she have been got ready; which was not so easy.
"Regent Anne had her suspicions; but the Princess was so
"indolent, so good: at last, when directly taxed with such a
"thing, the Princess burst into ingenuous weeping; quite
"disarmed Regent Anne's suspicions; — but found she had
"now better take L'Estoc's advice, and proceed at once.
"Which she did.

"And so, on the morrow morning, 5th December 1741, by
"aid of the Preobrazinsky Regiment, and the motions usual
"on such occasions, — in fact by merely pulling out the props
"from an undermined state of matters, — she reduced said
"state gently to ruin, ready for carting to Siberia, like its
"foregoers; and was hereby Czarina of All the Russias, pros-
"perously enough for the rest of her life. Twenty years or
"rather more. An indolent, orthodox, plump creature, dis-
"inclined to cruelty; 'not an ounce of nun's flesh in her
"composition,' said the wits. She maintained the Friedrich
"Treaty, indignant at Botta and his plots; was well with
"Friedrich, or might have been kept so by management, for
"there was no cause of quarrel, but the reverse, between the

"Countries, — could Friedrich have held his witty tongue,
"when eavesdroppers were by. But he could not always;
"though he tried. And sarcastic quizzing (especially if it be
"truth too), on certain female topics, what Improper-Female,
"Czarina of All the Russias, could stand it? The history is
"but a distressing one, a disgusting one, in human affairs.
"Elizabeth was orthodox, too, and Friedrich not, 'the horrid
"man!' The fact is, — fact dismally indubitable, though it is
"huddled into discreet dimness, and all details of it (as to
"what Friedrich's witticisms were, and the like) are refused
"us in the Prussian Books, — indignation, owing to such dis-
"mal cause, became fixed hate on the Czarina's part; and
"there followed terrible results at last: A Czarina risen to the
"cannibal pitch upon a man, in his extreme need; — '*infâme*
"*Catin du Nord*,' thinks the man! Friedrich's wit cost him
"dear; him, and half a million others still dearer, twenty
"years hence." — Till which time we will gladly leave the
Czarina and it.

Major von Winterfeld had been in Russia before
this; and had wooed his fair Malzahn there. He is
the same Winterfeld whom we once saw dining by the
wayside with the late Friedrich Wilhelm, on that last
Review Journey his Majesty made. A Captain in the
Potsdam Giants at that time; always in great favour
with the late King; and in still greater with the present, — who finds in him, we can dimly discover, and
pretty much in him alone, a soul somewhat like his
own; the one real "peer" he had about him. A man
of little education; bred in camps; yet of a proud natural eminency, and rugged nobleness of genius and
mind. Let readers mark this fiery hero-spirit, lying
buried in those dull Books, like lightning among clay.
Here is another anecdote of his Russian business:

"Winterfeld had gone, in Friedrich Wilhelm's time, with
"a party of Prussian drill-sergeants for Petersburg" (year
not given); "and duly delivered them there. He naturally
"saw much of Feldmarschall Münnich, naturally saw the

"Step-daughter of the Feldmarschall, a shining beauty in
"Petersburg; Winterfeld himself a man of shining gifts, and
"character; and one of the handsomest tall men in the world.
"Mutual love between the Fräulein and him was the rapid
"result. But how to obtain marriage? Winterfeld cannot
"marry, without leave had of his superiors: you, fair
"Malzahn, are Hof-Dame of Princess Elizabeth, all your for-
"tune the jewels you wear; and it is too possible she will not
"let you go!
"They agreed to be patient, to be silent; to watch warily
"till Winterfeld got home to Prussia, till the Fräulein Malzahn
"could also contrive to get home. Winterfeld once home,
" and the King's consent had, the Fräulein applied to Princess
"Elizabeth for leave of absence: 'A few months, to see my
"friends in Deutschland, your Highness!' Princess Elizabeth
"looked hard at her; answered evasively, this and that. At
"last, being often importuned, she answered plainly, 'I al-
"most feel convinced thou wilt never come back!' Protesta-
"tions from the Fräulein were not wanting: — 'Well then,'
"said Elizabeth, 'if thou art so sure of it, leave me thy jewels
"in pledge. Why not?' The poor Fräulein could not say
"why; had to leave her jewels, which were her whole fine
"fortune, 'worth 100,000 rubles' (20,000 *l*.); and is now the
"brave Wife of Winterfeld; — but could never, by direct
" entreaty or circuitous interest and negotiation, get back the
"least item of her jewels. Elizabeth, as Princess and as
"Czarina, was alike deaf on that subject. Now or henceforth
"that proved an impossible private enterprise for Winterfeld,
"though he had so easily succeeded in the public one."*

The new Czarina was not unmerciful. Münnich
and Company were tried for life; were condemned to
die, and did appear on the scaffold (29th January
1742), ready for that extreme penalty; but were there,
on the sudden, pardoned or half-pardoned by a merciful new Czarina, and sent to Siberia and outer darkness. Whither Bieren had preceded them. To outer darkness also, though a milder destiny had been intended

* Retzow, *Charakteristik des siebenjährigen Krieges* (Berlin, 1802), i.
45 n.

them at first, went Anton Ulrich and his Household. Towards native Germany at first; they had got as far as Riga on the way to Germany, but were detained there, for a long while (owing to suspicions, to Botta Plots, or I know not what), till finally they were recalled into Russian exile. Strict enough exile, seclusion about Archangel and elsewhere; in convents, in obscure uncomfortable places: — little Iwan, after vicissitudes, even went underground; grew to manhood, and got killed (partly by accident, not quite by murder), some twenty-three years hence, in his dungeon in the Fortress of Schlüsselburg, below the level of the Ladoga waters there. Unluckier Household, which once seemed the luckiest of the world, was never known. Canted suddenly, in this way, from the very top of Fortune's wheel to the very bottom; never to rise more; — and did not even die, at least not all die, for thirty or forty years after.*

This is the Chétardie-L'Estoc conspiracy, of 5th December 1741; the pitching up of Princess Elizabeth, and the pitching down of Anton Ulrich and his Münnichs, who had before pitched Bieren down. After which, matters remained more stationary, at Petersburg: Czarina Elizabeth, fat indolent soul, floated with a certain native buoyancy, with something of bulky steadiness, in the turbid plunge of things, and did not sink. On the contrary, her reign, so-called, was pros-

* Anton Ulrich, not till 15th May 1775 (two Daughters of his went, after this, to "Horstens, a poor Country-House in Jutland," whither Catherine II. had manumitted them, with pension; — she had wished Anton Ulrich to go home, many years before; but he would not, from shame). — Iwan had perished, 5th August 1764 (Catherine II. blamed for his death, but without cause). Iwan's Mother, Princess Anne, (mercifully) 18th March 1746. See Russian Histories, *Tooke, Castéra*, &c., — none of which, except *Munnstein*, is good for much, or to be trusted without scrutiny.

perous, though stupid; her big dark Countries, kindled already into growth, went on growing rather. And, for certain, she herself went on growing, in orthodox devotions of spiritual type (and in strangely heterodox ditto of *non*-spiritual!); in indolent mansuetudes (fell rages, if you cut on the *raws* at all); in perpetual incongruity; and, alas, at last in brandy-and-water, — till, as "*infâme Catin du Nord*," she became terribly important to some persons!

At her accession, and for two years following, Czarina Elizabeth, in spite of real disinclination that way, had a War on her hands: the Swedish War (August 1741 — August 1743), which, after long threatening on the Swedish side, had broken out into unwelcome actuality, in Anton Ulrich's time; and which could not, with all the Czarina's industry, be got rid of or staved off; Sweden being bent upon the thing, reason or no reason. War not to be spoken of, except on compulsion, in the most voluminous History! It was the unwisest of wars, we should say, and in practice probably the contemptiblest; if there were not one other Swedish War coming, which vies with it in these particulars, of which we shall be obliged to speak, more or less, at a future stage. Of this present Russian-Swedish war, having happily almost nothing to do with it, we can, except in the way of transient chronology, refrain altogether from speaking or thinking.

Poor Sweden, since it shot Karl XII. in the trenches at Fredericshall, could not get a King again; and is very anarchic under its Phantasm King and free National Palaver, — Senate with subaltern Houses; — which generally has French gold in its pocket, and noise instead of wisdom in its head. Scandalous to think of or behold. The French, desirous to keep Russia in play during these high Belleisle adventures now on foot, had, after much egging, bribing, flattering, persuaded vain Sweden into this War with Russia. "At Narva they were 80,000, we 8,000; and what became of them!" cry the Swedes always. Yes, my friends, but you had a Captain at Narva; you had not yet shot your Captain when you did Narva! "Faction of Hats," "Faction of Caps" (that is, *nightcaps*, as being somnolent and disinclined to France and War): seldom did a once valiant far-shining Nation sink to such depths, since they shot their Captain, and said to Anarchy, "*Thou* art Captaincy, we see, and the Divine thing!" Of the Wars and businesses of such a set of mortals let us shun speaking, where possible.

Mannstein gives impartial account, pleasantly clear and compact, to such as may be curious about this Swedish-Russian War; and, in the didactic point of view, it is not without value. To us the interesting circumstance is, that it does not interfere with our Silesian operations at all; and may be figured as a mere accompaniment of rumbling discord, or vacant far-off noise, going on in those Northern parts, — to which therefore we hope to be strangers in time coming. Here are some dates, which the reader may take with him, should they chance to illustrate anything:

"*August 4th*, 1741. The Swedes declare War: 'Will re-"cover their lost portions of Finland, will' &c. &c. They had "long been meditating it; they had Turk negotiations going "on, diligent emissaries to the Turk (a certain Major Sinclair "for one, whom the Russians waylaid and assassinated to get "sight of his Papers), during the late Turk-Russian War; "but could conclude nothing while that was in activity; con-"cluded only after that was done, — striking the iron when

"grown *cold*. A chief point in their Manifesto was the assas-
"sination of this Sinclair; scandal and atrocity, of which
"there is no doubt now the Russians were guilty. Various
"pretexts for the War: — prime movers to it, practically,
"were the French, intent on keeping Russia employed while
"their Belleisle German adventure went on, and who had
"even bargained with third-parties to get up a War there, as
"we shall see.
"*September* 3*d*, 1741. At Wilmanstrand, — key of Wy-
"borg, their frontier stronghold in Finland, which was under
"Siege, — the Swedes (about 5,000 of them, for they had no-
"thing to live upon, and lay scattered about in fractions) made
"fight, or skirmish, against a Russian attacking party:
"Swedes, rather victorious on their hill-top, rushed down;
"and totally lost their bit of victory, their Wilmanstrand,
"their Wyborg, and even the War itself; — for this was, in
"literal truth, the only fighting done by them in the entire
"course of it, which lasted near two years more. The rest of
"it was retreat, capitulation, loss on loss without stroke
"struck; till they had lost all Finland, and were like to lose
"Sweden itself, — Dalecarlian mutiny bursting out ('Ye
"traitors, misgovernors, worthy of death!'), with invasive
"Danes to rear of it; — and had to call in the very Russians
"to save them from worse. Czarina Elizabeth at the time of
"her accession, six months after Wilmanstrand, had made
"truce, was eager to make peace: 'By no means!' answered
"Sweden, taking arms again, or rather taking legs again;
"and rushing ruin-ward, at the old rate, still without stroke.
"*June* 28*th*, 1743. They did halt; made Peace of Abo
"(Truce and Preliminaries signed there, that day: Peace
"itself, August 17th); Czarina magnanimously restoring most
"of their Finland (thinking to herself, 'Not done enough for
"me yet; cook it a little yet!'); — and settling who their
"next King was to be, among other friendly things. And in
"November following, Keith, in his Russian galleys, with
"some 10,000 Russians on board, arrived in Stockholm; pro-
"tective against Danes and mutinous Dalecarles; staid there
"till June of next year 1744."* Is not this a War!

* Adelung, ii. 445. Mannstein, pp. 297 (Wilmanstrand Affair, himself
present) — 365 (Peace) — 373 (Keith's *return* with his galleys). Comte de
Hordt (present also, on the Swedish side, and subsequently a Soldier of

On the Russian side, General Keith, under Field-marshal Lacy as chief in command (the same Keith whom we saw at Oczakow under Münnich, some time ago), had a great deal of the work and management; which was of a highly miscellaneous kind, commanding fleets of gunboats, and much else; and readers of *Mannstein* can still judge, — much more could King Friedrich, earnestly watching the affair itself as it went on, — whether Keith did not do it in a solid and quietly eminent and valiant manner. Sagacious, skilful, imperturbable, without fear and without noise; a man quietly ever ready. He had quelled, once, walking direct into the heart of it, a ferocious Russian mutiny, or uproar from below, which would have ruined everything in few minutes more.* He suffered, with excellent silence, now and afterwards, much ill usage from above withal; — till Friedrich himself, in the third year hence, was lucky enough to get him as General. Friedrich's Sister Ulrique, the marriage of Princess Ulrique, — that also, as it chanced, had something to do with this Peace of Abo. But we anticipate too far.

Friedrich's), *Mémoires* (Berlin, 1789), i. 18-88. The murder of Sinclair (done by "four Russian subalterns, two miles from Naumburg in Silesia, 17th June 1739, about 7 P. M.") is amply detailed from Documents, in a late Book: Weber, *Aus Vier Jahrhunderten* (Leipzig, 1858), i. 274-279.

* Mannstein, p. 130 (no date, April — May 1742).

CHAPTER IX.

FRIEDRICH RETURNS TO SILESIA.

FRIEDRICH staid only three weeks at home; moving about, from Berlin to Potsdam, to Reinsberg and back: all the gay world is in Berlin, at this Carnival time; but Friedrich has more to do with business, of a manifold and over-earnest nature, than with Carnival gaieties. French Valori is here, "my fat Valori," who is beginning to be rather a favourite of Friedrich's: with Excellency Valori, and with the other Foreign Excellencies, there was diplomatic passaging in these weeks; and we gather from Valori, in the inverse way (Valori fallen sulky), that it was not ill done on Friedrich's part. He had some private consultation with the Old Dessauer, too; "probably on military points," thinks Valori. At least there was noticed more of the drill-sergeant than before, in his handling of the Army, when he returned to Silesia, continues the sulky one. "Troops and generals did not know him again," — so excessively strict was he grown, on the sudden. And truly "he got into details which were beneath, not only "a Prince who has great views, but even a simple "Captain of Infantry," — according to my (Valori's) military notions and experiences! *—

The truth is, Friedrich begins to see, more clearly than he did with *Gloire* dazzling him, that his position is an exceedingly grave one, full of risk, in the then mood and condition of the world; that he, in the whole

* Valori, i. 99.

world, has no sure friend but his Army; and that in
regard to *it* he cannot be too vigilant! The world is
ominous to this youngest of the Kings more than to
another. Sounds as of general Political Earthquake
grumble audibly to him from the deeps: all Europe
likely, in any event, to get to loggerheads on this
Austrian Pragmatic matter; the Nations all watching
him, to see what he will make of it: — fugleman he
to the European Nations, just about bursting up on
such an adventure. It may be a glorious position, or
a not glorious; but, for certain, it is a dangerous one,
and awfully solitary! —

Fuglemen the world and its Nations always have,
when simultaneously bent anywhither, wisely or unwisely; and it is natural that the most adventurous
spirit take that post. Friedrich has not sought the
post; but following his own objects, has got it; and
will be ignominiously lost, and trampled to annihilation
under the hoofs of the world, if he do not mind! To
keep well ahead; — to be rapid as possible; that were
good: — to step aside were still better! And Friedrich
we find is very anxious for that; "would be content
"with the Duchy of Glogau, and join Austria;" but
there is not the least chance that way. His Special
Envoy to Vienna, Gotter, and along with him Borck
the regular Minister, are come home; all negotiation
hopeless at Vienna; and nothing but indignant war-
preparation going on there, with the most animated
diligence, and more success than had seemed possible.
That is the law of Friedrich's Silesian Adventure:
"Forward, therefore, on these terms; others there are
not; waste no words!" Friedrich recognises to himself
what the law is; pushes stiffly forward, with a fine

silence on all that is not practical, really with a fine steadiness of hope, and audacity against discouragements. Of his anxieties, which could not well be wanting, but which it is royal to keep strictly under lock and key, of these there is no hint to Jordan or to anybody; and only through accidental chinks, on close scrutiny, can we discover that they exist. Symptom of despondency, of misgiving or repenting about his Enterprise, there is none anywhere. Friedrich's fine gifts of *silence* (which go deeper than the lips) are noticeable here, as always; and highly they availed Friedrich in leading his life, though now inconvenient to Biographers writing of the same! —

It was not on matters of drill, as Valori supposes, that Friedrich had been consulting with the Old Dessauer: this time it was on another matter. Friedrich has two next Neighbours greatly interested, none more so, in the Pragmatic Question: Kur-Sachsen, Polish King, a foolish greedy creature, who is extremely uncertain about his course in it (and indeed always continued so, now against Friedrich, now for him, and again against); and Kur-Hanover, our little George of England, whose course is certain as that of the very stars, and direct against Friedrich at this time, as indeed, at all times not exceptional, it is apt to be. Both these Potentates must be attended to, in one's absence; method to be gentle but effectual; the Old Dessauer to do it: — and this is what these consultings had turned upon; and in a month or two, readers, and an astonished Gazetteer world, will see what comes of them.

It was February 19th when Friedrich left Berlin; the 21st he spends at Glogau, inspecting the Blockade there, and not ill content with the measures taken:

"Press that Wallis all you can," enjoins he: "Hunger seems to be slow about it! Summon him again, were your new Artillery come up; threaten with bombardment; but spare the Town, if possible. Artillery is coming: let us have done here, and soon!" Next day he arrives, not at Breslau as some had expected, but at Schweidnitz sidewards; a strong little Town, at least an elaborately fortified, of which we shall hear much in time coming. It lies a day's ride west of Breslau; and will be quieter for business than a big gazing Capital would be, — 'were Breslau even one's own city; which it is not, though perhaps tending to be. Breslau is in transition circumstances at present; a little uncertain *whose* it is, under its Münchows and new managers: Breslau he did not visit at all on this occasion. To Schweidnitz certain new regiments had been ordered, there to be disposed of in reinforcing: there, "in the Count Hoberg's Mansion," he principally lodges for six weeks to come; shooting out on continual excursions; but always returning to Schweidnitz, as the centre, again.

Algarotti, home from Turin (not much of a success there, but always melodious for talk), had travelled with him; Algarotti, and not long after, Jordan and Maupertuis, bear him company, that the vacant moments too be beautiful. We can fancy he has a very busy, very anxious, but not an unpleasant time. He goes rapidly about, visiting his posts, — chiefly about the Neisse Valley; Neisse being the prime object, were the weather once come for siege-work. He is in many Towns (specified in *Rödenbeck* and the Books, but which may be anonymous here); doubtless on many Steeples and Hill-tops; questioning intelligent natives, diligently using his own eyes: intent to make personal acquaintance with this new Country, — where, little as he yet dreams of it, the deadly struggles of his Life lie waiting him, and which he will know to great perfection before all is done!

Neisse lies deep enough in Prussian environment; like Brieg, like Glogau, strictly blockaded; our posts thereabouts, among the Mountains, thought to be impregnable. Nevertheless, what new thing is this? Here are swarms of loose Hussar-Pandour people, wild Austrian Irregulars, who come pouring out of Glatz Country; disturbing the Prussian posts towards that quarter; and do not let us want for Small War (*Kleine Krieg*) so-called. General Browne, it appears, is got back to Glatz at this early season, he and a General Lentulus busy there; and these are the compliments they send! A very troublesome set of fellows, infesting one's purlieus in winged predatory fashion; swooping down like a cloud of vulturous harpies on the sudden; fierce enough, if the chance favour; then to wing again, if it do not. Communication, especially reconnoitring, is not safe in their neighbourhood. Prussian Infantry, even in small parties, generally beats them; Prussian Horse not, but is oftener beaten, — not drilled for this rabble and their ways. In pitched fight they are not dangerous, rather are despicable to the disciplined man; but can, on occasion, do a great deal of mischief.

Thus, it was not long after Friedrich's coming into these parts, when he learnt with sorrow that a Body of "500 Horse and 500 Foot" (or say it were only 300 of each kind, which is the fact*) had eluded our posts

---

* Orlich, t. 79; *Œuvres de Frédéric*, ii. 68.

in the Mountains, and actually got into Neisse, "The "Foot will be of little consequence," writes Friedrich; "but the Horse, which will disturb our communications, "are a considerable mischief." This was on the 5th of March. And about a week before, on the 27th of February, there had well nigh a far graver thing befallen, — namely the capture of Friedrich himself, and the sudden end of all these operations.

Skirmish of Baumgarten, 27*th February* 1741.

In most of the Anecdote-Books there used to figure, and still does, insisting on some belief from simple persons, a wonderful Story in very vague condition: How once "in the Silesian Wars," the King, in those Upper Neisse regions, in the Wartha district between Glatz and Neisse, was, one day, within an inch of being taken, — clouds of Hussars suddenly rising round him, as he rode reconnoitring, with next to no escort, only an adjutant or so in attendance. How he shot away, keeping well in the shade; and ere long whisked into a Convent or Abbey, the beautiful Abbey of Kamenz in those parts; and found Tobias Stusche, excellent Abbot of the place, to whom he candidly disclosed his situation. How the excellent Tobias thereupon instantly ordered the bells to be rung for a mass extraordinary, Monks not knowing why; and, after bells, made his appearance in high costume, much to the wonder of his Monks, with a *second* Abbot, also in high costume, but of shortish stature, whom they never saw before or after. Which two Abbots, or at least Tobias, proceeded to do the so-called divine office there and then; letting loose the big chant especially, and the growl of organs, in a singularly expressive manner. How the Pandours arrived in clouds, meanwhile; entered, in searching parties, more or less reverent of the mass; searched high and low; but found nothing, and were obliged to take Tobias's blessing at last, and go their ways. How the Second Abbot thereupon swore eternal friendship with Tobias, in the private apartments; and rode off as — as a rescued Majesty, determined to be more cautious in Pandour Countries for the future!* — Which story, as to the body of it, is all myth; though, as is oftenest the case, there lies in it some soul of fact too. The History-Books, which had not much heeded the little fact, would have nothing to do with this account of it. Nevertheless the people stuck to their Myth; so that Dryasdust (in punishment for his sinful blindness to the human and divine significance of facts) was driven to investigate the business; and did at last victoriously bring it home to the small occurrence now called *Skirmish of Baumgarten*, which had nearly become so great in the History of the World, — to the following effect.

There are Two Valleys with roads that lead from that Southwest quarter of Silesia towards Glatz, each with a little Town at the end of it, looking up into it: Wartha the name of the one; Silberberg that of the other. Through the Wartha Valley, which is southernmost, young Neisse River comes rushing down, — the blue mountains thereabouts very pretty, on a clear spring day, says my touring friend. Both at Wartha,

---

* Hildebrandt, *Anekdoten*, i. 1-7. Pandour proper is a *foot*-soldier (tall raw-boned ill-washed biped, in copious Turk breeches, rather barish in the top parts of him; carries a very long musket, and has several pistols and butcher's-knives stuck in his girdle): specifically a footman; but readers will permit me to use him withal, as here, in the generic sense.

and at Silberberg the little Town which looks into the mouth of the northernmost Valley, the Prussians have a post. Old Derschau, Malplaquet Derschau, with headquarters at Frankenstein, some seven or eight miles nearer Schweidnitz, has not failed in that precaution. Friedrich wished to visit Silberberg and Wartha; set out accordingly, 27th February, with small escort carelessly as usual: the Pandour people had wind of it; knew his habits on such occasions; and, gliding through other roadless valleys, under an adventurous Captain, had determined to whirl him off. And they were in fact not far from succeeding, had not a mistake happened.

Silberberg, and Wartha the southernmost, which stands upon the Neisse River (rushing out there into the plainer country), are each about seven or eight miles from Frankenstein, the Headquarters; and there are relays of posts, capable of supporting one another, all the way from Frankenstein to each. Friedrich rode to Silberberg first; examined the post, found it right; then rode across to Wartha, seven or eight miles southward; examined Wartha likewise; after which, he sat down to dinner in that little Town, with an Officer or two for company, — having, I suppose, found all right in both the posts. In the way hither, he had made some change in the relay-arrangements, which at first involved some diminution of his own escort, and then some marching about and redistributing: so that, externally, it seemed as if the Principal Relay-party were now marching on Baumgarten, an intermediate Village, — at least so the Pandour Captain understands the movements going on; and crouches into the due thickets in consequence, not doubting but the King himself is for Baumgarten, and will be at hand presently. Principal relay-party, a squadron of Schulenburg's Dragoons, with a stupid Major over them, is not quite got into Baumgarten, when "with horrible cries, the Pandour Captain with about 500 Horse," plunges out of cover, direct upon the throat of it; — and Friedrich, at Wartha, is but just begun dining when tumult of distant musketry breaks in upon him. With Friedrich himself, at this time, as I count, there might be 150 Horse; in Wartha post itself are at least "forty hussars and fifty foot." By no means "nothing but a single adjutant," as the Myth bears.

The stupid Major ought to have beaten this rabble, though above two to one of him. But he could not, though he tried considerably; on the contrary, he was himself beaten; obliged to make off, leaving "ten dragoons killed, sixteen prisoners, one standard and two kettle-drums:" — victory and all this plunder, ye Pandour gentry; but evidently no King. The Pandour gentry, on the instant, made off too, alarm being abroad; got into some side valley, with their prisoners and drum-and-standard honours and vanished from view of mankind.

Friedrich had started from dinner; got his escort under way, with the forty hussars and the fifty foot, and what small force was attainable; and hurried towards the scene. He did see, by the road, another strongish party of Pandours; dashed them across the Neisse River out of sight; — but, getting to Baumgarten, found the field silent, and ten dead men upon it. "I always told you those Schulenburg Dragoons were good for nothing!" writes he to the Old Dessauer; but gradually withal, on comparing notes, finds what a danger he had run, and how rash and foolish he had been. "An *étourderie* (foolish trick)," he calls it, writing to Jordan; "a black eye;" and will avoid the like. Vienna got its two kettle-drums and flag; extremely glad to see them; and even sang *Te-deum* upon them, to general edification.* This is the naked primordial substance out of which the above Myth grew to its present luxuriance in the popular imagination. Place, the little Village of Baumgarten; day, 27th February 1741. Of Tobias Stusche or the Convent of Kamenz, not one authentic word on this occasion. Tobias did get promotions, favours in coming years: a worthy Abbot, deserving promotion on general grounds; and master of a Convent very picturesque, but twelve miles from the present scene of action.

Aspects of Breslau.

Friedrich avoided visiting Breslau, probably for the reasons above given; though there are important interests of his there, especially his chief Magazine; and issues of moment are silently working forward. Here are contemporary Excerpts (in abridged form), which are authentic, and of significance to a lively reader:

"*Breslau, Middle of January* 1741. The Prussian Envoy, "Herr von Gotter, had appeared here, returning from Vienna; "Gotter, and then Borck, who made no secret in Breslau "society, That not the slightest hope of a peaceable result "existed, as society might have flattered itself; but that war "and battle would have to decide this matter. A Saxon "Ambassador was also here, waiting some time; message "thought to be insignificant: — probably some vague ad- "monitory stuff again from Kur-Sachsen (Polish King, son of "August the Strong, a very insignificant man), who acts as

* Orlich, i. 62 64.

"*Reichs-Vicarius* in those Northern parts." For the reader is to know, there are Reichs-Vicars more than one (nay more than two on this occasion, with considerable jarring going on about them); and I could say much about their dignities, limits, duties,* — if indeed there were any duties, except dramatic ones! But the Reich itself, and Vicarship along with it, are fallen into a nearly imaginary condition; and the Regensburg Diet (not Princes now, but mere Delegates of Princes, mostly Bombazine People), which, "ever since 1663," has sat continual, instead of now and then, is become an Enchanted Wiggery, strange to look upon, under those earnest stars. "As King Friedrich did not call at Breslau," after those Neisse bombardments, "but rolled past, straight "homewards, the three Excellencies all departed, — Borck "and Gotter to Berlin, the Saxon home again with his in- "significant message.

"*January* 19*th*. Schwerin too was here in the course of the "winter, to see how the magazines and other war-preparations "were going on: Breslau outwardly and inwardly is whirling "with business, and offers phenomena. For instance, it is "known that the Army-Chest, heaps of silver and gold in it, "lies in the Scultet Garden-House, where the King lodged; "and that only one sentry walks there, and that in the guard- "house itself, which is some way off, there are only thirty "men. January] 19th, about 9 of the clock,** alarm rises, "That 2,000 *Diebs-Gesindel* (Collective Thief-rabble of Breslau "and dependencies) are close by; intending a stroke upon "said Garden-House and Army-Chest! Perhaps this rumour "sprang of its own accord; — or perhaps not quite? It had "been very rife; and ran high; not without remonstrances in "Town-Hall, and the like, which we can imagine. Issue was, "The Officer on post at Scultet's loaded his treasure in carts; "conveyed it, that same night, to the interior of the City, in "fact to the *Oberamts-Haus* (Government-House that was);— "which doubtless was a step in the right direction. For now "the Two Feld-Kriegs-Commissariat Gentlemen (one of "whom is the expert Münchow, son of our old Cüstrin friend), "supreme Prussian Authorities here, do likewise shift out of "their inns; and take old Schaffgotsch's apartments in the

* Adelung, II. 143, &c.; Köhler, *Reichs-Historic*, pp. 585-589.
** *Helden-Geschichte*, I. 700.

"same Oberamts-Haus; mutely symbolling that perhaps *they*
" are likely to become a kind of Government. And the reader
" can conceive how, in such an element, the function of
" governing would of itself fall more and more into their hands.
" They were consummately polite, discreet, friendly towards
" all people; and did in effect manage their business, tax-
" gatherings in money and in kind, with a perfection and pre-
" cision which made the evil a minimum.

"*February 17th.* * * This day also, there arrived at
" Breslau, by boat up the Oder, ten heavy cannon, three
" mortars, and ammunition of powder, bombshells, balls, as
" much as loaded fifty wagons; the whole of which were, in
" like manner, forwarded to Ohlau. This day, as on other
" days before and after. Great Magazines forming here; the
" Military chiefly at Ohlau; at Breslau the Provender part,—
" and this latter under noteworthy circumstances. In the
" Dom-Island, namely; which is definable (in a case of such
" necessity) as being 'outside the walls.' Especially as the
" Reverend Fathers have mostly glided into corners, and left
" the place vacant. In the Dom-Island, it certainly is; and
" such a stock, — all bought for money down, and spurred for-
" ward while the roads were under frost, — 'such a stock as
" was not thought to be in all Silesia,' says exaggerative
" wonder. The vacant edifices in the Dom-Island are filled to
" the neck with meal and corn; the Prussian brigade now
" quartering there ('within the walls,' in a sense) to guard the
" same. And in the Bishop's Garden" (poor Sinzendorf, far
enough away and in no want of it just now) "are mere hay-
" mows, bigger than houses: who can object, — in a case of
" necessity? No man, unless he politically meddle, is meddled
" with; politically meddling, you are at once picked up; as
" one or two are, — clapped into gentle arrest, or, like old
" Schaffgotsch, and even Sinzendorf before long, requested to
" leave the Country till it get settled. Rigour there is, but
" not intentional injustice on Münchow's part, and there is a
" studious avoidance of harsh manner.

"*February-March.* Considerable recruiting in Schlesien:
" six hundred recruits have enlisted in Breslau alone. Also
" his Prussian Majesty has sent a supply of Protestant
" Preachers, ordained for the occasion, to minister where
" needed; — which is piously acknowledged as a god-send in

"various parts of Silesia. Twelve came first, all Berliners; "soon afterwards, others from diffcrent parts, till, in the end, "there were about Sixty in all. Rigorous, punctilious "avoidance of offence to the Catholic minorities, or of what- "ever least thing Silesian Law does not permit, is enjoined "upon them; 'to preach in barns or town-halls, where by "Law you have no Church.' Their salary is about 30*l.* a "year; they are all put under supervision of the Chaplain of "Margraf Karl's Regiment" (a judicious Chaplain, I have no doubt, and fit to be a Bishop); and so far as appears, mere benefit is got of them by Schlesien as well as by Friedrich, in this function. Friedrich is careful to keep the balance level between Catholic and Protestant; but it has hung at such an angle, for a long while past! In general we observe, the Catholic Dignitaries, and the zealous or fanatic of that creed, especially the Jesuits, are apt to be against him: as for the non-fanatic, they expect better government, secular advantage; these latter weigh doubtfully, and with less weight whichever way. In the general population, who are Protestant, he recognises friends; — and has sent them Sixty Preachers, which by Law was their due long since. Here follow two little traits, comic or tragicomic, with which we can conclude:

"Detached Jesuit parties, here and there, seem to have "mischief in hand in a small way, encouraging deserters and "the like; — and we keep an eye on them. No discontent "elsewhere, at least none audible; on the contrary, much en- "listing on the part of the Silesian youth, with other good "symptoms. But in the Dom, there is, singular to say, a "Goblin found walking, one night; — advancing, not with airs "from Heaven, upon the Prussian sentry there! The Prussian "sentry handles arms; pokes determinedly into the Goblin, "and, finding him solid, ever more determinedly, till the "Goblin shrieked 'Jesus Maria!' and was hauled to the "Guardhouse for investigation." A weak Goblin; doubtless of the valet kind; worth only a little whipping; but testifies what the spirit is.

"Another time, two deserter Frenchmen getting hanged" (such the law in aggravated cases), "certain polite Jesuits, "who had by permission been praying and extreme-unctioning "about them, came to thank the Colonel after all was over.

"Colonel, a grave practical man, needs no 'thanks;' would,
"however, 'advise your Reverences to teach your people
"that perjury is not permissible, that an oath sworn ought to
"be kept;' and in fine 'would advise you Holy Fathers
"hereabouts, and others, to have a care lest you get into'—
"And twitching his reins, rode away without saying into
"what."*

Austria is standing to Arms.

Schwerin has been doing his best in this interim; collecting magazines with double diligence while the roads are hard, taking up the Key-positions far and wide, from the Jablunka round to the Frontier Valleys of Glatz again. He was through Jablunka, at one time; on into Mähren, as far as Olmütz; levying contributions, emitting patents: but as to intimidating her Hungarian Majesty, if that was the intention, or changing her mind at all, that is not the issue got. Austria has still strength, and Pragmatic Sanction and the Laws of Nature have! Very fixed is her Hungarian Majesty's determination, to part with no inch of Territory, but to drive the intrusive Prussians home well punished.

How she has got the funds is, to this day, a mystery; — unless George and Walpole, from their Secret-Service Moneys, have smuggled her somewhat? For the Parliament is not sitting, and there will be such jargonings, such delays: a preliminary 100,000*l*., say by degrees 200,000*l*., — we should not miss it, and in her Majesty's hands it would go far! Hints in the English Dryasdust we have; but nothing definite; and we are left to our guesses.** A romantic story, first

---

* *Helden-Geschichte*, i. 723.
** Tindal (xx. 497) says expressly 200,000*l*., but gives no date or other particular.

set current by Voltaire, has gone the round of the world, and still appears in all Histories: How in England, there was a Subscription set on foot for her Hungarian Majesty; outcome of the enthusiasm of English Ladies of quality, — old Sarah Duchess of Marlborough putting down her name for 40,000*l*., or indeed putting down the ready sum itself; magnanimous veteran that she was. Voltaire says, omitting date and circumstance, but speaking as if it were indubitable, and a thing you could see with eyes: "The Duchess "of Marlborough, widow of him who had fought for Karl VI." (and with such signal returns of gratitude from the said Karl VI.), "assembled the principal "Ladies of London; who engaged to furnish 100,000*l*. "among them; the Duchess herself putting down" (*en deposa*, tabling *in corpore*) "40,000*l*. of it. The Queen "of Hungary had the greatness of soul to refuse this "money; — needing only, as she intimated, what the "Nation in Parliament assembled might please to offer "her."*

One is sorry to run athwart such a piece of mutual magnanimity; but the fact is, on considering a little and asking evidence, it turns out to be mythical. One Dilworth, an innocent English soul (from whom our grandfathers used to learn *Arithmetic*, I think), writing on the spot some years after Voltaire, has this useful passage: "It is the great failing of a strong imagination "to catch greedily at wonders. Voltaire was misin-"formed; and would perhaps learn, by a second inquiry, "a truth less splendid and amusing. A Contribution "was, by Newswriters upon their own authority, fruit-"lessly proposed. It ended in nothing: the Parliament

* Voltaire, *Œuvres* (*Siècle de Louis XV*, c. 6), xxviii. 79.

"voted a supply;"— that did it, Mr. Dilworth; supplies enough; and many of them! "Fruitlessly, by News-writers on their own authority;" that is the sad fact.*

It is certain, little George, who considers Pragmatic Sanction as the Keystone of Nature in a manner, has been venturing far deeper than purse for that adorable object; and indeed has been diving, secretly, in muddier waters than we expected, to a dangerous extent, on behalf of it, at this very time. In the first days of March, Friedrich has heard from his Minister at Petersburg of a *detestable Project*,** — project for "Partitioning the Prussian Kingdom," no less; for fairly cutting into Friedrich, and paring him down to the safe pitch, as an enemy to Pragmatic and mankind. They say, a Treaty, Draught of a Treaty, for that express object, is now ready; and lies at Petersburg, only waiting signature. Here is a Project! Contracting parties (Russian signature still wanting) are: Kur-Sachsen; her Hungarian Majesty; King George; and that Regent Anne (*Mrs.* Anton Ulrich, so to speak), who sits in a Liddle of undress, — impatient of Political objects, but sensible to the charms of handsome men. To the charms of Count Lynar, especially; the handsomest of Danish noblemen (more an ancient Roman than a Dane),

---

* *The Life and Heroick Actions of Frederick III.* (*sic*, a common blunder): by W. H. Dilworth, M.A. (London 1758), p. 25. A poor little Book, one of many coming out on that subject just then (for a reason we shall see on getting thither); which contains, of available now, the above sentence and no more. Indeed its brethren, one of them by Samuel Johnson (*impraxsus*, the imprisoned giant), do not even contain that, and have gone wholly to zero. — Neither little Dilworth nor big Voltaire give the least shadow of specific date; but both evidently mean, Spring 1742 (not 1741).

** Orlich, i. 83 (scrap of Note to Old Dessauer; no date allowed us; "early in March").

whom the Polish Majesty, calculating cause and effect, had despatched to her, with that view, in the dead of winter lately. To whom she has given ear; — dismissing her Münnich, as we saw above; — and is ready for signing, or perhaps has signed!* Friedrich's astonishment, on hearing of this "detestable Project," was great. However, he takes his measures on it; — right lucky that he has the Old Dessauer, and machinery for acting on Kur-Sachsen and the Britannic Majesty. "Get your machinery in gear!" is naturally his first order. And the Old Dessauer does it, with effect: of which by and by.

Never did I hear, before or since, of such a plunge into the muddy unfathomable, on the part of little George, who was an honourable creature, and dubitative to excess: and truly this rash plunge might have cost him dear, had not he directly scrambled out again. Or did Friedrich exaggerate to himself his Uncle's real share in the matter? I always guess, there had been more of loose talk, of hypothesis and fond hope, in regard to George's share, than of determinate fact or procedure on his own part. The transaction, having had to be dropped on the sudden, remains somewhat dark; but, in substance, it is not doubtful;** and Parliament itself took afterwards to poking into it, though with little effect. Kur-Sachsen's objects in the adventure were of the earth, earthy; but on George's part it was pure adoration of Pragmatic Sanction, anxiety for the Keystone of Nature, and lest Chaos come again. In comparison with such transcendent divings, what is a little Secret-Service money! —

The Count Lynar of this adventure, who had well

* *Œuvres de Frédéric,* ii. 68.   ** Tindal, xx. 497.

nigh done such a feat in Diplomacy, may turn up transiently again. A conspicuous, more or less ridiculous person of those times. Büsching (our Geographical friend) had gone with him, as Excellency's Chaplain, in this Russian Journey; which is a memorable one to Büsching; and still presents vividly, through his Book, those haggard Baltic Coasts in mid-winter, to readers who have business there. Such a Journey for grimness of outlook, upon pine-tufts and frozen sand; for cold (the Count's very tobacco-pipe freezing in his mouth), for hardship, for bad lodging, and extremity of dirt in the unfreezable kinds, as seldom was. They met, one day on the road, a Lord Hyndford, English Ambassador just returning from Petersburg, with his fourgons and vehicles, and arrangements for sleep and victual, in an enviably luxurious condition, — whom we shall meet, to our cost. They saw, in the body, old Field-marshal Lacy, and dined with him, at Riga; who advised brandy schnapps; a recipe rejected by Büsching. And other memorabilia, which by accident hang about this Lynar.* — All through Regent Anne's time he continued a dangerous object to Friedrich; and it was a relief when Elizabeth *Catin* became Autocrat, instead of Deshabille Anne and her Lynar. Adieu to him, for fifteen years or more.

Of Friedrich's military operations, of his magazines, posts, diligent plannings and gallopings about, in those weeks; of all this the reader can form some notion by looking on the map and remembering what has gone before: but that subterranean growling which attended him, prophetic of Earthquake, that universal breaking

* Büsching, *Beytrãge*, vi. 132-164.

forth of Bedlams, now fallen so extinct, no reader can imagine. Bedlams totally extinct to everybody; but which were then very real, and raged wide as the world, high as the stars, to a hideous degree among the then sons of men; — unimaginable now by any mortal.

And, alas, this is one of the grand difficulties for my readers and me; Friedrich's Life-element having fallen into such a dismal condition. Most dismal, dark, ugly, that Austrian-Succession Business, and its worldwide battlings, throttlings and intriguings: not Dismal Swamp, under a coverlid of London Fog, could be uglier! A Section of "History" so-called, which human nature shrinks from; of which the extant generation already knows nothing, and is impatient of hearing anything! Truly, Oblivion is very due to such an Epoch: and from me far be it to awaken, beyond need, its sordid Bedlams, happily extinct. But without Life-element, no Life can be intelligible; and till Friedrich and one or two others are extricated from it, Dismal Swamp cannot be quite filled in. Courage, reader! — Our Constitutional Historian makes this farther reflection:

"English moneys, desperate Russian intrigues, Treaties "made and Treaties broken — If instead of Pragmatic Sanc- "tion with eleven Potentates guaranteeing, Maria Theresa "had at this time had 200,000 soldiers and a full treasury (as "Prince Eugene used to advise the late Kaiser), how different "might it have been with her, and with the whole world that "fell upon one another's throats in her quarrel! Some eight "years of the most disastrous War; and except the falling of "Silesia to its new place, no result gained by it. War at any "rate inevitable, you object? English-Spanish War having "been obliged to kindle itself; French sure to fall in, on the "Spanish side; sure to fall upon Hanover, so soon as beaten "at sea, and thus to involve all Europe? Well, it is too likely.

"But, even in that case, the poor English would have gone "upon their necessary Spanish War, by the direct road and "with their eyes open, instead of somnambulating and stum- "bling over the chimney-tops; and the settlement might "have come far sooner, and far cheaper to mankind. — Nay, "we are to admit that the new place for Silesia was, likewise, "the place appointed it by just Heaven; and Friedrich's too "was a necessary War. Heaven makes use of Shadow-hunt- "ing Kaisers too; and its ways in this mad world are through "the great Deep."

The Young Dessauer captures Glogau (March 9th); the Old Dessauer, by his Camp of Göttin (April 2d), checkmates certain Designing Persons.

Money somewhere her Hungarian Majesty has got; that is one thing evident. She has an actual Army on foot, "drawn out of Italy," or whence she could; formidable Army, says rumour, and getting well equipped; — and here are the Pandour Precursors of it, coming down like storm-clouds through the Glatz valleys; — nearly finishing the War for her at a stroke, the other day, had accident favoured; — and have thrown reinforcement of 600 into Neisse. Friedrich is not insensible to these things; and amid such alarms from far and from near, is becoming eager to have, at least, Glogau in his hand. Glogau, he is of opinion, could now, and should, straight-way be done.

Glogau is not a strong place; after all the repair- ing, it could stand little siege, were we careless of hurting it. But Wallis is obstinate; refuses Free With- drawal; will hold out to the uttermost, though his meal is running low. He pretends there is relief coming; relief just at hand; — and once, in midnight time, "lets off a rocket and fires six guns," alarming Prince

Leopold as if relief were just in the neighbourhood. A tough industrious military man; stiff to his purpose, and not without shift.

Friedrich thinks the place might be had by assault: "Open trenches; set your batteries going, which need not injure the Town; need only alarm Wallis, and *terrify* it; then, under cover of this noise and feint of cannonading, storm with vigour." Leopold, the Young Dessauer, is cautious; wants petards if he must storm, wants two new battalions if he must open trenches; — he gets these requisites, and is still cunctatory. Friedrich has himself got the notion, "from clear intelligence," true or not, that relief to Glogau is actually on way; and under such imminences, Russian and other, in so ticklish a state of the world, he becomes more and more impatient that this thing were done. In the first week of March, still hurrying about on inspection-business, he writes, from four or five different places ("Mollwitz near Brieg" is one of them, a Village we shall soon know better), Note after Note to Leopold; who still makes difficulties, and is not yet perfect to the last finish in his preparations. "Preparations!" answers Friedrich impatiently (date *Mollwitz*, 5th *March*, the third or fourth impatient Note he has sent); and adds, just while quitting Mollwitz for Ohlau, this Postscript in his own hand:

P.S. "I am sorry you have not understood me! They "have, in Böhmen, a regular enterprise on hand for the rescue "of Glogau. I have Infantry enough to meet them; but "Cavalry is quite wanting. You must therefore, without "delay, begin the siege. Let us finish there, I pray you!"*

* Orlich, i. 70.

And next day, Monday 6th, to cut the matter short, he despatches his General-Adjutant Goltz in person (the distance is above seventy miles), with this Note wholly in autograph, which nothing vocal on Leopold's part will answer:

"*Ohlau, 6th March.* As I am certainly informed that the "Enemy will make some attempt, I hereby with all distinct- "ness command, That, so soon as the petards are come" (which they are), "you attack Glogau. And you must make "your Arrangement (*Disposition*) for more than one attack; "so that, if one fail, the other shall certainly succeed. I hope "you will put off no longer; — otherwise the blame of all the "mischief that might arise out of longer delay must lie on you "alone." *

Goltz arrived with this emphatic Piece, Tuesday Evening, after his course of seventy miles: this did at last rouse our cautious Young Dessauer; and so there is next obtainable, on much compression, the following authentic Excerpt:

"*Glogau, 8th March* 1741. His Durchlaucht the Prince "Leopold summoned all the Generals at noon; and informed "them That, this very night, Glogau must be won. He gave "them their Instructions in writing: where each was to post "himself; with what detachments; how to proceed. There "are to be Three Attacks: one up stream, coming on with the "River to its left; one down stream, River to its right; and a "third from the landward side, perpendicular to the other "two. The very captains that shall go foremost are speci- "fied; at what hour each is to leave quarters, so that all be "ready simultaneously, waiting in the posts assigned; — "against what points to advance out of these, and storm "Rampart and Wall. Places, times, particulars, everything "is fixed with mathematical exactitude: 'Be steady, be cor- "rect, especially be silent; and so far as Law of Nature will "permit, be simultaneous! When the big steeple of Glogau "peals Midnight, — Forward, with the first stroke; with the

* Orlich, i. 71.

"second, much more with the twelfth stroke, be one and all of you, in the utmost silence, advancing! And, under pain of death, two things: Not one shot till you are in; No plundering when you are.' — In this manner is the silent three-sided avalanche to be let go. Whereupon," says my Dryasdust, "the Generals retired; and had, for one item, their fire-arms all cleaned, and new-loaded." *

Without plans of Glogau, and more detail and study than the reader would consent to, there can no Narrative be given. Glogau has Ramparts, due Ring-fence, palisaded and repaired by Wallis; inside of this is an old Town-Wall, which will need petards: there are about 1,000 men under Wallis, and altogether on the works, not to count a mortar or two, fifty-eight big guns. The reader must conceive a poor Town under blockade, in the wintry night-time, with its tough Count Wallis; ill off for the necessaries of life; Town shrouded in darkness, and creeping quietly to its bed. This on the one hand: and on the other hand, Prussian battalions marching up, at 10 o'clock or later, with the utmost softness of step; "taking post behind the ordinary field-watches;" and at length, all standing ranked, in the invisible dark; silent, like machinery, like a sleeping avalanche: Husht! — No sentry from the walls dreams of such a thing. "Twelve!" sings out the steeple of Glogau; and in grim whisper the word is "*Vorwärts!*" and the three-winged avalanche is in motion.

They reach their glacises, their ditches, covered ways, correct as mathematics; tear out chevaux-de-frise, hew down palisades, in the given number of minutes: Swift, ye Regiment's-carpenters; smite your best! Four

* *Helden-Geschichte,* i. 823; ii. 165.

cannon-shot do now boom out upon them; which go high over their heads, little dreaming how close at hand they are. The glacis is thirty feet high, of stiff slope, and slippery with frost: no matter, the avalanche, led on by Leopold in person, by Margraf Karl the King's Cousin, by Adjutant Golz and the chief personages, rushes up with strange impetus; hews down a second palisade; surges in; — Wallis's sentries extinct, or driven to their main guards. There is a singular fire in the besieging party. For example, Four Grenadiers, — I think of this First Column, which succeeded sooner, certainly of the Regiment Glasenapp, — four grenadiers, owing to slippery or other accidents, in climbing the glacis, had fallen a few steps behind the general body; and on getting to the top, took the wrong course, and rushed along rightward instead of leftward. Rightward, the first thing they come upon is a mass of Austrians still ranked in arms; Fifty-two men, as it turned out, with their Captain over them. Slight stutter ensues on the part of the Four Grenadiers; but they give one another the hint, and dash forward: "Prisoners?" ask they sternly, as if all Prussia had been at their rear. The Fifty-two, in the darkness, in the danger and alarm, answer "Yes." — "Pile arms, then!" Three of the grenadiers stand to see that done; the fourth runs off for force, and happily gets back with it before the comedy had become tragic for his comrades. "I must make acquaintance with these four men," writes Friedrich, on hearing of it; and he did reward them by present, by promotion to sergeantcy (to ensigncy one of them), or what else they were fit for. Grenadiers of Glasenapp: these are the men Friedrich heard swearing-in under his window, one memorable morning when he burst into tears! At half-past Twelve, the Ramparts, on all sides, are ours.

The Gates of the Town, under axe and petard, can make little resistance, to Leopold's Column or the other two. A hole is soon cut in the Town-Gate, where Leopold is; and gallant Wallis, who had rallied behind it, with his Artillery-General and what they could get together, fires through the opening, kills four men; but is then (by order, and not till then) fired upon, and obliged to draw back, with his Artillery-General mortally hurt. Inside he attempts another rally, some 200 with him; and here and there perhaps a house-window tries to give shot; but it is to no purpose, not the least stand can be made. Poor Wallis is rapidly swept back, into the Market-place, into the Main Guardhouse; and there piles arms: "Glogau yours, Ihr Herren, and we prisoners of War!" The steeple had not yet quite struck One. Here has been a good hour's-work!

Glogau, as in a dream, or half-awake, and timidly peeping from behind window-curtains, finds that it is a Town taken. Glogau easily consoles itself, I hear, or even is generally glad; Prussian discipline being so perfect, and ingress now free for the necessaries of life. There was no plundering; not the least insult: no townsman was hurt; not even in houses where soldiers had tried firing from windows. The Prussian Battalions rendezvous in the Market-place, and go peaceably about their patrolling, and other business; and meddle with nothing else. They lost, in killed, ten men; had of killed and wounded, forty-eight; the Austrians rather more.* Wallis was to have been set free on parole;

* Orlich, i. 75, 78; *Helden-Geschichte,* i. 829: irreconcilable otherwise, in some slight points.

but was not, — in retaliation for some severity of General Browne's in the interim (picking up of two Silesian Noblemen, suspected of Prussian tendency, and locking them in Brünn over the Hills), — and had to go to Berlin, till that was repaired. To the wounded Artillery-General there was every tenderness shown, but he died in few days. The other Prisoners were marched to the Cüstrin-Stettin quarter; "and many of them took Prussian service."

And this is the Scalade of Glogau: a shining feat of those days; which had great rumour in the Gazettes, and over all the then feverish Nations, though it has now fallen dim again, as feats do. Its importance at that time, its utility to Friedrich's affairs, was undeniable; and it filled Friedrich with the highest satisfaction, and with admiration to overflowing. Done, 9th March 1741; in one hour, the very earliest of the day.

Goltz posted back to Schweidnitz with the news; got thither about 5 P.M.; and was received, naturally, with open arms. Friedrich in person marched out, next morning, to make *Feu-de-joie* and *Te-Deum*-ing; — there was Royal Letter to Leopold, which flamed through all the Newspapers, and can still be read in innumerable Books; Letter omissible in this place. We remark only how punctual the King is, to reward in money as well as praise and not the high only, but the low that had deserved: to Prince Leopold he presents 2,000*l.*; to each private soldier who had been of the storm, say half-a-guinea, — doubling and quadrupling, in the special cases, to as high as twenty guineas, of our present money. To the old Gazetteers, and their readers everywhere, this of Glogau is a very effulgent business; bursting out on them, like sudden Bude-light, in the uncertain stagnancy and expectancy of mankind. Friedrich himself writes of it to the Old Dessauer:

"The more I think of the Glogau business, the more important I find it. Prince Leopold has achieved the prettiest military stroke (*die schönste Action*) that has been done in this Century. From my heart I congratulate you on having such a Son. In boldness of resolution, in plan, in execution, it is alike admirable; and quite gives a turn to my affairs." *

And indeed, it is a perfect example of Prussian discipline, and military quality in all kinds; such as it would be difficult to match elsewhere. Most potently correct; coming out everywhere with the completeness and exactitude of mathematics; and has in it such a fund of martial fire, not only ready to blaze out (which can be exampled elsewhere), but capable of bottling itself *in*, and of lying silently ready. Which is much rarer; and very essential in soldiering! Due a little to the *Old* Dessauer, may we not say, as well as to the Young? Friedrich Wilhelm is fallen silent; but his heavy labours, and military and other drillings to Prussian mankind, still speak with an audible voice.

About three weeks after this of Glogau, Leopold the Old Dessauer, over in Brandenburg, does another thing which is important to Friedrich, and of great rumour in the world. Steps out, namely, with a force of 36,000 men, horse, foot and artillery, completely equipped in all points; and takes Camp, at this early season, at a place called Göttin, not far from Magde-

* Date, 13th March 1741 (Orlich, i. 77).

burg, handy at once for Saxony and for Hanover; and continues there encamped, — "merely for review purposes." Readers can figure what an astonishment it was to Kur-Sachsen and British George; and how it struck the wind out of their Russian Partition-Dream, and awoke them to a sense of the awful fact! — Capable of being slit in pieces, and themselves partitioned, at a day's warning, as it were! It was on April 2d, that Leopold, with the first division of the 36,000, planted his flag near Göttin. No doubt it was the "detestable Project," that had brought him out, at so early a season for tent life, and nobody could then guess why. He steadily paraded here, all summer; keeping his 36,000 well in drill, since there was nothing else needed of him.

The Camp at Göttin flamed greatly abroad through the timorous imaginations of mankind, that Year; and in the Newspapers are many details of it. And, besides the important general fact, there is still one little point worth special mention: namely, that old Field-marshal Katte (Father of poor Lieutenant Katte whom we knew) was of it; and perhaps even got his death by it: "Chief Commander of the Cavalry here," such honour had he; but died at his post, in a couple of months, "at Rekahn, May 31st;"* poor old gentleman, perhaps unequal to the hardships of field-life at so early a season of the year.

Friedrich takes the Field, with some Pomp; goes into the Mountains, — but comes fast back.

At Glogau there was Homaging, on the very morrow after the storm; on the second day, the superfluous

* *Militair-Lexikon*, ii. 254.

regiments marched off: no want of vigorous activity to settle matters on their new footing there. General Kalkstein (Friedrich's old Tutor, whom readers have forgotten again) is to be Commandant of Glogau; an office of honour, which can be done by deputy except in cases of real stress. The place is to be thoroughly new-fortified, — which important point they commit to Engineer Wallrave, a strong-headed heavy-built Dutch Officer, long since acquired to the service, on account of his excellence in that line; who did, now and afterwards, a great deal of excellent engineering for Friedrich; but for himself (being of deep stomach withal, and of life too dissolute) made a tragic thing of it ultimately. As will be seen, if we have leisure.

In seven or eight days, Prince Leopold, having wound up his Glogau affairs, and completed the new preliminaries there, joins the King at Schweidnitz. In the highest favour, as was natural. Kalkstein is to take a main hand in the Siege of Neisse; for which operation it is hoped there will soon be weather, if not favourable yet supportable. What of the force was superfluous at Glogau had at once marched off, as we observed; and is now getting re-distributed where needful. There is much shifting about; strengthening of posts, giving up of posts: the whole of which readers shall imagine for themselves, — except only two points that are worth remembering: *First*, that Kalkstein with about 12,000 takes post at Grotkau, some twenty-five miles north of Neisse, ready to move on, and open trenches, when required: and *second*, that Holstein-Beck gets posted at Frankenstein (chief place of that Baumgarten Skirmish), say thirty-five miles west-by-north of Neisse; and has some 8 or 10,000 Horse and

Foot thereabouts, spread up and down, — who will be much wanted, and not procurable, on an occasion that is coming.

Friedrich has given up the Jablunka Pass; called-in the Jablunka and remoter posts; anxious to concentrate, before the Enemy get nigh. That is the King's notion; and surely a reasonable one; the *area* of the Prussian Army, as I guess it from the Maps, being above 2,000 square miles, beginning at Breslau only and leaving out Glogau. Schwerin thinks differently; but without good basis. Both are agreed, The Austrian Army cannot take the field till the forage come," till the new grass spring, which its cavalry find convenient. That is the fair supposition; but in that both are mistaken, and Schwerin the more dangerously of the two. — Meanwhile, the Pandour swarms are observably getting rifer, and of stormier quality; and they seem to harbour farther to the East than formerly, and not to come all out of Glatz. Which perhaps are symptomatic circumstances? The worst effect of these preliminary Pandour clouds is, Your scout-service cannot live among them; they hinder reconnoitring, and keep the Enemy veiled from you. Of that sore mischief Friedrich had, first and last, ample experience at their hands! This is but the first instalment of Pandours to Friedrich; and the mere foretaste of what they can do in the veiling way.

Behind the Mountains, in this manner, all is inane darkness to Friedrich and Schwerin. They know only that Neipperg is rendezvousing at Olmütz; and judge that he will still spend many weeks upon it; the real facts being: That Neipperg, — "who arrived in Olmütz on the 10th of March," the very day while Glogau was Homaging, — has been, he and those above him and those under him, driving preparations forward at a furious rate. That Neipperg held, — I think at Steinberg his hithermost post, some twenty miles hither of Olmütz, — a Council of War, "all the Generals and even Lentulus from Glatz, present at it," day not given; where the unanimous decision was, "March straightway; save Neisse, since Glogau is gone!" — and in fine, That on the 26th, Neipperg took the road accordingly, "in spite of furious snow blowing in his face;" and is ever since (30,000 strong, says rumour, but perhaps 10,000 of them mere Pandours) unweariedly climbing the Mountains, laboriously jingling forward with his heavy guns and ammunition-wagons: "contending with the steep snowy icy roads;" — intent upon saving Neisse. This is the fact; profoundly unknown to Friedrich and Schwerin; who will be much surprised, when it becomes patent to them at the wrong time.

Schweidnitz, 27th March. This day Friedrich, with considerable apparatus, pomp and processional cymballing, greatly the reverse of his ulterior use and wont in such cases, quitted Schweidnitz and his Algarottis; solemnly opening Campaign in this manner; and drove off for Ottmachau, having work there for to-morrow.

The Siege of Neisse is now to proceed forthwith; trenches to be opened, April 4th. Friedrich is still of opinion, that his posts lie too wide apart; that especially Schwerin, who is spread among the Hills in Jägerndorf Country, ought to come down, and take closer order for covering the Siege.* Schwerin answers,

* *Œuvres de Frédéric*, II. 70.

That if the King will spare him a reinforcement of
eight squadrons and nine battalions (say 1,200 Horse,
9,000 Foot), he will maintain himself where he is,
and no Enemy shall get across the Mountains at all.
That is Schwerin's notion; who surely is something of
a judge. Friedrich assents; will himself conduct the
reinforcement to Schwerin, and survey matters, with
his own eyes, up yonder. Friedrich marches from
Ottmachau, accordingly, 29th March; — Kalkstein,
Holstein-Beck, and others are to be rendezvoused
before Neisse, in the interim; trenches ready for
opening on the sixth day hence; — and in this manner, climbs these Mountains, and sees Jägerndorf
Country for the first time.

Beautiful blue world of Hills, ridge piled on ridge
behind that Neisse region; fruitful valleys lapped in
them, with grim stone Castles and busy little Towns
disclosing themselves as we advance: that is Jägerndorf Country, — which Uncle George of Anspach,
hundreds of years ago, purchased with his own money;
which we have now come to lay hold of as his Heir!
Friedrich, I believe, thinks little of all this, and does
not remember Uncle George at all. But such are the
facts; and the Country, regarded or not, is very blue
and beautiful, with the Spring sun shining on it; or
with the sudden Spring storms gathering wildly on the
peaks, as if for permanent investiture, but vanishing
again straightway, leaving only a powdering of snow.

He met Schwerin at Neustadt, half way to Jägerndorf; whither they proceeded next day. "What news
have you of the Enemy?" was Friedrich's first question.
Schwerin has no news whatever; only that the Enemy
is far off, hanging in long thin straggle from Olmütz

westward. "I have a spy out," said Schwerin; "but he has not returned yet," — nor ever will, he might have added. An invincible Predecessor has compelled what next follows into human intelligibility, and into the Diary Form, for their behoof; — readers of an idler turn can skip: but this confused hurry-scurry of marches issues in something which all will have to attend to.

"*Jägerndorf*, 2d *April* 1741. This is the day when the Old
"Dessauer makes appearance with the first brigades of his
"Camp at Göttin. Friedrich is satisfied with what he has seen
"of Jägerndorf matters; and intends returning towards
"Neisse, there to commence on the 4th. He is giving his
"final orders, and on the point of setting off, when — Seven
"Austrian Deserters, 'dragoons of Lichtenstein,' come in;
"and report, That Neipperg's Army is within a few miles!
"And scarcely had they done answering and explaining, when
"sounds rise of musketry and cannon, from our outposts on
"that side; intimating that here is Neipperg's Army itself.
"Seldom in his life was Friedrich in an uglier situation. In
"Jägerndorf, an open Town, are only some three or four
"thousand men, 'with three fieldpieces, and as much powder
"as will charge them forty times.' Happily these proved
"only the Pandour outskirts of Neipperg's Army, scouring
"about to reconnoitre, and not difficult to beat; the real
"body of it is ascertained to be at Freudenthal, fifteen miles
"to westward, southwestward; making towards Neisse, it is
"guessed, by the other or western road, which is the nearer
"to Glatz and to the Austrian force there.

"Had Neipperg known what was in Jägerndorf — ! But he
"does not know. He marches on, next morning, at his usual
"slow rate; wide clouds of Pandours accompanying and pre-
"ceding him; skirmishing in upon all places" (upon Jägerndorf, for instance, though fifteen miles wide of their road),
"to ascertain if Prussians are there. One can judge whether
"Friedrich and Schwerin were thankful when the huge alarm
"produced nothing! 'The mountain,' as Friedrich says,

"'gave birth to a mouse;'—nay it was a 'mouse' of essential
"vital use to Friedrich and Schwerin; a warning, That they
"must instantly collect themselves, men and goods; and
"begone one and all out of these parts, double-quick towards
"Neisse. Not now with the hope of besieging Neisse,—far
"from that;—but of getting their wide-scattered posts to-
"gether thereabouts, and escaping destruction in detail!

"*April 4th, Headquarters Neustadt.* By violent exertion,
"with the sacrifice only of some remote little storehouses, all
"is rendezvoused at Jägerndorf, within two days; and this
"day they march; King and vanguard reaching Neustadt,
"some twenty-five miles forward, some twenty still from
"Neisse. At Neustadt, the posts that had stood in that
"neighbourhood are all assembled, and march with the King
"tomorrow. Of Neipperg, except by transitory contact with
"his Pandour clouds, they have seen nothing: his road is
"pretty much parallel to theirs, and some fifteen miles left-
"ward, Glatzward; goes through Zuckmantel, Ziegenhals,
"straight upon Neisse.* Neipperg's men are wearied with
"the long climb out of Mähren; and he struggles towards
"Neisse as the first object;—holding upon Glatz and Leu-
"tulus with his left. Numerous orders have been speeded
"from the King's quarters, at Jägerndorf, and here at Neu-
"stadt; order especially to Holstein-Beck at Frankenstein,
"and to Kalkstein at Grotkau, How they are to unite, first
"with one another; and then to cross Neisse River, and unite
"with the King,—to which end there is already a Bridge
"laid for them, or about to be laid in good time.

"*April 5th, Headquarters Steinau.* Steinau is a little Town,
"twenty miles east of Neisse, on the road to Kosel" (strongish
place, on the Oder, some forty miles farther east): "here
"Friedrich, with the main body, take their quarters; rear-
"guard being still at Neustadt. Temporary Bridge there is,
"ready or all but ready, at Sorgau" (twelve miles to north of

---

* Zuckmantel, "Twitch-Cloak," occurs more than once as a Town's name in those regions: name which, says my Dryasdust without smile visible, it got from robberies done on travellers, "twitchings of your cloak," with stand-and-deliver, as you cross those wild mountain spaces. (Zeiller, *Beschreibung des Königreichs Boheim:* Frankfurt, 1650;—a rather worthless old Book, like the rest of Zeiller's in that kind.)

us, on our left): "by this Kalkstein, with his 10,000, comes "punctually across; while other brigades from the Kosel side "are also punctual in getting in; which is a great comfort: "but of Holstein-Beck there is no vestige, nor did there ever "appear any. Holstein, 'whom none of the repeated orders "sent him could reach,' says Friedrich, 'remained com- "fortably in his quarters; and looked at the Enemy rushing "past him to right and left, without troubling his head with "them.'* The too easy-minded Holstein! Austrian Deserters "inform us, That General Neipperg arrived today with his "Army in Neisse; and has there been joined by Lentulus with "the Glatz force, chiefly cavalry, a good many thousands. "We may be attacked, then, this very night, if they are "diligent? Friedrich marks out ground and plan in such case, "and how and where each is to rank himself. There came "nothing of attack: but the poor little Village of Steinau, "with so many troops in it and baggage-drivers stumbling "about, takes fire; burns to ashes; 'and we had great diffi- "culty in saving the artillery and powder through the narrow "streets, with the houses all burning on each hand.'" Fancy it, — and the poor shrieking inhabitants; gone to silence long since with their shrieks, not the least whisper left of them. "The Prussians bivouack on the field, each in the place that "has been marked out. Night extremely cold."

In this poor Steinau was a Schloss, which also went up in fire; disclosing certain mysteries of an almost mythical nature to the German Public. It was the Schloss of a Gräfin von Callenberg; a dreadful old Dowager of Medea-Messalina type, who "always wore pistols about her;" pistols, and latterly, with more and more constancy, a brandy-bottle;— who has been much on the tongues of men for a generation back. Herr Nüssler (readers recollect shifty Nüssler) knew her, in the way of business, at one time; with pity, if also with horror. Some weeks ago, she was, by the Austrian Commandant at Neisse, summoned out of this Schloss, as in correspondence with Prussian Officers: peasants breaking in, tied her with ropes to the bed where she was; put bed and her into a farm-cart, and in that scandalous manner delivered her at Neisse to the Commandant; by which adventure, and its rages and unspeakabilities, the poor old Callenberg is since

* Œuvres de Frédéric, ii. 70.

dead. And now the very Schloss is dead; and there is finis to a human dust-vortex, such as is sometimes noisy for a time. Perhaps Nüssler may again pass that way, if we wait.*

"*April 6th,* *Headquarters Friedland.* To Friedland on "the 6th; — and do not, as expected, get away next morning. "Friedland is ten miles down the Neisse, which makes a bend "of near ninety degrees opposite Steinau; and runs thence "straight north for the Oder, which it reaches some dozen "miles or more above Brieg. Both Steinau and Friedland are "a good distance from the River; Friedland, the nearer of "the two, with Sorgau Bridge direct west of it, is perhaps "eight miles from that important structure. There, being "now tolerably rendezvoused, and in strength for action, "Friedrich purposes to cross Neisse River tomorrow; hoping "perhaps to meet Holstein-Beck, and incorporate him; "anxious, at any rate, to get between the Austrians and "Ohlau, where his heavy Artillery, his Ammunition, not to "mention other indispensables, are lying. The peculiarity "of Neipperg at this time is, that the ground he occupies "bears no proportion to the ground he commands. His re-"gular Horse are supposed to be the best in the world; and of "the Pandour kind, who live, horse and man, mainly upon "nothing (which means upon theft), his supplies are unlimited. "He sits like a volcanic reservoir, therefore, not like a com-"mon fire of such and such intensity and power to burn; — "casts the ashes of him, on all sides, to many miles distance.

"*Friday, 7th April, Friedland* (still Headquarters). Un-"luckily, on trying, there is no passage to be had at Sorgau. "The Officer on charge there still holds the Bridge, but has "been obliged to break away the farther end of it; 'Lentulus "and Dragoons, several thousands strong' (such is the report), "having taken post there. Friedrich commands that the "Bridge be reinstated; fieldpieces to defend it; Prince Leo-"pold to cross, and clear the ways. All Friday, Friedrich "waiting at Friedland, was spent in these details. Leopold "in due force started for Sorgau, himself with Cavalry in the "van; Leopold did storm across, and go charging and "fencing, some space, on the other side; but, seeing that it "was in truth Lentulus, and Dragoons without limit, had to "send report accordingly; and then to wind himself to this

* Büsching, *Beyträge,* ii. 273 et sqq.

"side again, on new order from the King. What is to be "done, then? Here is no crossing. Friedrich decides to go "down the River; he himself to Löwen, perhaps near twenty "miles farther down, but where there is a Bridge and High- "way leading over; Prince Leopold, with the heavier divi- "sions and baggages, to Michelau, some miles nearer, and "there to build his Pontoons and cross. Which was effected, "with success. And so,

"*Saturday, 8th April*, With great punctuality, the King "and Leopold met at Michelau, both well across the Neisse. "Here on Pontoons, Leopold had got across about noon; and "precisely as he was finishing, the King's Column, which "had crossed at Löwen, and come up the left bank again, "arrived. The King, much content with Leopold's be- "haviour, nominates him General of Infantry, a stage higher "in promotion, there and then. Brieg Blockade is, as "natural, given up; the Blockading Body joining with the "King, this morning, while he passed that way. From "Holstein-Beck not the least whisper, — nor to him, if we "knew it.

"Neipperg has quitted Neisse; but walks invisible within "clouds of Pandours; nothing but guessing as to Neipperg's "motions. Rightly swift, and awake to his business, Neipperg "might have done, might still do, a stroke upon us here. "But he takes it easy; marches hardly five miles a day, since "he quitted Neisse again. From Michelau, Friedrich for his "part turns southwestward, in quest of Holstein and other "interests; marches towards Grotkau, not intending much "farther that night. Thick snow blowing in their faces, no- "thing to be seen ahead, the Prussian column tramps along.* "In Leipe, a little Hamlet sidewards of the road, short way "from Grotkau, our Hussar Vanguard had found Austrian "Hussars; captured forty, and from them learned that the "Austrian Army is in Grotkau; that they took Grotkau half "an hour before, and are there! A poor Lieutenant Mitschepfal "(whom I think Friedrich used to know in Reinsberg) lay in "Grotkau, 'with some sixty recruits and deserters,' says "Friedrich, — and with several hundreds of camp-labourers "(intended for the trenches, which will *not* now be opened): "— Mitschepfal made a stout defence; but, after three hours

* *Œuvres de Frédéric*, ii. 156.

"of it, had to give in: and there is nothing now for us at
"Grotkau. 'Halt,' therefore! Neipperg is evidently pushing
"towards Ohlau, towards Breslau, though in a leisurely
"way; there it will behove us to get the start of him, if
"humanly possible: To the right about, therefore, without
"delay! The Prussians repass Leipe (much to the wonder of
"its simple people); get along, some seven miles farther, on
"the road for Ohlau; and quarter, that night, in what handy
"villages there are; the King's Corps in two Villages, which
"he calls 'Pogrel and Alsen' " — which are to be found still
on the Map as "Pogarell and Alzenau," on the road from
Löwen towards Ohlau.

This is the end of that March into the Mountains,
with Neisse Siege hanging triumphant ahead. These
are the King's quarters, this wintry Spring night,
Saturday 8th April 1741; and it is to be guessed there
is more of care than of sleep provided for him there.
Seldom, in his life, was Friedrich in a more critical
position; and he well knows it, none better. And
could have his remorses upon it, — were these of the
least use in present circumstances. Here are two
Letters which he wrote that night; veiling, we perceive, a very grim world of thoughts; betokening, however, a mind made up. Jordan, Prince August Wilhelm Heir-Apparent, and other fine individuals who
shone in the Schweidnitz circle lately, are in Breslau,
safe sheltered against this bad juncture; Maupertuis
was not so lucky as to go with them.

The King to Prince August Wilhelm (in Breslau).

"Pogarell, 8th April 1741.
"My dearest Brother, — The Enemy has just got into
"Silesia; We are not more than a mile (*quart de mille*) from
"them. To-morrow must decide our fortune.

"If I die, do not forget a Brother who has always loved
"you very tenderly. I recommend to you my most dear
"Mother, my Domestics, and my First Battalion" (*Lifeguard*

of Foot, men picked from his own old Ruppin Regiment and from the disbanded Giants, star of all the Battalions).* "Eichel and Schuhmacher" (Two of the Three Clerks) "are "informed of all my testamentary wishes. Remember me al- "ways, you; but console yourself for my death: the glory of "the Prussian arms, and the honour of the House have set me "in action, and will guide me to my last moment. You are "my sole Heir: I recommend to you, in dying, those whom "I have the most loved during my life: Keyserling, Jordan, "Wartensleben; Hacke, who is a very honest man; Freders- "dorf" (Factotum), "and Eichel, in whom you may place "entire confidence. I bequeath 8,000 crowns (1,200*l*.), which "I have with me, to my Domestics; but all that I have else- "where depends on you. To each of my Brothers and Sisters "make a present in my name; a thousand affectionate regards "(*amitiés et compliments*) to my Sister of Baireuth. You know "what I think on their score; and you know better than I "could tell you, the tenderness and all the sentiments of most "inviolable friendship with which I am,
"Dearest Brother,
"Your faithful Brother and Servant till death,
"Fédéric." **

The King to M. Jordan (in Breslau).
"Pogarell, 8th April 1741.

"My dear Jordan, — We are going to fight tomorrow. "Thou knowest the chances of war; the life of Kings not more "regarded than that of private people. I know not what will "happen to me.
"If my destiny is finished, remember a friend, who loves "thee always tenderly: if Heaven prolong my days, I will "write to thee after tomorrow, and thou wilt hear of our "victory. Adieu, dear friend; I shall love thee till death. —
"Fédéric." ***

The King, we incidentally discover somewhere, "had no sleep that night;" none, "nor the next night either," — such a crisis coming, still not come.

* See Preuss, i. 144, iv. 309; Nicolai, *Beschreibung von Berlin*, iii. 1252.
** *Œuvres de Frédéric*, xxvi. 85; List of Friedrich's Testamentary ar- rangements in Note there, — Six in all, at different times, besides this.
*** *Œuvres de Frédéric*, xvii. 98.

CHAPTER X.

BATTLE OF MOLLWITZ.

"TOMORROW," Sunday, did not prove the Day of Fight, after all. Being a day of wild drifting snow, so that you could not see twenty paces, there was nothing for it but to sit quiet. The King makes all his dispositions; sketches out punctually, to the last item, where each is to station himself, how the Army is to advance in Four Columns, ready for Neipperg wherever he may be, — towards Ohlau at any rate, whither it is not doubted Neipperg is bent. These snowy six-and-thirty hours at Pogarell were probably, since the Cüstrin time, the most anxious of Friedrich's life.

Neipperg, for his part, struggles forward a few miles, this Sunday, April 9th; the Prussians rest under shelter in the wild weather. Neipperg's headquarters, this night, are a small Village or Hamlet, called Mollwitz; there and in the adjacent Hamlets, chiefly in Laugwitz and Grüningen, his Army lodges itself: — he is now fairly got between us and Ohlau, — if, in the blowing drift, we knew it, or he knew it. But, in this confusion of the elements, neither party knows of the other: Neipperg has appointed that tomorow, Monday 10th, shall be a rest-day: — appointment which could by no means be kept, as it turned out!

Friedrich had despatched messengers to Ohlau, that the force there should join him; messengers are all captured. The like message had already gone to Brieg, some days before, and the Blockading Body, a good few thousands strong, quitted Brieg, as we saw, and effected their junction with him. All day, this Sunday 9th, it still snows and blows; you cannot see a yard before you. No hope now of Holstein-Beck. Not the least news from any quarter; Ohlau uncertain, too likely the wrong way: What is to be done? We are cut off from our Magazines, have only provision for one other day. "Had this weather lasted," says an Austrian reporter of these things, "his Majesty "would have passed his time very ill."*

Of the Battle of Mollwitz, as indeed of all Friedrich's Battles, there are ample accounts new and old, of perfect authenticity and scientific exactitude; so that in regard to military points the due clearness is, on study, completely attainable. But as to personal or human details, we are driven back upon a miscellany of sources; most of which, indeed all of which except Nicolai, when he sparingly gives us anything, are of questionable nature; and, without intending to be dishonest, do run out into the mythical, and require to be used with caution. The latest and notablest of these, in regard to Mollwitz, is the Pamphlet of a Dr. Fuchs; from which, in spite of its amazing quality, we expect to glean a serviceable item here and there.** It is definable as probably the most chaotic Pamphlet

* *Feldzüge der Preussen* (the complete Title is, *Sammlung ungedruckter Nachrichten so die Geschichte der Feldzüge der Preussen von 1740 bis 1779 erläutern*, or in English words, *Collection of unprinted Narratives which elucidate the Prussian Campaigns from 1740 to 1779*: 5 voll. Dresden, 1782-5), i. 33. Excellent Narratives, modest, brief, effective (from Private Diaries and the like; many of them given also in *Scyfarth*); well worth perusal by the studious military man, and creditably characteristic of the Prussian writers of them, and actors in them.

** *Jubelschrift zur Feier* (Centenary) *der Schlacht bei Mollwitz*, 10 April 1741, von Dr. Medicinæ Fuchs (Brieg, 10th April 1841).

ever written; and in many places, by dint of uncorrected printing, bad grammar, bad spelling, bad sense, and in short, of intrinsic darkness in so vivacious a humour, it has become abstruse as Sanscrit; and really is a sharp test of what knowledge you otherwise have of the subject. Might perhaps be used in that way, by the Examining Military Boards, in Prussia and elsewhere, if no other use lie in it? Fuchs's own contributions, mere ignorance, folly and credulity, are not worth interpreting: but he has printed, and in the same abstruse form, one or two curious Parish Manuscripts, particularly a "*History*" of this War, privately jotted down by the then Schoolmaster of Mollwitz, a good simple accurate old fellow-creature; through whose eyes it is here and there worth while to look. In regard to Fuchs himself, a late Tourist says:

"This 'Centenary-Celebration Pamphlet' (Celebration it-"self, so obtuse was the Country, did not take effect) was by "a zealous, noisy but not wise, old Medical Gentleman of "these parts, called Dr. Fuchs (*Fox*); who had set his heart "on raising, by subscription, a proper National Monument "on the Field of Mollwitz, and so closing his old career. "Subscriptions did not take, in that April 1841, nor in the "following months or twelvemonths: the zealous Doctor, "therefore, indignantly drew his own purse; got a big Obelisk "of Granite hewn ready, with suitable Inscription on it; "carted his big Obelisk from the quarries of Strehlen; assem-"bled the Country round it, on Mollwitz Field; and pas-"sionately discoursed and pleaded, That at least the Country "should bring block-and-tackle, with proper frame-work, "and set up this Obelisk on the Pedestal he had there built "for it. The Country listened cheerfully (for the old Doctor "was a popular man, clever though flighty); but the Country "was again obtuse in the way of active furtherance, and "would not even bring block-and-tackle. The old Doctor "had to answer, 'Well, then!' and go on his way on more

"serious errands. The cattle have much undermined, and
"rubbed down, his poor Pedestal, which is of rubble-work;
"his Obelisk still lies mournfully horizontal, uninjured; —
"and really ought to be set up, by some parish-rate, or effort
"of the community otherwise." *

From the old Mollwitz Schoolmaster we distill the following:

"*Mollwitz, Sunday, 9th April.* Country, for two days back,
"was in new alarm by the Austrian Garrison of Brieg now left
"at liberty, who sallied out upon the Villages about, and
"plundered black-cattle, sheep, grain, and whatever they
"could come at. But this day (Sunday) in Mollwitz the whole
"Austrian Army was upon us. First, there went 300 Hussars
"through the Village to Grüningen, who quartered them-
"selves there; and rushed hither and thither into houses,
"robbing and plundering. From one they took his best horses,
"from another they took linen, clothes, and other furnitures
"and victual. General Neuburg" (Neipperg) "halted here
"at Mollwitz, with the whole Army; before the Village, in
"mind to quarter. And quarter was settled, so that a *Bauer*"
(Plough-Farmer) "got four to five companies to lodge, and a
"*Gärtner*" (Spade-Farmer) "two or three hundred cavalry.
"The houses were full of Officers, the *Gürte*" (Garths) "and
"the Fields full of horsemen and baggage; and all round, you
"saw nothing but fires burning; the *Zäune*" (wooden railings)
"were instantly torn down for firewood; the hay, straw,
"barley and haver, were eaten away, and brought to nothing;
"and everything from the barns was carried out. And, as the
"whole Army could not lodge itself with us, 1,100 Infantry
"quartered at Laugwitz; Bärzdorf got 400 Cavalry; and this
"day, nobody knew what would come of it." **

Monday morning, the Prussians are up betimes;
King Friedrich, as above noted, had not, or had hardly
at all, slept during those two nights, such his anxieties.
This morning, all is calm, sleeked out into spotless
white; Pogarell and the world are wrapt as in a

* Tourist's Note (Brieg, 1858).   ** Extract in *Fuchs*, p. 6.

winding-sheet, near two feet of snow on the ground. Air hard and crisp; a hot sun possible about noon season. "By daybreak" we are all astir, rendezvousing, ranking, — into Four Columns; ready to advance in that fashion for battle, or for deploying into battle, wherever the Enemy turn up. The orders were all given overnight, two nights ago; were all understood, too, and known to be rhadamanthine; and, down to the lowest pioneer, no man is uncertain what to do. If we but knew where the Enemy is; on which side of us; what doing, what intending?

Scouts, General-Adjutants are out on the quest; to no purpose hitherto. One young General-Adjutant, Saldern, whose name we shall know again, has ridden northward, has pulled bridle some way north of Pogarell; hangs, gazing diligently through his spyglass, there; — can see nothing but a Plain of silent snow, with sparse bearding of bushes (nothing like a hedge in these countries), and here and there a tree, the miserable skeleton of a poplar: — when happily, owing to an Austrian Dragoon — Be pleased to accept (in abridged form) the poor old Schoolmaster's account of a small thing!

"Austrian Dragoon of the regiment Althan, native of "Kriesewitz in this neighbourhood, who was billeted in Chris- "topher Schönwitz's, had been much in want of a clean shirt, "and other interior outfit; and had, last night, imperatively "despatched the man Schölzke, a farm-servant of the said "Christopher's, off to his, the Dragoon's, Father in Kriese- "witz, to procure such shirt or outfit, and to return early "with the same; under penalty of — Schölzke and his master "dare not think under what penalty. Schölzke, floundering "homewards with the outfit from Kriesewitz, flounders at this "moment into Saldern's sphere of vision: 'Whence, whi- "ther?' asks Saldern: 'Dost thou know where the Austrians "are?' 'Recht gut: in Mollwitz, whither I am going!' Saldern takes him to the King, — and that was the first clear light his Majesty had on the matter." * That or something equivalent, indisputably was; Saldern and "a Peasant," the account of it in all the Books.

The King says to this Peasant, "Thou shalt ride with me today!" And Schölzke, Ploschke others call him, — heavy-footed rational biped knowing the ground there practically, every yard of it, — did, as appears, attend the King all morning; and do service, that was recognisable long years afterwards. "For always," say the Books, "when the King "held review here, Ploschke failed not to make appearance "on the field of Pogarell, and get recognition and a gift from "his Majesty."

At break of day, the ranking and arranging began. Pogarell clock is near striking ten, when the last squadron or battalion quits Pogarell; and the Four Columns, punctiliously correct, are all under way. Two on each side of Ohlau Highway; steadily advancing, with pioneers ahead to clear any obstacle there may be. Few obstacles; here and there a little ditch (where Ploschke's advice may be good, under the sleek of the snow), no fences, smooth wide Plain, nothing you would even call a knoll in it for many miles ahead and around. Mollwitz is some seven miles north from Pogarell; intermediate lie dusty fractions of Villages more than one; two miles or more from Mollwitz we come to Pampitz on our left, the next considerable, if any of them can be counted considerable.

"All these Dorfs, and indeed most German ones," says my Tourist, "are made on one type; an agglomerate of dusty "farmyards, with their stalls and barns; all the farmyards "huddled together in two rows; a broad negligent road be-"tween, seldom mended, never swept except by the elements.

* Fuchs, pp. 6, 7.

"Generally there is nothing to be seen, on each hand, but
"thatched roofs, dead clay walls and rude wooden gates;
"sometimes a poor public-house, with probable beer in it;
"never any shop, nowhere any patch of swept pavement, or
"trim gathering-place for natives of a social gossipy turn: the
"road lies sleepy, littery, good only for utilitarian purposes.
"In the middle of the Village stands Church and Churchyard,
"with probably some gnarled trees around it: Church often
"larger than you expected; the Churchyard, always fenced
"with high stone-and-mortar wall, is usually the principal
"military post of the place. Mollwitz, at the present day,
"has something of whitewash here and there; one of the
"farmer people, or more, wearing a civilised prosperous look.
"The belfry offers you a pleasant view: the roofs and steeples
"of Brieg, pleasantly visible to eastward; villages dotted
"about, Laugwitz, Bürzdorf, Hermsdorf, clear to your in-
"quiring: and to westward, and to southward, tops of Hill-
"country in the distance. Westward, twenty miles off, are
"pleasant Hills; and among them, if you look well, shadowy
"Town-spires, which you are assured are Strehlen, a place
"also of interest in Friedrich's History. — Your belfry itself,
"in Mollwitz, is old, but not unsound; and the big iron clock
"grunts heavily at your ear, or perhaps bursts out in a too
"deafening manner, while you study the topographics. Pam-
"pitz, too, seems prosperous, in its littery way; the Church
"is bigger and newer," — owing to an accident we shall hear
of soon; — "Country all about seems farmed with some in-
"dustry, but with shallow ploughing; liable to drought. It
"is very sandy in quality; shorn of umbrage; painfully naked
"to an English eye." That is the big champaign, coated
with two feet of snow, where a great Action is now to go
forward.

Neipperg, all this while, is much at his ease on
this white resting day. He is just sitting down to
dinner at the Dorfschulze's (Village Provost, or minia-
ture Mayor of Mollwitz), a composed man; when —
rockets or projectiles, and successive anxious sputterings
from the steeple-tops of Brieg, are hastily reported:
What can it mean? Means little perhaps; — Neipperg

sends out a Hussar party to ascertain, and composedly sets himself to dine. In a little while his Hussar party will come galloping back, faster than it went; faster and fewer; — and there will be news for Neipperg during dinner! Better have had one idle fellow, one of your 20,000, on the Belfry-top here looking out, though it was a rest-day? —

The truth is, the Prussian advance goes on with punctilious exactitude, by no means rapidly. Colonel Count von Rothenburg, — the same whom we lately heard of in Paris as a miracle of gambling, — he now here, in a new capacity, is warily leading the Vanguard of Dragoons; warily, with the Four Columns well to rear of him: the Austrian Hussar party came upon Rothenburg, not two miles from Mollwitz; and suddenly drew bridle. Them Rothenburg tumbles to the right-about, and chases;— finds, on advancing, the Austrian Army totally unaware. It is thought, had Rothenburg dashed forward, and sent word to the rearward to dash forward at their swiftest, the Austrian Army might have been cut in pieces here, and never have got together to try battle at all. But Rothenburg had no orders; nay, had orders Not to get into fighting; — nor had Friedrich himself, in this his first Battle, learned that feline or leonine promptitude of spring which he subsequently manifested. Far from it! Indeed this punctilious deliberation, and slow exactitude as on the review-ground, is wonderful and noteworthy at the first start of Friedrich; — the faithful apprentice-hand still rigorous to the rules of the old shop. Ten years hence, twenty years hence, had Friedrich found Neipperg in this condition, Neipperg's account had been soon settled! — Rothenburg drove back the

Hussars, all manner of successive Hussar parties, and kept steadily ahead of the main battle, as he had been bidden.

Pampitz Village being now passed, and in rear of them to left, the Prussian Columns halt for some instants; burst into field-music; take to deploying themselves into line. There is solemn wheeling, shooting-out to right and left, done with spotless precision: once in line, — in two lines, "each three men deep," lines many yards apart, — they will advance on Mollwitz; still solemnly, field-music guiding, and banners spread. Which will be a work of time. That the King's frugal field-dinner was shot away, from its camp-table near Pampitz (as Fuchs has heard), is evidently mythical; and even impossible, the Austrians having yet no cannon within miles of him; and being intent on dining comfortably themselves, not on firing at other people's dinners.

Fancy Neipperg's state of mind, busy beginning dinner in the little Schulze's, or Town-Provost's house, when the Hussars dashed in at full gallop, shouting "*Der Feind*, The Enemy! All in march there; vanguard this side of Pampitz; killed forty of us!" — Quick, your Plan of Battle, then? Whitherward; How; What? answer or perish! Neipperg was infinitely struck; dropt knife and fork: "Send for Römer, General of the Horse!" Römer did the indispensable: a swift man, not apt to lose head. Römer's battle-plan, I should hope, is already made; or it will fare ill with Neipperg and him. But beat, ye drummers; gallop, ye aides-de-camp as for life! The first thing is to get our Force together; and it lies scattered about, in Three other

Villages besides Mollwitz, miles apart. Neipperg's trumpets clangour, his aides-de-camp gallop: he has his left wing formed, and the other parts in a state of rapid genesis, Horse and Foot pouring in from Laugwitz, Bärzdorf, Grüningen, before the Prussians have quite done deploying themselves, and got well within shot of him. Römer, by birth a Saxon gentleman, by all accounts a superior soldier and excellent General of Horse, commands this Austrian left wing; General Göldlein,* a Swiss veteran of good parts, presiding over the Infantry in that quarter. Neipperg himself, were he once complete, will command the right wing.

Neipperg is to be in two lines, as the Prussians are, with horse on each wing, which is orthodox military order. His length of front, I should guess, must have been something better than two English miles: a sluggish Brook, called of Laugwitz, from the Village of that name which lies some way across, is on his right hand; sluggish, boggy; stagnating towards the Oder in those parts: — improved farming has, in our time, mostly dried the strip of bog, and made it into coarse meadow, which is rather a relief amid the dry sandy element. Neipperg's right is covered by that. His left rests on the Hamlet of Grüningen, a mile-and-half north-east of Mollwitz; — meant to have rested on Hermsdorf nearly east, but the Prussians have already taken that up. The sun coming more and more round to west of south (for it is now past noon) shines right in Neipperg's face, and is against him: how the wind is, nobody mentions, — probably there was no wind. His regular Cavalry, 8,600, outnumbers twice or more that of the Prussians, not to mention their

* (Anonymous) *Maria Theresa* (already cited), p. 8n.

quality; and he has fewer Infantry, somewhat in proportion; — the entire force on each side is scarcely above 20,000, the Prussians slightly in majority by count. In field-pieces Neipperg is greatly outnumbered; the Prussians having about three score, he only eighteen.* And now here *are* the Prussians, close upon our left wing, not yet in contact with the right, — which in fact is not yet got into existence; — thank Heaven they have not come before our left got into existence, as our right (if you knew it) has not yet quite finished doing! —

The Prussians, though so ready for deploying, have had their own difficulties and delays. Between the boggy Brook of Laugwitz on their left, and the Village of Hermsdorf, two miles distant, on which their right wing is to lean, there proves not to be room enough;** and then, owing to mistake of Schulenburg (our old pipeclay friend, who commands the right wing of Horse here, and is not up in time), there is too much room. Not room enough for all the Infantry, we say: the last Three Battalions of the front line therefore, the three on the outmost right, wheel round, and stand athwart; *en potence* (as soldiers say), or at right angles to the first line; hanging to it like a kind of lid in that part, — between Schulenburg and them, — had Schulenburg come up. Thus are the three battalions got rid of at least; "they cap the First Prussian Line rectangularly, like a lid," says my Authority, — lid which does not reach to the Second Line by a good way. This accidental arrangement had material effects on the right wing. Unfortunate Schulenburg did at last come

* Kausler, *Atlas der merkwürdigsten Schlachten*, p. 232.
** Œuvres de Frédéric, ii. 73.

up: — had he miscalculated the distances, then? Once on the ground, he will find he does not reach to Hermsdorf after all, and that there is now too much room! What his degree of fault was I know not; Friedrich has long been dissatisfied with these Dragoons of Schulenburg; "good for nothing, I always told you" (at that Skirmish of Baumgarten): and now here is the General himself fallen blundering! — In respect of Horse, the Austrians are more than two to one; to make out our deficiency, the King, imitating something he had read about Gustavus Adolphus, intercalates the Horse-Squadrons, on each wing, with two Battalions of Grenadiers, and *so* lengthens them; — "a manœuvre not likely to be again imitated," he admits.

All these movements and arrangements are effected above a mile from Mollwitz, no Enemy yet visible. Once effected, we advance again with music sounding, sixty pieces of artillery well in front, steady, steady! — across the floor of snow which is soon beaten smooth enough, the stage, this day, of a great adventure. And now there is the Enemy's left wing, Römer and his Horse; their right wing wider away, and not yet, by a good space, within cannon-range of us. It is towards Two of the afternoon; Schulenburg now on his ground, laments that he will not reach to Hermsdorf; — but it may be dangerous now to attempt repairing that error? At Two of the clock, being now fairly within distance, we salute Römer and the Austrian left, with all our sixty cannon; and the sound of drums and clarionets is drowned in universal artillery thunder. Incessant, for they take (by order) to "swift-shooting," which is almost of the swiftness of musketry in our

Prussian practice; and from sixty cannon, going at that rate, we may fancy some effect. The Austrian Horse of the left wing do not like it; all the less as the Austrians, rather short of artillery, have nothing yet to reply with.

No Cavalry can stand long there, getting shivered in that way; in such a noise, were there nothing more. "Are we to stand here like milestones, then, and be all shot without a stroke struck?" "Steady!" answers Römer. But nothing can keep them steady: "To be shot like dogs (*wie Hunde*)! For God's sake (*Um Gottes Willen*), lead us forward, then, to have a stroke at them!" — in tones ever more plangent, plaintively indignant; growing ungovernable. And Römer can get no orders; Neipperg is on the extreme right, many things still to settle there; and here is the cannon-thunder going, and soon their very musketry will open. And — and there is Schulenburg, for one thing, stretching himself out eastwards (rightwards) to get hold of Hermsdorf; thinking this an opportunity for the manœuvre. "Forward!" cries Römer; and his Thirty Squadrons, like bottled whirlwind now at last let loose, dash upon Schulenburg's poor Ten (five of them of Schulenburg's own regiment), — who are turned sideways too, trotting towards Hermsdorf, at the wrong moment, — and dash them into wild ruin. That must have been a charge! That was the beginning of hours of chaos, seemingly irretrievable, in that Prussian right wing.

For the Prussian Horse fly wildly; and it is in vain to rally. The King is among them; has come in hot haste, conjuring and commanding: poor Schulenburg addresses his own regiment, "Oh shame, shame! shall it be told, then?" rallies his own regiment, and some others; charges fiercely in with them again; gets a sabre-slash across the face, — does not mind the sabre-slash, small bandaging will do; — gets a bullet through the head (or through the heart, it is not said which);* and falls down dead; his regiment going to the winds again, and *his* care of it and of other things concluding in this honourable manner. Nothing can rally that right wing; or the more you rally, the worse it fares: they are clearly no match for Römer, these Prussian Horse. They fly along the front of their own First Line of Infantry, they fly between the Two Lines; Römer chasing, — till the fire of the Infantry (intolerable to our enemies, and hitting some even of our fugitive friends) repels him. For the notable point in all this was the conduct of the Infantry; and how it stood in these wild vortexes of ruin; impregnable, immovable, as if every man of it were stone; and steadily poured out deluges of fire, — "five Prussian shots for two Austrian:" — such is perfect discipline against imperfect; and the iron ramrod against the wooden.

The intolerable fire repels Römer, when he trenches on the Infantry: however, he captures nine of the Prussian sixty guns; has scattered their Horse to the winds; and charges again and again, hoping to break the Infantry too, — till a bullet kills him, the gallant Römer; and some other has to charge and try. It was thought, had Göldlein with his Austrian Infantry advanced to support Römer at this juncture, the Battle had been gained. Five times, before Römer fell and after, the Austrians charged here; tried the Second Line too;

* *Helden-Geschichte,* i. 899.

tried once to take Prince Leopold in rear there. But Prince Leopold faced round, gave intolerable fire; on one face as on the other, he, or the Prussian Infantry anywhere, is not to be broken. "Prince Friedrich," one of the Margraves of Schwedt, King's Cousin, whom we did not know before, fell in these wild rallyings and wrestlings; "by a cannon-ball, at the King's hand," not said otherwise where. He had come as Volunteer, few weeks ago, out of Holland, where he was a rising General: he has met his fate here, — and Margraf Karl, his Brother, who also gets wounded, will be a mournful man to-night.

The Prussian Horse, this right wing of it, is a ruined body; boiling in wild disorder, flooding rapidly away to rearward, — which is the safest direction to retreat upon. They "sweep away the King's person with them," say some cautious people; others say, what is the fact, that Schwerin entreated, and as it were commanded, the King to go; the Battle being, to all appearance, irretrievable. Go he did, with small escort, and on a long ride, — to Oppeln, a Prussian post, thirty-five miles rearward, where there is a Bridge over the Oder and a safe country beyond. So much is indubitable; and that he despatched an Aide-de-Camp to gallop into Brandenburg, and tell the Old Dessauer, "Bestir yourself! Here all seems lost!" — and vanished from the Field, doubtless in very desperate humour. Upon which the extraneous world has babbled a good deal, "Cowardice! Wanted courage: Haha!" in its usual foolish way; not worth answer from him or from us. Friedrich's demeanour, in that disaster of his right wing, was furious despair rather; and neither Schulenburg nor Margraf Friedrich, nor any of the captains, killed or left living, was supposed to have sinned by "cowardice" in a visible degree! —

Indisputable it is, though there is deep mystery upon it, the King vanishes from Mollwitz Field at this point for sixteen hours, into the regions of Myth, "into Fairyland," as would once have been said; but reappears unharmed in tomorrow's daylight: at which time, not sooner, readers shall hear what little is to be said of this obscure and much-disfigured small affair. For the present we hasten back to Mollwitz, — where the murderous thunder rages unabated all this while; the very noise of it alarming mankind for thirty miles round. At Breslau, which is thirty good miles off, horrible dull grumble was heard from the southern quarter ("still better, if you put a staff in the ground, and set your ear to it"); and from the steeple-tops, there was dim cloudland of powder-smoke discernible in the horizon there. "At Liegnitz," which is twice the distance, "the earth sensibly shook," * — at least the air did, and the nerves of men.

"Had Göldlein but advanced with his Foot, in "support of gallant Römer!" say the Austrian Books. But Göldlein did not advance; nor is it certain he would have found advantage in so doing: Göldlein, where he stands, has difficulty enough to hold his own. For the notable circumstance, miraculous to military men, still is, How the Prussian Foot (men who had never been in fire, but whom Friedrich Wilhelm had drilled for twenty years) stand their ground, in this distraction of the Horse. Not even the Two outlying Grenadier Battalions will give way: those poor intercalated Grenadiers, when their Horse fled on the right

* *Helden-Geschichte;* and Jordan's Letter, infrà.

and on the left, they stand there, like a fixed stonedam in that wild whirlpool of ruin. They fix bayonets, "bring their two field-pieces to flank" (Winterfeld was Captain there), and, from small arms and big, deliver such a fire as was very unexpected. Nothing to be made of Winterfeld and them. They invincibly hurl back charge after charge; and, with dogged steadiness, manœuvre themselves into the general Line again; or into contact with the Three superfluous Battalions, arranged *en potence*, whom we heard of. Those Three, ranked athwart in this right wing ("like a lid," between First Line and Second), maintained themselves in like impregnable fashion, — Winterfeld commanding; — and proved unexpectedly, thinks Friedrich, the saving of the whole. For they also stood their ground immovable, like rocks; steadily spouting fire-torrents. Five successive charges storm upon them, fruitless: "Steady, *meine Kinder*; fix bayonets, handle ramrods! There is the Horse-deluge thundering in upon you; reserve your fire, till you see the whites of their eyes, and get the word; then give it them, and again give it them; see whether any man or any horse can stand it!"

Neipperg, soon after Römer fell, had ordered Göldlein forward: Göldlein with his Infantry did advance, gallantly enough; but to no purpose. Göldlein was soon shot dead; and his Infantry had to fall back again, ineffectual or worse. Iron ramrods against wooden; five shots to two: what is there but falling back? Neipperg sent fresh Horse from his right wing, with Berlichingen, a new famed General of Horse; Neipperg is furiously bent to improve his advantage, to break those Prussians, who are mere musketeers left bare, and thinks that will settle the account: but it could in no wise be done. The Austrian Horse, after their fifth trial, renounce charging; fairly refuse to charge any more; and withdraw dispirited out of ball-range, or in search of things not impracticable. The Hussar part of them did something of plunder to rearward; — and, besides poor Maupertuis's adventure (of which by and by), and an attempt on the Prussian baggage and knapsacks, which proved to be "too well guarded," — "burnt the Church of Pampitz," as some small consolation. The Prussians had stript their knapsacks, and left them in Pampitz: the Austrians, it was noticed, stript theirs in the Field; built walls of them, and fired behind the same, in a kneeling, more or less protected posture, — which did not avail them much.

In fact, the Austrian Infantry too, all Austrians, hour after hour, are getting wearier of it: neither Infantry nor Cavalry can stand being riddled by swift shot in that manner. In spite of their knapsack walls, various regiments have shrunk out of ball-range; and several cannot, by any persuasion, be got to come into it again. Others, who do reluctantly advance, — see what a figure they make; man after man edging away as he can, so that the regiment "stands forty to eighty "men deep, with lanes through it every two or three "yards;" permeable everywhere to Cavalry, if we had them; and turning nothing to the enemy but colour-sergeants and bare poles of a regiment! And Römer is dead, and Göldlein of the Infantry is dead. And on their right wing, skirted by that marshy Brook of Laugwitz, — Austrian right wing had been weakened by detachments, when Berlichingen rode off to succeed Römer, — the Austrians are suffering: Posadowsky's

Horse (among whom is Rothenburg, once vanguard), strengthened by remnants who have rallied here, are at last prospering, after reverses. And the Prussian fire of small arms, at such rate, has lasted now for five hours. The Austrian Army, becoming instead of a web a mere series of flying tatters, forming into stripes or lanes in the way we see, appears to have had about enough.

These symptoms are not hidden from Schwerin. His own ammunition, too, he knows is running scarce, and fighters here and there are searching the slain for cartridges: Schwerin closes his ranks, trims and tightens himself a little; breaks forth into universal field-music, and with banners spread, starts in mass wholly, "Forwards!" Forwards toward these Austrians and the setting sun.

An intelligent Austrian Officer, writing next week from Neisse,* confesses he never saw anything more beautiful. "I can well say, I never in my life saw "anything more beautiful. They marched with the "greatest steadiness, arrow-straight, and their front "like a line (*schnurgleich*), as if they had been upon "parade. The glitter of their clear arms shone strangely "in the setting sun, and the fire from them went on "no otherwise than a continued peal of thunder." Grand picture indeed; but not to be enjoyed as a Work of Art, for it is coming upon us! "The spirits of our "Army sank altogether," continues he; "the Foot "plainly giving way, Horse refusing to come forward, "all this wavering towards dissolution:" — so that Neipperg, to avoid worse, gives the word to go; and they roll off at double-quick time, through Mollwitz,

* *Feldzüge der Preussen* (above cited), i. 38.

over Laugwitz Bridge and Brook, towards Grotkau by what routes they can. The sun is just sunk; a quarter to eight, says the intelligent Austrian Officer, — while the Austrian Army, much to its amazement, tumbles forth in this bad fashion.

They had lost nine of their own cannon, and all of those Prussian nine which they once had, except one: eight cannon *minus*, in all. Prisoners of them were few, and none of much mark: two Feldmarshals, Römer and Göldlein, lie among the dead; four more of that rank are wounded. Four standards too are gone; certain kettle-drums and the like trophies, not in great number. Lieutenant-General Browne was of these retreating Austrians; a little fact worth noting: of his actions this day, or of his thoughts (which latter surely must have been considerable), no hint anywhere. The Austrians were not much chased; though they might have been, — fresh Cavalry (two Ohlau regiments, drawn hither by the sound* having hung about to rear of them, for some time past; unable to get into the Fight, or to do any good till now. Schwerin, they say, though he had two wounds, was for pursuing vigorously: but Leopold of Anhalt over-persuaded him; urged the darkness, the uncertainty. Berlichingen, with their own Horse, still partly covered their rear; and the Prussians, Ohlauers included, were but weak in that branch of the service. Pursuit lasted little more than two miles, and was never hot. The loss of men, on both sides, was not far from equal, and rather in favour of the Austrian side: — Austrians counted in killed, wounded and missing, 4,410 men; Prussians

---

* Interesting correct account of their movements and adventures this day and some previous days, in Nicolai, *Anekdoten*, ii. 142-148.

4,613;* — but the Prussians bivouacked on the ground, or quartered in these Villages, with victory to crown them, and the thought that their hard day's-work had been well done. Besides Margraf Friedrich, Volunteer from Holland, there lay among the slain Colonel Count von Finckenstein (Old Tutor's Son), King's friend from boyhood, and much loved. He was of the six whom we saw consulting at the door at Reinsberg, during a certain ague-fit; and he now rests silent here, while the matter has only come thus far.

Such was Mollwitz, the first Battle for Silesia; which had to cost many Battles first and last. Silesia will be gained, we can expect, by fighting of this kind in an honest cause. But here is something already gained, which is considerable, and about which there is no doubt. A new Military Power, it would appear, has come upon the scene; the Gazetteer-and-Diplomatic world will have to make itself familiar with a name not much heard of hitherto among the Nations. "A Nation which can fight," think the Gazetteers; "fight almost as the very Swedes did; and is led on by its King too, — who may prove, in his way, a very Charles XII., or small Macedonia's Madman, for aught one knows?" In which latter branch of their prognostic the Gazetteers were much out. —

The Fame of this Battle, which is now so sunk out of memory, was great in Europe; and struck, like a huge war-gong, with long resonance, through the general ear. M. de Voltaire had run across to Lille in those Spring days: there is a good Troop of Players

---

* Orlich, I. 108; Kausler, p. 235, correct; *Helden-Geschichte*, I. 695, incorrect.

in Lille; a Niece, Madame Denis, wife of some Military Commissariat Denis, important in those parts, can lodge the divine Emilie and me: — and one could at last see *Mahomet*, after five years of struggling, get upon the boards, if not yet in Paris by a great way, yet in Lille, which is something. *Mahomet* is getting upon the boards on those terms; and has proceeded, not amiss, through an Act or two, when a Note from the King of Prussia was handed to Voltaire, announcing the victory of Mollwitz. Which delightful Note Voltaire stopt the performance till he read to the Audience: "Bravissimo!" answered the Audience. "You will see," said M. de Voltaire to the friends about him, "this Piece at Moll-"witz will make mine succeed:" which proved to be the fact.* For the French are Anti-Austrian; and smell great things in the wind. "'That man is mad, your Most Christian Majesty?" "Not quite; or at any rate not mad only!" think Louis and his Belle-isle now.

Dimly poring in those old Books, and squeezing one's way into face-to-face view of the extinct Time, we begin to notice what a clangorous rumour was in Mollwitz to the then generation of mankind; — betokening many things; universal European War, as the first thing. Which duly came to pass; as did, at a slower rate, the ulterior thing, not yet so apparent, that indeed a new hour had struck on the Time Horologe, that a New Epoch had risen. Yes, my friends. New Charles XII. or not, here truly has a new Man and King come upon the scene: capable perhaps of doing something? Slumberous Europe, rotting amid its blind pedantries, its lazy hypocrisies, conscious

* Voltaire, *Œuvres* (*Vie Privée*), ii. 74.

and unconscious: this man is capable of shaking it a little out of its stupid refuges of lies, and ignominious wrappages and bed-clothes, which will be its grave-clothes otherwise; and of intimating to it, afar off, that there is still a Veracity in Things, and a Mendacity in Sham-Things, and that the difference of the two is infinitely more considerable than was supposed.

This Mollwitz is a most deliberate, regulated, ponderously impressive (*gravitätisch*) Feat of Arms, as the reader sees; done all by Regulation methods, with orthodox exactitude; in a slow, weighty, almost pedantic, but highly irrefragable manner. It is the triumph of Prussian Discipline; of military orthodoxy well put in practice: the honest outcome of good natural stuff in those Brandenburgers, and of the supreme virtues of Drill. Neipperg and his Austrians had much despised Prussian soldiering: "Keep our soup hot," cried they, on running out this day to rank themselves, "hot a little, till we drive these fellows to the Devil!" That was their opinion, about noon this day: but that is an opinion they have renounced for all remaining days and years. — It is a Victory due properly to Friedrich Wilhelm, and the Old Dessauer, who are far away from it. Friedrich Wilhelm, though dead, fights here, and the others only do his bidding on this occasion. His Son, as yet, adds nothing of his own; though he will ever henceforth begin largely adding, — right careful withal to lose nothing, for the Friedrich Wilhelm contribution is invaluable, and the basis of everything: — but it is curious to see in what contrast this first Battle of Friedrich's is with his latter and last ones.

Considering the Battle of Mollwitz, and then, in contrast, the intricate Pragmatic Sanction, and what their consequences were and their antecedents, it is curious once more! This, then, is what the Pragmatic Sanction has come to? Twenty years of world-wide diplomacy, cunningly-devised spider-threads overnetting all the world, have issued here. Your Congresses of Cambray, of Soissons, your Grumkow-Seckendorf Machiavelisms, all these might as well have lain in their bed. Real Pragmatic Sanction would have been, A well-trained Army and your Treasury full. Your Treasury is empty (nothing in it but those foolish 200,000 English guineas, and the passionate cry for more): and your Army is not trained as this Prussian one; cannot keep its ground against this one. Of all those long-headed Potentates, simple Friedrich Wilhelm, son of Nature, who had the honesty to do what Nature taught him, has come out gainer. You all laughed at him as a fool: do you begin to see now who was wise, who fool? He has an Army that "advances on "you with glittering musketry, steady as on the "parade-ground, and pours out fire like one continuous "thunderpeal;" so that, strange as it seems, you find there will actually be nothing for you but — taking to your heels, shall we say? — rolling off with despatch, as second-best! These things are of singular omen. Here stands one that will avenge Friedrich Wilhelm, — if Friedrich Wilhelm were not already sufficiently avenged by the mere verdict of facts, which is palpably coming out, as Time peels the wiggeries away from them more and more. Mollwitz and such places are full of veracity; and no head is so thick as to resist conviction in that kind.

Of Friedrich's Disappearance into Fairyland, in the interim; and of Maupertuis's similar Adventure.

Of the King's Flight, or sudden disappearance into Fairyland, during this First Battle, the King himself, who alone could have told us fully, maintained always rigorous silence, and nowhere drops the least hint. So that the small fact has come down to us involved in a great bulk of fabulous cobwebs, mostly of an ill-natured character, set a-going by Voltaire, Valori and others (which fabulous process, in the good-natured form, still continues itself); and, except for Nicolai's good industry (in his *Anekdoten*-Book), we should have difficulty even in guessing, not to say understanding, as is now partly possible. The few real particulars, — and those do verify themselves, and hang perfectly together, when the big globe of fable is burnt off from them, — are to the following effect.

"Battle lost," said Schwerin, "but what is the loss of a Battle to that of your Majesty's own Person? For Heaven's sake, go; get across the Oder; be you safe, till this decide itself!" That was reasonable counsel. If defeated, Schwerin can hope to retreat upon Ohlau, upon Breslau, and save the Magazines. This side the Oder, all will be movements, a whirlpool of Hussars; but beyond the Oder, all is quiet, open. To Ohlau, to Glogau, nay home to Brandenburg and the Old Dessauer with his Camp at Göttin, the road is free, by the other side of the Oder. — Schwerin and Prince Leopold urging him, the King did ride away; at what hour, with what suite, nor with what adventures (not mostly fabulous) is not known: — but it was towards Löwen, fifteen miles off (where he crossed Neisse

River, the other day); and thence towards Oppeln, on the Oder, eighteen miles farther; and the pace was swift. Leopold, on reflection, ordered off a Squadron of Gens d'Armes to overtake his Majesty, at Löwen or sooner; which they never did. Passing Pampitz, the King threw Fredersdorf a word, who was among the baggage there: "To Oppeln; bring the Purse, the Privy Writings; swift!" Which Fredersdorf, and the Clerks (and another Herr, who became Nicolai's Father-in-law in after years) did; and joined the King at Löwen; but I hope stopped there.

The King's suite was small, names not given; but by the time he got to Löwen, being joined by cavalry fugitives and the like, it had got to be seventy persons: too many for the King. He selected what was his of them; ordered the gates to be shut behind him on all others, and again rode away. The Leopold Squadron of Gens d'Armes did not arrive till after his departure; and having here lost trace of him, called halt, and billeted for the night. The King speeds silently to Oppeln on his excellent bay horse, the worse-mounted gradually giving in. At Oppeln is a Bridge over the Oder, a free Country beyond: Regiment La Motte lay, and as the King thinks, still lies in Oppeln; — but in that he is mistaken. Regiment La Motte is with the baggage at Pampitz, all this day; and a wandering Hussar Party, some sixty Austrians, have taken possession of Oppeln. The King, and the few who had not yet broken down, arrive at the Gate of Oppeln, late, under cloud of night: "Who goes?" cried the sentry from within. "Prussians! A Prussian Courier!" answer they; — and are fired upon through the gratings; and immediately draw back, and vanish unhurt into Night again. "Had those Hussars only let him in!" said Austria afterwards: but they had not such luck. It was at this point, according to Valori, that the King burst forth into audible ejaculations of a lamentable nature. There is no getting over, then, even to Brandenburg, and in an insolvent condition. Not open insolvency and bankrupt disgrace; no, ruin, and an Austrian jail, is the one outlook. "*O mon Dieu*, O God, it is too much (*c'en est trop*)!" with other the like snatches of lamentation;* which are not inconceivable in a young man, sleepless for the third night, in these circumstances; but which Valori knows nothing of, except by malicious rumour from the valet class, — who have misinformed Valori about several other points.

The King riding diligently, with or without ejaculations, back towards Löwen, comes at an early hour to the Mill of Hilbersdorf, within a mile-and-half of that place. He alights at the Mill; sends one of his attendants, almost the only one now left, to inquire what is in Löwen. The answer, we know, is: "A squadron of Gens d'Armes there; furthermore, a Prussian Adjutant come to say, Victory at Mollwitz!" Upon which the King mounts again; — issues into daylight, and concludes these mythical adventures. That "in Löwen, in "the shop at the corner of the Market-place, Widow "Panzern, subsequently Wife Something-else, made his "Majesty a cup of coffee, and served a roast fowl "along with it," cannot but be welcome news, if true; and that "his Majesty got to Mollwitz again before "dark that same day,"** is liable to no controversy.

In this way was Friedrich snatched by Morgante

* Valori, l. 104.   ** Fuchs, p. 11.

into Fairyland, carried by Diana to the top of Pindus (or even by Proserpine to Tartarus, through a bad sixteen hours), till the Battle-whirlwind subsided. Friendly imaginative spirits would, in the antique time, have so construed it: but these moderns were malicious-valetish, not friendly; and wrapped the matter in mere stupid worlds of cobweb, which require burning. Friedrich himself was stone-silent on this matter, al! his life after; but is understood never quite to have pardoned Schwerin for the ill-luck of giving him such advice.*

Friedrich's adventure is not the only one of that kind at Mollwitz; there is another equally indubitable, — which will remain obscure, half-mythical to the end of the world. The truth is, that Right Wing of the Prussian Army was fallen chaotic, ruined; and no man, not even one who had seen it, can give account of what went on there. The sage Maupertuis, for example, had climbed some tree or place of impregnability ("tree," Voltaire calls it, though that is hardly probable), hoping to see the Battle there. And he did see it, much too clearly at last! In such a tide of charging and chasing, on that Right Wing and round all the Field in the Prussian rear; in such wide bickering and boiling of Horse-currents, — which fling out, round all the Prussian rear quarters, such a spray of Austrian Hussars for one element, — Maupertuis, I have no doubt, wishes much he were at home, doing his sines and tangents. An Austrian Hussar-party gets

* Nicolai, ii. 180-195 (the one true account); Levoaux, i. 194; Valori, i. 104; &c. &c. (the myth in various stages). Most distractedly mythical of all, with the truth clear before it, is the latest version, just come out, in *Was sich die Schlesier vom alten Fritz erzählten* (Brieg, 1860), pp. 113-125

sight of him, on his tree or other standpoint (Voltaire says elsewhere he was mounted on an ass, the malicious spirit!) — too certain, the Austrian Hussars got sight of him: his purse, gold watch, all he has of movable is given frankly; all will not do. There are frills about the man, fine laces, cloth; a goodish yellow wig on him, for one thing: — their Slavonic dialect, too fatally intelligible by the pantomime accompanying it, forces sage Maupertuis from his tree or standpoint; the big red face flurried into scarlet, I can fancy; or scarlet and ashy-white mixed; and — Let us draw a veil over it! He is next seen shirtless, the once very haughty, blustery, and now much-humiliated man; still conscious of supreme acumen, insight, and pure science; and, though an Austrian prisoner and a monster of rags, struggling to believe that he is a genius and the Trismegistus of mankind. What a pickle! The sage Maupertuis, as was natural, keeps passionately asking, of gods and men, for an Officer with some tincture of philosophy, or even who could speak French. Such Officer is at last found; humanely advances him money, a shirt and suit of clothes; but can in no wise dispense with his going to Vienna as prisoner. Thither he went accordingly; still in a mythical condition. Of Voltaire's laughing, there is no end; and he changes the myth from time to time, on new rumours coming; and there is no truth to be had from him."*

Thus much is certain: at Vienna, Maupertuis, Prisoner on parole, glided about for some time in deep eclipse, till the Newspapers began babbling of him. He confessed then that he was Maupertuis, Flattener

---

* Voltaire, *Œuvres* (*Vie Privée*), ii. 33-4; and see his *Letters* for some weeks after the event.

of the Earth; but for the rest, "told rather a blind story about himself," says Robinson; spoke as if he had been of the King's suite, "riding with the King," when that Hussar accident befel; — rather a blind story, true story being too sad. The Vienna Sovereignties, in the turn things had taken, were extremely kind; Grand-Duke Franz handsomely pulled out his own watch, hearing what road the Maupertuis one had gone; dismissed the Maupertuis, with that and other gifts, home: — to Brittany (not to Prussia), till times calmed for engrafting the Sciences.*

On Wednesday, Friedrich writes this Note to his Sister; the first utterance we have from him, since those wild roamings about Oppeln and Hilbersdorf Mill:

King to Wilhelmina (at Baireuth; two days after Mollwitz.)

"Ohlau, 12th April 1741.

"My dearest Sister, — I have the satisfaction to inform "you that we have yesterday" (day before yesterday; but some of us have only had one sleep!) "totally beaten the "Austrians. They have lost more than 5,000 men, killed, "wounded and prisoners. We have lost Prince Friedrich, "Brother of Margraf Karl; General Schulenburg, Wartens-"leben of the Carabineers, and many other Officers. Our "troops did miracles; and the result shows as much. It was "one of the rudest Battles fought within memory of man.

"I am sure you will take part in this happiness; and that "you will not doubt of the tenderness with which I am, my "dearest Sister," — Yours wholly, — Fédéric.**

And on the same day there comes, from Breslau, Jordan's Answer to the late anxious little Note from

* *Helden-Geschichte*, i. 902; Robinson's Despatch (Vienna, 22d April 1741, x. s.); Voltaire, *ubi suprà*.
** *Œuvres*, xxvii. i. 101.

Pogarell; anxieties now gone, and smoky misery changed into splendour of flame:

> *Jordan to the King* (finds him at Ohlau).
> "Breslau, 11th April 1741.
>
> "Sire — Yesterday I was in terrible alarms. The sound of "the cannon heard, the smoke of powder visible from the "steeple-tops here; all led us to suspect that there was a "Battle going on. Glorious confirmation of it this morning! "Nothing but rejoicing among all the Protestant inhabitants; "who had begun to be in apprehension, from the rumours "which the other party took pleasure in spreading. Persons "who were in the Battle cannot enough celebrate the coolness "and bravery of your Majesty. For myself, I am at the over-"flowing point. I have run about all day, announcing this "glorious news to the Berliners who are here. In my life I "have never felt a more perfect satisfaction.
>
> "M. de Camas is here, very ill for the last two days; attack "of fever: the Doctor hopes to bring him through," — which proved beyond the Doctor: the good Camas died here three days hence (age sixty-three); an excellent German Frenchman, of much sense, dignity and honesty; familiar to Friedrich from infancy onwards, and no doubt regretted by him as deserved. The Widow Camas, a fine old Lady, German by birth, will again come in view. Jordan continues:
>
> "One finds, at the corner of every street, an orator of the "Plebs celebrating the warlike feats of your Majesty's troops. "I have often, in my idleness, assisted at these discourses: "not artistic eloquence, it must be owned, but spurting rude "from the heart." * * *
>
> Jordan adds in his next Note: "This morning (14th) I "quitted M. de Camas; who, it is thought, cannot last the "day. I have hardly left him during his illness;"* — and so let that scene close.

Neipperg, meanwhile, had fallen back on Neisse; taken up a strong encampment in that neighbourhood; he lies thereabouts, all summer; stretched out, as it were, in a kind of vigilant dog-sleep on the threshold,

* *Œuvres de Frédéric,* xvii. 99.

keeping watch over Neisse, and tries fighting no more at this time, or indeed ever after, to speak of. And always, I think, with disadvantage, when he does try a little. He had been Grand-Duke Franz's Tutor in War-matters; had got into trouble at Belgrad once before, and was almost hanged by the Turks. George II. had occasionally the benefit of him, in coming years. Be not too severe on the poor man, as the Vienna public was; he had some faculty, though not enough. "Governor of Luxemburg," before long: there, for most part, let him peacefully drill, and spend the remainder of his poor life. Friedrich says, neither Neipperg nor himself, at this time, knew the least of War; and that it would be hard to settle which of them made the more blunders in their Silesian tussle.

Friedrich, in about three weeks hence, was fully ready for opening trenches upon Brieg; did open trenches, accordingly, by moonlight, in a grand nocturnal manner (as readers shall see anon); and, by vigorous cannonading, — Maréchal de Belleisle having come, by this time, to enjoy the fine spectacle, — soon got possession of Brieg, and held it thenceforth. Neisse now alone remained, with Neipperg vigilantly stretched upon the threshold of it. But the Maréchal de Belleisle, we say, had come; that was the weighty circumstance. And before Neisse can be thought of, there is a whole Europe bickering aloft into conflict; embattling itself from end to end, in sequel of Mollwitz Battle; and such a preliminary sea of negotiating, diplomatic finessing, pulse-feeling, projecting and palavering, with Friedrich for centre all summer, as — as I wish readers could imagine without my speaking of it farther! But they cannot.

CHAPTER XI.

THE BURSTING FORTH OF BEDLAMS: BELLEISLE AND THE BREAKERS OF PRAGMATIC SANCTION.

THE Battle of Mollwitz went off like a signal-shot among the Nations; intimating that they were, one and all, to go battling. Which they did, with a witness; making a terrible thing of it, over all the world, for above seven years to come. Foolish Nations; doomed to settle their jarring accounts in that terrible manner! Nay, the fewest of them had any accounts, except imaginary ones, to settle there at all; and they went into the adventure *gratis*, spurred on by spectralities of the sick brain, by phantasms of hope, phantasms of terror; and had, strictly speaking, no actual business in it whatever.

Not that Mollwitz kindled Europe; Europe was already kindled for some two years past; — especially since the late Kaiser died, and his Pragmatic Sanction was superadded to the other troubles afoot. But ever since that Image of *Jenkins's Ear* had at last blazed up in the slow English brain, like a fiery constellation or Sign in the Heavens, symbolic of such injustices and unendurabilities, and had lighted the Spanish-English War, Europe was slowly but pretty surely taking fire. France "could not see Spain humbled," she said: England (in its own dim feeling, and also in the fact of things) could not do at all without considerably humbling Spain. France, endlessly interested in that Spanish-English matter, was already sending out fleets, firing shots, — almost, or altogether, putting forth her hand in it. "In which case, will not, must not, Austria help us?" thought England, — and was asking, daily, at Vienna (with intense earnestness, but without the least result), through Excellency Robinson, there, when the late Kaiser died. Died, poor gentleman; — and left his big Austrian Heritages lying, as it were, in the open market-place; elaborately tied by diplomatic pack-thread and Pragmatic Sanction; but not otherwise protected against the assembled cupidities of mankind! Independently of Mollwitz, or of Silesia altogether, it was next to impossible that Europe could long avoid blazing out; especially unless the Spanish-English quarrel got quenched, of which there was no likelihood.

But, if not as cause, then as signal, or as signal and cause together (which it properly was), the Battle of Mollwitz gave the finishing stroke, and set all in motion. This was "the little stone broken loose from the mountain;" this, rather than the late Kaiser's Death, which Friedrich defined in that manner. Or at least, this was the first *leap* it took; hitting other stones big and little, which again hit others with their leaping and rolling, — till the whole mountain-side was in motion under law of gravity, and you behold one wide stone-torrent thundering towards the valleys; shivering woods, farms, habitations clean away with it: fatal to any Image of composite Clay and Brass which it may meet!

There is, accordingly, from this point, a change in Friedrich's Silesian Adventure; which becomes infinitely more complicated for him, — and for those that write of him, no less! Friedrich's business henceforth is not to be done by direct fighting, but rather by waiting to see how, and on what side, others will fight: nor can we describe or understand Friedrich's business, except as in connexion with the immense, obsolete, and indeed delirious Phenomenon called Austrian-Succession War, upon which it is difficult to say any human word. If History, driven upon Dismal Swamp with its horrors and perils, can get across unsunk, she will be lucky!

For, directly on the back of Mollwitz, there ensued, first, an explosion of Diplomatic activity such as was never seen before; Excellencies from the four winds taking wing towards Friedrich; and talking and insinuating, and fencing and fugling, after their sort, in that Silesian Camp of his, the centre being there. A universal rookery of Diplomatists;— whose loud cackle and cawing is now as if gone mad to us; their work wholly fallen putrescent and avoidable, dead to all creatures. And secondly, in the train of that, there ensued a universal European War, the French and the English being chief parties in it; which abounds in battles and feats of arms, spirited but delirious, and cannot be got stilled for seven or eight years to come; and in which Friedrich and his War swim only as an intermittent Episode henceforth. What to do with such a War; how extricate the Episode, and leave the War lying? The War was at first a good deal mad; and is now, to men's imagination, fallen wholly so; who indeed have managed mostly to forget it; only the Episode (reduced thereby to an *un*intelligible state) retaining still some claims on them.

It is singular into what oblivion the huge Phenomenon called Austrian-Succession War has fallen; which, within a hundred years ago or little more, filled all mortal hearts! The English were principals on one side; did themselves fight in it, with their customary fire, and their customary guidance ("courageous Wooden Pole with Cocked Hat," as our friend called it); and paid all the expenses, which were extremely considerable, and are felt in men's pockets to this day: but the English have more completely forgotten it than any other People. "Battle of Dettingen, Battle of Fontenoy, — what, in the Devil's name, were we ever doing there?" the impatient Englishman asks; and can give no answer, except the general one: "Fit of insanity; *Delirium Tremens*, perhaps *Furens*; — don't think of it!" Of Philippi and Arbela educated Englishmen can render account; and I am told young gentlemen entering the Army are pointedly required to say who commanded at Aigos-Potamos and wrecked the Peloponnesian War: but of Dettingen and Fontenoy, where is the living Englishman that has the least notion, or seeks for any? The Austrian-Succession War did veritably rage for eight years, at a terrific rate, deforming the face of Earth and Heaven; the English paying the piper always, and founding their National Debt thereby: — but not even that could prove mnemonic to them; and they have dropped the Austrian-Succession War, with one accord, into the general dust-bin, and are content it should lie there. They have not, in their language, the least approach to an intelligible account of it: How it went on, whitherward, whence; why it was there at all, — are points dark to the English, and on which they do not wish to be informed. They have quitted the matter, as an unintelligible huge English-and-Foreign Delirium (which in good part it was); Delirium unintelligible to them; tedious, not to say in parts, as those of the Austrian Subsidies, hideous and disgusting to them;— happily now fallen extinct; and capable of being skipped, in one's inquiries into the wonders of this England and this World. Which, in fact, is a practical conclusion not so unwise as it looks.

"Wars are not memorable," says Sauerteig, "however big "they may have been, whatever rages and miseries they may "have occasioned, or however many hundreds of thousands "they may have been the death of,— except, when they have "something of World-History in them withal. If they are "found to have been the travail-throes of great or consider- "able changes, which continue permanent in the world, men "of some curiosity cannot but inquire into them, keep memory "of them. But if they were travail-throes that had no birth, "who of mortals would remember them? Unless perhaps the "feats of prowess, virtue, valour and endurance, they might "accidentally give rise to, were very great indeed. Much "greater than the most were, which came out in that Austrian- "Succession case! Wars otherwise are mere futile transitory "dust-whirlwinds stilled in blood; extensive fits of human in- "sanity, such as we know are too apt to break out; — such as "it rather beseems a faithful Son of the House of Adam *not* to "speak about again; as in houses where the grandfather was "hanged, the topic of ropes is fitly avoided.

"Never again will that War, with its deliriums, mad out- "lays of blood, treasure, and of hope and terror, and far- "spread human destruction, rise into visual life in any imagi- "nation of living man. In vain shall Dryasdust strive: things "mad, chaotic and without ascertainable purpose or result, "cannot be fixed into human memories. Fix them there by "never so many Documentary Histories, elaborate long-eared "Pedantries, and cunning threads, the poor human memory "has an alchemy against such ill usage; — it forgets them "again; grows to know them as a mere torpor, a stupidity "and horror, and instinctively flies from Dryasdust and "them."

Alive to any considerable degree, in the poor

human imagination, this Editor does not expect or even wish the Austrian-Succession War to be. Enough for him if it could be understood sufficiently to render his poor History of Friedrich intelligible. For it enwraps Friedrich like a world-vortex henceforth; modifies every step of his existence henceforth; and apart from it, there is no understanding of his business or him. "So much as sticks to Friedrich:" that was our original bargain! Assist loyally, O reader, and we will try to make the indispensable a minimum for you.

Who was to blame for the Austrian-Succession War?

The first point to be noted is, Where did it originate? To which the answer mainly is, With that lean Gentleman whom we saw with Papers, in the Œil-de-Bœuf on New-year's day last. With Monseigneur the Maréchal de Belleisle principally; with the ambitious cupidities and baseless vanities of the French Court and Nation, as represented by Belleisle. George II.'s Spanish War, if you will examine, had a real necessity in it. Jenkins's Ear was the ridiculous outside figure this matter had: Jenkins's Ear was one final item of it; but the poor English People, in their wrath and bellowings about that small item, were intrinsically meaning: "Settle the account; let us have that account cleared up and liquidated: it has lain too long!" And seldom were a People more in the right, as readers shall yet see.

The English-Spanish War had a basis to stand on in this Universe. The like had the Prussian-Austrian one; so all men now admit. If Friedrich had not business there, what man ever had in an enterprise he ventured on? Friedrich, after such trial and proof as has seldom been, got his claims on Schlesien allowed by the Destinies. His claims on Schlesien; — and on infinitely higher things; which were found to be his and his Nation's, though he had not been consciously thinking of them in making that adventure. For, as my poor Friend insists, there *are* Laws valid in Earth and in Heaven; and the great soul of the world is just. Friedrich had business in this War; and Maria Theresa *versus* Friedrich had likewise cause to appear in court, and do her utmost pleading against him.

But if we ask, What Belleisle, or France and Louis XV. had to do there? the answer is rigorously, Nothing. Their own windy vanities, ambitions, sanctioned not by fact and the Almighty Powers, but by phantasm and the babble of Versailles; transcendent self-conceit, intrinsically insane; pretensions over their fellow-creatures which were without basis anywhere in Nature, except in the French brain alone: it was this that brought Belleisle and France into a German War. And Belleisle and France having gone into an Anti-Pragmatic War, the unlucky George and his England were dragged into a Pragmatic one, — quitting their own business, on the Spanish Main, and hurrying to Germany, — in terror as at Doomsday, and zeal to save the Keystone of Nature there. That is the notable point in regard to this War: That France is to be called the author of it, who, alone of all the parties, had no business there whatever. And the wages due to France for such a piece of industry, — the reader will yet see what wages France and the other parties got, at the tail of the affair. For that too is apparent in our day.

April—May 1741.

We have often said, the Spanish-English War was itself likely to have kindled Europe; and again Friedrich's Silesian War was itself likely, — France being nearly sure to interfere. But if both these Wars were necessary ones, and if France interfered in either of them on the wrong side, the blame will be to France, not to the necessary Wars. France could, in no way, have interfered in a more barefacedly unjust and gratuitous manner, than she now did; nor, on any terms, have so palpably made herself the author of the conflagration of deliriums that ensued for above Seven years henceforth. Nay for above Twenty years, — the settlement of this Silesian Pragmatic-Antipragmatic matter (and of Jenkins's Ear, incidentally, *along* with this!) not having fairly completed itself till 1763.

How Belleisle made Visit to Teutschland; and there was no fit Henry the Fowler to welcome him.

It is very wrong to keep Enchanted Wiggeries sitting in this world, as if they were things still alive! By a species of "conservatism," which gets praised in our Time, but which is only a slothful cowardice, base indifference to truth, and hatred to trouble in comparison with lies that sit quiet, men now extensively practise this method of procedure; — little dreaming how bad and fatal it at all times is. When the brains are out, things really ought to die; — no matter what lovely things they were, and still affect to be, the brains being out, they actually ought in all cases to die, and with their best speed get buried. Men had noses, at one time; and smelt the horror of a deceased reality fallen putrid, of a once dear verity become mendacious, phantasmal; but they have, to an immense degree, lost that organ since, and are now living comfortably cheek-by-jowl with lies. Lies of that sad "conservative" kind, — and indeed of all kinds whatsoever: for that kind is a general mother; and *breeds*, with a fecundity that is appalling, did you heed it much! —

It was pity that the "Holy Romish Reich, Teutsch by Nation," had not got itself buried some ages before. Once it had brains and life, but now they were out. Under the sway of Barbarossa, under our old Anti-chaotic friend Henry the Fowler, how different had it been! No field for a Belleisle, to come and sow tares; no rotten thatch for a French Sungod to go sailing about in the middle of, and set fire to! Henry, when the Hungarian Pan-Slavonic Savagery came upon him, had got ready in the interim; and a mangy dog was the "tribute" he gave them; followed by the due extent of broken crowns, since they would not be content with that. That was the due of Belleisle too, — had there been a Henry to meet him with it, on his crossing the marches, in Trier Country, in Spring 1741: "There, you anarchic Upholstery-Belus, fancying yourself God of the Sun; there is what Teutschland owes you. Go home with that; and mind your own business, which I am told is plentiful, if you had eye for it!"

But the sad truth is, for above Four Centuries now — and especially for Three, since little Kaiser Karl IV. "gave away all the moneys of it," in his pressing occasions, — this Holy Romish Reich, Teutsch by Nation, has been more and ever more becoming an imaginary quantity; the Kaisership of it not capable of being worn by anybody, except a Hapsburger who had resources otherwise his own. The fact is palpable. And

Austria, an Anti-Reformation Entity, "conservative" in that bad sense, of slothfully abhorring trouble in comparison with lies, had not found the poison more malodorous in this particular than in many others. And had cherished its "Holy Romish Reich" grown *unholy*, phantasmal, like so much else in Austrian things; and had held firm grip of it, these Three Hundred years; and found it a furthersome and suitable thing, though sensible it was more and more becoming an Enchanted Wiggery pure and simple. Nor have the consequences failed; they never do. Belleisle, Louis XIV., Henri II., François I.: it is long since the French have known this state of matters; and been in the habit of breaking in upon it, fomenting internal discontents, getting up unjust Wars, — with or without advantage to France, but with endless disadvantage to Germany. Schmalkaldic War; Thirty-Years War; Louis XIV.'s Wars, which brought Alsace and the other fine cuttings; late Polish-Election War, and its Lorraine; Austrian-Succession War: many are the wars kindled on poor Teutschland, by neighbour France; and large is the sum of woes to Europe and to it, chargeable to that score. Which appears even yet not to be completed? — Perhaps not, even yet. For it is the penalty of being loyal to Enchanted Wiggeries; of living cheek-by-jowl with lies of a peaceable quality, and stuffing your nostrils, and searing your soul, against the accursed odour they all have! — For I can assure you, the curse of Heaven does dwell in one and all of them; and the son of Adam cannot too soon get quit of their bad partnership, cost him what it may.

Belleisle's Journey as Sungod began in March, —

"end of March 1741," no date of a day to be had for that memorable thing: — and he went gyrating about through the German Courts, for almost a year afterwards; his course rather erratic, but always in a splendour as of Belus, with those Hundred-and-thirty French Lords and Valets, and the glory of Most Christian King irradiating him. Very diligent for the first six months, till September or October next, which we may call his *seed-time;* and by no means resting, after nine or twelve months, while the harrowing and hoeing went on. In January 1742, he had the great satisfaction to see a Bavarian Kaiser got, instead of an Austrian; and everywhere the fruit of his diligent husbandry begin to *beard* fairly above ground, into a crop of facts (like armed men from dragon's teeth), and "the pleasure of the" — *whom* was it the pleasure of! — "prosper in his hands." Belleisle was a pretty man; but I doubt it was not "the Lord" he was doing the pleasure of, on this occasion, but a very Different Personage, disguised to resemble him in poor Belleisle's eyes! —

Austria was not dangerous to France in late times, and now least of all; how far from it, — humbled by the loss of Lorraine; and now as it were bankrupt, itself in danger from all the world. And France, so far as express Treaties could bind a Nation, was bound to maintain Austria in its present possessions. The bitter loss of Lorraine had been sweetened to the late Kaiser by that solitary drop of consolation; — as his Failure of a Life had been, poor man; "Failure the most of me has been; but I have got Pragmatic Sanction, thanks to Heaven, and even France has signed it!" Loss of Lorraine, loss of Elsass, loss of the Three Bishopricks; since Karl V.'s times, not to speak of earlier, there has

April–May 1741.

been mere loss on loss: — and now is the time to consummate it, think Belleisle and France, in spite of Treaties.

Towards humbling or extinguishing Austria, Belleisle has two preliminary things to do: *First*, Break the Pragmatic Sanction, and get everybody to break it; *second*, Guide the *Kaiserwahl* (Election of a Kaiser), so that it issue, not in Grand-Duke Franz, Maria Theresa's Husband, as all expect it will, but in another party friendly to France: — say, in Karl Albert of Bavaria, whose Family have long been good clients of ours, dependent on us for a living in the Political World. Belleisle, there is little doubt, had from the first cast his eye on this unlucky Karl Albert for Kaiser; but is uncertain as to carrying him. Belleisle will take another, if he must; Kur-Sachsen, for example; — any other, and all others, only not the Grand-Duke: that is a point already fixed with Belleisle, though he keeps it well in the background, and is careful not to hint it till the time come.

In regard to Pragmatic Sanction, Belleisle and France found no difficulty, — or the difficulty only (which we hope must have been considerable) of eating their own Covenant in behalf of Pragmatic Sanction; and declaring, which they did without visible blush, That it was a Covenant including, if not expressly, then tacitly, as all human covenants do, this clause, "*Salvo jure tertii* (Saving the rights of Third Parties)," — that is, of Electors of Bavaria, and others who may object against it! O soul of honour, O first Nation of the Universe, was there ever such a subterfuge? Here is a field of flowering corn, the biggest in the world, begirt with elaborate ring-fence, many miles of firm oak-paling pitched and buttressed; — the poor gentleman now dead gave you his Lorraine, and almost his life, for swearing to keep up said paling. And you do keep it up, — all except six yards; through which the biggest team on the highway can drive freely, and the paltriest cadger's ass can step in for a bellyful!

It appears, the first Nation of the Universe had, at an early period of their consultations, hit upon this of *Salvo jure tertii*, as the method of eating their Covenant, before an enlightened public.* And they persisted in it, there being no other for them. An enlightened public grinned sardonically, and was not taken in; but, as so many others were eating their Covenants, under equally poor substerfuges, the enlightened public could not grin long on any individual, — could only gape mutely, with astonishment, on all. A glorious example of veracity and human nobleness, set by the gods of this lower world to their gazing populations, who could read in the Gazettes! What is truth, falsity, human Kingship, human Swindlership? Are the Ten Commandments only a figuré of speech, then? And it was some beggarly Attorney-*Devil* that built this sublunary world and us? Questions might rise; had long been rising; — but now there was about enough, and the *response* to them was falling due; and Belleisle himself, what is very notable, had been appointed, to get ready the response. Belleisle (little as Belleisle dreamt of it, in these high Enterprises) was ushering in, by way of response, a *Ragnarök*, or Twilight of the Gods,

* 20th January 1741, in their Note of Ceremony, recognising Maria Theresa as Queen of Hungary, Note which had been due so very long (*Adelung*, ii. 206)[,] there is ominous silence on Pragmatic Sanction; "beginning of March," there is virtual avowal of *Salvo jure* (ib. 279); — open avowal on Belleisle's advent (ib. 305).

which, as "French Revolution, or Apotheosis of *Sansculottism*," is now well known; — and that is something to consider of!

Downbreak of Pragmatic Sanction; Manner of the chief Artists in handling their Covenants.

The operation once accomplished on its own Pragmatic Covenant, France found no difficulty with the others. Everybody was disposed to eat his Covenant who could see advantage in so doing, after that admirable example. The difficulty of France and Belleisle rather was, to keep the hungry parties back: "Don't eat your Covenant *till* the proper time; patience, we say!" A most sad Miscellany of Royalties, coming all to the point, "Will you eat your Covenant, Will you keep it?" — and eating, nearly all; in fact, wholly all that needed to eat.

On the first Invasion of Silesia, Maria Theresa had indignantly complained in every Court; and pointing to Pragmatic Sanction, had demanded that such Law of Nature be complied with, according to covenant. What Maria Theresa got by this circuit of the Courts, everybody still knows. Except England, which was willing, and Holland, which was unwilling, all Courts had answered, more or less uneasily: "Law of Nature, — humph: yes!" — and, far from doing anything, not one of them would with certainty promise to do anything. From England alone and her little King (to whom Pragmatic Sanction is the Palladium of Human Freedoms and the Keystone of Nature) could she get the least help. The rest hung back; would not open heart or pocket; waited till they saw. They do now see; now that Belleisle has done his feat of Covenant-eating! —

Eleven great Powers, some count Thirteen, some Twelve,* — but no two agree, and hardly one agrees with himself; — enough, the Powers of Europe, from Naples and Madrid to Russia and Sweden, have all signed it, let us say a Dozen or Baker's-Dozen of them. And except our little English Paladin alone, whose interest and indeed salvation seemed to him to lie that way, and who needed no Pragmatic Covenant to guide him, nobody whatever distinguished himself by keeping it. Between December 1740, when Maria Theresa set up her cries in all Courts, on to April 1741, England, painfully dragging Holland with her, had alone of the Baker's-Dozen spoken word of disapproval; much less done act of hindrance. Two especially (France and Bavaria, not to mention Spain) had done the reverse, and disowned, and declared against, Pragmatic Sanction. And after the Battle of Mollwitz, when the "little stone" took its first leap, and set all thundering, then came, like the inrush of a fashion, throughout that high Miscellany or Baker's-Dozen, the general eating of Covenants (which was again quickened in August, for a reason we shall see): and before November of that Year, there was no Covenant left to eat. Of the Baker's-Dozen nobody remained but little George the Paladin, dragging Holland painfully along with him; — and Pragmatic Sanction had gone to water, like ice in a June day, and its beautiful crystalline qualities and prismatic colours were forever vanished from the world. Will the reader note a point or two, a personage or two, in this sordid process, — not for the

* Schöll, ii. 286; Adelung, *list,* ii. 127.

April—May 1741.

process's sake, which is very sordid and smells badly, but for his own sake, to elucidate his own course a little, in the intricacies now coming or come upon him and me?

1º. *Elector of Bavaria.* — Karl Albert of Baiern is by some counted as a Signer of the Pragmatic Sanction, and by others not; which occasions that discrepancy of sum-total in the Books. And he did once, in a sense, sign it, he and his Brother of Köln; but, before the late Kaiser's death, he had openly drawn back from it again: and counted himself a Non-signer. Signer or not, he, for his part, lost no moment (but rather the contrary) in openly protesting against it, and signifying that he never would acknowledge it. Of this the reader saw something, at the time of her Hungarian Majesty's Accession. Date and circumstances of it, which deserve remembering, are more precisely these: October 20th, 1740, Karl Albert's Ambassador, Perusa by name, wrote to Karl from Vienna, announcing that the Kaiser was just dead. From München, on the 21st, Karl Albert, anticipating such an event, but not yet knowing it, orders Perusa, in *case* of the Kaiser's decease, which was considered probable at München, to demand instant audience of the proper party (Kanzler Sinzendorf), and there openly lodge his Protest. Which Perusa did, punctually in all points, — no moment *lost*, but rather the contrary, as we said! Let poor Karl Albert have what benefit there is in that fact. He was, of all the Anti-Pragmatic Covenant-Breakers (if he ever fairly were such), the only one that proceeded honourably, openly and at once, in the matter; and he was, of them all, by far the most unfortunate.

This is the poor gentleman whom Belleisle had

settled on for being Kaiser. And Kaiser he became; to his frightful sorrow, as it proved: his crown like a crown of burning iron, or little better! There is little of him in the Books, nor does one desire much: a tall aquiline type of man; much the gentleman in aspect; and in reality, of decorous serious deportment, and the wish to be high and dignified. He had a kind of right, too, in the Anti-Pragmatic sense; and was come of Imperial kindred, — Kaiser Ludwig the Bavarian, and Kaiser Rupert of the Pfalz, called Rupert *Klemm*, or Rupert Smith's-vice, if any reader now remember him, were both of his ancestors. He might fairly pretend to Kaisership and to Austrian ownership, — had he otherwise been equal to such enterprises. But, in all ambitions and attempts, howsoever grounded otherwise, there is this strict question on the threshold: "Are you of weight for the adventure; are not you far too light for it?" Ambitious persons often slur this question; and get squelched to pieces, by bringing the Twelve Labours of Hercules on Unherculean backs! Not every one is so lucky as our Friedrich in that particular, — whose back, though with difficulty, held out. Which poor Karl Albert's never had much likelihood to do. Few mortals in any age have offered such an example of the tragedies which Ambition has in store for her votaries; and what a matter Hope *Fulfilled* may be to the unreflecting Son of Adam.

We said, he had a kind of right to Austria, withal. He descended by the female line from Kaiser Ferdinand I. (as did Kur-Sachsen, though by a younger Daughter than Karl Albert's Ancestress); and he appealed to Kaiser Ferdinand's Settlement of the Succession, as a higher than any subsequent Pragmatic could be. Upon which there hangs an incident; still famous to German readers. Karl Albert, getting into Public Argument in this way, naturally instructed Perusa to demand sight of Kaiser Ferdinand's Last Will, the tenor of which was known by authentic Copy in München, if not elsewhere among the kindred. After some delay, Perusa (4th November 1740), summoning the other Excellencies to witness, got sight of the Will: to his horror, there stood, in the cardinal passage, instead of "*männliche*" (male descendants), "*eheliche*" (lawfully-begotten descendants), — fatal to Karl Albert's claim! Nor could he *prove* that the Parchment had been scraped or altered, though he kept trying and examining for some days. He withdrew thereupon, by order, straightway from Vienna; testifying in dumb-show what he thought. "It is your Copy that is false," cried the Vienna people: "it has been foisted on you, with this wrong word in it; done by somebody (your friend, the Excellency Herr von Hartmann, shall we guess?), wishing to curry favour with ambitious foolish persons!" Such was the Austrian story. Perhaps in München itself their Copyist was not known; — for aught I learn, the Copy was made long since, and the Copyist dead. Hartmann, named as Copyist by the Vienna people, made emphatic public answer, "Never did I copy it, or see it!" And there rose great argument, which is not yet quite ended, as to the question, "Original falsified, or Copy falsified?" — and the modern vote, I believe, rather clearly is, That the Austrian Officials had done it — in a case of necessity.* Possible? "But you will lose your soul!" said

---

* Adelung, II. 150-154 (14th-20th November 1740), gives the public facts, without commentary. Hormayr (*Anemonen aus dem Tagebuch eines alten*

the Parson once to a poor old Gentlewoman, English by Nation, who refused, in dying, to contradict some domestic fiction, to give up some domestic secret: "But you will lose your soul, Madam!" — "'Tush, what signifies my poor silly soul, compared with the honour of the family?" —

2⁰. *King Friedrich.* — King Friedrich may be taken as the Anti-Pragmatic next in order of time. He too lost not a moment, and proceeded openly; no quirking to be charged upon him. His account of himself in this matter always was: "By the Treaty of Wusterhausen, 1726, unquestionably Prussia undertook to guarantee Pragmatic Sanction; the late Kaiser undertaking in return, by the same Treaty, to secure Berg and Jülich to Prussia, and to have some progress made in it within six months from signing. And, unquestionably also, the late Kaiser did thereupon, or even had already done, precisely the reverse; namely, secured, so far as in him was possible, Berg and Jülich to Kur-Pfalz. Such Treaty, having in this way done suicide, is dead and become zero: and I am free, in respect of Pragmatic Sanction, to do whatever shall seem good to me. My wish was, and would still be, To maintain Pragmatic Sanction, and even to support it by 100,000 men, and secure the Election of the Grand-Duke to the Kaisership, — were my claims on Silesia once liquidated. But these have no concern with Pragmatic Sanction, for or against: these are good against whoever may fall Heir to the House of Austria,

---

Pilgersmannes, Jena, 1845, i. 162-169, our old Hormayr of the *Austrian Plutarch*, but now Anonymous, and in Opposition humour) considers the case nearly proved against Austria, and that Bartenstein and one Bessel, a pillar of the Church, were concerned in it.

or to Silesia: and my intention is, that the strong hand, so long clenched upon my rights, shall open itself by this favourable opportunity, and give them out." That is Friedrich's case. And in truth the jury everywhere has to find, — so soon as instructed, which is a long process in some sections of it (in England, for example), — That Pragmatic Sanction has not, except helpless lamentations, "Alas that *you* should be here to insist upon your rights, and to open fists long closed!" — the least word to say to Friedrich.

3°. *Termagant of Spain.* — Perhaps the most distracted of the Anti-Pragmatic subterfuges was that used by Spain, when the She-dragon or Termagant saw good to eat her Covenant; which was at a very early stage. The Termagant's poor Husband is a Bourbon, not a Hapsburg at all: "But has not he fallen heir to the Spanish Hapsburgs; become all one as they an *alter-ego* of the Spanish Hapsburgs?" asks she. "And the Austrian Hapsburgs being out, do not the Spanish Hapsburgs come in? He, I say, this *Bourbon*-Hapsburg, he is the real Hapsburg, now that the Austrian Branch is gone; President he of the Golden Fleece" (which a certain "Archduchess," Maria Theresa, has been meddling with); "Proprietor, he, of Austrian Italy, and of all or most things Austrian!" — and produces Documentary Covenants of Philip II. with his Austrian Cousins; "to which Philip," said the Termagant, "we Bourbons surely, if you consider it, are Heir and Alter-Ego!" Is not this a curious case of testamentary right; human greed obliterating personal identity itself?

Belleisle had a great deal of difficulty, keeping the Termagant back till things were ripe. Her hope practically was, Baby Carlos being prosperous King of Naples this long while, to get the Milanese for another Baby she has, — Baby Philip, whom she once thought of making Pope; — and she is eager beyond measure to have a stroke at the Milanese. "Wait!" hoarsely whispers Belleisle to her; and she can scarcely wait. Maria Theresa's Note of Announcement, "New Queen of Hungary may it please you!" the French, as we saw, were very long in answering. The Termagant did not answer it at all; complained, on the contrary, "What is this, Madam! Golden Fleece, you?" — and, early in March, informed mankind that she was Spanish Hapsburg, the genuine article; and sent off Excellency Montijos, a little man of great expense, to assist at the Election of a proper Kaiser, and be useful to Belleisle in the great things now ahead.*

4°. *King of Poland.* — The most ticklish card in Belleisle's game, and probably the greatest fool of these Anti-Pragmatic Dozen, was Kur-Sachsen, King of Poland. He, like Karl Albert Kur-Baiern, derives from Kaiser Ferdinand, though by a *younger* Daughter, and has a like claim on the Austrian Succession; claim nullified, however, by that small circumstance itself, but which he would fain mend by one makeshift or another; and thinks always it must surely be good for something. This is August III., this King of Poland, as readers know; son of August the Strong: Papa made him change to the Catholic religion so-called, — for the sake of getting Poland, which proves a very poor possession to him. Who knows what damage the

* Spain's Golden-Fleece pretensions, 17th January 1741 (Adelung, ii. 233, 234); "Publishes at Paris," in March (ib. 293); and on the 23d March, accredits Montijos (ib. 293): Italian War, held back by Belleisle and the English Fleets, cannot get begun till October following.

poor creature may have got by that sad operation; — which all Saxony sighed to the heart on hearing of; for it was always hoped he had some real religion, and would deliver them from that Babylonish Captivity again! He married Kaiser Joseph I.'s Daughter, — Maria Theresa's Cousin, and by an Elder Brother; — this, too, ought surely to be something in the Anti-Pragmatic line? It is true, Kur-Baiern has to Wife another Daughter of Kaiser Joseph's; but she is the younger: "I am senior *there*, at least!" thinks the foolish man.

Too true, he had finally, in past years, to sign Pragmatic Sanction; no help for it, no hope without it, in that Polish-Election time. He will have to eat his Covenant, therefore, as the first step in Anti-Pragmatism; and he is extremely in doubt as to the How, sometimes as to the Whether. And shifts and whirls, accordingly, at a great rate, in these months and years; now on Maria Theresa's side, deluded by shadows from Vienna, and getting into Russian Partition-Treaties; anon tickled by Belleisle into the reverse posture; then again reversing. An idle, easy-tempered, yet greedy creature, who, what with religious apostasy in early manhood, what with flaccid ambitions since, and idle gapings after shadows, has lost helm in this world; and will make a very bad voyage for self and country.

His Palinurus and chief Counsellor, at present and afterwards, is a Count von Brühl, once Page to August the Strong; now risen to such height: Brühl of the Threehundred and Sixty-five suits of clothes; whom it has grown wearisome even to laugh at. A cunning little wretch, they say, and of deft tongue; but surely among the unwisest of all the Sons of Adam in that day, and such a Palinurus as seldom steered before. Kur-Sachsen, being Reichs-Vicar in the Northern Parts, — (Kur-Baiern and Kur-Pfalz, as friends and good Wittelsbacher Cousins surely ought, in a crisis like this, have agreed to be *Joint*-Vicars in the Southern Parts, and no longer quarrel upon it), — Kur-Sachsen has a good deal to do in the Election preludings, formalities and prearrangements; and is capable, as Kur-Pfalz and Cousin always are, of serving as chisel to Belleisle's mallet, in such points, which will plentifully turn up.

5°. *King of Sardinia.* — Reichs-Vicar in Italian Parts is Charles Amadeus King of Sardinia (tough old Victor's Son, whom we have heard of): an office mostly honorary; suitable to the important individual who keeps the Door of the Alps. Charles Amadeus had signed the Pragmatic Sanction; but eats his Covenant, like the others, on example of France; — having, as he now bethinks himself, claims on the Milanese. There are two claimants on the Milanese, then; the Spanish Termagant, and he? Yes; and they will have their difficulties, their extensive tusslings in Italian War and otherwise, to make an adjustment of it; and will give Belleisle (at least the Doorkeeper will) an immensity of trouble, in years coming.

In this way do the Pragmatic people eat their own Covenant, one after the other, and are not ashamed; — till all have eaten, or as good as eaten; and, almost within year and day, Pragmatic Sanction is a vanished quantity; and poor Kaiser Karl's life-labour is not worth the sheep-skin and stationery it cost him. History reports in sum, That "nobody kept the Pragmatic

Sanction; that the few" (strictly speaking, the one) "who acted by it, would have done precisely the same, "though there had never been such a Document in "existence." To George II., it is, was and will be, the Keystone of Nature, the true Anti-French palladium of mankind; and he, dragging the unwilling Dutch after him, will do great things for it: but nobody else does anything at all. Might we hope to bid adieu to it, in this manner, and never to mention it again! —

Document more futile there had not been in Nature, nor will be. Friedrich had not yet fought at Mollwitz in assertion of his Silesian claim, when the poor Pope, — poor soul, who had no Covenant to eat, but took pattern by others, — claimed, in solemn Allocution, Parma and Piacenza for the Holy See.* All the world is claiming. Of the Court of Würtemberg and its Protestings, and "extensive Deduction" about nothing at all, we do not speak;** nor of Montmorency claiming Luxemburg, of which he is Titular "Duke; nor of Monsignore di Guastalla claiming Mantua; nor of — In brief, the fences are now down; a broad French gap in those miles of elaborate paling, which are good only as fire-wood henceforth, and any ass may rush in and claim a bellyful. Great are the works of Belleisle! —

Concerning the Imperial Election (Kaiserwahl) *that is to be; Candidates for Kaisership.*

At equal step with the ruining of Pragmatic Sanction, goes on that spoiling of Grand-Duke Franz's Election to the Kaisership: these two operations run parallel; or rather, under different forms, they are one and the

---
* Adelung, II. 376 (5th April 1741). ** Ibid. 195, 403.

same operation. "To assist, as a Most Christian neighbour ought, in picking out the fit Kaiser," was Belleisle's ostensible mission; and indeed this does include virtually his whole errand. Till three months after Belleisle's appearance in the business, Grand-Duke Franz never doubted but he should be Kaiser; Friedrich's offers to help him in it he had scorned, as the offer of a fifth wheel to his chariot, already rushing on with four. "Here is Kur-Böhmen, Austria's own vote," counts the Grand-Duke; "Kur-Sachsen, doing Prussian-Partition Treaties for us; Kur-Trier, our fat little Schönborn, Austrian to the bone; Kur-Mainz, important chairman, regulator of the Conclave; here are Four Electors for us: then also Kur-Pfalz, he surely, in return for the Berg-Jülich service; finally, and liable to no question, Kur-Hanover, little George of England with his endless guineas and resources, a little Jack-the-Giantkiller, greater than all Giants, Paladin of the Pragmatic and us: here are Six Electors of the Nine. Let Brandenburg and the Bavarian Couple, Kur-Baiern and Kur-Köln, do their pleasure!" This was Grand-Duke Franz's calculation.

By the time Belleisle had been three months in Germany, the Grand-Duke's notion had changed; and he began "applying to the Sea-Powers," "to Russia," and all round. In Belleisle's sixth month, the Grand-Duke, after such demolition of Pragmatic, and such disasters and contradictions as had been, saw his case to be desperate; though he still stuck to it, Austrian-like, — or rather, Austria for him stuck to it, the Grand-Duke being careless of such things; — and indeed, privately, never did give in, even *after* the Election, as we shall have to note.

The Reich itself being mainly a Phantasm or Enchanted Wiggery, its "Kaiser-Choosing" (*Kaiserwahl*), — now getting under way at Frankfurt, with preliminary outskirts at Regensburg, and in the Chancery of Mainz, — is very phantasmal, not to say ghastly; and forbidding, not inviting, to the human eye. Nine Kurfürsts, Choosers of Teutschland's real Captain; in none of whom is there much thought for Teutschland or its interests, — and indeed in hardly more than One of whom (Prussian Friedrich, if readers will know it) is there the least thought that way; but, in general, much indifference to things divine or diabolic, and thought for one's own paltry profits and losses only! So it has long been; and so it now is, more than usual. — Consider again, are Enchanted Wiggeries a beautiful thing, in this extremely earnest World? —

The Kaiserwahl is an affair depending much on processions, proclamations, on delusions optical, acoustic; on palaverings, manœuvrings, holdings back, then hasty pushings forward; and indeed is mainly, in more senses than one, under guidance of the Prince of the Power of the Air. Unbeautiful, like a World-Parliament of Nightmares (if the reader could conceive such a thing); huge formless, tongueless monsters of that species, doing their "three readings," — under Presidency or chief-pipership as above! Belleisle, for his part, is consummately skilful, and manages as only himself could. Keeps his game well hidden, not a hint or whisper of it except in studied proportions; spreads out his lines, his birdlime; tickles, entices, astonishes; goes his rounds, like a subtle Fowler taking captive the minds of men; a Phœbus-Apollo, god of melody and of the sun, filling his net with birds.

I believe, old Kur-Pfalz, for the sake of French neighbourhood, and Berg-and-Jülich, were there nothing more, was very helpful to him; — in March past, when the Election was to have been, when it would have gone at once in favour of the Grand-Duke, Kur-Pfalz got the Election "postponed a little." Postponing, procrastinating; then again pushing violently on, when things are ripe: Belleisle has only to give signal to a fit Kur-Pfalz. In all Kurfürst Courts, the French Ambassadors sing diligently to the tune Belleisle sets them; and Courts give ear, or will do, when the charmer himself arrives.

Kur-Sachsen, as above hinted, was his most delicate operation, in the charming or trout-tickling way. And Kur-Sachsen, — and poor Saxony, ever since, — knows if he did not do it well! "Deduct this Kur-Sachsen from the Austrian side," calculates Belleisle; "add him to ours, it is almost an equality of votes. Kur-Baiern, our own Imperial Candidate; Kur-Köln, his Brother; Kur-Pfalz, by genealogy his Cousin (not to mention Berg-Jülich matters): here are three Wittelsbachers, knit together; three sure votes; King Friedrich, Kur-Brandenburg, there is a fourth; — and if Kur-Sachsen would join?" But who knows if Kur-Sachsen will! The poor soul has himself thoughts of being Kaiser; then no thoughts, and again some: thoughts which Belleisle knows how to handle. "Yes, Kaiser you, your Majesty; excellent!" And sets to consider the methods: "Hm, ha, — hm! Think, your Majesty: ought not that Bohemian Vote to be excluded, for one thing? Kur-Böhmen is fallen into the distaff, Maria Theresa herself cannot vote. Surely question will rise, Whether distaff can, validly, hand it over to distaff's

April—May 1741.

husband, as they are about doing? Whether, in fact, Kur-Böhmen is not in abeyance for this time?" "So!" answered Kur-Sachsen, Reichs-Vicarius. And thereupon meetings were summoned; Nightmare Committees sat on this matter under the Reichs-Vicar, slowly hatching it; and at length brought out, "Kur-Böhmen *not* transferable by the distaff; Kur-Böhmen in abeyance for this time." Greatly to the joy of Belleisle; infinitely to the chagrin of her Hungarian Majesty, — who declared it a crying injustice (though I believe legally done in every point); and by and by, even made it a plea of Nullity, destructive to the Election altogether, when her Hungarian Majesty's affairs looked up again, and the world would listen to Austrian sophistries and obstinacies. This was an essential service from Kur-Sachsen.*

After which Kur-Sachsen's own poor Kaisership died away into "Hm, ha, hm!" again, with a grateful Belleisle. Who nevertheless dexterously retained Kur-Sachsen as ally; tickling the poor wretch with other baits. Of the Kaiser he had really meant all along, there was dead silence, except between the parties; no whisper heard, for six months after it had been agreed upon; none, for two or near three months after formal settlement, and signing and sealing. Karl Albert's Treaty with Belleisle was, 18th May 1741; and he did not declare himself a Candidate till 1st-14th July following.** Belleisle understands the Nightmare Parliaments, the electioneering art, and how to deal with

---

* Began, indistinctly, "in March" (1741); languid "for some months" (Adelung, ii. 292); "November 4th," was settled in the negative, "Kur-Böhmen not to have a vote" (*Maria Theresiens Leben*, p. 47 n.).

** Adelung, ii. 357, 421.

Enchanted Wiggeries. More perfect master, in that sad art, has not turned up on record to one's afflicted mind. Such a Sungod, and doing such a Scavengerism! Belleisle, in the sixth month (end of August 1741) feels sure of a majority. How Belleisle managed, after that, to checkmate George of England, and make even George vote for him, and the Kaiserwahl to be unanimous against Grand-Duke Franz, will be seen. Great are Belleisle's doings in this world, if they were useful either to God or man, or to Belleisle himself first of all! —

Teutschland to be carved into something of Symmetry, should the Belleisle Enterprises succeed.

Belleisle's schemes, in the rear of all this labour, are grandiose to a degree. Men wonder at the First Napoleon's mad notions in that kind. But no Napoleon, in the fire of the revolutionary element; no Sham-Napoleon, in the ashes of it; hardly a Parisian Journalist of imaginative turn, speculating on the First Nation of the Universe and what its place is, — could go higher than did this grandiose Belleisle; a man with clear thoughts in his head, under a torpid Louis XV. Let me see, thinks Belleisle. Germany with our Bavarian for Kaiser; Germany to be cut into, say, Four little Kingdoms: 1⁰. Bavaria with the lean Kaiserhood; 2⁰. Saxony, fattened by its share of Austria; 3⁰. Prussia the like; 4⁰. Austria itself, shorn down as above, and shoved out to the remote Hungarian parts: *voilà*. These, not reckoning Hanover, which perhaps we cannot get just yet, are Four pretty Sovereignties. Three, or Two, of these hireable by gold, it is to be hoped. And will not France have a glorious time of it; playing master of the revels there, egging one against the other! Yes, Germany is then, what Nature designed it, a Province of France: little George of Hanover himself, and who knows but England after him, may one day find their fate inevitable, like the others. O Louis, O my King, is not this an outlook? Louis le Grand was great; but you are likely to be Louis the Grandest; and here is a World shaped, at last, after the real pattern!

Such are, in sad truth, Belleisle's schemes; not yet entirely hatched into daylight or articulation; but becoming articulate, to himself and others, more and more. Reader, keep them well in mind: I had rather not speak of them again. They are essential to our Story; but they are afflictively vain, contrary to the Laws of Fact; and can, now or henceforth, in no wise be. My friend, it was not Beelzebub, nor Mephistopheles, nor Autolycus-Apollo that built this world and us; it was Another. And you will get your crown well rapped, M. le Maréchal, for so forgetting that fact! France is an extremely pretty creature; but this of making France the supreme Governor and God's-Vicegerent of Nations, is, was and remains, one of the maddest notions. France at its ideal *best*, and with a demigod for King over it, were by no means fit for such function; nay of many Nations, is eminently the unfittest for it. And France at its *worst* or nearly so, with a Louis XV. over it by way of demigod — O Belleisle, what kind of France is this; shining in your grandiose imagination, in such contrast to the stingy fact: like a creature consisting of two enormous wings, five hundred yards in potential extent, and no body bigger than that of a common Cock, weighing three pounds avoirdupois. Cock with his own gizzard much out of sorts, too!

It was 'early in March'* when Belleisle, the Artificial Sungod, quitted Paris on this errand. He came by the Moselle road; called on the Rhine Kurfürsts, Köln, Trier, Mainz; dazzling them, so far as possible, with his splendour for the mind and for the eye. He proceeded next to Dresden, which is a main card; and where there is immense manipulation needed, and the most delicate trout-tickling; this being a skittish fish, and an important, though a foolish. Belleisle was at Dresden when the Battle of Mollwitz fell out: what a windfall into Belleisle's game! He ran across to Friedrich at Mollwitz, to congratulate, to consult, — as we shall see anon.

Belleisle, I am informed, in this preliminary Tour of his, speaks only, or hints only (except in the proper quarters), of Election Business; of the need there perhaps is, on the part of an Age growing in liberal ideas, to exclude the Austrian Grand-Duke; to curb that ponderous, harsh, ungenerous House of Austria, too long lording it over generous Germany; and to set up some better House, — Bavaria, for example; Saxony, for example? Of his plans in the rear of this he is silent; speaks only by hints, by innuendos, to the proper parties. But ripening or ripe, plans do lie to rear; far-stretching, high-soaring; in part, dark at Versailles; — darkly fermenting, not yet developed, in Belleisle's own head; only the Future Kaiser a luminous

* Adelung, ii. 305.

fixed point, shooting beams across the grandiose Creation-Process going on there.

By the end of August 1741, Belleisle had become certain of his game; 24th January, he saw himself as if winner. Before August, he had got his Electors manipulated, tickled to his purpose, by the witchery of a Phœbus-Autolycus or Diplomatic Sungod; majority secured for a Bavarian Kaiser, and against an Austrian one. And in the course of that Month, — what was still more considerable! — he was getting, under mild pretexts, about a Hundred Thousand armed Frenchmen gently wafted over upon the soil of Germany. Two complete French Armies, 40,000 each (*plus* their Reserves), one over the Upper Rhine, one over the Lower; about which we shall hear a great deal in time coming! Under mild pretexts: "Peaceable as lambs, don't you observe? Merely to protect Freedom of Election, in this fine neighbour country; and as allies to our Friend of Bavaria, should he chance to be new Kaiser, and to persist in his modest claims otherwise." This was his crowning stroke. Which finished straightway the remnants of Pragmatic Sanction and of every obstacle; and in a shining manner swept the roads clear. And so, on January 24th following, the Election, long held back by Belleisle's manœuvrings, actually takes effect, — in favour of Karl Albert, our invaluable Bavarian Friend. Austria is left-solitary in the Reich; Pragmatic Sanction, Keystone of Nature, which Belleisle and France had sworn to keep in, is openly torn out by Belleisle and by France and the majority of mankind; and Belleisle sees himself, to all appearance, winner.

This was the harvest reaped by Belleisle, within

year and day; after endless manoeuvring, such as only a Belleisle in the character of Diplomatic Sungod could do. Beyond question, the distracted ambitions of several German Princes have been kindled by Belleisle; what we called the rotten thatch of Germany is well on fire. This diligent sowing in the Reich, — to judge by the 100,000 armed men here, and the counter hundreds of thousands arming, — has been a pretty stroke of dragon's-teeth husbandry on Belleisle's part.

Belleisle on Visit to Friedrich; sees Friedrich besiege Brieg, with Effect.

It was April 26th, when Maréchal de Belleisle, with his Brother the Chevalier, with Valori and other bright accompaniment, arrived in Friedrich's Camp. "Camp of Mollwitz," so named; between Mollwitz and Brieg; where Friedrich is still resting, in a vigilant expectant condition; and, except it be the taking of Brieg, has nothing military on hand. Wednesday, 26th April, the distinguished Excellency, — escorted for the last three miles by 120 Horse, and the other customary ceremonies, — makes his appearance: no doubt an interesting one to Friedrich, for this and the days next following. Their talk is not reported anywhere: nor is it said with exactitude how far, whether wholly now, or only in part now, Belleisle expounded his sublime ideas to Friedrich; or what precise reception they got. Friedrich himself writes long afterwards of the event; but, as usual, without precision, except in general effect. Now, or some time after, Friedrich says he found Belleisle, one morning, with brow clouded, knit into intense meditation: "Have you had bad news, M. le Maréchal?" asks Friedrich. "No, oh no! I am considering what we shall make of that Moravia?" — "Moravia; Hm!" Friedrich suppresses the glance that is rising to his eyes: "Can't you give it to Saxony, then? Buy Saxony into the Plan with it!" "Excellent," answers Belleisle, and unpuckers his stern brow again.

Friedrich thinks highly, and about this time often says so, of the man Belleisle: but as to the man's effulgencies, and wide-winged Plans, none is less seduced by them than Friedrich: "Your chickens are not hatched, M. le Maréchal; some of us hope they never will be, — though the incubation-process may have uses for some of us!" Friedrich knows that the Kaisership given to any other than Grand-Duke Franz will be mostly an imaginary quantity. "A grand Symbolic Cloak in the eyes of the vulgar; but empty of all things, empty even of cash, for the last Two Hundred Years: Austria can wear it to advantage; no other mortal. Hang it on Austria, which is a solid human figure, — so." And Friedrich wishes, and hopes always, Maria Theresa will agree with him, and get it for her Husband. "But to hang it on Bavaria, which is a lean bare pole? Oh, M. le Maréchal! — And those Four Kingdoms of yours: what a brood of poultry, those? Chickens happily yet *un*hatched; — eggs addle, I should venture to hope: — only do go on incubating, M. le Maréchal!" That is Friedrich's notion of the thing. Belleisle stayed with Friedrich "a few days," say the Books. After which, Friedrich, finding Belleisle too winged a creature, corresponded, in preference, with Fleury and the Head Sources; — who are always intensely enough concerned about those "aces" falling to him, and how the same are to be "shared."*

Instead of parade or review in honour of Belleisle, there happened to be a far grander military show, of the practical kind. The Siege of Brieg, the Opening of the Trenches before Brieg, chanced to be just ready, on Belleisle's arrival; — and would have taken effect, we find, that very night, April 26th, had not a sudden wintry outburst, or "tempest of extraordinary violence," prevented. Next night, night of the 27th-28th, under shine of the full Moon, in the open champaign country, on both sides of the River, it did take effect. An uncommonly fine thing of its sort; as one can still see by reading Friedrich's strict Program for it, — a most minute, precise and all-anticipating Program, which still interests military men, as Friedrich's first Piece in that kind, — and comparing therewith the Narratives of the performance which ensued.**

Kalkstein, Friedrich's old Tutor, is Captain of the Siege; under him Jeetz, long used to blockading about Brieg. The silvery Oder has its due bridges for communication; all is in readiness, and waiting manifold as in the slip, — and there is Engineer Walrave, our Glogau Dutch friend, who shall, at the right instant, "with his straw-rope (*Strohseil*) mark out the first parallel," and be swift about it! There are 2,000 diggers, with the due implements, fascines, equipments; duly divided, into Twelve equal Parties, and "always

---

* Details, in *Helden-Geschichte*, i. 912, 962, 916; in *Œuvres de Frédéric*, ii. 79, 80; &c.

** *Ordre und Dispositionen* (sic), *wornach sich der General-Lieutenant von Kalckstein bei Eröffnung der Trancheen* &c. (*Œuvres de Frédéric*, xxx. 39-44): the Program. *Helden-Geschichte*, i. 916-28: the Narrative.

two spademen to one pickman" (which indicates soft sandy ground): these, with the escorting or covering battalions, Twelve Parties they also, on both sides of the River, are to be in their several stations at the fixed moments; man, musket, mattock, strictly exact. They are to advance at Midnight; the covering battalions so many yards ahead: no speaking is permissible, nor the least tobacco-smoking; no drum to be allowed for fear of accident; no firing, unless you are fired on. The covering battalions are all to "lie flat, so soon as "they get to their ground, all but the Officers and "sentries." To rear of these, stand Walrave and assistants, silent, with their straw-rope; — silent, then anon swift, and in whisper or almost by dumb-show, "Now, then!" After whom the diggers, fascine-men, workers, each in his kind, shall fall-to, silently, and dig and work as for life.

All which is done; exact as clockwork: beautiful to see, or half-see, and speak of to your Belleisle, in the serene moonlight! Half an hour's marching, half an hour's swift digging: the Town-clock of Brieg was hardly striking One, when "they had dug themselves in." And, before daybreak, they had, in two batteries, fifty cannon in position, with a proper set of mortars (other side the River), — ready to astonish Piccolomini and his Austrians; who had not had the least whisper of them, all night, though it was full moon. Graf von Piccolomini, an active gallant person, had refused terms, some time before; and was hopefully intent on doing his best. And now, suddenly, there rose round Piccolomini such a tornado of cannonading and bombardment, day after day, always "three guns of ours playing against one of theirs," that his guns got ruined;

that "his hay-magazines took fire," — and the Schloss itself, which was adjacent to them, took fire (a sad thing to Friedrich, who commanded pause, that they might try quenching, but in vain); — and that in short, Piccolomini, could not stand it; but on the 4th of May, precisely after one week's experience, hung out the white flag, and "beat chamade at 3 of the afternoon." He was allowed to march out, next morning, with escort to Neisse; parole pledged, Not to serve against us for two years coming.

Friedrich in person (I rather guess, Belleisle not now at his side) saw the Garrison march out; — kept Piccolomini to dinner; a gallant Piccolomini, who had hoped to do better, but could not. This was a pretty enough piece of Siege-practice. Torstenson, with his Swedes, had furiously besieged Brieg in 1642, a hundred years ago; and could do nothing to it. Nothing, but withdraw again, futile; leaving 1,400 of his people dead. Friedrich, the Austrian Garrison once out, set instantly about repairing the works, and improving them into impregnability, — our ugly friend Walrave presiding over that operation too.

Belleisle, we may believe, so long as he continued, was full of polite wonder over these things; perhaps had critical advices here and there, which would be politely received. It is certain he came out extremely brilliant, gifted and agreeable, in the eyes of Friedrich; who often afterwards, not in the very strictest language, calls him a great man, great soldier, and by far the considerablest person you French have. It is no less certain, Belleisle displayed, so far as displayable, his magnificent Diplomatic Ware to the best advantage.

To which, we perceive, the young King answered, "Magnificent, indeed!" but would not bite all at once; and rather preferred corresponding with Fleury, on business points, keeping the matter dextrously hanging, in an illuminated element of hope and contingency, for the present.

Belleisle, after we know not how many days, returned to Dresden; perfected his work at Dresden, or shoved it well forward, with "that Moravia" as bait. "Yes, King of Moravia, you, your Polish Majesty, shall be!" — and it is said the simple creature did so style himself, by and by, in certain rare Manifestoes, which still exist in the cabinets of the curious. Belleisle next, after only a few days, went to München; to operate on Karl Albert Kur-Baiern, a willing subject. And, in short, Belleisle whirled along incessantly, torch in hand; making his "circuit of the German Courts," — details of said circuit not to be followed by us farther. One small thing only I have found rememberable; probably true, though vague. At München, still more out at Nymphenburg, the fine Country-Palace not far off, there was of course long conferencing, long consulting, secret and intense, between Belleisle with his people and Karl Albert with his. Karl Albert, as we know, was himself willing. But a certain Baron von Unertl, — heavy-built Bavarian of the old type, an old stager in the Bavarian Ministries, — was of far other disposition. One day, out at Nymphenburg, Unertl got to the Council-room, while Belleisle and Company were there: Unertl found the Apartment locked, absolutely no admittance; and heard voices, the Kurfürst's and French voices, eagerly at work inside. "Admit me, Gracious Herr; *um Gottes Willen,* me!" No admission. Unertl, in despair, rushed round to the garden side of the Apartment; desperately snatched a ladder; set it up to the window, and conjured the Gracious Highness: "For the love of Heaven, my *Allergnädigster*, don't! Have no trade with those French! Remember your illustrious Father, Kurfürst Max, in the Eugene-Marlborough time, what a job he made of it, building actual architecture on *their* big promises, which proved mere acres of gilt balloon!" * Words terribly prophetic; but they were without effect on Karl Albert.

The rest of Belleisle's inflammatory circuitings and extensive travellings, for he had many first and last in this matter, shall be left to the fancy of the reader. May 18th, he made formal Treaty with Karl Albert: Treaty of Nymphenburg, "Karl Albert to be Kaiser; Bavaria, with Austria Proper added to it, a Kingdom; French armies, French moneys, and other fine items."** Treaty to be kept dead secret; King Friedrich, for the present, would not accede. *** June 25th, after some preliminary survey of the place, Belleisle made his Entry into Frankfurt: magnificent in the extreme. And still did not rest there; but had to rush about, back to Versailles, to Dresden, hither, thither: it was not till the last day of July that he fairly took up his abode in Frankfurt; and, — the Election eggs, so to speak, being now all laid, — set himself to hatch the same. A process which lasted him six months longer, with curious phenomena to mankind. Not till the middle of August did he bring those 80,000 Armed Frenchmen across the Rhine, "to secure peace in those parts, and

---

* Hormayr, *Anemonen*, (cited above), ii. 152.
** Given in *Adelung*, ii. 359. *** Ibid. 421.

freedom of voting." Not till November 4th had Kur-Sachsen, with the Nightmares, finished that important problem of the Bohemian Vote, "Bohemian Vote *excluded* for this time;" — after which all was ready, though still not in the least hurry. November 20th, came the first actual "Election-Conference (*Wahl-Conferenz*)" in the Römer at Frankfurt; to which succeeded Two Months more of conferrings (upon almost nothing at all): and finally, 24th January 1742, came the Election itself, Karl Albert the man; poor wretch, who never saw another good day in this world.

Belleisle during those six months was rather high and airy, extremely magnificent; but did not want discretion: "more like a Kurfürst than an Ambassador;" capable of "visiting Kur-Mainz, with servants purposely in *old* liveries," — where the case needed old, where Kur-Mainz needed snubbing; not otherwise.*
"The Maréchal de Belleisle," says an Eyewitness, of some fame in those days, "comes out in a variety of "parts, among us here; plays now the General, now "the Philosopher, now the Minister of State, now the "French Marquis; — and does them all to perfection. "Surely a master in his art. His Brother the Chevalier "is one of the sensiblest and best-trained persons you "can see. He has a penetrating intellect; is always "occupied, and full of great schemes; and has never-"theless a staid kind of manner. He is one of the "most important Personages here; and in all things his "Brother's right hand."** In Frankfurt, both Belleisle and his Brother were much respected, the Brother especially, as men of dignified behaviour and shining qua-

* Buchholtz, ii. 57 n.
** Von Loen, *Kleine Schriften* (cited in Adelung, ii. 400).

lities; but as to their Hundred-and-thirty French Lords and other Valetry, these by their extravagancies and excesses (*Ausschweifungen*) made themselves extremely detestable, it would appear.*

---

* Buchholz, ii. 54; in Adelung, ii. 398 n., a French *brocard* on the subject, of sufficient emphasis.

CHAPTER XII.

SORROWS OF HIS BRITANNIC MAJESTY.

GEORGE II. did not hear of Mollwitz for above a fortnight after it fell out; but he had no need of Mollwitz to kindle his wrath or his activity in that matter.* George II. had seen, all along, with natural manifold aversion and indignation, these high attempts of his Nephew. "Who is this new little King, that will not let himself be snubbed, and laughed at, and led by the nose, as his Father did; but seems to be taking a road of his own, and tacitly defying us all? A very high conduct indeed, for a Sovereign of that magnitude. Aspires seemingly to be the leader among German Princes; to reduce Hanover and us, — us, with the gold of England in our breeches-pocket, — to the second place? A reverend old Bishop of Liége, twitched by the rochet, and shaken hither and thither, like a reverend old clothes-screen, till he agree to stand still and conform. And now a Silesia seized upon; a Pragmatic Sanction kicked to the winds: the whole world to be turned topsyturvy, and Hanover and us, with our breeches-pocket, reduced to — —?"

The emotions, the prognosticatings, and distracted procedures of his Britannic Majesty, of which we have ourselves seen somewhat, in this fermentation of the elements, are copiously set down for us by the English Dryasdust (mostly in unintelligible form): but, except

* Mollwitz first heard of in London, April 25th (14th); Subsidy of 300,000*l.* voted same day. *London Gazette* (April 11th-14th, 1741); *Commons Journals,* xxiii. 705.

for sane purposes, one must be careful not to dwell on them, to the sorrow of readers. Seldom was there such a feat of Somnambulism, as that by the English and their King in the next Twenty Years. To extract the particle of sanity from it, and see how the poor English did get their own errand done withal, and Jenkins's Ear avenged,— that is the one interesting point; Dryasdust and the Nightmares shall, to all time, be welcome to the others. Here are some Excerpts, a select few; which will perhaps be our readiest expedient. These do, under certain main aspects, shadow forth the intricate posture of King George and his Nation, when Belleisle, as Protagonistes or Chief Bully, stept down into the ring, in that manner; asking, "Is there an Antagonistes, then, or Chief Defender?" I will label them, number them; and, with the minimum of needful commentary, leave them to imaginative readers.

No. 1. *Snatch of Parliamentary Eloquence by Mr. Viner* (19th April 1741).

The fuliginous explosions, more or less volcanic, which went on in Parliament and in English society, against Friedrich's Silesian Enterprise, for long years from this date, are now all dead and avoidable,— though they have left their effects among us to this day. Perhaps readers would like to see the one reasonable word I have fallen in with, of opposite tendency; Mr. Viner's word, at the first starting of that question: plainly sensible word, which, had it been attended to (as it was not), might have saved us so much nonsense, not of idle talk only, but of extremely serious deed which ensued thereupon!

"*London*, 19*th April* 1741. This day" (Mollwitz not yet known, Camp of Göttin too well known!) "King George, in " his own high person, comes down to the House of Lords,— "which, like the Other House, is sunk painfully in Walpole "Controversies, Spanish-War Controversies, of a merely "domestic nature;—and informs both Honourable Houses,

April—May 1741.

"with extreme caution, naming nobody, That he much wishes "they would think of helping him in these alarming cir- "cumstances of the Celestial Balance, ready apparently to go "heels uppermost. To which the general answer is, 'Yes, "surely!' — with a vote of 300,000 *l.* for her Hungarian "Majesty, a few days hence. From those continents of Par- "liamentary tufa, now fallen so waste and mournful, here "is one little piece which ought to be extricated into day- "light:

'*Mr. Viner* (on his legs): * *   "If I mistake not the true 'intention of the Address proposed,' in answer to his Majesty's most gracious Speech from the Throne, 'we are invited to ' declare that we will oppose the King of Prussia in his attempts ' upon Silesia: a declaration in which I see not how any man ' can concur who *knows not* the nature of his Prussian Majesty's 'Claim, and the Laws of the German Empire' (*nor do I, Mr. V.*)! 'It ought therefore, Sir, to have been the first 'endeavour of those by whom this Address has been so 'zealously supported, to show that his Prussian Majesty's 'Claim, so publicly explained' (*by Kanzler Ludwig, of Halle, who, it seems, has staggered or convinced Mr. Viner*), 'so firmly 'urged, and so strongly supported, is *without* foundation and 'reason, and is only one of those imaginary titles which Ambi- 'tion may always find to the dominions of another.' (*Hear, Mr. Viner!*)"*

A most indispensable thing, surely. Which was never done, nor can ever be done, but was assumed as either un- necessary or else done of its own accord, by that Collective Wisdom of England (with a sage George II. at the head of it); who plunged into Dettingen, Fontenoy, Austrian Sub- sidies, Aix-la-Chapelle, and foundation of the English National Debt, among other strange things, in con- sequence!—

Upon that of Kanzler Ludwig, and the "so public Explanation" (which we slightly heard of long since), here is another Note,—unless readers prefer to skip it:

* Tindal, xx. 491, gives the Royal Speech (*date* in a very slobbery condition); see also Coxe, *House of Austria*, iii. 365. Viner's Fragment of a Speech is in Thackeray, *Life of Chatham*, i. 87.

"That the Diplomatic and Political world is universally in
"travail at this time, no reader need be told; Europe every-
"where in dim anxiety, heavy-laden expectation (which to us
"has fallen so vacant); looking towards inevitable changes
"and the huge inane. All in travail; — and already uttering
"printed Manifestoes, Patents, Deductions, and other public
"travail-*shrieks* of that kind. Printed; not to speak of the
"unprinted, of the oral which vanished on the spot; or even
"of the written which were shot forth by breathless estafettes,
"and unhappily did not vanish, but lie in archives, still
"humming upon us, 'Won't you read me, then?' — Alas,
"except on compulsion, No! Life being precious (and time,
"which is the stuff of life), No! —

"At Reinsberg as elsewhere, at Reinsberg first of all, it
"had been felt, in October last, that there would be Mani-
"festoes needed; learned Proof, the more irrefragable the
"better, of our Right to Silesia. It was settled there, Let
"Ludwig, Kanzler of the University of Halle, do it." (Herr
Kanzler Ludwig, monster of Antiquarian, Legal and other
Learning there: wealthy, too, and close-fisted; whom we have
seen obliged to open his closed fist, and to do building in the
Friedrich Strasse, before now; Nüssler, his son-in-law, having
no money: — as careless readers have perhaps forgotten?)
"Ludwig set about his new task with a proud joy. Ludwig
"knows that story, if he know anything. Long years ago
"he put forth a Chapter upon it; weighty Chapter; in a Book
"of weight, said judges; — Book weighing, in pounds avoir-
"dupois and otherwise, none of us now knows what:* — but,
"in after years, it used to be said by flatterers of the Kanzler,
"'Herr Kanzler, see the effect of Learning. It was you, it
"was your weighty Book, that caused all this World-tumult,
"and flung the Nations into one another's hair!' Upon which
"the old Kanzler would blush: 'You do me too much
"honour!'

"Ludwig, directly on order given, gathered out his docu-

* Title of this weighty Performance (see Preuss, *Thronbesteigung*, p.
432) is, or was (size not given), *Germania Princeps* (Halæ, 1702). Preuss
says farther, "That Book ii. c. 3 handles the Prussian claims: Jägerndorf
"being § 13; Liegnitz, § 14; Oppeln and Ratibor, § 16; — and that Ludwig
"had sent a Copy of this Argument" (weighty Performance altogether?
Or Book ii. c. 3 of it, which would have had a better chance?) "to King
"Friedrich, on the death of Kaiser Karl VI."

April—May 1741.

"ments again, in the King's name this time; and promised "something weighty by Newyear's day at latest." Doubtless to the joy of Nüssler, who has still no regular appointment, though well deserving one. "And sure enough, on January "7th, at Berlin, 'in three languages,' Ludwig's *Deduction* had "come out; an eager Public waiting for it;* — and at Berlin "it was generally thought to be conclusive. I have looked "into Ludwig's Deduction, stern duty urging, in this instance "for one: such portions as I read are nothing like so stupid as "was expected; and in fact, are not to be called stupid at all, "but fit for their purpose, and moderately intelligible to those "who need them," — which happily we do not in this place.

Judicious Mr. Viner availed nothing against the Proposed Address; any more than he would against the Atlantic Tide, coming-in unanimous, under influence of the Moon itself, — as indeed this Address, and the triumphant Subsidy which was voted in the rear of it, may be said to have done.** Subsidy of 300,000*l.* to her Hungarian Majesty; which, with the 200,000*l.* already gone that road, makes a handsome Half-million for the present Year. The first gush of the Britannic Fountain, — which flowed like an Amalthea's Horn for seven years to come; refreshing Austria, and all thirsty Pragmatic Nations, to defend the Keystone of this Universe. Unluckily every guinea of it went, at the same time, to encourage Austria in scorning King Friedrich's offers to it; which perhaps are just offers, thinks Mr. Viner; which once listened to, Pragmatic Sanction would be safe.***

---

* Title is, *Rechtsgegründetes Eigenthum* (in the Latin copies), *Patrimonium*, and *Propriété fondée en Droit* in the French copies) des &c., — that is to say, *Legal Right of Property in the Royal-Electoral House of Brandenburg to the Duchies and Principalities of Jägerndorf, Liegnitz, Brieg, Wohlau* (Berlin, 7th January 1741).

** Coxe, iii. 265.

*** Mr. Viner was of Popham, or Popholm, in Lincolnshire, for which County he sat then, and for many years before and after', — from about

This Parliament is strong for Pragmatic Sanction, and has high resentments against Walpole; in both which points the New Parliament, just getting elected, will rival and surpass it, — especially in the latter point, that of uprooting Walpole, which the Nation is bent on, with a singular fury. Pragmatic Sanction like to be ruined; and Walpole furiously thrown out: what a pair of sorrows for poor George! During his late Caroline's time, all went peaceably, and that of "governing" was a mere pleasure; Walpole and Caroline cunningly doing that for him, and making him believe he was doing it. But now has come the crisis, the collapse; and his poor Majesty left alone to deal with it! —

No. 2. *Constitutional Historian on the Phenomenon of Walpole in England.*

"For above Ten Years, Walpole himself," says my Constitutional Historian (unpublished), "for almost Twenty "Years, Walpole virtually and through others, has what "they call 'governed' England; that is to say, has adjusted "the conflicting Parliamentary Chaos into counterpoise, by "what methods he had; and allowed England, with Walpole "atop, to jumble whither it would and could. Of crooked "things made straight by Walpole, of heroic performance or "intention, legislative or administrative, by Walpole, nobody "ever heard; never of the least handbreadth gained from the "Night-Realm in England, on Walpole's part: enough if he "could manage to keep the Parish Constable walking, and "himself float atop. Which task (though intrinsically zero "for the Community, but all-important to the Walpole, of

---

1713 till 1761, when he died. A solid, instructed man, say his contemporaries. "He was a friend of Bolingbroke's and had a house near Bolingbroke's Battersea one." He is Great-great-grandfather to the present Mr. Viner, and to the Countess De Grey and Ripon; which is an interesting little fact.

"Constitutional Countries) is a task almost beyond the faculty of man, if the careless reader knew it!

"This task Walpole did, — in a sturdy, deep-bellied, long-headed, John-Bull fashion, not unworthy of recognition. A man of very forcible natural eyesight, strong natural heart, — courage in him to all lengths; a very block of oak, or of oak-root, for natural strength. He was always very quiet with it, too; given to digest his victuals, and be peaceable with everybody. He had no rule, that stood in place of many: To keep out of every business which it was possible for human wisdom to stave aside. 'What good will you get of going into that? Parliamentary criticism, argument and botheration! Leave well alone. And even leave ill alone: — are you the tradesman to tinker leaky vessels in England? You will not want for work. Mind your pudding, and say little!' At home and abroad, that was the safe secret. For, in Foreign Politics, his rule was analogous: 'Mind your own affairs. You are an Island, you can do without Foreign Politics; Peace, keep Peace with everybody: what, in the Devil's name, have you to do with those dog-worryings over Seas? Once more, mind your pudding!' Not so bad a rule; indeed it is the better part of an extremely good one; — and you might reckon it the real rule for a pious Britannic Island (reverent of God, and contemptuous of the Devil) in times of general Downbreak and Spiritual Bankruptcy, when quarrellings of Sovereigns are apt to be mere dog-worryings, and Devil's work, not good to interfere in.

"In this manner, Walpole, by solid John-Bull faculty (and methods of his own), had balanced the Parliamentary swaggings and clashings, for a great while; and England had jumbled whither it could, always in a stupid, but also in a peaceable way. As to those same 'methods of his own,' they were — in fact they were Bribery. Actual purchase of votes by money slipt into the hand. Go straight to the point. 'The direct real method this,' thinks Walpole: 'is there in reality any other?' A terrible question to Constitutional Countries; which, I hear, has never been resolved in the negative, by the modern improvements of science. Changes of form have introduced themselves; the outward process, I hear, is now quite different. According as the fashions and conditions alter, — according as you have a

"Fourth Estate developed, or a Fourth Estate still in the grub "stage and only developing, — much variation of outward "process is conceivable.

"But Votes, under pain of Death Official, are necessary "to your poor Walpole: and votes, I hear, are still bidden "for, and bought. You may buy them by money down (which "is felony, and theft simple, against the poor Nation); or by "preferments and appointments of the unmeritorious man, — "which is felony double-distilled (far deadlier, though more "refined), and theft most compound; theft, not of the poor "Nation's money, but of its soul and body so far, and of *all* "its moneys and temporal and spiritual interests whatsoever; "theft, you may say, of collops cut from its side, and poison "put into its heart, poor Nation! Or again, you may buy, not "of the Third Estate in such ways, but of the Fourth, or of " the Fourth and Third together, in other still more felonious "and deadly, though refined ways. But doing claptraps, "namely; letting off Parliamentary blue-lights, to awaken "the Sleeping Swineries, and charm them into diapason for "you, — what a music! Or, without claptrap or previous "felony of your own, you may feloniously, in the pinch of "things, make truce with the evident Demagogos, and Son of " Nox and of Perdition, who has got 'within those walls' of "yours, and is grown important to you by the Awakened "Swineries, risen into alt, that follow him. Him you may, in "your dire hunger of votes, consent to comply with; his "Anarchies you will pass for him into 'Laws,' as you are "pleased to term them; — instead of pointing to the whipping-"post, and to his wicked long ears, which are so fit to be "nailed there, and of sternly recommending silence, which "were the salutary thing. — Buying may be done in a great "variety of ways. The question, How you buy? is not, on "the moral side, an important one. Nay, as there is a beauty "in going straight to the point, and by that course there is "likely to be the minimum of mendacity for you, perhaps the "direct money-method is a shade *less* damnable than any of "the others since discovered; — while, in regard to practical "damage resulting, it is of childlike harmlessness in com-"parison!

"That was Walpole's method; with this to aid his great "natural faculty, long-headed, deep-bellied, suitable to the

April—May 1741.

"English Parliament and Nation, he went along with perfect
"success for ten or twenty years. And it might have been for
"longer, — had not the English Nation accidentally come to
"wish, that it should *cease* jumbling *no*whither; and try to
"jumble *some*whither, at least for a little while, or important
"business that had risen for England in a certain quarter.
"Had it not been for Jenkins's Ear blazing out in the dark
"English brain, Walpole might have lasted still a long while.
"But his fate lay there: — the first Business vital to England
"which might turn up; and this chanced to be the Spanish
"War. How vital, readers shall see anon. Walpole, know-
"ing well enough in what state his War apparatus was, and
"that of all his Apparatuses there was none in a working
"state, but the Parliamentary one, — resisted the Spanish
"War; stood in the door against it, with a rhinoceros deter-
"mination, nay almost something of a mastiff's; resolute not
"to admit it, to admit death as soon. Doubtless he had a
"feeling it would be death, the sagacious man; — and such it
"is now proving; the Walpole Ministry dying by inches from
"it; dying hard, but irremediably.

"The English Nation was immensely astonished, which
"Walpole was not, any more than at the other Laws of
"Nature, to find Walpole's War-apparatus in such a condi-
"tion. All his Apparatuses, Walpole guesses, are in no
"better, if it be not the Parliamentary one. The English
"Nation is immensely astonished, which Walpole again is not,
"to find that his Parliamentary Apparatus has been kept in
"gear and smooth going by the use of *oil:* 'Miraculous Scandal
"of Scandals!' thinks the English Nation. 'Miracle? Law of
"Nature, you fools!' thinks Walpole. And in fact there is
"such a storm roaring in England, in those and in the late
"and the coming months, as threatens to be dangerous to
"high roofs, — dangerous to Walpole's head at one time.
"Storm such as had not been witnessed in men's memory; all
"manner of Counties and Constituencies, with solemn indig-
"nations charging their representatives to search into that
"miraculous Scandal of Scandals, Law of Nature, or whatever
"it may be; and abate the same, at their peril.

"To the now reader there is something almost pathetic in
"these solemn indignations, and high resolves to have Purity
"of Parliament and thorough Administrative Reform, in spite

"of Nature and the Constitutional Stars;— and nothing I
"have met with, not even the Prussian Dryasdust, is so un-
"sufferably wearisome, or can pretend to equal in depth of
"dull inanity, to ingenuous living readers, as our poor English
"Dryasdust's interminable, often-repeated Narratives, volume
"after volume, of the debatings and colleaguings, the tossings
"and tumults, fruitless and endless, in Nation and National
"Palaver, which ensued thereupon. Walpole (in about a
"year hence),* though he stuck to the ground like a rhino-
"ceros, was got rolled out. And a Successor, and series of
"Successors, in the bright brand-new state, was got rolled in;
"with immense shouting from mankind: — but up to this date
"we have no reason to believe that the Laws of Nature were
"got abrogated on that occasion, or that the constitutional
"stars have much altered their courses since."

That Walpole will probably be lost, goes much home to the Royal bosom, in these troublous Spring months of 1741, as it has done and will do. And here, emerging from the Spanish Main just now, is a second sorrow, which might quite transfix the Royal bosom, and drive Majesty itself to despair; awakening such insoluble questions, — furnishing such proof, that Walpole and a good few other persons (persons, and also things, and ideas and practices, deep-rooted in the Country) stand much in need of being lost, if England is to go a good road!

The Spanish War being of moment to us here, we will let our Constitutional Historian explain, in his own dialect, How it was so vital to England; and shall even subjoin what he gives as History of it, such being so admirably succinct, for one quality.

* February 13th (2d), 1742, quitting the House after bad usage there, said he would never enter it again; nor did: February 22d, resigned in favour of Pulteney and Company (Tindal, xx. 530; Thackeray, i. 45).

April—May 1741.

No. 3. *Of the Spanish War, or the Jenkins's-Ear Question.*

"There was real cause for a War with Spain. It is one of "the few cases, this, of a war from necessity. Spain, by "Decree of the Pope,— some Pope long ago, whose name we "will not remember, in solemn Conclave, drawing accurately "'his Meridian Line,' on I know not what Telluric or Uranic "principles, no doubt with great accuracy, 'between Portugal "and Spain,'— was proprietor of all those Seas and Con- "tinents. And now England, in the interim, by Decree of "the Eternal Destinies, had clearly come to have property "there, too; and to be practically much concerned in that "theoretic question of the Pope's Meridian. There was no "reconciling of theory with fact. 'Ours indisputably,'' said "Spain, with loud articulate voice; 'Holiness the Pope made "it ours!'— while fact and the English, by Decree of the "Eternal Destinies, had been grumbling inarticulately the "other way, for almost Two Hundred years past, and no "result had.

"In Oliver Cromwell's time, it used to be said, 'With "Spain, in Europe, there may be peace or war; but between "the Tropics it is always war.' A state of things well re- "cognised by Oliver, and acted on, according to his op- "portunities. No settlement was had in Oliver's brief time; "nor could any be got since, when it was becoming yearly "more pressing. Bucaniers, desperate naval gentlemen living "on *boucan*, or hung beef; who are also called Flibustiers "(*Flibûtiers*, "Freebooters," in French pronunciation, which "is since grown strangely into *Filibusters*, Fillibustiers, and " other mad forms, in the Yankee Newspapers now current): "readers have heard of those dumb methods of protest. Dumb "and furious; which could bring no settlement; but which did "astonish the Pope's Decree, slashing it with cutlasses and "sea-cannon, in that manner, and circuitously forwarded a " settlement. Settlement was becoming yearly more needful: "and, ever since the Treaty of Utrecht especially, there had "been an incessant haggle going on, to produce one; without "the least effect hitherto. What embassyings, bargainings, "bargain-breakings; what galloping of estafettes; acres of "diplomatic paper, now fallen to the spiders, who always "privately were the real owners! Not in the Treaty of Utrecht,

"not in the Congresses of Cambray, of Soissons, Convention
"of Pardo, by Ripperda, Horace Walpole, or the wagging of
"wigs, could this matter be settled at all. Near two hundred
"years of chronic misery; — and had there been, under any
"of those wigs, a Head capable of reading the Heavenly Man-
"dates, with heart capable of following them, the misery
"might have been briefly ended, by a direct method. With
"what immense saving in all kinds, compared with the oblique
"method gone upon! In quantity of bloodshed needed, of
"money, of idle talk and estafettes, not to speak higher con-
"siderations, the saving had been incalculable. For it was
"England's one Cause of War during the Century we are now
"upon; and poor England's course, when at last driven into
"it, went ambiguously circling round the whole Universe,
"instead of straight to the mark. Had Oliver Cromwell lived
"ten years longer;— but Oliver Cromwell did not live; and,
"instead of Heroic Heads, there came in Constitutional Wigs,
"which makes a great difference.

"The pretensions of Spain to keep Half the World locked
"up in embargo were entirely chimerical; plainly contra-
"dictory to the Laws of Nature; and no amount of Pope's
"Donation Acts, or Ceremonial in Rota or Propaganda, could
"redeem them from untenability, in the modern days. To lie
"like a dog in the manger over South America, and say
"snarling, 'None of you shall trade here, though I cannot!'
"— what Pope or body of Popes can sanction such a proce-
"dure? Had England had a Head, instead of Wigs, amid its
"diplomatists, England, as the chief party interested, would
"have long since intimated gently to such dog in the manger:
"'Dog, will you be so obliging as rise! I am grieved to say,
"we shall have to do unpleasant things otherwise. Dogs have
"doors for their hutches: but to pretend barring the Tropic
"of Cancer, — that is too big a door for any dog. Can nobody
"but you have business here, then, which is not displeasing to
"the gods? We bid you rise!' And in this mode there is no
"doubt the dog, bark and bite as he might, would have ended
"by rising; not only England, but all the Universe being
"against him. And furthermore, I compute with certainty,
"the quantity of fighting needed to obtain such result would,
"by this mode, have been a minimum. The clear right being
"there, and now also the clear might, why take refuge in

"diplomatic wiggeries, in Assiento-Treaties, and Arrange-
"ments which are *not* analogous to the facts; which are but
"wigged mendacities, therefore; and will but aggravate in
"quantity and in quality the fighting yet needed? Fighting
"is but (as has been well said) a battering out of the men-
"dacities, pretences, and imaginary elements: well battered
"out, these, like dust and chaff, fly torrent-wise along the
"winds, and darken all the sky; but these once gone, there
"remain the facts and their visible relation to one another,
"and peace is sure.

"The Assiento Treaty being fixed upon, the English ought
"to have kept it. But the English did not, in any measure;
"nor could pretend to have done. They were entitled to
"supply Negroes, in such and such number, annually to the
"Spanish Plantations; and besides this delightful branch of
"trade, to have the privilege of selling certain quantities of
"their manufactured articles on those coasts; quantities re-
"gulated briefly by this stipulation, That their Assiento Ship
"was to be of 600 tons burden, so many and no more. The
"Assiento ship was duly of 600 tons accordingly, promise kept
"faithfully to the eye; but the Assiento Ship was attended
"and escorted by provision-sloops, small craft said to be of
"the most indispensable nature to it. Which provision-sloops,
"and indispensable small craft, not only carried merchandise
"as well, but went and came to Jamaica and back, under
"various pretexts, with ever new supplies of merchandise;
"converting the Assiento ship into a Floating Shop, the Tons
"burden and Tons sale of which set arithmetic at defiance.
"This was the fact, perfectly well known in England, veiled
"over by mere smuggler pretences, and obstinately persisted
"in, so profitable was it. Perfectly well known in Spain also,
"and to the Spanish-Guarda-Costas and Sea-captains in those
"parts; who were naturally kept in a perennial state of rage
"by it, — and disposed to fly out into flame upon it, when a
"bad case turned up! Such a case that of Jenkins had seemed
"to them; and their mode of treating it, by tearing off Mr.
"Jenkins's Ear, proved to be, — bad shall we say, or good?
"— intolerable to England's thick skin; and brought matters
"to a crisis, in the ways we saw." * * *

The Jenkins's-Ear Question, which then looked so

mad to everybody, how sane has it now grown to my Constitutional Friend! In abstruse ludicrous form, there lay immense questions involved in it; which were serious enough, certain enough, though invisible to everybody. Half the World lay hidden in embryo under it. Colonial-Empire, whose is it to be? Shall Half the World be England's, for industrial purposes; which is innocent, laudable, conformable to the Multiplication-table at least, and other plain Laws? Or shall it be Spain's, for arrogant-torpid sham-devotional purposes, contradictory to every Law? The incalculable Yankee Nation itself, biggest Phenomenon (once thought beautifullest) of these Ages, — this too, little as careless readers on either side of the sea now know it, lay involved. Shall there be a Yankee Nation, shall there not be; shall the New World be of Spanish type, shall it be of English? Issues which we may call immense. Among the then extant Sons of Adam, where was he who could in the faintest degree surmise what issues lay in the Jenkins's-Ear Question! And it is curious to consider now, with what fierce deep-breathed doggedness the poor English Nation, drawn by their instincts, held fast upon it, and would take no denial, as if *they* had surmised and seen. For the instincts of simple guileless persons (liable to be counted *stupid*, by the unwary) are sometimes of prophetic nature, and spring from the deep places of this Universe! — — My Constitutional Friend entitles his next Section, *Carthagena;* but might more fitly have headed it (for such in reality it is, Carthagena proving the evanescent point of that sad business),

April—May 1741.

Succinct History of the Spanish War, which began in 1739; and ended — When did it end?

1°. *War, and Porto-Bello (November* 1739 — *March* 1740).
— "November 4th, 1739, War was at length (after above
"four months obscure quasi-declaring of it, in the shape of
"Orders in Council, Letters of Marque, and so on) got openly
"declared; 'Heralds at Arms at the usual places' blowing
"trumpets upon it, and reading the royal Manifesto, date of
"which is five days earlier, 'Kensington, October 30th (19th).'
"The principal Events that ensue, arrange themselves under
"Three Heads, this of Porto-Bello being the *first;* and (by in-
"tense smelting) are dateable as follows:*

"Wednesday Evening, 1st December 1739, Admiral Ver-
"non, our chosen Anti-Spaniard, finding, a while ago, that he
"had missed the Azogue Ships on the Coast of Spain, and
"must try America and the Spanish Main, in that view arrives
"at Porto-Bello. Next day, December 2d, Vernon attacks
"Porto-Bello; attacks certain Castles so-called, with furious
"broadsiding, followed by scalading; gets surrender (on the
"3d); — seamen have allowance instead of plunder; — blows
"up what Castles there are; and returns to Port Royal in
"Jamaica.

"Never-imagined joy in England, and fame to Vernon,
"when the news came: 'Took it with Six Ships,' cry they;
"'the scurvy Ministry, who had heard him, in the fire of Par-
"liamentary debate, say Six, would grant him no more: in-
"vincible Vernon!' Nay, Next Year, I see, 'London was
"illuminated on the Anniversary of Porto-Bello:' — day
"settled in permanence, as one of the High-tides of the
"Calendar, it would appear. And 'Vernon's Birthday'
"withal, — how touching is stupidity when loyal! — was
"celebrated amazingly in all the chief Towns, like a kind of
"Christmas, when it came round; Nature having deigned to
"produce such a man, for a poor Nation in difficulties. In-
"vincible Vernon, it is thought by Gazetteers, 'will look in at
"Carthagena shortly;' much more important Place, where a
"certain Governor Don Blas has been insolent withal, and
"written Vernon letters.

* *Gentleman's Magazine,* ix. 551, x. 124, 142, 144, 350; Tindal, xx. 430-3, 442; &c.

"2⁰. *Preliminaries to Carthagena* (*March— November* 1740.)
"— Monday, 14th March 1740, Vernon did, accordingly, look
"in on Carthagena;* cast anchor in the shallow waste of surfs
"there, that Monday; and tried some bombarding, with bomb-
"ketches and the like, from Thursday till Saturday following.
"Vernon hopes he did hit the Jesuits' College, South Bastion,
"Custom-house and other principal edifices; but found that
"there was no getting near enough on that seaward side.
"Found that you must force the Interior Harbour, — a big In-
"land Gulf or Lake, which gushes in by what they call *Little*
"*Mouth* (Boca-Chica), and has its Booms, Castles and De-
"fences, which are numerous and strongish; — and that, for
"this end, you must have Seven or Eight Thousand Land
"Forces, as well as an addition of Ships. On Saturday
"Evening, therefore, Vernon calls-in his bomb-ketches; sails
"past, examining these things; and goes forth on other small
"adventures. For example, —

"Saturday, 3d April 1740, 'about 10 at night,' Opens can-
"nonade on Chagres (place often enough taken, by cutlass
"and pistol, in the Bucanier times); and, on Monday 5th, gets
"surrender of Chagres: 'Custom-house crammed with goods,
"which we set fire to.' On news of which, there is again, in
"England, joy over the day of small things. The poor English
"People are set on this business of avenging Jenkins's Ear,
"and of having the Ocean Highway unbarred; and hope al-
"ways it can be done by the Walpole Apparatuses, which
"ought to be in working order, and are not! 'Support this
"hero, you Walpole and Company, in his Carthagena views:
"it will be better for you!'

"Walpole and Company, aware of that fact, do take some
"trouble about it; and now, may not we say, *Paullo majora
"canamus?* All through that Summer 1740" — while King
Friedrich went rushing about, to Strasburg, to Wesel; doing
his Herstals and Practicalities, with a light high hand, in almost an entertaining manner; and intent, still more, on his
Voltaires and a Life to the Muses, — "there was, in England,
"serious heavy tumult of activity, secret and public. In the
"Dockyards, on the Drill-grounds, what a stir: Camp in the
"Isle of Wight, not to mention Portsmouth and the Sea-
"industries; 6,000 Marines are to be embarked, as well as

* *Gentleman's Magazine*, x. 350.

April—May 1741.

"Land Regiments, — can anybody guess whither? America "itself is to furnish 'one Regiment, with Scotch Officers to "discipline it,' if they can.

"Here is real haste and effort; but by no means such speed "as could be wished; multiplex confusions and contradictions "occurring, as is usual, when your machinery runs foul. Nor "are the Gazetteers without their guesses, though they study "to be discreet. 'Here is something considerable in the wind; "a grand idea, for certain;' — and to men of discernment, it "points surely towards Carthagena and heroic Vernon out "yonder? Government is dumb altogether; and lays oc- "casional embargo; trying hard (without success), in the "delays that occurred, to keep it secret from Don Blas and "others. The outcome of all which was,

"3⁰. *Carthagena itself (November* 1740 — *April* 1741). — On "November 6th, — by no means, 'July 3d,' as your first fond "programs bore; which delay was itself likely to be fatal, un- "less the Almanac, and course of the Tropical Seasons would "delay along with you! — we say, On Sunday, 6th November "1740" (Kaiser Karl's Funeral just over, and great thoughts going on at Reinsberg), "Rear-Admiral Sir Chaloner Ogle,— "so many weeks and months after the set time, — does sail "from St. Helen's (guessed, for Carthagena); all people send- "ing blessings with him. Twenty-five big Ships of the Line, "with three Half-Regiments on board; fireships, bomb- "ketches, in abundance; and eighty Transports, with 6,000 "drilled Marines: a Sea-and-Land Force, fit to strengthen "Hero Vernon with a witness, and realize his Carthagena "views. A very great day at Portsmouth and St. Helen's for "these Sunday folk.*

"Most obscure among the other items in that Armada of "Sir Chaloner's, just taking leave of England; most obscure "of the items then, but now most noticeable, or almost alone "noticeable, is a young Surgeon's-Mate, — one Tobias "Smollett; looking over the waters there and the fading "coasts, not without thoughts. A proud, soft-hearted, though "somewhat stern-visaged, caustic and indignant young gen- "tleman. Apt to be caustic in speech, having sorrows of his

---

* Tindal, xx. 463 (*Lists* &c. there; date wrong, "31st October," instead of 26th (o. s.), many things wrong, and all things left loose and flabby, and not right! As is poor Tindal's way).

"own under lock and key, on this and subsequent occasions.
"Excellent Tobias; he has, little as he hopes it, something
"considerable by way of mission in this Expedition, and in
"this Universe generally. Mission to take Portraiture of
"English Seamanhood, with the due grimness, due fidelity;
"and convey the same to remote generations, before it vanish.
"Courage, my brave young Tobias; through endless sorrows,
"contradictions, toils and confusions, you will do your errand
"in some measure; and that will be something! —

"Five weeks before (29th September 1740, which was also
"several months beyond time set), there had sailed, strictly
"hidden by embargoes which were little effectual, another
"Expedition, all Naval; intended to be subsidiary to this one:
"Commodore Anson's, of Three inconsiderable Ships; who is
"to go round Cape Horn, if he can; to bombard Spanish Ame-
"rica from the other side; and stretch out a hand to Vernon in
"his grand Carthagena or ulterior views. Together they may
"do some execution, if we judge by the old Bucanier and
"Queen-Elizabeth experiences? Anson's Expedition has be-
"come famous in the world, though Vernon got no good of it."

Well! Here truly was a business; not so ill-contrived.
Somebody of head must have been at the centre of this: and it
might, in result, have astonished the Spaniard, and tumbled
him much topsy-turvy in those latitudes, — had the machinery
for executing it been well in gear. Under Friedrich Wilhelm's
captaincy and management, every person, every item, correct
to its time, to its place, to its function, what a thing! But with
mere Walpole Machinery: alas, it was far too wide a Plan
for Machinery of that kind, habitually out of order, and only
used to be as correct as — as it could. Those *delays* themselves, first to Anson, then to Ogle, since the Tropical Almanac
would not delay along with them, had thrown both Enterprises into weather such as all-but meant impossibility in
those latitudes! This was irremediable; — had not been remediable, by efforts and pushings here and there. The best
of management, as under Anson, could not get the better of
this; worst of management, as in the other case, was likely to
make a fine thing of it! Let us hasten on:

"January 20th, 1741, We arrive, through much rough
"weather and other confused hardships, at Port Royal in
"Jamaica; find Vernon waiting on the slip; the American

"Regiment, tolerably drilled by the Scotch Lieutenants, in
"full readiness and equipment; a body of Negroes super-
"added, by way of pioneer labourers fit for those hot climates.
"One sad loss there had been on the voyage hither: Land
"forces had lost their Commander, and did not find another.
"General Cathcart had died of sickness on the voyage; a
"Charles Lord Cathcart, who was understood to possess some
"knowledge of his business; and his Successor, one Went-
"worth, did not happen to have any. Which was reckoned
"unlucky, by the more observant. Vernon, though in haste
"for Carthagena, is in some anxiety about a powerful French
"Fleet which has been manœuvring in those waters for some
"time; intent on no good that Vernon can imagine. The first
"thing now is, See into that French Fleet. French Fleet, on
"our going to look in the proper Island, is found to be all off
";for home; men 'mostly starved or otherwise dead,' we hear;
"so that now, after this last short delay, — To Carthagena,
"with all sail.

"Wednesday Evening, 15th March 1741, We anchor in the
"Playa Grande, the waste surfy Shallow which washes Cartha-
"gena seaward; 124 sail of us, big and little. We find Don
"Blas in a very prepared posture. Don Blas has been doing
"his best, this twelvemonth past; plugging up that Boca-
"Chica (*Little-Mouth*) Ingate, with batteries, booms, great
"ships; and has castles not a few thereabouts and in the In-
"terior Lake or Harbour; all which he has put in tolerable de-
"fence, so far as can be judged: not an inactive, if an insolent
"Don. We spend the next five days in considering and
"surveying these Performances of his: What is to be done
"with them; how, in the first place, we may force Boca-Chica;
"and get in upon his Interior Castles and him. After con-
"sideration, and plan fixed:

"Monday, 20th March, Sir Chaloner, with broadsides,
"sweeps away some small defences which lie to left of Boca-
"Chica" (to our *left*, to Boca-Chica's *right*, if anybody cares to
be,particular). "Whereupon the Troops land, some of them
"that same evening; and, within the next two days, are all
"ashore, implements, Negroes and the rest; building bat-
"teries, felling wood; intent to capture Boca-Chica Castle,
"and demolish the War-Ships, Booms, and fry of Fascine and
"other Batteries; and thereby to get in upon Don Blas, and

"have a stroke at his Interior Castles and Carthagena itself.
"Till April 5th, here are sixteen days of furious intricate work;
"not ill done:— the physical labour itself, the building of bat-
"teries, with Boca-Chica firing on you over the woods, is
"scarcely doable by Europeans in that season; and the
"Negroes, who are able for it, 'fling down their burdens, and
"scamper, whenever a gun goes off.' Furious fighting, too,
"there was, by seamen and landsmen; not ill done, consider-
"ing circumstances.

"On the sixteenth day, April 5th" (King Friedrich hurrying
from the Mountains, that same day, towards Steinau, which
took fire with him at night), "Boca-Chica Castle and the in-
"tricate War-Ships, Booms, and Castles thereabouts (Don
"Blas running off when the push became intense), are at last
"got. So that now, through Boca-Chica, we enter the Interior
"Harbour or Harbours. 'Harbours' which are of wide extent,
"and deep enough; being in fact a Lake, or rather Pair of
"Lakes, with Castles (*Castello Grande*, 'Castle Grand,' the
"chief of them), with War-Ships sunk or afloat, and mis-
"cellaneous obstructions: beyond all which, at the farther
"shore, some five miles off, Carthagena itself does at last lie
"potentially accessible; and we hope to get in upon Don Blas
"and it. There ensue five days of intricate sea-work; not
"much of broadsiding, mainly tugging-out of sunk War-Ships
"and the like, to get along-side of Castle Grand, which is the
"chief obstruction.

"April 10th, Castle Grand itself is got; nobody found in it
"when we storm. Don Blas and the Spaniards seem much in
"terror; burning any Ships they still have, near Carthagena;
"as if there were no chance now left." This is the very day of
Mollwitz Battle; near about the hour when Schwerin broke
into field-music, and advanced with thunderous glitter against
the evening sun! "Carthagena Expedition is, at length, fairly
"in contact with its Problem,— the question rising, 'Do you
"understand it, then?'

"Up to this point, mistakes of management had been made
"good by obstinate energy of execution; clear victory had
"gone on so far, the Capture of Carthagena now seemingly at
"hand. One thing was unfortunate: 'the able Mr. Moor'
"(meritorious Captain of Foot, who, by accident, had spent

"some study on his business), 'the one real Engineer we had,' "got killed in that Boca-Chica struggle: an end to poor Moor! "So that the Siege of Carthagena will have to go on *without* "Engineer science henceforth. May be important, that, — "who knows? Another thing was still more palpably import-"ant: Sea-General Vernon had an undisguised contempt for "Land-General Wentworth. 'A mere blockhead, whose Bro-"ther has a Borough,' thinks Vernon (himself an Opposition "Member, of high-sniffing, angry, not too magnanimous "turn);—and withdraws now to his Ships; intimating: 'Do "your Problem, then; I have set you down beside it, which "was my part of the affair!'— Let us give the attack of Fort "Lazar, and end this sad business.

"Sunday, 16th April, Wentworth, once master of the Up-"permost Lake or Harbour (what the Natives call the *Surgi-*"*dero*, or Anchorage Proper), had disembarked, high up to the "right, a good way south of Carthagena; meaning to attack "therefrom a certain Fort Lazar, which stands on a Hill be-"tween Carthagena and him: this Hill and Fort once his, he "has Carthagena under his cannon; Carthagena in his pocket, "as it were. 'Fort not to be had without batteries,' thinks "Wentworth; though the sickly rainy season has set in. "'Batteries? Scaling-ladders, you mean!' answers Vernon, "with undisguised contempt. For the two are, by this time, "almost in open quarrel. Wentworth starts building bat-"teries, in spite of the rain-deluges; then stops building; — "decides to do it by scalade, after all. And, at two in the "morning of this Sunday, April 16th, sets forth, in certain "columns, — by roads ill-known, with arrangements that do "*not* fit like clock-work, — to storm said Hill and Fort. The "English are an obstinate people; and strenuous execution "will sometimes amend defects of plan, — sometimes not.

"The obstinate English, nothing in them but sullen fire of "valour, which has to burn *un*luminous, did, after mistake on "mistake, climb the rocks or heights of Lazar Hill, in spite of "the world and Don Blas's cannonading; but found, when "atop, That Fort Lazar, raining cannon-shot, was still divided "from them by chasms; that the scaling-ladders had not come "(never did come, owing to indiscipline somewhere), — and "that, without wings as of eagles, they could not reach Fort "Lazar at all! For about four hours, they struggled with a

"desperate doggedness, to overcome the chasms, to wrench
"aside the Laws of Nature, and do something useful for them-
"selves; patiently, though sulkily; regardless of the storm of
"shot which killed 600 of them, the while. At length, finding
"the Laws of Nature too strong for them, they descended
"gloomily; 'in gloomy silence,' marched home to their tents
"again, — in a humour too deep for words.
"Yes; and we find they fell sick in multitudes, that night;
"and, 'in two days more, were reduced from 6,645 to 3,200
"effective;' Vernon, from the sea, looking disdainfully on: —
"and it became evident that the big Project had gone to water;
"and that nothing would remain but to return straightway to
"Jamaica, in bankrupt condition. Which accordingly was
"set about. And ten days hence (April 26th), the final party
"of them did get on board, — punctual to take 'three tents,'
"their last rag of Siege-furniture, along with them; 'lest Don
"Blas have trophies," thinks poor Wentworth. And sailed
"away, with their sad Siege finished in such fashion. Stre-
"nuous Siege; which, had the War-Sciences been foolishness,
"and the Laws of Nature and the rigours of Arithmetic and
"Geometry been stretchable entities, might have succeeded
"better!" * —

"Evening of April 26th:" — I perceive it was in
the very hours while Belleisle arrived in Friedrich's
Camp of Mollwitz; eve of that Siege of Brieg, which
we saw performing itself with punctual regard to said
Laws and rigours, and issuing in so different a manner!
Nothing that my Constitutional Historian has said
equals in pungent enormity the matter-of-fact Picture,
left by Tobias Smollett, of the sick and wounded, in
the interim which followed that attempt on Fort Lazar
and the Laws of Nature:

"As for the sick and wounded," says Tobias, "they were,
"next day, sent on board of the transports and vessels called

* Smollett's Account, *Miscellaneous Works* (Edinburgh, 1806), iv.
445-469, is that of a highly intelligent Eyewitness, credible and intelligible
in every particular.

"hospital-ships; where they languished in want of every ne-
"cessary comfort and accommodation. They were destitute
"of surgeons, nurses, cooks and proper provision; they were
"pent up between decks in small vessels, where they had not
"room to sit upright; they wallowed in filth; myriads of
"maggots were hatched in the putrefaction of their sores,
"which had no other dressing than that of being washed by
"themselves with their own allowance of brandy; and nothing
"was heard but groans, lamentations and the language of
"despair, invoking death to deliver them from their miseries.
"What served to encourage this despondence, was the prospect
"of those poor wretches who had strength and opportunity to
"look around them; for there they beheld the naked bodies of
"their fellow-soldiers and comrades floating up and down the
"harbour, [affording prey to the carrion-crows and sharks,
"which tore them in pieces without interruption, and con-
"tributing by their stench to the mortality that prevailed.

"This picture cannot fail to be shocking to the humane
"reader, especially when he is informed, that while those
"miserable objects cried in vain for assistance, and actually
"perished for want of proper attendance, every ship of war in
"the fleet could have spared a couple of surgeons for their re-
"lief; and many young gentlemen of that profession solicited
"their captains in vain for leave to go and administer help to
"the sick and wounded. The necessities of the poor people
"were well known; the remedy was easy and apparent; but
"the discord between the chiefs was inflamed to such a degree
"of diabolical rancour, that the one chose rather to see his
"men perish than ask help of the other, who disdained to offer
"his assistance unasked, though it might have saved the lives
"of his fellow-subjects."[*]

In such an amazing condition is the English
Fighting Apparatus under Walpole, being 'important
for England's self only; while the Talking Apparatus,
important for Walpole, is in such excellent gearing, so
well kept in repair and oil! By Wentworth's blame,
who had no knowledge of war; by Vernon's, who sat

[*] Smollett, *ibid*. (Anderson's Edition), iv. 466.

famous on the Opposition side, yet wanted loyalty of mind; by one's blame and another's, *whose* it is idle arguing, here is how your Fighting Apparatus performs in the hour when needed. Unfortunate General, or General's Cocked-Hat (a brave heart too, they say, though of brain too vacant, too opaque); unfortunate Admiral (much blown away by vanity, ill-nature, and Parliamentary wind); — doubly unfortunate Nation, that employs such to lead its armaments! How the English Nation took it? The English Nation has had much of this kind to take, first and last; and apparently will yet have. "Gloomy silence," like that of the poor men going home to their tents, is our only dialect towards it.

This is a dreadful business, this of the wrecked Carthagena Expedition; such a force of war-munitions in every kind, — including the rare kind, human Courage and force of heart, only not human Captaincy, the rarest kind, — as could have swallowed South America at discretion, had there been Captains over it. Has gone blundering down into Orcus and the shark's belly, in that unutterable manner. Might have been didactic to England, more than it was; England's skin being very thick against lessons of that nature. Might have broken the heart of a little Sovereign Gentleman, Curator of England, had he gone hypochondriacally into it; which he was far from doing, brisk little Gentleman; looking out elsewhither, with those eyes *à fleur de tête*, and nothing of insoluble admitted into the brain that dwelt inside.

What became subsequently of the Spanish War,

we in vain inquire of History-Books. The War did not die for many years to come, but neither did it publicly live; it disappears at this point: a River Niger, seen once flowing broad enough; but issuing — Does it issue nowhere, then! Where does it issue? Except for my Constitutional Historian, still unpublished, I should never have known where. — By the time these disastrous Carthagena tidings reached England, his Britannic Majesty was in Hanover; involved, he, and all his State-doctors, English and Hanoverian, in awful contemplation on Pragmatic Sanction, Kaiser-Wahl, Celestial Balance, and the saving of Nature's Keystone, should this still prove possible to human effort and contrivance. In which imminency of Doomsday itself, the small English-Spanish matter, which the Official people, and his Majesty as much as any, had bitterly disliked, was quite let go, and dropped out of view. Forgotten by Official people; left to the dumb English Nation, whose concern it was, to administer as it could.

Anson, — with his three ships gone to two, gone ultimately to one, — is henceforth what Spanish War there officially is. Anson could not meet those Vernon-Wentworth gentlemen "from the other side of the Isthmus of Darien," the gentlemen, with their Enterprise, being already bankrupt and away. Anson, with three inconsiderable ships, which rotted gradually into one, could not himself settle the Spanish War: but he did, on his own score, a series of things, ending in beautiful finis of the Acapulco Ship, which were of considerable detriment, and of highly considerable disgrace, to Spain; — and were, and are long likely to be, memorable among the Sea-heroisms of the world.

Giving proof that real Captains, taciturn Sons of Anak, are still born in England; and Sea-kings, equal to any that were. Luckily, too, he had some chaplain or ship's-surgeon on board, who saw good to write account of that memorable *Voyage* of his; and did it, in brief, perspicuous terms, wise and credible: a real Poem in its kind, or Romance all Fact; one of the pleasantest little Books in the World's Library at this date. Anson sheds some tincture of heroic beauty over that otherwise altogether hideous puddle of mismanagement, platitude, disaster; and vindicates, in a pathetically potential way, the honour of his poor Nation a little.

Apart from Official Anson, the Spanish War fell mainly, we may say, into the hands of — of Mr. Jenkins himself, and such Friends of his, at Wapping, Bristol and the Seaports, as might be disposed to go privateering. In which course, after some crosses at first, and great complaints of losses *to* Spanish Privateers, Wapping and Bristol did at length eminently get the upper hand; and thus carried on this Spanish War (or Spanish-French, Spain and France having got into one boat), for long years coming, in an entirely inarticulate, but by no means quite ineffectual manner, — indeed to the ultimate clearance of the Seas from both French and Spaniard, within the next twenty years. Readers shall take this little Excerpt, dated Three Years hence, and set it twinkling in the night of their imaginations:

Bristol, Monday, 21st (10th) September 1744. * * "No-"thing is to be seen here but rejoicings for the number of "French prizes brought into this port. Our Sailors are in "high spirits, and full of money; and while on shore, spend "their whole time in carousing, visiting their Mistresses, going "to plays, serenading, &c., dressed out with laced hats, tossels "(sic), swords with sword-knots, and every other way of "spending their money."*

Carthagena, Walpole, Viners: here are Sorrows for a Britannic Majesty; — and these are nothing like all. But poor readers should have some respite; brief breathing-time, were it only to use their pocket-handkerchiefs, and summon new courage!

* Extract of a Letter from Bristol, in *Gentleman's Magazine*, xlv. 504.

CHAPTER XIII.

SMALL-WAR: FIRST EMERGENCE OF ZIETHEN THE HUSSAR GENERAL INTO NOTICE.

AFTER Brieg, Friedrich undertook nothing military, except strict vigilance of Neipperg, for a couple of months or more. Military, especially offensive operations, are not the methods just now. Rest on your oars; see how this seething Ocean of European Politics, and Peace or War, will settle itself into currents, into set winds; by which of them a man may steer, who happens to have a fixed port in view. Neipperg, too, is glad to be quiescent; "my Infantry hopelessly inferior," he writes to headquarters: "Could not one hire 10,000 Saxons, think you," — or do several other chimerical things, for help? Except with his Pandour people, working what mischief they can, Neipperg does nothing. But this Hungarian rabble is extensively industrious, scouring the country far and wide; and gives a great deal of trouble both to Friedrich and the peaceable inhabitants. So that there is plenty of Small War always going on: — not mentionable here, any passage of it, except perhaps one, at a place called Rothschloss; which concerns a remarkable Prussian Hussar Major, their famed Ziethen, and is still remembered by the Prussian public.

We have heard of Captain, now Major Ziethen, how Friedrich Wilhelm sent him to the Rhine Campaign, six years ago, to learn the Hussar Art from the

Austrians there. One Baronay (*Baroniay*, or even *Baranyai*, as others write him), an excellent hand, taught him the Art; — and how well he has learned, Baronay now sadly experiences. The Affair of Rothschloss (in abridged form) befel as follows:

"In these Small-War businesses, Baronay, Austrian Major-"General of Hussars, had been exceedingly mischievous "hitherto. It was but the other day, a Prussian regular party "had to go out upon him, just in time; and to *re*-wrench "'sixty cartloads of meal,' wrenched by him from suffering "individuals; with which he was making off to Neisse, when "the Prussians" (from their Camp of Mollwitz, where they still are) "came in sight.

"And now again (May 16th) news is, That Baronay, and "1400 Hussars with him, has another considerable set of meal-"carts, — in the Village of Rothschloss, about twenty miles "southward, Frankenstein way; and means to march with "them Neisse-ward tomorrow. Two marches or so will bring "him home; if Prussian diligence prevent not. 'Go in-"stantly,' orders Friedrich, — appointing Winterfeld to do "it: Winterfeld with 300 dragoons, with Ziethen and Hussars "to the amount of 600; which is more than one to two of "Austrians.

"Winterfeld and Ziethen march that same day; are in the "neighbourhood of Rothschloss by nightfall; and take their "measures, — block the road to Neisse, and do the other ne-"cessary things. And go in upon Baronay next morning, at "the due rate, fiery men both of them; sweep poor Baronay "away, *minus* the meal; who finds even his road blocked "(bridge bursting into cannon-shot upon him, at one point),— "instead of bridge a stream, or slow current of quagmire for "him, — and is in imminent hazard. Ziethen's behaviour was "superlative (details of it unintelligible off the ground); and "Baronay fled totally in wreck; — his own horse shot, and at "the moment no other to be had; swam the quagmire, or "swashed through it, 'by help of a tree;' and had a near miss "of capture. Recovering himself on the other side, Baronay, "we can fancy, gave a grin of various expression, as he got "into saddle again: 'The arrow so near killing was feathered "from one's own wing, too!' — And indeed, a day or two "after, he wrote Ziethen a handsome Letter to that effect."*

Ziethen, for minor good feats, had been made Lieutenant-Colonel, the very day he marched; his Commission dates May 16th, 1741; and on the morrow he handsels it in this pretty manner. He is now forty-two: much held down hitherto; being a man of inarticulate turn, hot and abrupt in his ways, — liable always to multifarious obstruction, and unjust contradiction from his fellow-creatures. But Winterfeld's report on this occasion was emphatic; and Ziethen shoots rapidly up henceforth; Colonel within the year, General in 1744; and more and more esteemed by Friedrich during their subsequent long life together.

Though perhaps the two most opposite men in Nature, and standing so far apart, they fully recognised one another in their several spheres. For Ziethen too had good eyesight, though in abstruse sort: — rugged simple son of the moorlands; nourished, body and soul, on orthodox frugal oatmeal (so to speak), with a large sprinkling of fire and iron thrown in! A man born poor: son of some poor Squirelet in the Ruppin Country; — "used to walk five miles into Ruppin on "Saturday nights," in early life, "and have his hair "done into club, which had to last him till the week "following."** A big-headed, thick-lipped, decidedly ugly little man. And yet so beautiful in his ugliness: wise, resolute, true, with a dash of high uncomplaining

---

* *Helden-Geschichte*, i. 927; Orlich, i. 120. *The Life of General de Zieten* (English Translation, very ill printed, Berlin, 1803), *by Frau von Blumenthal* (a vaguish eloquent Lady, but with access to information, being a connexion of Z.'s), p. 84.
** *Militair-Lexikon*, iv. 310.

sorrow in him; — not the "bleached nigger" at all, as Print-Collectors sometimes call him! No; but (on those oatmeal terms) the Socrates-Odysseus, the valiant pious Stoic, and much-enduring man. One of the best Hussar-Captains ever built. By degrees King Friedrich and he grew to be, — with considerable tiffs now and then, and intervals of gloom and eclipse, — what we might call sworn friends. On which and on general grounds, Ziethen has become, like Friedrich himself, a kind of mythical person with the soldiery and common people; more of a demigod than any other of Friedrich's Captains.

Friedrich is always eagerly in quest of men like Ziethen; specially so at this time. He has meditated much on the bad figure his Cavalry made at Mollwitz; and is already drilling them anew in multiplex ways, during those leisure days he now has, — with evident success on the next trial, this very Summer. And, as his wont is, will not rest satisfied there. But strives incessantly, for a series of summers and years to come, till he bring them to perfection; or to the likeness of his own thought, which probably was not far from that. Till at length it can be said his success became world-famous; and he had such Seidlitzes and Ziethens as were not seen before or since.

END OF VOL. VI.

PRINTING OFFICE OF THE PUBLISHER.

www.ingramcontent.com/pod-product-compliance
Lightning Source LLC
Chambersburg PA
CBHW030551300426
44111CB00009B/934